# Beyond the Stars 5

# Beyond the Stars 5
## Themes and Ideologies in American Popular Film

edited by

Paul Loukides

and

Linda K. Fuller

Bowling Green State University Popular Press
Bowling Green, OH 43403

Library of Congress Catalogue Card No.: 89-82334

ISBN: 0-87972-701-2 clothbound
0-87972-702-0 paperback

Cover design by Dumm Art

# Dedication

To Pat Browne, whose support for the Beyond the Stars Series has been unwavering. It has been a great pleasure and honor to work with her.

Paul Loukides
Albion College
Albion, MI

Linda K. Fuller
Worcester State College
Worcester, MA

# Contents

# Introduction

## American Themes, American Dreams

To undergraduate students sitting through the films and clips of a course on film and American culture, it seems nearly inconceivable that the racism and sexism of past mainstream Hollywood films went virtually unquestioned and unchallenged by white Americans, including those who thought they were without racial or gender prejudices. How could thoughtful, well-meaning people not react to the racism of *Birth of a Nation,* or *Gunga Din* or *African Queen*? Or not notice that in the movies the war in the Pacific was a race war while the European one was an ideological war. Students who have become sensitive to patterns of sexism in American films wonder how audiences could disregard the male condescension to females in *Casablanca* or why audiences didn't groan aloud at nearly every June Allyson role.

But convincing students that we rarely question our own mainstream cultural premises is still easier than getting them to recognize that in all probability their children and their grandchildren will be amused and appalled by the films that the current generation of filmgoers accepts without question. Every generation views its own values as givens, while every subsequent generation is tempted to judge the past from its own perspective.

It takes no great insight to recognize that, for the most part, the thematic and ideological dimensions of popular film typically go unexamined and unremarked except in those instances where offense is given or some new ground broken. Issues of race, gender, family values, violence and sexuality are currently in vogue as ideologically important dimensions of film. With the House Un-American Activities Committee (HUAC) gone, the Legion of Decency moribund, and World War II becoming a subject for study rather than a living memory, there is no powerful group currently committed to gauging whether American films are sufficiently anticommunist, properly punishing of pre- and extramarital sex, or consistent in presenting America as a democratic melting pot where differences of ethnic origins and class are put aside for the common good.

It is not unreasonable to suggest that if we are ever really to understand the relationship of American popular film to American society as a whole, we need to move beyond single issue assessments of the themes and ideologies of popular film toward a broader understanding of the belief systems that these films embody. This is not to say that current scholarship on issues of race, gender, family, and so forth are without value; rather, what is being suggested here is the need to cast much wider nets and/or perhaps many more smaller nets into the sea of popular film.

What is being promoted here is that the tools provided by semiotics, deconstruction, anthropological ritual analysis, discourse analysis, cultural studies, and poststructuralist critical theory be brought to bear not only on the currently fashionable themes and ideologies of popular film but also on whatever appears in the whole texture and text of American cinema. That is, the study of film and American culture needs to turn more distinctly toward social/anthropological analysis not only of the surface or manifest themes and ideologies of popular film but of the most submerged or embedded manifestations of our culture within the films we consume. To do this, we must systematically catalog and describe the conventions of popular film—particularly those conventions whose presence is, in this historical moment, utterly unremarkable.

In the process of soliciting and reading manuscripts for this final volume of a series on the conventions of American popular film—*Beyond the Stars 5: Themes and Ideologies in American Popular Film*—it quickly became apparent that this would be the most difficult volume of the project. First, there were many fewer would-be contributors to this book, and second, many of the proposed papers either addressed those thematic or ideological issues currently in fashion or recounted the life cycles of once fashionable but now discredited ideologies.

Each of the earlier volumes of the series had a fair share of papers that illuminated previously unexplored regions of the psyche of popular film. Why was a call for papers on conventional themes and ideologies in popular film producing fewer new analyses of neglected themes and ideologies than those calls that had asked for papers on stock characters, stock plot conventions, and the conventions of the material world or movie locales?

The answer to that question is simple but important. The film scholars who had written for the prior volumes had uncovered many of the fundamental themes and ideologies of American popular film precisely by looking at conventions of plot, character, locale, and physical objects both within and across film genres. From an anthropological perspective, the discovery of popular themes and ideologies in conventions of plot, character, locales, and physical objects certainly makes sense; the deepest rooted beliefs of a culture, its cosmologies, are manifested in the everyday stuff of ordinary life. To look for belief systems, themes, or ideologies in and of themselves is typically to find only those that are—for whatever reason—currently being self-consciously aired in public discourse. All the rest, our most important views of the world, are not hung out like banners of meaning, but are embedded in the minutia of characters, actions, places, and objects within the world of film. It is in the conventions of character and plot, place, and objects, as well as in overtly stated conventional themes and ideologies that we can discover the central beliefs of American film and American culture.

To illustrate, a quick look at two recent popular films can serve as examples. For most viewers, films like *When Harry Met Sally* and *Thelma and Louise* carry their burdens of themes or ideologies on the surface. The central tension of *When Harry Met Sally* is the overtly gender one, which allows the film to explore and at least seemingly resolve the conflict between love, friendship, and sexuality in an open textuality and public debate. But at least as interesting for the popular culturist is the world of the film itself and the thematic motifs or cosmologies that are embedded and suggested indirectly in the film.

To take but three of the most obvious cultural sets within the film, recall the role of sports in the movie, the ways in which telephones are used, and how a wedding provides the social setting for the resolution of sexual/romantic problems. If weddings do, indeed, demonstrate the triumph of hope over experience, the choice of a wedding scene for the climax of the film is not entirely inappropriate. But we might also remember that weddings are commonly used in films as occasions when the surfacing of unexpressed emotions is not only allowed but expected. Weddings, as ritual occasions that celebrate traditional values, act as signs that the complexities of love can be resolved and affirmed. In the movies, weddings invite weddings because they reaffirm traditional values.

The sport scenes of the film are not, of course, simply scenes for further expository dialogue; they are also occasions for rituals of male bonding and, in the comedic continuation of conversation during the "wave," a demonstration of the greater social bonding of mass sporting events. In the same way, the telephone intimacy within the film seems practically a commercial for AT&T where Americans can "reach out and touch somebody" through the nearly invisible intermediation of technology, thus validating that particular technology in ways that seem quite different from any that occurred in films of the '30s and '40s.

More than enough has been written about the sexual politics of *Thelma and Louise,* but where should we look for commentary on the relation of social class and big convertibles or social classes and redneck bars? Where should we turn to begin to understand how American films treat the (rare) deaths of sympathetic characters? How does the film fit the tradition of road films, and how are we to read the evolving cultural value of Levi jeans as they relate to women's liberation?

Are those topics worth writing and thinking about? Indeed they are. One might even venture to say that those subjects—and hundreds of others like them—are the most important topics to be addressed by film scholars. Until such time as we regularly and systematically examine the conventional components of film both across and within genres, we cannot begin to understand how much they have to tell us.

Like clumsy anthropologists who do not recognize the value of discarded chicken bones, or the scorch marks of an ancient campfire, we tend to neglect what is commonplace and thus miss important clues to the puzzle of how popular film reflects the most fundamental dreams and cosmologies of our culture.

The essays in this collection are about a mere handful of the conventional themes and ideologies that have appeared in American popular film over nearly a century. No essay in this volume addresses the celebration of consumerism in popular film or the ways in which films have dealt with homosexuality or real religious faith. The innocent child/bad seed theme hasn't been touched, nor the redeeming/corrupting influence of education. Racism, antisemitism, colonialism, and imperialism, to mention just a few enduring thematic/ideological motifs of popular film, are barely represented here. There is, in short, much that remains to be done to chart the growth and evolution of the most conventional themes and ideologies of American film.

The essays in *Beyond the Stars 5: Themes and Ideologies in American Popular Film* reflect a small but important sampling of the conventional themes and ideologies manifest in the movies. The book's first section focuses on issues of family and gender, beginning with Parley Ann Boswell's study of motherhood. It continues with Mark J. Charney's analysis of how the family is being redefined in films of the '80s and '90s. Devoney Looser and Jennifer Machiorlatti each explore the power relationships of men and women in film and the ways in which films define and deal with "deviant" female behavior.

In the section on warfare, Ralph R. Donald discusses what he aptly calls the "Ugly American" syndrome in films about the Vietnam war. Rick Clifton Moore recounts the uneasy place of ideologic pacifism in

American film, while Richard L. Stromgren explores the complex history of irony and satire in Hollywood's treatment of war.

Further explorations of the insider/outsider themes can be found in those films which portray the winners and losers of our competitive society. Carolyn Anderson explores the ways in which popular films deal with and avoid issues of class mobility, while William Brigham discusses how the dispossessed—the homeless—are presented in American film. Howard Good points out that the American success myth is a recurrent motif in more than seventy years of baseball biopics and Martin F. Norden closely delineates how people with physical disabilities are typically misrepresented in popular film.

The final selections present a glimpse of a variety of changing ideological and thematic fashions. Linda K. Fuller recounts the history of McCarthyism, anticommunist films, and anti-McCarthyist movies. Dealing with monsters of quite a different type, Gary Hoppenstand delves into the particular role of hedonism in the contemporary horror film. Greg Metcalf's subject is the counter-culture of the 1960s and how Hollywood has marginalized the period. In the final essay of this group, Philip J. Skerry looks at two contemporary westerns and how their apocalyptic vision relates to the traditions of that genre.

The small sample of recurrent themes and ideologies presented here suggests how much we need to continue to explore how American values and American movies interrelate.

# "Like a Tiger in the Trees": Mothers Redeemed in Contemporary American Film

**Parley Ann Boswell**

> Oh, rubbish! You have no power here! Be gone, before somebody drops a house on you, too!"
>
> —Glinda (Billie Burke),
> *The Wizard of Oz*

> I am waiting like a tiger in the trees, now ready to leap out and cut her spirit loose.
>
> —Ying-Ying St. Clair (France Nuyen),
> *The Joy Luck Club*

Many American moviewatchers can remember the point in our childhoods, perhaps after having watched *The Wizard of Oz* several times, when we noticed that all of the characters in Dorothy's black-and-white Kansas had their parallel characters in the Land of Oz: Professor Marvel and the Wizard, Miss Gulch and the Wicked Witch of the West, the three farmhands and Dorothy's three travelling companions in Oz, Glinda the Witch of the North and . . . who?

For those of us who have tried to make perfect sense of Dorothy's trip, we discover, as we try to fit all the characters into place, that there is no character in Kansas who resembles Glinda, that she is, of all the Oz characters, singular. Why doesn't Glinda have a parallel in Kansas? Who might Glinda be? In order to answer these questions, we might ask another question: If Glinda is unique, how is she different from the other characters?

Glinda is different from the other characters because she attends to the needs of the lonely adolescent Dorothy in ways that they do not. We know that Dorothy has no parents, and during the early Kansas scenes we see that the people she lives with—the farmhands, her aunt and uncle—are too busy to pay attention to the little girl's problems. When the orphan Dorothy wishes to be over the rainbow, she is looking as much for comfort and attention as for anything else. When she travels to a place far away, she finds in the Good Witch the one person who will protect, guide, love, and instruct her. In other words, Glinda—singularly beautiful, wise, and powerful among clowns, buffoons, and hags—just *might* be the mother little Dorothy of Kansas so desperately wants and needs.[1]

Although we may not necessarily understand this dynamic when we first watch the film, there are many times in this American classic when Glinda takes on the role of "dream mother," one of a limited number of mother types that Hollywood films have offered to their audiences through the years. What seems to distinguish Hollywood mothers is precisely what Glinda the fantasy-mother represents: whether dead or alive, they are inaccessible, mysterious, somehow unworldly, and often very powerful.

Indeed, until very recently in American films, the ideal mother has been either a dead dream mother (Glinda seems to be the only one who floats in a bubble to her child's defense—most are unseen and silent, only mentioned), or a bad, negligent mother. Only since the 1980s has the pattern of dead, absent, or mean mothers begun to change in any significant way in Hollywood films. Since about 1980, mothers in American films have gradually redeemed themselves. No longer are movie mothers silent projections of their children's dreams or nightmares. American movie mothers are beginning to speak for themselves, and their narratives speak clearly to a change in Hollywood's approach toward mothers and motherhood.

In "Jane Austen and the Tradition of the Absent Mother," Susan Peck MacDonald points out that many women novelists of the nineteenth century created young heroines (Jane Eyre, Catherine Earnshaw, Maggie Tulliver) who "[did] not have strong supportive mothers" (Davidson and Broner 59). MacDonald's description could appropriately describe the same phenomenon in American film history. In literature and in film, however, not only heroines have had to muddle through without the help of their mothers. Shakespeare never allows any of his characters to have good mothers (if any), and plenty of male characters—Huck Finn, Peter Pan, Holden Caulfield, Jem Finch, and almost every male character in an American western—have deceased or preoccupied mothers.[2] In fact, for every "good mother" who shows up in American films between the 1930s and 1980, there are three or four bad or missing mothers. The lists are almost endless. Motherless characters show up in most Disney movies and most films based on childrens' literature: *The Adventures of Huckleberry Finn* (1939), *The Adventures of Tom Sawyer* (1938), *The Secret Garden* (1949, 1992), *The Chalk Garden* (1964). Several major Hollywood productions involve death scenes of mothers (whether on or off screen), which become important to plot or character development: *Gone with the Wind* (1939), *Doctor Zhivago* (1965), *The Godfather* (1972), *The Color Purple* (1985), and more recent Hollywood productions such as *Housekeeping* (1987), *Rain Man* (1988), and *Sleepless in Seattle* (1993). And perhaps the definitive dead mother in Hollywood is Mrs. Bates, Norman Bates's mother in *Psycho* (1960).

Bad mothers in Hollywood movies come in two varieties: either malevolent (often emasculating) or merely negligent. Some films that include really mean mothers are *Citizen Kane* (1941), *Now, Voyager* (1942), *East of Eden* (1955), *Rebel without a Cause* (1955), *A Kiss before Dying* (1956), *The Three Faces of Eve* (1957), *Suddenly Last Summer* (1959), *Marnie* (1964), *A Patch of Blue* (1965), *The Graduate* (1967), *Ordinary People* (1980), *The Grifters* (1990), and *The Prince of Tides* (1991). Films in which mothers are portrayed as negligent (and therefore wanting or bad) include *Imitation of Life* (1934, 1959), *Mildred Pierce* (1945), *Gypsy* (1962), *The Exorcist* (1973), *Close Encounters of the Third Kind* (1977), *Kramer vs. Kramer* (1979), *E.T.* (1982), *The Karate Kid* (1984), and most recently, *Home Alone* (1990), *My Own Private Idaho* (1991), and *Radio Flyer* (1992).

There are so many missing or bad mothers in Hollywood films through the years that to say why becomes a monumental task. Critics like MacDonald, Faludi, and Adrienne Rich are useful to our understanding of the missing mother. Again, MacDonald's discussion of nineteenth-century fiction could help us to understand the ideological context out of which motherless films have been the norm. Literary mothers are missing, she writes, not

> from the impotence or unimportance of mothers but from the *almost excessive power of motherhood* . . . if she is dead or absent, the good mother can remain an ideal without her presence disrupting or preventing the necessary drama of the novel. If the mother is to be present . . . the mother must be flawed in some way. (Davidson and Broner 59; italics mine)

If most of the stories presented to us through film are stories about the journey of the human spirit, we cannot allow our mothers to come with us on this journey because they will help us too much, we will all understand too much, and we will not have our own struggles or our own stories.

In Hollywood films, then, mothers have the most power to do good when they are missing or dead. But what of the equally substantial group of bad or negligent mothers who show up in Hollywood productions? Why are so many movie mothers portrayed as mean-spirited, twisted, or indifferent to their children? The answers to these questions are, again, to be found in the literary heritage of film and in the ideological contexts out of which Hollywood films have been produced.

Bad or ineffective mothers have been a staple in much of world literature, from *Medea* to fairy tales that include evil stepmothers.[3] Certainly, American literature has its share of mothers who are suspect or silently peculiar, perhaps best exemplified by Hester Prynne in *The Scarlet Letter*. In the same way that Hollywood has reflected and promoted other stereotypes and values of American culture through the years, so has the movie industry perpetuated the bad or pathetic mother.

Ironically, the industry that has prided itself on celebrating the institution of the American family over the years is the same industry that often shows us the dark side of this institution: the family with a bad mother. In fact, if we remember mothers in American movies, we most often think of the bad ones. Why? Because Hollywood films have always been uneasy and uneven concerning institutions; American films have always given us mixed signals about the values we are experiencing. Motherhood gives us a good example of this difficulty with institutional constructions: mothers are powerful but silent, bad but important. To gauge the institution of motherhood in the movies underscores one of the great paradoxical characteristics of Hollywood films: like other institutions it propounds to glorify or glamorize—marriage, law, religion—Hollywood more often than not undercuts the value of the institution by suggesting its powerlessness.

As film scholar Mary Ann Doane has pointed out, fatherhood is often portrayed as a social institution (fathers represent "issues of identity, legality, inheritance"), but motherhood is represented as an obvious, non-negotiable fact:

> Everyone has a mother, and furthermore, all mothers are essentially the same, each possessing the undeniable quality of motherliness. In Western culture, there is something *obvious* about the maternal which has no counterpart in the paternal. (70)

If a protagonist in a Hollywood movie has a mother, then the Hollywood formula requires that the mother be either bad or powerless. What Hollywood most often does to mother characters is use them to subvert the ideal of a strong family unit. Why mothers? Precisely for the same reason that mothers are often missing on film: mothers are so powerful that to portray them as anything less than saintly will allow other characters—especially their children—to become the focus and strength of the stories on film. Fathers come and go; they can be good or evil. But when we see mothers on the screen who contribute to the film in some negative or hostile way, we have a monumental conflict.

Doane also suggests that many American films that include mother characters have been designated "melodramas," which "foreground sacrifice and suffering" and which suggest "a lack of social power" by providing passive examples of "the mother/child relation" (73). The most memorable Hollywood mothers are the bad ones because Hollywood films need bad mothers to play against good children, grown or not. Mothers who either constrict their children or are mute to help them (usually because the social tide is too strong, as in *Stella Dallas*), represent, by Hollywood standards, melodrama of the highest order. "The term 'melodramatic,'" writes Doane, "in colloquial language connotes excess, the artifice of theatricality" (71).

There are other, more practical reasons for the great number of bad-mother roles in Hollywood productions. Through the decades, roles for women, playing mothers or not, have been scarce, particularly during certain times (post–World War II, the 1980s). Molly Haskell has written that, with the decline of the Hollywood star system in the late 1950s, actresses "lost much of their economic leverage," and as a result, the 1960s and early '70s became a "most disheartening" time for actresses, who had to take roles that were predominantly those of "whores, quasi-whores, jilted mistresses, emotional cripples, spinsters, psychotics . . . and shrill mothers" (232-38 passim.).

Even during the late '70s, when there seemed to be a resurgance of movies about women's independence (*An Unmarried Woman* [1978], *Alice Doesn't Live Here Anymore* [1974]), and stories about aggressive career women (*The China Syndrome* [1979], *Julia* [1977]), these were women's stories, not mothers' stories. In fact, as Susan Faludi has pointed out, the late 1970s and early 1980s saw a series of "backlash" films against career women *and* mothers alike. Mothers, especially, were absent in a series of "man-boy body-swapping films . . . *18 Again, Like Father, Like Son, . . . Big.* . . . In such films as *Field of Dreams, Indiana Jones and the Last Crusade, Dad* . . . mother dies or disappears from the scene, leaving father . . . and son to form a spiritually restorative bond" (138).[4]

This would all seem to describe the Hollywood approach to the institution of motherhood—except for one part of the theory that we cannot account for—those points in American movies when mothers *do* have voices and stories. Just enough American films do include strong, effective mothers that to categorize all film mothers as either dead or bad begins to look puzzling and unbalanced. In the same way that we cannot find a parallel character in Kansas for Glinda, we have been left with this singular flaw in our explanation of the treatment of mothers in the movies: some of the people on these journeys *are* mothers. Where are their stories? Again, we look to literary and feminist critics to help us.

In her essay on the novels of Toni Morrison, Marianne Hirsch points out that, although "feminist writing and scholarship has explored motherhood . . . nearly all of those perspectives have belonged to daughters. . . . [T]he 'great unwritten story' remains the story of the mother herself, told in her own voice" (Gates and Appiah 261). The same might be said of film narratives: there have been movies about mothers and their children, but almost all of these are stories told by the children, or presented in narratives that favor the children's perspectives, for example, in *Desert Bloom* (1986), *Men Don't Leave* (1990), *Staying Together* (1989), *Gas Food Lodging (1992),* and *Mermaids (1990).*

We know how difficult finding a strong, significant mother character can be in a Hollywood production, but to find a film in which the mother's perspective is the dominant one, or the mother's voice carries the narrative, would seem almost impossible. However, there *are* such films. If we listen and watch closely enough, we will see and hear mothers telling their stories in American movies, beginning with a few films before 1980. By the middle 1990s, there are a number of remarkable mothers' stories for American film audiences to experience—enough for a growing chorus of mothers' voices.

One of the first mother's voices we hear in American movies is that of Ginger Rogers, whose war bride character in *Tender Comrade* (1943) tells us her story as she endures loneliness, fear, and ultimately widowhood during World War II. When her son is born near the end of the movie, he becomes her solace and her victory. The film itself is one of several World War II melodramas; what distinguishes it from others like *Since You Went Away* (1944), and *To Each His Own* (1946) is the first-person narrative by Rogers's character.[5]

We hear other mothers tell pieces of their stories through the years in *I Remember Mama* (1948), *A Tree Grows in Brooklyn* (1945), *A Summer Place* (1959), and, especially in *A Raisin in the Sun* (1961), where the mother's voice is the strongest and surest of all of the characters'. We hear mothers tell about their pasts in *Norma Rae* (1979) and *Clara's Heart* (1988); we hear them hope for the future in *Guess Who's Coming to Dinner?* (1967) and *Breaking Away* (1979), a movie that includes one of the most expressive and wisest of mothers in the movies (Barbara Barrie), who, in order to encourage a sense of adventure in her son, shows him her unused but valid passport, "So, you see, I think you should go [bicycle racing]. I think you should come home singing and with a trophy. I think you should do all of these things while you can."

In the 1970s we hear from strong farm mothers in *Sounder* (1972) and *Heartland* (1979); in the 1980s, we see a series of rural American mothers who take care of their families either alone or as the stronger of two parents in *Places in the Heart* (1984), *The River* (1984), and *Country* (1984). In all of these films, mothers become central both to their children and to the audience, because it is through the mothers that we understand the other relationships and dynamics of plot. We hear mothers of the Holocaust tell their stories in *Sophie's Choice* (1982) and *Enemies: A Love Story* (1989); we hear the girlhood stories of mothers in *The Trip to Bountiful* (1985) and *Bright Lights, Big City* (1988). In *Tell Me a Riddle* (1980), we follow the flashbacks of a dying mother/grandmother as she remembers her life as a young woman in Russia and America.

By the end of the 1980s, and into the 1990s, there is a series of American productions in which mothers are the main characters of films. Often, their being mothers is integral to the plots, as in *Not Without My Daughter* (1991) and *Lorenzo's Oil* (1992). Even in the stories still told by their children, these mothers are not frightening, evil, or dead. We have flesh-and-blood mothers who have a variety of occupations, interests, and flaws. In *Mermaids,* Mrs. Flax (Cher) cannot stay in one town long enough to put down roots. In *This Is My Life* (1992), Dotty (Judith Kavner) is an aspiring stand-up comic whose two daughters must patiently abide their mother's struggles with show business. In *Boyz N the Hood* (1991), Tre's mother, Reva (Angela Bassett), works all day and attends graduate school at night. And the former cocktail waitress Sarah Connor becomes a rebel warrior in *The Terminator* (1984).

As more and more women become visible and vocal in the public sphere and in the workplace in the larger American society, Hollywood has also seen a (slight) growth of numbers of professional women in the film industry.[6] As more women writers, editors, directors, and producers become involved in the production of American movies, the films themselves change to reflect the female point of view. Just as the institution of American literature has finally acknowledged women's (and mothers') voices and stories in the works of Kate Chopin, Tillie Olsen, Louise Erdrich, and Toni Morrison, women as mothers, very much alive and active, are finally speaking to us on film, largely due to the efforts of women filmmakers and writers.[7]

Most recently, *The Piano* (a 1992 international production with a largely American cast) and *Angie* (1993) have as their main characters women who are mothers, and who tell us their own stories. *The Joy Luck*

*Club* (1993) allows us to hear not one but a series of mothers who tell their stories themselves. *The Joy Luck Club* is a most remarkable and important film for our purposes. Considering the history of dead, dreaded, mean, conniving, and pathetic mothers in so many earlier American movies, this film might serve as a refreshing model of how Hollywood films can offer to us wise, funny, admirable mothers whose stories are formidable, haunting, and more powerful than any wave of Glinda's wand.

*The Joy Luck Club* weaves the stories of four Chinese mothers, all now living in San Francisco, with those of their four adult Chinese American daughters. The film is predominantly a series of flashbacks, precipitated by a going-away party for the one daughter among them, June Woo, whose mother, Suyuan, has died. On behalf of her deceased mother, June is on her way to China to meet for the first time her mother's twin daughters—June's half-sisters—whom Suyuan left behind as she fled during the 1949 revolution.

During the film, we see the stories of all four American daughters, especially the stories of their complicated relationships with their mothers. However, the film takes its name from a card club created by the four mothers, and it is the remembrances of the three living mothers, An-mei, Lindo, and Ying-Ying, that become the center of the film, both visually and thematically. The mothers' flashbacks of their lives in prerevolutionary China and of the war serve many purposes in the film. Most especially, the mothers' stories help the audience to understand the complexities of their lives and their relationships to their children. We begin to understand, in the same way their daughters do, that long before these women were living in America raising American daughters, they were children, daughters themselves, in China.

These mothers allow us to experience their memories, their hopes, and their fears, both for themselves and for their daughters. When Lena St. Clair, married daughter of Ying-Ying, begins to have marital problems, her mother remembers her own tragic first marriage in China. The memory gives her the power to confront Lena about her bad marriage. We see Ying-Ying waiting to talk to Lena in a darkened bedroom, and we hear her vow to help save her confused, brokenhearted child: "I am waiting like a tiger in the trees, now ready to leap out and cut her spirit loose." The strength of Ying-Ying's narrative is the key to Lena's empowerment and happiness.

The ancient Greeks, Freud, and modern feminists have all suggested that our mothers are our first and most important teachers. What *The Joy Luck Club* and other films that include the narratives of mother characters allow us to experience is not only the ultimate power of storytelling but also the strength of teaching by example. Thus, instead of supplying us with an endless series of one-dimensional mother characters whose purposes are to foil, fool, or diminish other characters, Hollywood has begun to provide us with characters who are not just mother figures but real people. The most recent Hollywood mothers are not icons or monoliths but are flesh and blood. Hearing their own stories teaches us to see them as characters who embody human traits, both admirable and flawed.

As Adrienne Rich has pointed out, "motherhood" is an institution, quite different from the act of mothering. Like all institutions, motherhood changes—however slowly—to accommodate the changing needs of the society that has created it. In American culture, it is possible to gauge Hollywood's version of motherhood: we have come from unreal dream mother Glinda to perceptive, sad Ying-Ying; we have gone from silent, muzzled victim-mother Stella Dallas (1937, 1990) to vital, savvy Reva in *Boyz N the Hood.*

If Glinda represents the traditional institutional portrait of Hollywood motherhood, then Ying-Ying represents mothering in contemporary American film. If, as *The Joy Luck Club* suggests, mothers use the power of storytelling to teach and comfort their children, then Ying-Ying is a promising indication that Hollywood will portray mothers, not motherhood. Ying-Ying and the other recent mothers in these films are truly redeemed ideals in Hollywood films. They seem to understand, better than the Hollywood tradition that helped create them, that their power on film is not in a bubble or with a wand but with narrative and action. Perhaps we will learn more about Hollywood and about ourselves by listening to these mothers. They have a great deal to teach us.

## Notes

I am grateful to the following: S. Carey, L. Coleman, B. Funk, J. Gittes, K. & T. Hutson, L. & S. Hutson, P. Loukides, and J. Standerfer.

1. Glinda has many characteristics of a mother, not a "fairy godmother," in this film. She is much more affectionate than either Dorothy's aunt or uncle. Glinda holds and kisses Dorothy, and she even helps dress her. Most important, Glinda does not merely grant Dorothy's wish to go home; she makes Dorothy learn this on her own. A mother, not a fairy godmother, makes us learn on our own. For more on the development of the Glinda character in the film, see Fricke, et. al., and McClelland.

2. Two good studies of missing mothers in Shakespeare are Rose and Schotz. Other important studies of mothers in literature and in society are the collection edited by Davidson and Broner; on women's and mother's roles in American film, see Haskell, Silverman, and Williams.

3. The evil stepmother, in literature or on film, is a character who deserves her own chapter in a book. See especially Rich.

4. Faludi's chapter "Fatal and Fetal Visions: The Backlash in the Movies" is a particularly insightful and thorough treatment of Hollywood films of the 1980s.

5. For more on womens' and mothers' films of the 1940s, see the chapter "The Moving Image: Pathos and the Maternal" in Mary Ann Doane, *The Desire to Desire: The Woman's Film of the 1940s.*

6. Women writers and directors are still exceptional in Hollywood, although there are more than there were in 1980. Still, as Faludi points out, even roles for actresses are fewer than they used to be: ". . . in 1990 . . . men . . . were now receiving more than twice as many roles as women" (138).

7. For example, several very recent movies with healthy living mothers have been either written or directed by women: *This Is My Life* (written and directed by Nora Ephron); *The Piano* (written and directed by Jane Campion); *Angie* (directed by Martha Coolidge); and *The Joy Luck Club* (co-written by Amy Tan).

## Works Cited

Davidson, Cathy N., and E.M. Broner, eds. *The Lost Tradition: Mothers and Daughters in Literature.* New York: Ungar, 1980.

Doane, Mary Ann. *The Desire to Desire: The Woman's Film of the 1940s.* Bloomington: Indiana UP, 1987.

Faludi, Susan. *Backlash: The Undeclared War Against American Women.* New York: Doubleday, 1991.

Fricke, John, Jay Scarfone, and William Stillman. *The Wizard of Oz.* New York: Warner, 1989.

Gates, Henry Louis, Jr., and K.A. Appiah, eds. *Toni Morrison: Critical Perspectives Past and Present.* New York: Amistad, 1993.

Haskell, Molly. *From Reverence to Rape: The Treatment of Women in the Movies.* New York: Holt, 1987.

Hirsch, Marianne. "Maternal Narratives: 'Cruel Enough to Stop the Blood.'" Gates and K.A. Appiah 261-73.

MacDonald, Susan Peck. "Jane Austen and the Tradition of the Absent Mother." Davidson and Broner 58-69.

McClelland, Doug. *Down the Yellow Brick Road.* New York: Pyramid, 1976.

Rich, Adrienne. *Of Woman Born: Motherhood as Experience and Institution.* New York: Norton, 1976.

Rose, Mary Beth. "Where Are the Mothers in Shakespeare? Options for Gender Representation in the English Renaissance." *Shakespeare Quarterly* 42 (1991): 291-314.

Schotz, Myra Glazer. "The Great Unwritten Story: Mothers and Daughters in Shakespeare." Davidson and Broner 44-54.

Silverman, Sheldon. "Hollywood's Murdering Mothers: The Rationalization of Psychotic Mother-Love." *Beyond the Stars: Studies in American Popular Film.* Vol 1. Ed. Paul Loukides and Linda K. Fuller. Bowling Green, OH: Bowling Green State University Popular Press, 1990.

Walker, Alice. *In Search of Our Mothers' Gardens.* New York: Harcourt, 1983.

Williams, Linda. "'Something Else Besides a Mother': *Stella Dallas* and the Maternal Melodrama." *Cinema Journal* 24 (1984): 2-27.

## Filmography

| Year | Film | Director |
|---|---|---|
| 1934 | *Imitation of Life* | John Stahl |
| 1937 | *Stella Dallas* | King Vidor |
| 1938 | *The Adventures of Tom Sawyer* | Norman Taurog |
| 1939 | *The Adventures of Huckleberry Finn* | Richard Thorpe |
| 1939 | *Gone with the Wind* | Victor Fleming |
| 1939 | *The Wizard of Oz* | Victor Fleming |
| 1941 | *Citizen Kane* | Orson Welles |
| 1942 | *Now Voyager* | Irving Rapper |
| 1943 | *Tender Comrade* | Edward Dmytryk |
| 1944 | *Since You Went Away* | John Cromwell |
| 1945 | *Mildred Pierce* | Michael Curtiz |
| 1945 | *A Tree Grows in Brooklyn* | Joel Hardy |
| 1946 | *To Each His Own* | Mitchell Leisen |
| 1948 | *I Remember Mama* | George Stevens |
| 1949 | *The Secret Garden* | Fred M. Wilcox |
| 1955 | *East of Eden* | Elia Kazan |
| 1955 | *Rebel without a Cause* | Nicholas Ray |
| 1956 | *A Kiss before Dying* | Gerd Oswald |
| 1957 | *The Three Faces of Eve* | Nunnally Johnson |
| 1959 | *Suddenly Last Summer* | Joseph L. Mankiewicz |
| 1959 | *A Summer Place* | Delmer Daves |
| 1959 | *Imitation of Life* | Douglas Sirk |

| | | |
|---|---|---|
| 1960 | *Psycho* | Alfred Hitchcock |
| 1961 | *A Raisin in the Sun* | Daniel Petrie |
| 1962 | *Gypsy* | Mervyn LeRoy |
| 1964 | *The Chalk Garden* | Ronald Neame |
| 1964 | *Marnie* | Alfred Hitchcock |
| 1965 | *Doctor Zhivago* | David Lean |
| 1965 | *A Patch of Blue* | Guy Green |
| 1967 | *Guess Who's Coming to Dinner?* | Stanley Kramer |
| 1967 | *The Graduate* | Mike Nichols |
| 1972 | *The Godfather* | Francis Coppola |
| 1972 | *Sounder* | Martin Ritt |
| 1973 | *The Exorcist* | William Friedkin |
| 1974 | *Alice Doesn't Live Here Anymore* | Martin Scorsese |
| 1977 | *Close Encounters of the 3rd Kind* | Steven Spielberg |
| 1977 | *Julia* | Fred Zinnemann |
| 1978 | *An Unmarried Woman* | Paul Mazursky |
| 1979 | *Breaking Away* | Peter Yates |
| 1979 | *The China Syndrome* | James Bridges |
| 1979 | *Heartland* | Richard Pearce |
| 1979 | *Kramer vs. Kramer* | Robert Benton |
| 1979 | *Norma Rae* | Martin Ritt |
| 1980 | *Ordinary People* | Robert Redford |
| 1980 | *Tell Me A Riddle* | Lee Grant |
| 1982 | *E.T. The Extra-Terrestrial* | Steven Spielberg |
| 1982 | *Sophie's Choice* | Alan J. Pakula |
| 1984 | *Country* | Richard Pierce |
| 1884 | *The Karate Kid* | John Avildsen |
| 1984 | *Places in the Heart* | Robert Benton |
| 1984 | *The River* | Mark Rydell |
| 1984 | *The Terminator* | James Cameron |
| 1985 | *The Color Purple* | Steven Spielberg |
| 1985 | *The Trip to Bountiful* | Peter Masterson |
| 1986 | *Desert Bloom* | Eugene Corr |
| 1987 | *Housekeeping* | Bill Forsythe |
| 1987 | *Like Father, Like Son* | Rod Daniel |
| 1988 | *Big* | Penny Marshall |
| 1988 | *Bright Lights, Big City* | James Bridges |
| 1988 | *Clara's Heart* | Robert Mulligan |
| 1988 | *18 Again* | Paul Flaherty |
| 1988 | *Rain Man* | Barry Levinson |
| 1989 | *Dad* | Gary David Goldberg |
| 1989 | *Enemies: A Love Story* | Paul Mazursky |

| | | |
|---|---|---|
| 1989 | *Field of Dreams* | Phil Alden Robinson |
| 1989 | *Indiana Jones and the Last Crusade* | Steven Spielberg |
| 1989 | *Staying Together* | Lee Grant |
| 1990 | *The Grifters* | Stephen Frears |
| 1990 | *Home Alone* | John Hughes |
| 1990 | *Men Don't Leave* | Paul Brickman |
| 1990 | *Mermaids* | Richard Benjamin |
| 1990 | *Stella* | John Erman |
| 1991 | *Boyz N The Hood* | John Singleton |
| 1991 | *My Own Private Idaho* | Gus Van Sant |
| 1991 | *Not Without My Daughter* | Brian Gilbert |
| 1991 | *The Prince of Tides* | Barbra Streisand |
| 1992 | *Gas Food Lodging* | Allison Anders |
| 1992 | *Lorenzo's Oil* | George Miller |
| 1992 | *Radio Flyer* | Richard Donner |
| 1992 | *This is My Life* | Nora Ephron |
| 1993 | *Angie* | Martha Coolidge |
| 1993 | *The Joy Luck Club* | Wayne Wang |
| 1993 | *The Piano* | Jane Campion |
| 1993 | *Sleepless in Seattle* | Nora Ephron |

# "It's a Cold World Out There": Redefining the Family in Contemporary American Film

**Mark J. Charney**

A couple take down their volleyball net and wonder what to do with the two dozen eggs left by their group of college friends, hoping that their last remaining guest will stay for at least one more night. Several upwardly mobile young professionals sit around a breakfast table and for a moment consider the possibilities of living in one house together—forever. A social misfit is captured on screen in freeze frame, clicking his heels after discovering not only that the prom queen of the high school he attends finds him more attractive than the school jock, but also that he can be accepted by a group of students very different from himself. Six recent college graduates catch glimpses of their own reflections as they gaze into the window of their old haunt, realizing that, as much as they would like, their tight-knit group may not maintain its insularity in the face of "real world" demands. Three teenagers hitchhike on the New Jersey turnpike, finding that lasting relationships can be forged by the most ridiculous of circumstances. A group of five stand gazing at the Grand Canyon, marveling as much at the bond that exists between them as the miracle of nature they face.

These conclusions to John Sayles's *Return of the Secaucus Seven* (1980), Lawrence Kasdan's *The Big Chill* (1983), John Hughes's *The Breakfast Club* (1985), Joel Schumacher's *St. Elmo's Fire* (1985), Whit Stillman's *Metropolitan* (1990), and Lawrence Kasdan's *Grand Canyon* (1991), respectively, indicate a new convention in films that Sayles helped to create in the 1980s. Each of the films proves that in American cinema, water often runs deeper than blood. Developing a surrogate family beyond the ties of blood and marriage has become a popular dramatic staple in recent movies. When the bonds defined are already established as the story begins, as in *St. Elmo's Fire* and *The Big Chill*, much of the drama results from testing the strength of the connection. Other times, as in *The Breakfast Club* and *Grand Canyon*, the process of forming these bonds creates the drama. But both types of films show audiences that connections between friends can be at least as strong as those within the family, primarily because such relationships are rooted in spiritual need, not familial obligation—in the heart, not the blood or the legal bond.

Films such as these illustrate the ideology of the extended family in contemporary cinema. This trend does not include adventure movies, particularly war films such as *Platoon* or westerns such as *Silverado* where the formation and trial of surrogate families depend on fulfilling primarily temporary needs, or buddy pictures such as *Thelma and Louise* and the *Lethal Weapon* trilogy, which borrow from traditional formulas to recreate the idea of family. Instead, the extended family film creates its own set of structures. A group of people, usually similar in age, are brought together for any number of reasons—a reunion, a Saturday detention, a Christmas holiday—either bonding for the first time or renewing old friendships. A few days together usually not only strengthens lifelong friendships but also solves significant individual problems. The groups are usually defined by the variety of personalities within them and almost always include a central couple (extended family mother and father) around which the gathering revolves, an irresponsible and even dangerous rebel, and outsiders unacceptable by the standards of the extended family. The appeal of these films lies in their ability to convince audiences that the connections between members of the groups are believable, and that the individual problems can be solved by temporary group interaction. As this connection grows slicker, more romantic, and less realistic in films made after *Return of the Secaucus Seven*, the popularity of these films continues to increase.

Although he was not singularly responsible for the extended family movement in cinema, John Sayles created the prototype in his *Return of the Secaucus Seven*. Made for only $90,000, the movie tells the story of seven college friends who meet in Vermont for an annual weekend reunion. The film revolves around a couple, Mike and Kate (Bruce MacDonald and Maggie Renzi), who work as teachers, and five of their friends: J.T. (Adam Lefevre), an aspiring country singer with a reputation for promiscuity; Irene (Jean Passanante), J.T.'s old girlfriend who now writes speeches for a senatorial candidate; Francis (Maggie Cousineau), a medical school student who seeks companionship and a permanent attachment; Maura (Karen Trott), a social worker who recently broke off a lengthy relationship with Jeff (Mark Arnott), a drug rehabilitation counselor who is also Maura's ex and J.T.'s best friend. These friends have dubbed themselves the Secaucus Seven because several years ago they had been arrested in Secaucus, New Jersey, on their way to a march in Washington—ironically not for protesting but for just resembling demonstrators. This arrest created friendships that have led to an annual reunion, even though career choices and life changes seem to be pushing the seven apart.

Although Maura greets the group with news of her breakup with Jeff by sarcastically asking, "What's a reunion without a little drama," Sayles downplays the individual relationship problems to concentrate more heavily on the bond that exists between these seven friends. They arrive separately and in pairs, break off into subgroups, discuss each other, regroup, and discuss each other again. In fact, Sayles is careful to keep the characters in groups of twos and threes so that they can feed the audience exposition about the other off-screen characters. When not in smaller groups, the seven are usually seen together—along with their dates, friends, and high school buddies. The drama lies not in one conflict or on a central relationship, but within the honest connection these seven share and the comfortable ways in which they react to each other's patterns and eccentricities.

To give background information about the group and to define further the relationship of the seven within it, Sayles uses several outsiders with whom the audience can identify. Irene's new boyfriend Chip (Gordon Clapp) is the most significant. His nervousness over meeting Irene's "extended family" prompts Irene to give advice that only heightens his anxiety: "These are my best friends. You get all kinda points just for being with me. So relax." One moment reminding Chip to be himself and the next encouraging him to act more relaxed, Irene is as nervous about Chip's acceptance as he is, maybe even more. The outsider role, as exemplified by Chip, becomes a character type within the "extended family" film who helps the director deliver exposition smoothly and provides an opportunity to create audience empathy.

Although *Return of the Secaucus Seven* lacks a central plot, especially in conventional narrative terms, several subplots drive the narrative by creating tension between the characters. Maura arrives, having recently broken up with Jeff, and has sex almost immediately with Jeff's best friend J.T. Jeff, who is supposedly attending a family reunion, shows up unexpectedly, forcing the trio to discuss their infidelities. Irene's past relationship with J.T., a second subplot, causes Chip distress, while Francis, who longs to sleep with J.T., settles for Ron—with whom Irene had made love the year before. Because Mike and Katie have the only stable relationship and are the hosts for the weekend, they serve as the center around which the other subplots revolve. Their evening discussions in bed heighten their centrality to the group, for not only do they arrange the reunion, but they also referee the interactions and evaluate their progress.

The untangling of these subplots demonstrates the group's ability to listen sympathetically to one another; support one another's emotional needs; and ultimately forgive each other's indiscretions and mini-betrayals. For example, everyone listens to Maura's complaints about her recent breakup with Jeff without taking sides. Even Jeff's best friend, J.T., remains neutral, assuring Maura, "You're my friend too." And when Jeff shows up unexpectedly, he is as welcome as Maura. Jeff even forgives J.T. for sleeping with his ex-girlfriend, just as Chip forgives Irene when he discovers her past fling with Ron. Members of the group also offer each other financial as well as emotional support. Irene insists on funding J.T.'s move to Los Angeles as an investment in his music career, and Maura pays his bus fare. The friendship shared by the Secaucus Seven is built on unconditional support. They treat each other with respect and affection. While they don't always condone or forget each other's indiscretions, they are ultimately willing to forgive and to help one another recover for the sake of their mutual friendship. The unconditional acceptance they feel for one another overpowers their interpersonal jealousies and animosities, and resembles the acceptance normally found within the family.

Lawrence Kasdan borrows heavily from *Return of the Secaucus Seven* in his multimillion-dollar success, *The Big Chill.* From Running Dog shoes to sexual infidelity, Kasdan imitates Sayles's pattern almost stitch by stitch, sewing seven thirtysomething college friends into a similar, though more fashionable, piece of cloth. Kasdan transforms the Secaucus Seven into seven postsixties liberals whose spontaneous reunion results from the suicide of their mutual friend Alex. As in *Return of the Secaucus Seven*, the reunion centers around a stable couple, Sarah (Glenn Close) and Harold (Kevin Kline), who are upscale, attractive versions of Katie and Mike (doctor and entrepreneur rather than teachers); but unlike Katie and Mike, Sarah and Harold have bought into respectability. They are married, have several children, and own a small plantation replete with columns and draped with Spanish moss. Although Sarah and Harold admittedly feel guilt and a little regret over their financial success, they assuage their consciences by providing a temporary home for friends such as Alex and his girlfriend Chloe (Meg Tilly), and, indeed, it was in their guest house that Alex committed suicide.

Several of the college friends resemble characters from *Secaucus Seven.* Meg (Mary Kay Place), a Houston lawyer who uses the weekend in part to find a potential surrogate father to help her conceive, seems most like Francis—who hopes in *Secaucus Seven* to begin a relationship with J.T. but ends up with Ron Desjardins. Both characters are strong, isolated women who lament that they are fulfilling themselves professionally but not emotionally. Nick (William Hurt), the drug dealer in *The Big Chill*, is very much like J.T., the womanizer in *Secaucus Seven*, not only because he is equally attractive to members of the opposite sex, but also because he too is an aimless wanderer who lives more for the moment than the future. Sam (Tom Berenger), a Los Angeles actor who plays J.T. Lancer on a popular television series, also resembles a successful version of *Secaucus Seven*'s J.T., who is bound for L.A. hoping to find stardom. Karen (Jobeth Williams), trapped in an unhappy marriage to a husband who she feels is insensitive to her needs, resembles Maura, who breaks with longtime boyfriend Jeff before she suffers a similar fate. Karen sleeps with Sam, hoping to satisfy her needs, unfulfilled by marriage, just as Maura sleeps with J.T., to fill the void Jeff has left in her life. And Michael (Jeff Goldblum), who works as a writer for *People* magazine, rounds out the seven.

Both films, using similar character types and film techniques, establish the same premise: that renewing friendships in spite of pressures to let them finally fade is as significant as furthering familial bonds. And despite its all-star cast and lavish settings, *The Big Chill* is linked to *Return of the Secaucus Seven* by structural and contextual concerns, as well as similar characters.

Although the relationship traumas differ in the two films, the tenor of the reunion is the same and the structure almost identical. Both films concentrate on one weekend—from a Friday to a Sunday—to identify character conflicts and relationships, and both directors give the illusion of plotlessness in their efforts to avoid building to a conventional climax. Kasdan incorporates activities similar to those in *Secaucus Seven* to define the relationships between individual members of the group. A volleyball game in *Secaucus Seven* becomes a football game in *The Big Chill;* a cookout is transformed into a spaghetti dinner; a drunken night in the bar becomes a late night marijuana fest at the plantation. Even the scenes around the breakfast tables seem similar. Like Sayles, Kasdan affects an easygoing style loosely arranged around the conversations among the seven friends; in fact, both directors organize subplots effectively by creating focal activities where the central characters meet (football games, dinners, breakfasts), then finding reasons for the seven to break into satellite groups again, thus furthering the intrigue within the large group.

Kasdan also uses innovative methods of revealing characterization, such as using a video camera for characters to interview themselves and each other, and filming individual scenes of guests unpacking their suitcases, each with specific items that indicate both character quirks and weekend plans. For example, Meg brings calculators, day planners, and several packs of Merit cigarettes, while Michael empties a suitcase of cologne, hair-dressing materials, and condoms. Even the rooms to which they are assigned indicate character and/or further plot. Karen and Don share twin beds—not pushed together—Meg has an isolated attic bedroom, and Michael sleeps in one of Sarah's son's beds—shaped humorously like an airplane. Because of this economy of character depiction, Kasdan leads audiences to assume a great deal about each of the seven before the weekend actually begins.

But the seven college friends in *The Big Chill* share more than trauma and missed opportunities. They also share a bond, one so strong that outsiders are even more excluded from their group than they are in *Secaucus Seven*. In Sayles's film, members of the group treat outsiders such as Chip warmly because he is dating Irene. Mike, Katie, and Francis may analyze his potential as a suitor for Irene and joke about his apparent conservatism, but even high school friends such as Ron and Howie are included in some events simply based on their past friendship with Mike. Although it is apparent that none of these characters will ever be a part of the *Secaucus Seven* (nor would they necessarily want to be), few are made to feel unwelcome or permanently excluded. This is not the case with an outsider in *The Big Chill* parallel to Chip from *Secaucus Seven*: Karen's husband, Richard.

When Kasdan first introduces Richard, we see his reaction as Karen waves to her old love-interest, Sam Weber. As she leans back at the funeral in the church pew after waving to Sam, we see Richard lean up in a paranoid gesture to catch a glimpse of the man he has probably heard much about, especially considering Karen's continued interest in the television star. After the funeral, Richard stammers when he tries to remember either the name of Sam's show or the night when he and his boys supposedly watch it on TV, embarrassing both Karen and Sam. And in the car alone with Karen, Richard chides her for misrepresenting her friends. "They're nothing like you said. I'd love to hear how you describe me to them." As Karen looks sadly away from Richard and out the window, we can safely guess how she has described Richard to her college friends: responsible, secure, and a good provider, but also dull, conservative, and distant.

In later scenes before Richard escapes from the group into his comfortable role as father, Kasdan treats Richard almost punitively. Not only is he much more conservatively dressed than the other seven, but he is often made to look like a buffoon by members of the group. At the reception after the funeral, Richard talks about advertising to Nick, the most unlikely candidate of the seven to express interest about the subject, indicating that he has no sense of audience. When Sarah asks Karen if she should push their twin beds together, Karen responds immediately with a "Why?"—suggesting that Richard is uninterested in her or possibly just uninteresting sexually. And when Sam and Nick discuss Karen late Friday evening, Nick offers a warning based on what he has seen of Richard: "Be careful what you want or you will surely get it," implying that Richard is the retribution for Karen's obsessive need for marriage and security. Richard is neither as hip as Nick nor as comforting as Harold. He shares none of Sam's exciting sexual allure or Nick's street-smart savvy. Kasdan presents him as a conservative businessman who openly illustrates little warmth for the group and less ability to judge and/or relate to others. And the audience laughs at him along with the seven who feel that he will never be a part of their group—Karen or no Karen.

Although the treatment of the group, the structure of the film, and the definition of outsiders is similar in *The Big Chill* and *Return of the Secaucus Seven*, the much larger budget of Kasdan's film affects several thematic differences in the two movies. Sayles's group of seven are no longer radical hippies, and none of them shares the financial success or the good looks of the friends in *The Big Chill*. Lawyer, doctor, entrepreneur, actor—each of the seven in *The Big Chill* has made more money than most of the Secaucus Seven put together and it shows, not only in their more confident attitudes but in their secure stations in life. Although they joke with each other about "selling out," this recognition that they have disregarded their dreams and ignored their dedication to 1960s causes is more a catalyst for conversations about personal disappointments than it is serious self-criticism. As Harold says, "Fuck 'em if they can't take a joke." In fact, all of them are preppies but Nick, whose uncertainty about his future is decided after a weekend with his old college buddies. Along with this shift in ideology, *The Big Chill* also boasts bigger production values, a slicker look, a great '60s soundtrack, and recognizable, likable actors. In *Return of the Secaucus Seven*, audiences enjoy meeting the group; in *The Big Chill* audiences would like to join the group.

But this attention to success and good looks subtly undermines much of what Kasdan tries to achieve in *The Big Chill*. Harold may assure Meg and the rest of the group that his home provides haven from the chill of the world, that they can be themselves around each other, but his promise becomes less honest as the movie progresses. In true sitcom fashion, each of the characters finds solutions to his or her problems after only one weekend together. Sarah overcomes her guilt over sleeping with Alex by encouraging her husband (very unrealistically) to sleep with Meg, and this, of course, may take care of Meg's conception problem. Kasdan leads audiences to believe that Meg will almost certainly bear a child based on this one sexual experience, not only because of Harold's role as nurturing father and provider, but also because they are using Sarah and Harold's "lucky" bed. Through their affair, Karen and Sam are both content to return to their previous lives more satisfied with their respective situations than they were before, while Nick will overcome drug addiction and possibly even impotence through his relationship with Alex's old girlfriend Chloe. Even Michael seems less superficial, abandoning his schemes to use his friends to fund a new restaurant and to provide material for *People* magazine articles.

They may readily admit that the real world is cold and lonely (as the title of the film suggests), but the group finds that a weekend together heals their emotional and physical inadequacies, so much so that when Harold asks about airport rides, Michael playfully answers, "We took a secret vote. We're not leaving. We're never leaving." And although audiences know he is joking, Kasdan drives home the point that the seven have a bond that neither time nor distance will break. Whereas Sayles ends *The Return of the Secaucus Seven* realistically, with characters disappearing before they have a chance to say goodbye and friends temporarily dividing loyalties, Kasdan opts for a conclusion that is more romantic, more appealing, and ultimately less honest.

The success of *The Big Chill* established a place in popular cinema for films that extol the importance of a network of friends helping one another sort out problems and overcome obstacles. Hollywood was quick to respond to the success of *The Big Chill* with John Hughes's *The Breakfast Club* and Joel Schumacher's *St. Elmo's Fire* in 1985. Both of these films adopt the idea that friends can serve as surrogate family and apply it to a younger crowd. Dubbed "Little Chills" by promotional magazines and advertising managers, they borrow and exploit the pattern created by Sayles in *Secaucus Seven* and popularized by Kasdan in *The Big Chill*. Although the structure of both films on the surface differs from those of the earlier films upon which they are modeled, the financial success of both movies can be attributed to their adherence to a "Big Chill" formula. *The Breakfast Club* introduces five, not seven characters, who have never previously spent time together, while *St. Elmo's Fire* centers around the magic number seven again, old college buddies who have recently graduated and all live and work in the Georgetown area of Washington, D.C. Both setups are fairly unrealistic. The five high schoolers in *The Breakfast Club* are sentenced to a full Saturday of detention in the high school library, each for committing some "crime" against the school and/or the system. Although they have never previously met, in the eight hours spent together, they learn to break down emotional barriers and reevaluate their criteria for friendship. The seven college graduates in *St. Elmo's Fire* are sentenced to detention for life. Choosing to spend the next several years together in Georgetown near their old university, all seven would rather sacrifice future career plans for the opportunity to attempt to recreate college days and to hang on unrealistically to old friendships.

Both *The Breakfast Club* and *St. Elmo's Fire* use the staples brought to this type of film by Kasdan: energizing, popular music, an attractive all-star cast, stylized montages, and lots of sexual pairing and subplotting. Yet these two films neither generate relationships that seem as truthful and honest as *Return of the Secaucus Seven*, nor evoke the same emotional power exhibited by *The Big Chill*. In other words, *The Breakfast Club* and *St. Elmo's Fire* focus upon style without including substance. They build the same body but neglect the heart, and although both films are entertaining, they sacrifice integrity and realism for spark and showmanship.

Possibly most unrealistic is how easily the characters in each film break down into types. To fulfill the detention assignment in *The Breakfast Club*—each student must write at least 1,000 words describing who they think they are—Brian categorizes the five who spend the day in detention: a jock, Andrew (Emilio Estevez); a prom queen, Claire (Molly Ringwald); a juvenile delinquent, Bender (Judd Nelson); a brain, Brian (Anthony Michael Hall); and a basket case, Allison (Ally Sheedy). The seven from *St. Elmo's Fire* also can ironically be examined as stereotypes, older versions of *The Breakfast Club*: a jock, now aspiring graduate student and lovesick waiter, Kirby (Emilio Estevez); a prom queen, now pretty girlfriend to an up-and-coming lawyer, Leslie (Ally Sheedy); a juvenile delinquent, now drug addict, alcoholic, and adulterer, Billy (Rob Lowe); a brain, now cynical, lovesick, embittered journalist, Kevin (Andrew McCarthy); and a basket case, now bank teller, who prostitutes herself for drugs, affection, and financial support, Jules (Demi Moore). *St. Elmo's Fire* also contains other new categories from *The Big Chill*—a liberal Jewish social worker, Wendy (Mare Winningham), who is the counterpart to Meg, and a yuppie Democrat turned Republican, Alec (Judd Nelson), who is a more successful version of Michael. Many of the same actors from *The Breakfast Club* repeat similar roles in *St. Elmo's Fire,* like Emilio Estevez, or graduate to new ones, like Judd Nelson. After the success of films like *The Breakfast Club,* grouping several of these young actors together became a publicity ploy. Dubbed the Brat Pack, partially because of their youth and popularity and partially because of their tendency to travel together on and off screen, these inexperienced actors illustrated in real life, as they do in each of these two films, the powerful draw of the extended family.

The five high schoolers in *The Breakfast Club* become a family of sorts in the course of their detention spent in the library for committing crimes against a system that all of them question. Hughes structures the film around the group's increasing need to confess great truths to one another and their desire to combat authority. In fact, the group bonds primarily because of an "us versus them" philosophy that sets student against adult and rebel against authority. The David Bowie quote that opens the film against an image of shattering glass reveals much about how these students react to adults in *The Breakfast Club:*

> And these children
> that you spit on
> as they try to change their worlds
> are immune to your consultations
> They're quite aware
> of what they're going through.

The five members of the "breakfast club," as they come to call themselves, serve as universal representations of youth in general and stand metaphorically against those who resist change. The tone is both conciliatory and accusatory–conciliatory within the group or among the "insiders," and accusatory with anyone not a member of the group or the "outsiders."

Like *Return of the Secaucus Seven* and *The Big Chill*, *The Breakfast Club* uses outsiders to emphasize the strength of the newly formed familial connection, but these outsiders are not restricted to the occasional visitor, the old high school friend, or the most recent date or marriage partner. Outsiders in Hughes's film are all people above 25, and he treats them much like adults in a Charlie Brown cartoon. Essentially faceless and voiceless, because they have no identities beyond their complaints, parents in the film are drivers who transport their children to and from detention, goad them with criticism, and ultimately, represent the source of their children's inadequacies.

Sporting a gray "Barry Manilow" leisure suit and a "Don't mess with the bull or you'll get the horns" philosophy, vice-principal Richard Vernon is the primary nonparental outsider featured in *The Breakfast Club*. Hughes, who also served as screenwriter for the film, treats him with the disdain afforded all adults by the breakfast club. Vernon is a nincompoop, a preening peacock who hates his job, detests his students, and has an inflated sense of superiority. Stopping before mirrors and reflective windows to check his profile at every opportunity, Vernon symbolizes the elements of authority that high school students detest most: conformity, mediocrity, and senseless power. Speaking only in clichés, Vernon hands out detention slips in a lame effort to communicate his authority and believes physical punishment is the only instigator of change. Alone with Bender late in the film, Vernon pushes him forcefully against a file cabinet, calls him a "gutless turd," and threatens to "knock his dick in the dirt" if Bender ridicules him in front of other students again. Corrupt to the core, Vernon is discovered by Carl, the janitor, illegally searching through employee files. By the end of the film Vernon has become a cartoon villain who has no power to see or hear even what goes on in the room next to him. Whether he is guzzling beer in the file room with Carl or ineffectively taunting Bender, his nemesis in the film, Vernon is an outsider who inspires the group to bond.

In the course of the film, Bender, the juvenile delinquent, surfaces as the leader of the club and the primary instigator of their status as a family (almost like a parent). Not only does he stand openly against Vernon in front of the other students, but his experience and his openly rebellious attitude appeal to the four who have been repressed by uncaring parents. Bender even stands physically in opposition to Vernon. Lighting matches on his teeth, sporting a gray coat and army boots, and walking with the swagger of a young James Dean, Bender, as played by Judd Nelson, ultimately represents the most romantic figure in the film. He gets the group high (most for the first time), leads them in a dance, takes them on illegal excursions outside of the library, and confronts Vernon physically. By the end of the film Bender has broken through all social barriers. Not only is the rich prom queen, Claire, enamored of him, but he has loudly and aggressively forced them to reexamine their shallow loyalties and at least temporarily reevaluate their status within the school.

This unrealistic but sentimental emphasis on change and bonding helped to make *The Breakfast Club* a popular success, especially with teen audiences. Like *The Big Chill*, *The Breakfast Club* offers respite from the cold world outside as represented by bogus authority figures such as Vernon. In one eight-hour period, consciousnesses are raised and popularity rankings broken down—partially as a protective gesture against blind authority and partially because *The Breakfast Club* implies that children are more open to questioning existing institutions than the adults who created them. Having gained their acceptance and affection, Brian becomes their collective voice, ending the battle with Vernon by turning the assignment against him. At the end of the film as Andrew kisses Allison, as Claire gives Bender a diamond earring, and as the

Simple Minds tune begins, "Don't You Forget About Me," Brian writes in response to their detention assignment, "We found out that each one of us is a brain, an athlete, a basket case, a princess, and a criminal. Does that answer your question?" The film's last shot is of Bender walking across a solitary football field, triumphant in the knowledge that he has helped to change five people's lives in one day. And considering how many Saturdays he will spend in detention, he may very well become the Mary Poppins of Shermer High School, spending his weekends teaching others to overcome the prejudices and senseless structures imposed upon them by their parents and teachers.

In *St. Elmo's Fire*, Joel Schumacher attempts to follow the formula established by *Secaucus Seven* and *The Big Chill* and popularized by *The Breakfast Club*. Like *Secaucus Seven* and *The Big Chill*, the film is about the trials of an established family of friends. But because he depicts seven lives without the structure offered by a Saturday detention or a spontaneous weekend reunion, his film wanders aimlessly from mini-trauma to mini-trauma, almost a series of sensational, unrealistic vignettes rather than a coherent whole. In fact, because he cannot fall back on a weekend reunion or one localized event, Schumacher uses this transition period, which spans only several weeks, as the event around which he organizes the crises within the characters' lives. *St. Elmo's Fire* is the only one of the films discussed here in which the group itself actually faces an identity crisis. Because of the instability in their lives and the incestuous sexual relationships among members of the seven, one central crisis revolves around whether the group will survive this difficult transition period. When Kevin is temporarily banned from the group because he sleeps with Leslie, loyal roommate Kirby remarks, "I always thought we'd be friends forever," to which Kevin responds, "Forever got a lot shorter, didn't it?" The lack of apparent support between these friends is one reason these affairs somehow seem wrong. When Leslie confronts Alec and Alec hits Kevin, Billy's response is that "it ain't a party till something gets broke." His absolute callousness reflects the way they "help" one another.

But in the spirit of the extended family film, this crisis is alleviated quickly and unrealistically. Through mutual admiration and support, everyone but Billy remains intact and in town. Alec forgives Kevin his indiscretion and both forgive Leslie hers, allowing her to "try life without miracles for awhile." They may realize that their days at their old bar, St. Elmo's Fire, are numbered, but the movie ends with characters proclaiming that they cannot remember a time when the seven of them were not together, and audiences are left with a slow-motion image of the seven in cap and gown, graduating again—a picture preserved in time by seven graduates who will never abandon each another no matter where or with whom they eventually live.

As in *Return of the Secaucus Seven* and *The Big Chill*, outsiders help to define the group's insularity. Although parents are not treated with the same universal disrespect exhibited in *The Breakfast Club*, Jules calls her stepmother "stepmonster" and longs to become more significant in her parents' lives. Wendy's father (Martin Balsam) attempts unsuccessfully to push her into a marriage with Howie, an up-and-coming manager in his greeting card empire, but neither Wendy's father nor Jules's stepmonster is evil—like the vice-principal in *The Breakfast Club*—only misinformed. The true outsiders are exemplified by Wendy's potential suitor and temporary fiancé, Howie. Like Richard from *The Big Chill*, Howie is treated by the seven with the disdain deserving of anyone not judged an "insider" to the group, primarily based on his appearance. Unlike the rest of the seven, Howie is overweight, sports a pair of horn-rimmed glasses, and dresses conservatively—so right away he is recognizably unacceptable. When Billy breaks Wendy's heart by joking about her virginity, she agrees to marry Howie to please her father and as a revenge tactic to upset Billy. Although he escorts Wendy to parties on more than one occasion, the group never considers Howie as seriously as the Secaucus Seven consider Chip or the college friends in *The Big Chill* evaluate Richard. When Wendy expresses concern over a fight between Billy and Felicia, Jules shares a laugh with Wendy at Howie's expense: "Go ahead with your evening with Howie, no matter what he looks like" (further evidence of their cruelty toward one another). And her advice to Wendy, based on Wendy's father's promise that he will give her a car if she will marry Howie, is "Get the car, fuck him, and if you don't like it, *then* break the engagement." With his conservative tie and tight-fitting sweater vest, Howie is simply not "cool" enough to be taken seriously by the group. In fact, unlike outsiders in other extended family films, he rarely utters a word. When Wendy breaks up with Howie and loses her virginity to Billy, right before he leaves friends, wife, and child to pursue a music career in New York (shades of J.T. in *Return of the Secaucus Seven*), the five ironically praise the maturity of both Wendy's and Billy's choices.

Although the seven never permanently resolve their career or relationship crises, each finds closure to his or her emotional problems partially based on familial support offered within the group. Alec and Kevin recover quickly from their antagonistic struggle for Leslie, allowing her the time and space to decide between them. Kirby fails to attract Dale (who, ironically, would be accepted in the group based on her appearance alone), but feels confident that he handled his juvenile crush with integrity. Billy finds comfort in assuring himself that his wife and child would be better off without him, and Wendy is satisfied to lose her virginity to Billy even if she cannot have him permanently. And Jules, whose crisis over her stepmonster's coma brings the seven back together, is assured by her peers that everyone is experiencing the same confusion and isolation she feels. As Billy breaks into the empty room where Jules has locked herself, he tells her the story of St. Elmo's fire, a corona of light that appears in the rigging of ships, thought to be guides through rough weather or troubled seas. Billy claims that the sailors made it all up. When he explains that there is no guiding fire, just static electricity on the sails, Billy is telling her that there is no magic and there are no guides. In spite of the family, members of the group must find their own ways through the storm.

Both *The Breakfast Club* and *St. Elmo's Fire* carry the idea of the extended family to unrealistic and occasionally laughable extremes, but the comfort offered by the idea of an extended family, one that willingly accepts members for who they are, makes these films successful at the box office. Both films incorporate elements of the earlier prototypes, although each changes details to appeal to the interests of specific audiences and to address the culture of specific periods. For example, all of the films discussed focus upon a character who resembles J.T. from *Secaucus Seven*, a rebel with or without a cause, but as the formula becomes slicker it also panders to increasingly younger audiences by building the significance and romanticism of this role while diminishing the role of stable, untraumatic couples such as Katie and Mike or Sarah and Harold. In *Secaucus Seven*, J.T. is a bit of a rake and attractively irresponsible, but he is not the handsome drug dealer in *The Big Chill*, the delinquent in *The Breakfast Club*, or the adulterer in *St. Elmo's Fire*. With each incarnation, the role demands someone who is more physically attractive to make up for his increasing spiritual unattractiveness. From J.T. to Billy, the role has shifted from realistic to unrealistic and from irresponsible to immoral.

Each of the films also shares a loose structure, one more concerned with character than plot development, and each (with the exception of *Secaucus Seven*) suggests that an extended family will not only protect members from the harsh world outside but will magically solve problems for the individuals within it. Still, as illustrated by *The Breakfast Club* and *St. Elmo's Fire*, with each incarnation, the driving force pulling the groups together is more contrived and the leaps made in terms of personal growth for each individual less believable.

Whit Stillman's *Metropolitan* proves that a 1990s director can still adhere to many of the formulas begun in *Return of the Secaucus Seven* but discover original ways to revitalize the material. He returns to a structure that realistically restricts time and space—the debutante season in New York over Christmas holidays—and he focuses upon a group of young prep school students who are attractive, rich, and articulate. But these students are bonded together not from desire or even overt friendship. Instead, during the busy social season, girls need escorts and this Christmas in Manhattan, one "not so long ago," they are facing a shortage so serious that they are willing to accept questionable outsider Tom (Edward Clements) into their group. Innocently waiting for a cab, Tom is dragged unwillingly to Sally's first debutante post-party, and the movie traces his introduction to the group, his gradual acceptance by its members, and the series of parties he attends until the group naturally dissolves. Unlike the other extended family movies examined thus far, the family in *Metropolitan* is temporary, created more by the bonds of social status and physical proximity than genuine friendship, and Stillman uses outsider Tom to introduce audiences to an upper-class world that would seem very foreign to the high schoolers in *The Breakfast Club* or the college grads in *St. Elmo's Fire*.

Through Tom's increasing interest in, and dependence upon, the group, Stillman illustrates the significance of even a temporary extended family. A Westsider who lives alone with his mother in a middle-class flat after his wealthy father left them for another woman, Tom has always professed an intense dislike of upper-class morality and lifestyle. But egged on by Nick to buy a tux and join the escorts, he finds the group too attractive to dismiss. Rather than try to convince audiences that Tom and his newfound friends are wiser than the adults who conveniently are never around, Stillman, unlike Hughes in *The Breakfast Club*, comically celebrates their immaturity. In a series of indistinguishable debutante parties, most held at Sally Fowler's parents' apartment, Tom discusses socialism, surrealism, social mobility, Jane Austen, and escort shortages with preppies who label themselves part of the SFRP, Sally Fowler Rat Pack.

Stillman's *Metropolitan* shares none of the pretenses of films such as *The Big Chill*, *The Breakfast Club*, and *St. Elmo's Fire* that a group will serve permanently as an extended family, one that will protect its members from the chill of the real world outside. In fact, the rat pack in which Tom temporarily finds respite deserts him almost as quickly as he is introduced to it. When Cynthia defends Sally against Tom and Nick's accusations of desertion by snapping, "You act as if her living room were our living room," Tom replies, "It *is* our living room." Sally proves his quick retort false, however, when she refuses to admit them to her apartment because she has begun sleeping with a record producer, and

Cynthia deserts the rat pack to join Rick von Slanicker's enemy camp. Nothing is resolved at the end, not Tom's contradictory feelings about the rat pack, nor Audrey's confusion about pursuing a relationship with Tom rather than going to France. Stillman breaks the pattern popularized by these extended family films by refusing to grant closure to the group's dilemmas within the film, or the relationships that develop within their time spent together. Instead, *Metropolitan* is a slice-of-life comedy, a three-week visit with a spoiled but well-intentioned group of prep school students. At the end of the Christmas holiday, no one is paired up, no one is better off, and very few of the students face permanent friendships with the exception of Charlie, Audrey, and Tom. Although they have been fighting for most of the film, the three form a bond that might be permanent. Charlie and Tom forget their differences in order to "rescue" Audrey, who, flattered by the romantic nature of their effort to save her, bonds more closely with the two "suitors," especially Tom. This bond resembles the one formed by the Secaucus Seven through their experiences in jail.

Stillman treats outsiders differently in *Metropolitan* than do directors such as Kasdan and Schumacher. Like *The Breakfast Club*, his characters discuss parents as outsiders who are rarely around. As Nick wisely puts it, "The most important thing to realize about parents is that there's nothing you can do with them." Much of the charm of *Metropolitan*, in fact, comes from attempts, especially from Nick, to protect the group from outsiders and, luckily for all of them, parents express little interest in their rat pack. But the students, unlike those in *The Breakfast Club*, do not resent their parents; they respect a mutual agreement to leave each other alone.

Stillman does offer a new twist on the extended family ideology; primarily because *Metropolitan* is essentially comic, not melodramatic, the rat pack is too young and silly for audiences to take seriously. Stillman casts unknowns in each of the roles who look as normal and real as the actors from *Return of the Secaucus Seven*, and his script genuinely captures the comedy and pathos involved in adolescence. Tom, for example, criticizes Jane Austen constantly before admitting proudly that he's never read her novels, just criticism about them. To protect Audrey's honor, Tom and Charlie not only take a cab from New York to New Jersey, costing them over one hundred dollars, but Tom pulls out a gun and waves it at Rick. Their discussions of the bourgeoisie and socialism are comically and hopelessly uninformed, as are their opinions about parents. Waking up Audrey's mother on the day of Audrey's disappearance, Nick remarks that "old people get up really early." Unlike *The Big Chill*, *The Breakfast Club*, and *St. Elmo's Fire*,

*Metropolitan* boasts neither a recognizable rock soundtrack nor a big budget, slick production look. Instead, Stillman concentrates on clever dialogue, solid acting, and an intimate directorial style.

If the members of *Metropolitan* (other than Tom) are permanently a part of any group, it is their allegiance to the class that has reared and rewarded them—at least financially and socially. When Tom and Charlie find themselves alone in a bar on a night they wanted to spend at Sally Fowler's, they encounter an older companion from Charlie's social class who reminisces with them about his own years as a debutante escort: "I wouldn't put too much stock in [parties]. You go to a party. You meet people and you say, 'These people are going to be my friends for the rest of my life.' And then you never see them again. I wonder, where do they go?" He refuses, however, to sympathize with Charlie's belief that the upper middle class (what he calls the UHB, the urban haute bourgeoisie, a more "socially precise" term than preppie) is "doomed to failure," saying that being doomed "would be far easier. No, we simply fail without being doomed." At the end of the film, with their rat pack days already behind them, Charlie, Audrey, and Tom may have learned this lesson, but *Metropolitan* resembles *Return of the Secaucus Seven* in that Stillman, like Sayles, is not interested in teaching either his characters or his audiences a lesson. Stillman succeeds instead at humorously defining a group within a social class foreign to most filmgoers (other than New Yorkers) in a manner that is both affectionate and critical, and he uses Tom to carry audiences into an extended family created and destroyed by social necessity.

*Grand Canyon* (1983), directed by Lawrence Kasdan (*The Big Chill*), also offers a twist on the familiar extended family film, but one less successful and original than Whit Stillman's *Metropolitan*. Like *Return of the Secaucus Seven* and *The Big Chill*, the plot revolves primarily around a central couple, Mack (Kevin Kline) and Claire (Mary McDonnell). Firmly entrenched in the upper middle class, Mack and Claire have one son, Roberto, who is about to leave home for summer camp and will soon leave permanently for college. The film begins with a crisis: Mack is almost robbed and mugged by a group of Los Angeles street thugs when returning home from a basketball game that he has just attended with his producer/best friend Davis (Steve Martin). Rescued by tow truck driver Simon (Danny Glover), Mack vows to keep in touch, and in the course of the next few weeks, helps to move Simon's sister to a safer neighborhood and fixes Simon up with Jane (Alfre Woodard), his secretary's best friend. Meanwhile, Davis is shot in the leg by a mugger, inspiring a temporary crisis of conscience (he plans to stop producing violent splatter films), Claire discovers an abandoned infant on one of her morning runs and wants to keep her, Roberto falls in love during summer camp, and Mack breaks off a brief affair with his secretary Dee (Mary Louise Parker). The film is filled with violence, both emotionally and physical, and the characters band together to protect themselves from what Davis at one point calls "the dehumanizing rage that has spread across this country as a pestilence."

The extended family in *Grand Canyon* is not the tight-knit group of thirtysomething friends celebrating a reunion in *Secaucus Seven* or *The Big Chill*, the band of adolescents sharing a Saturday detention in *The Breakfast Club* or a post-party discussion in *Metropolitan*, or the gang of college graduates facing "life choices" in *St. Elmo's Fire*. Instead, *Grand Canyon* is filled with characters who have already made choices and must learn to live with them—couples and singles who are in a position to reevaluate decisions made in their youth. Compared to earlier films that have depicted the extended family, *Grand Canyon* is more portentous and less optimistic. It contains none of the football/volleyball/dance sequences from movies like *The Big Chill* that help to bring members of the extended family together and provide entertainment for the audience. In fact, except for the last scene, audiences never see more than two or three members of the group together at one time, and in spite of all the violence, *Grand Canyon* is full of lofty discussions and angst-ridden personal confessions that focus upon individuals instead of groups. Unlike *Metropolitan*, *Grand Canyon* certainly has a moral: only through acts of selflessness and extended family support, such as Simon's efforts to protect Mack or Claire's willingness to accept responsibility for the child she discovers, will people pull themselves from the despair that has become the norm.

This "lesson" is probably best expressed in a flashback that depicts a memory, appropriately located on Miracle Mile, that saved Mack's life. A woman with a Pirates cap standing on the corner of Wilshire Boulevard pulls Mack from the path of an oncoming bus, and then disappears with a smile and a nod into the crowd. Filmed in slow-motion black-and-white with an angelic choir humming in the background, the scene is central to Mack's life and the film's overt message. The woman's selfless act, which originated simply from her desire to protect a stranger in need, is held up as the sort of behavior that prevents the world from seeming so destructive. Shaking his head, Simon responds after hearing the story, "The world's a bad place. Sometimes you just get lucky." But *Grand Canyon* suggests that luck originates through such selfless concern for others and a willingness to take chances.

The structure of *Grand Canyon*, then, is by necessity very different from films such as *The Breakfast Club* or *Metropolitan*. It most resembles *St. Elmo's Fire* in its effort to connect characters through mini-traumas, although the stories that define relationships in *Grand Canyon* would more likely be labeled maxi-traumas. The film moves from one vignette of physical violence to another, but Kasdan spends the majority of his screen time defining Mack and Claire, especially Mack, who forges connections with everyone including the infant that Claire discovers. In fact, Kasdan consistently ignores other characters who are central to the plot, so audiences rarely see Davis (except for comic relief), Dee, or Jane. Because of this screen preoccupation with Mack and Claire, other characters are presented as filtered through Mack's perspective, an oddly personal emphasis for a film about forming collective communities.

Kasdan incorporates several motifs that connect the characters and the city, from the helicopter that glides soundlessly above the city to the expressionistic dream sequences that help to define fears of the central characters. Images of flying offer characters possibilities both of escape and of freedom not afforded by the tight confines of city life. Time is occasionally disrupted too, often to indicate the inevitability of changes and the natural passages from childhood to adulthood. For example, time-lapse sequences push dawn into day surrealistically, and slow motion emphasizes the importance of a memory or a discovery. With the exception of Warren Zevon's song "Lawyers, Guns, and Money," which playfully sets a satiric tone for the film, most of the music is choir-based and ethereal, complementing the dreams and occasional temporal distortion, while sirens from ambulances and police cars constantly serve as background noise. By juxtaposing this expressionistic desire for escape, as illustrated by the dreams, the use of slow motion, and the choir music, with the sounds and sights of real city life, Kasdan creates a tone very different from the protective seclusion groups experience in most extended family films. In *Grand Canyon* the possibility of family is not strong enough to protect its characters from the big chill of the world outside.

*Grand Canyon* also differs from other films about the extended family in its presentation of the outsider. Since the film traces the making of such a family, anyone is potentially an insider, especially if Mack and Claire's philosophy of helping others truly holds. Only Dee is left truly an outsider by the film's end, not because she deserves exclusion, but because Mack, who has more or less brought the group together, cannot include her because of their aborted affair. Unlike films such as *The Big Chill*, in *Grand Canyon*, illicit sex realistically pushes people apart rather than bringing them together. When he tries to persuade her to continue to work for him, Dee looks at Mack accusingly and replies, "If you really didn't want this to happen, you shouldn't have fucked me." Still, near the end of the film when Dee is attacked in her car, the policeman who saves her becomes her confidant and possibly savior from isolation.

The rest of the characters too in *Grand Canyon* connect partially because of luck, which is also defined as "miracles" within the film, and partially because of effort on at least one person's part, in this case Mack. At the end of the movie when Simon takes Roberto, Mack, Claire and their new baby, Jane, and his nephew Otis to see the Grand Canyon, which has served as a metaphor in the film for freedom, nature, and escape, audiences realize that although this group may not have periodic reunions like the college friends in *The Big Chill*, they have connected in a potentially more significant way: after realistically facing the dangers of a world that works actively against happiness, they have bonded to help each other pursue individual and collective dreams. Only together, standing united in front of a natural wonder, do they realize that "it's not all bad."

In many ways, this ending is inappropriate for a movie that has avoided the formulaic tendency of the extended family film to provide automatic closure for each member of the group. In spite of its struggle to depict honestly the decay and violence of Los Angeles, *Grand Canyon* resorts to an ending that implies everyone can find happiness: Davis agrees to marry longtime love interest Vanessa; Mack and Claire resolve their differences and adopt the abandoned child; Simon and Jane fall quickly and passionately in love; Dee may be beginning a relationship with the handsome cop who rescues her; and even Otis, who has been traumatized by his family's move to Canoga Park, seems satisfied while gazing at the Grand Canyon. Kasdan cannot resist the temptation to suggest that this extended family, once formed, will solve each of its members' problems quickly and permanently. As the camera whips through the Grand Canyon and the credits roll, audiences are reminded of the first conversation between Simon and Mack, in which Simon refers to the natural wonder as mystical in its ability to communicate. He says that the canyon makes him realize what a joke people are and how little they mean: "The rocks—they are laughing at me. Me and my worries, they seem real humorous to that Grand Canyon." Kasdan hopes that, in the presence of the Grand Canyon, audiences, too, will realize how little their problems seem when juxtaposed against the majesty of nature, a message that ironically undermines the characters' struggles within the film itself.

The emphasis on the extended family in these and other recent films and television shows illustrates that a nation of people who are facing rising divorce rates and families broken by career choices find the prospect of a surrogate family both comforting and entertaining. Films made in earlier decades, such as *Rebel without a Cause* (1955), *Bob and Carol and Ted and Alice* (1969), and *Alice's Restaurant* (1969), also concentrate on forming bonds within isolated groups that were as strong or stronger than familial connections. But these groups are not only smaller than the ones defined in this essay, they are formed as a reaction to a specific crisis, such as the run-in with the law in *Alice's Restaurant*, the parental conflict in *Rebel without a Cause*, or the sexual experiments in *Bob and Carol.* The catalyst for bonding in the extended family film may be natural means, such as college in *The Big Chill* or *St. Elmo's Fire*, or unnatural, such as Saturday detention in *The Breakfast Club* or the debutante season in *Metropolitan*, but the significance lies primarily in the group's ability to form new family ties with several others for the "right" reasons—love, concern, affection—not personal gain to temporary sexual gratification. Whether permanent (*Return of the Secaucus Seven*) or temporary (*Metropolitan*), these groups fulfill a need that, in many cases, will not only replace the desire for family, but will also inspire personal and collective growth.

And this trend looks as if it will become even more popular in the 1990s. Kenneth Branagh released *Peter's Friends* in late 1992. Dubbed "a British" *Big Chill*, it tells the story of seven or so college roommates and fellow thespians who gather for a New Year's Even reunion. *Indian Summer* depicts twenty- and thirtysomethings, having a reunion at an old summer camp. *Reality Bites* examines the ways in which four roommates can avoid some of the perils associated with Generation X and its struggle to succeed in a society that denies comfort. The popularity of television shows such as *Beverly Hills 90210*, *Melrose Place*, and even MTV's "documentary," *Real Life*, indicates that the nation finds the romantic notion of a surrogate family, one that is less critical and more nurturing than the natural family, irresistible.

As long as directors continue to change the "extended family" formula to capture shifting cultures and experiment with the formula to produce films that stylistically and contextually reflect contemporary events, the ideology will continue to thrive. But in spite of exponential increases in the crime rate and national debt, each of the directors examined ends his film optimistically. The appeal, then, lies as much in the renewal of hope as the celebration of friendship. Even the rebellious loners in the films discussed (Nick in *The Big Chill*, Bender in *The Breakfast Club*, Billy in *St. Elmo's Fire*) must become a part of an extended family to be revitalized. The ideology of extended families not only represents mankind's capacity to rejuvenate through contact with others, but also implies that the human drive for love and companionship is stronger than forces in contemporary society that seem intent on driving families apart.

# Aggression, Confession, and the Psychiatric Profession: Ideologies of Gender and Agency in Recent "Woman's Films"

**Devoney Looser**

Dependent and love-starved female protagonists—merely waiting to be rescued by their leading men—have grown scarce in today's Hollywood. Contemporary popular films cast postmodern women in any number of realms not previously open to them, providing more options in relationships, families, and careers, as well as a few more possibilities for women who fall outside of a white, heterosexual, upper-middle-class purview. Woman and "object" are not simply synonymous in today's filmic ideological relations. Does this mean that we should declare "You've come a long way, baby" to Hollywood's postmodern woman? Who is she, what does she do, and whom does she represent? Has Hollywood managed to produce more positive (if not perfect) representations of women? Furthermore, "What does it mean to see in [popular cinema] a progressive film or position for women? How far is the film different? And how far . . . does it impinge on dominant conceptions of women?" (Cowie 104).

My investigation of these larger issues is admittedly a partial one, focused on only a sampling of "women's films" from what might be called the talking cure subgenre. These films include *Dancing in the Dark* (1986), *Heartburn* (1986), *Sleeping with the Enemy* (1991), and *House of Games* (1987), among others. Briefly, I argue that these films indeed offer particular kinds of progress for (some) women. Today's film women take narrative control in ways not formerly available—or not available to such a degree—in earlier mainstream images. As a result, we might conclude that these protagonists' acts of aggression and confession resist dominant discourses by exposing or eschewing the model of the passive, helpless, and needy female. To stop with that conclusion would surely be a mistake. On closer examination, we find that recent film representations of strong women often serve to hide rather than to overturn dominant gender ideologies. Refashioned contemporary discourses on women might be said to co-opt and redeploy the same old gender ideologies. This time around, however, we find those "same old" views in the mouths of the film women themselves, rather than in the mouths of their psychiatrists.

In Hollywood, the psychiatric couch is as likely to be a setting for seduction as for therapy, as reviewers David Ansen and Karen Springen have reminded us. Citing a long list of films, including *Spellbound* (1945), *Basic Instinct* (1991), *The Prince of Tides* (1991), and *Final Analysis* (1992), Ansen and Springen note, "In real life, the instances of sexual breach of conduct overwhelmingly involve male therapists and female patients. In the movies, almost every woman shrink succumbs to the man on the couch" (58). Just because male psychiatrists' sexual misconduct is not a popular film convention these days, however, does not mean that women patients have disappeared from the big screen. Today's Hollywood has by no means ignored the situation of the woman on the couch, particularly in what Molly Haskell has dubbed "the woman's film" or the weepies (154).

Although there has long been disagreement about what makes a woman's film, female protagonists generally provide the focus or the center of the universe (Haskell 154). In the woman's film, according to Haskell, "women spectators are moved, not by pity and fear but by self-pity and tears, to accept rather than reject, their lot" (154). Some critics have seen more to laud in these films than Haskell, concluding that the woman's film provides a place for female protagonists to become more fully subjects than objects. Hollywood's popular woman's films of the 1940s repeatedly tried to trace the shape of female subjectivity and desire within traditional forms and narrative conventions, according to Mary Ann Doane. Because of these attempts to capture female subjectivity on screen, certain contradictory gender ideologies become more apparent, Doane argues. In *The Desire to Desire: The Woman's Film of the 1940s,* Doane focused on these contradictions and investigated female subjectivity in a variety of woman's film subgenres (13).

Some critics have seen the female film protagonist as more clearly stationed on the object side of the subject/object equation. In the case of the talking cure film, this has been particularly true. Janet Walker's work on postwar filmic representations of psychiatry provides a good overview. As Walker argues, "the narrativized doctor-patient unit reiterates a configuration of power where the doctor is the authority who adjusts the help-seeking patient to a traditional marriage that she has somehow threatened, guiding her on the one path to both mental and marital health" ("Couching" 152). The female patient becomes the object to be brought to (or back to) traditional wife and/or mother status by the (male) doctor.

A number of 1940s woman's films illustrate Walker's point. In *Cat People* (1942), Dr. Judd hypnotizes his patient Irena, placing her under a bright spotlight in a darkened room, taking notes on her confessions, and determining (albeit incorrectly) the origins of her sexual problems. Her "real" problems are finally shown to be too mysterious for science. In *Possessed* (1947), the doctor administers a pseudo truth serum to the vulnerable Louise to bring her from a relatively mute state to compulsive confessionality. *Now, Voyager* (1942) involves a fatherly and friendly doctor who whisks away ugly duckling Charlotte Vale to an institution and (we assume) provokes her transformation to a popular striking socialite. As Doane has shown, each of these films involves a shift in our traditional expectations for the classical Hollywood "gaze."

> In the "woman's film," the erotic gaze becomes the medical gaze. The female body is located not so much as spectacle but as an element in the discourse of medicine, a manuscript to be read for the symptoms which betray her story, her identity. Hence the need, in these films, for the figure of the doctor as reader or interpreter, as the site of a knowledge which dominates and controls female subjectivity. ("Woman's Film" 290)

Doane's book utilizes Michel Foucault's theories on the medical gaze or "the clinical eyes of medical discourse."[1] Kaja Silverman agrees with Doane that the woman's psyche in these films proves an extension of her objectified body. Citing films such as *The Snake Pit* (1948), *Lady in the Dark (1944)* and *The Guilt of Janet Ames* (1948), Silverman concludes that "the 'talking cure' films also deprivilege the female psyche by denying to woman any possibility of arriving at self-knowledge except through the intervening agency of a doctor or analyst" (65). Critics agree that the doctor/analyst figure is a key—if not the key—to the early film woman's intended recovery.

By the mid-1970s, Haskell declared that the woman's film genre had died out (188). It is clear, however, that the woman's film experienced a rebirth of popularity in the late 1980s. For their mock "Siskel and Ebert" sketches, fictional characters Wayne Campbell and Garth Algar of *Saturday Night Live*'s "Wayne's World" even created a reviewers' category to describe films such as *Steel Magnolias.* They dubbed them "Chick Movies." The "chick movie" may be found in a variety of guises, but the "talking cure" woman's film provides one subgenre undergoing a great deal of ideological change. More and more, these films involve not just a doctor but a newly formulated confession and a "laudable" act of female aggression—usually against a not-so-laudable man. Some of these films do away with the figure of the doctor entirely, while keeping other plot elements of the talking cure genre intact.

Given the social and economic changes of the last decades and the increased possibilities for women's lives outside of wife/mother roles, we might expect to find that male psychiatrists who cure female patients have been displaced as a filmic trope. More work remains to be done to follow up on these and related issues in contemporary popular film. Christine Gledhill's 1980 article investigating the psychiatric situation and the protagonist's position in *Klute* (1971) provides a place to start. For Gledhill, "a key question is whether in these scenes [the female protagonist] is subject or object" (124). Gledhill concludes that this question cannot have an either/or answer; the camera positions suggest that the protagonist is a subject while the character is objectified. *Klute*'s heroine Bree Daniels is treated by a woman psychiatrist, but the narrative heavily relies on the guidance/protection of the "expert" male detective, Klute. After all, the film is not titled *Bree.* Has the status of women as subjects or objects in film become any clearer in the last decades? To what degree do film females function as self-starting agents or as barely disguised puppets? In other words, who "controls" the narrative situation in today's popular film? Have male/female ideologies changed much, if at all, in these more recent films? These are some questions that I believe deserve further exploration and with which I will begin in what follows.

### *The Psychiatric Profession*

Two recent variations of the popular talking cure/woman's film, *Heartburn* and *Dancing in the Dark,* illustrate the different ways in which the traditional representation of the psychiatric situation has indeed been displaced. Paramount's melodramatic comedy *Heartburn* stars Meryl Streep and Jack Nicholson, and *Dancing in the Dark* is a Canadian New World Pictures/Brightstar Films release, without any big celebrity cachet. Some might argue that *Dancing in the Dark* should not be included in a study of popular film because of its slow-paced art film style. Reviewers compared *Dancing in the Dark* to Bergman's and Chantal Ackerman's work in terms of style, tone, and plot.[2] This film, however, reached mass audiences in the United States on videotape, where it was marketed as a garden-variety domestic drama/horror film, using the advertising theme "Betrayal can take a lifetime. Revenge takes only a moment." Both films deal with marriage, adultery, aggression, and therapy. If either *Dancing in the Dark*'s protagonist Edna Cormick or *Heartburn*'s heroine Rachel Samstat can be said ultimately to triumph, however, traditional marriage no longer constitutes such a "cure."[3]

*Dancing in the Dark* is not a conventional film in many respects, though the psychiatric situation in the film is fairly conventional. After a domestic crisis, the protagonist/housewife Edna is institutionalized under the care of a white male psychiatrist. We do not definitively learn what the crisis was until the end of the film: Edna had murdered her adulterous husband Harry. The film is a combination of voice-over narration of the journal Edna compulsively fills in the institution and her flashbacks to domestic scenes; consequently, the narrative point-of-view is almost entirely Edna's. This in itself gives the doctor a reduced amount of space in which to interpret, but the situation of the doctor's authority is even more profoundly limited.

In keeping with the plot elements of the 1940s woman's film, Edna initially figures the doctor as a possible romantic attachment. But in Edna's case, the relationship to the doctor is not clearly elaborated or pursued. She is only once even shown in the same frame as the doctor. This lone scene is also the only time Edna speaks to her doctor. Edna's problem in the film becomes one of vision—of seeing her husband Harry's deception, seeing her role in their illusory marital bliss, and so on. Her conclusion, in whatever limbo state of sanity or madness we deem her, is that their relationship was a sham. The doctor's access to Edna's "vision," however, is completely barred. This narrative and spatial exile of the doctor is by no means an isolated incident. The first time we see the doctor, it is in subsequent parts—shoes, hands, and mouth—from Edna's point-of-view shot. Edna differs from the protagonists of the 1940s films in that she does *not* participate in allowing her doctor to formulate a "reading" of her. She remains a mystery to the medical apparatus. Only the film's viewers are privy to her voice-over confessions.

Rachel Samstat in *Heartburn* provides a different case. Having second thoughts on her wedding day about her impending marriage to Mark, Rachel (Meryl Streep) lies down in a back room of the chapel where she is visited by a dizzying number of friends and relatives who counsel her. One of the visitors is Vera (Maureen Stapleton), Rachel's therapist. Vera says she won't advise Rachel whether or not to marry, concluding that Rachel should do whatever she wants to do. Rachel says: "That's such a lie. All you therapists ever want is for us to get married and have babies. It's the closest you ever get to a cure." Vera answers: "I'm just trying to understand why you don't want to marry someone you love." Rachel then counters: "Because it doesn't work. Marriage doesn't work. You know what works? Divorce." Vera responds: "Divorce is only a temporary solution."

Throughout the film, these characters' interactions end with a Vera one-liner and an all-knowing shrug from Rachel. Vera does not encounter a crisis in the reading of her patient. The crisis (if it can be called one) is one of getting the patient to accept the therapist's readings. As one of *Heartburn*'s reviewers suggests, "Rachel has only the camera as her therapist" (Corliss 575). This reviewer's insight about the camera as psychiatrist is interesting, and it might just as well describe *Dancing in the Dark.* However, in *Heartburn,* another character takes up the role of psychiatrist where Vera leaves off: Rachel's friend and former co-worker, Richard (Jeff Daniels). Richard, like the traditional filmic doctor, appears at all of the film's crucial moments. He is everything to Rachel that the 1940s talking cure film would ask for from a psychiatrist. He reads her benevolently, encourages her to read herself, shows an interest in her child, offers her work, and it is suggested, tries to offer himself as an appropriate match.

Again, although to a lesser degree than Edna, Rachel does not listen to her "therapist" (and potential savior) Richard. The only advice Rachel takes from him is to read herself; at his suggestion, she begins to tape-record her thoughts about the joys of motherhood. All of the other attempts Richard makes to guide her life are rejected until the end of the film, when she may or may not be returning (for a second time) to her former job, which Richard has offered to give back to her. The events up to the end of the film seem to suggest that nothing romantic will happen between them; there are no foreshadowing sparks. If Richard fulfills more of the stereotypical narrative conventions of the medical reader/interpreter than Vera does, he proves no more effective in bringing about change in his patient. Neither Rachel nor Edna is changed by the outside help of the "clinical eyes of medical discourse." Change comes about through the protagonist's own investigation of vision.

### *Confession*

The investigation of vision that each "heroine" undertakes is, to greater and lesser degrees, the main framing device of many recent films in this genre. These films tend to involve at least one incident of flashback or voice-over.[4] This, of course, was not an uncommon feature, even among woman's films of the 1940s. Doane concludes that "voice-over, introduced in the beginning of the film as the possession of the female protagonist who purportedly controls the narration of her own past, is rarely sustained" (290). The difference is that in the films Doane studies, the narrative control is passed on to a male who cures or tames the protagonist. In these recent films, even when the voice-over or flashback is incidental to the plot, the female protagonist's narrative role is not usurped by another character. The situation is decidedly more complex.

The learned lessons of *Dancing in the Dark*'s Edna are ambiguous at best. She says that she has had only twelve hours of thoughts in her life—from the afternoon on which she learned about Harry's affair with his secretary to the moment she stabbed him late that same night. The revelation that raises Edna's consciousness comes in the form of a phone call from Dottie, a co-worker's wife. Dottie reports that Edna's husband was seen kissing his secretary in the office parking lot. As Dottie speaks, the camera focuses on Edna's face and the phone; we never know what Dottie looks like. Dottie has called because she decides that Edna "might like to know" what is going on. Edna literally sees no evidence of her husband Harry's affair; rather, she takes on Dottie's voice as her own, in a sense, and acts on it.

Edna recognizes the limits of reading another person or even oneself. Her confession, neither an illness nor a cure, continually focuses and refocuses her as *her own* object of knowledge. The confession is obviously for an audience (for those watching the film), but within the world of the film, there is no confession *to* anyone. In this sense the voice-over serves much the same purpose for *self*-reflection as a private journal might. Edna constantly points to the differences between what the magazines told her about marriage, what she did to make things domestically perfect according to this system, and how this illusory system failed her—or how she fails it. This is the tension that never gets resolved. Edna blames herself for her infertility and for her domestic imperfections, though she is compulsively neat. She also celebrates her sense of being freed, after the murder, from the impossible subject position of good wife. These twin impulses of blame and celebration are never reconciled.

Point-of-view and confession in *Heartburn* follow much more closely the conventions of classical Hollywood narrative. The film is traditionally paced and has much less of a focus on voice-over than does *Dancing in the Dark.* Rachel, like Edna, also experiences her "cure" as a listener. In Rachel's case, the turning point occurs in a beauty shop as she is getting a haircut. Rachel eavesdrops on her hairdresser's conversation with another beautician as they discuss a cheating boyfriend. Rachel can't help registering her husband Mark's behavior in the hairdresser's account of the signs she missed to indicate her boyfriend's infidelity. During this conversation, we see Rachel's face in the beauty-shop mirror as it slowly changes to an expression of horror and realization. Rachel leaves mid-coiffure and rushes home to dig through Mark's desk drawers for evidence of his adultery. She finds telltale receipts for flowers and hotel rooms. Again, Rachel's "cure" is reached from a passive position (motionless in her beauty-shop chair). The hairdresser is an inadvertent therapist—a ludicrous therapist. Rachel knows her situation when she is ready to know, spurred on by another woman's similar experience.

Some aspects of *Heartburn* suggest that the story we see is Rachel's own future creation. As she watches television, Rachel fantasizes seeing her life turned into the introductory summary to a *Masterpiece Theater*-like television program. In this way, Rachel's filmic daydreams create narratives of her own experiences. This evidence suggests that the viewer sees the story Rachel ultimately pieces together. Such a speculation aside, however, the point of view of the film clearly belongs to Rachel. Reviewers complained of the "tunnel vision point of view" (Corliss 575), and one reviewer pleaded for an "obligatory speech of . . . self-justification" from Mark (Sarris 572-73). Because the film is shot primarily from an observer camera position (as opposed to *Dancing in the Dark*'s largely point-of-view shots from Edna), it is curious that *Heartburn*'s reviewers found the film's emphasis on Rachel's viewpoint to be all-encompassing. The wish to hear or see Mark's side of the affair suggests that some viewers may rankle at the notion that Rachel alone is a competent reader of her situation. Conventional domestic melodramas have generally made the female character central. The change, then, is in the lack of a central, outside male interpreter (doctor, romantic partner, etc.). In *Heartburn*'s case, this lack seems to have created the illusion that the film is therefore less "objective."

Each of the female protagonists' confessions results from the failure of the male's fidelity or loyalty in the domestic sphere, as well as from the wife's inability to "see" this infidelity. In many other recent films of this genre, the psychiatric situation plays no part in the cure, but similar narrative devices of vision are employed. In *Sleeping with the Enemy,* Laura Burney (Julia Roberts) must see her way to an escape. For Margaret Ford (Lindsay Crouse) of *The House of Games,* she must see herself as the victim of a con artist and recognize in herself qualities she hadn't known existed. Babe MaGrath (Sissy Spacek) in *Crimes of the Heart* (1986) sees her situation for what it is when she views the pictures of herself with which her heartless husband intends to blackmail her. In *Mortal Thoughts* (1991), Cynthia (Demi Moore) sees her crime in a flashback at the end of the film, having blocked it out during questioning by a skeptical detective. These women are duped (at least) and abused (at most) by men they trusted. In each case, the epiphany to vision provokes aggression. These epiphanies occur in metonymic situations—through the confessions of other women to the protagonists or through the ventriloquism of their own stories onto fictitious women. These metonymic occurrences are what compel or even force the protagonists (and often the viewers) to "see." These visions, then, take the place of a traditional psychiatric reading.

What provokes both Edna and Rachel to act and to change their lives involves not the directive hand of a psychiatric authority (a reader) but rather involves the protagonists' consumption of another woman's reading. This pattern is by no means anomalous. *Mortal Thoughts*, for example, shows Cynthia (Moore) being questioned by a detective (Harvey Keitel) who takes on the doctoring role in the film. Cynthia claims not to have killed Jimmy (Bruce Willis). Instead, she confesses to being an accessory in the murder. Cynthia blames it on Jimmy's abused wife, Joyce (Glenne Headley). It is only at the end of the film, after pointed eye contact with her friend Joyce, that Cynthia remembers what really happened. Cynthia herself stabbed Jimmy as he attempted to rape her. For the first time, the viewers see with Cynthia her role in the murder as an extended flashback with her voice-over saying, "Oh my god. What am I doing?" She goes back into the police station and confesses. This confession appears not to have resulted from detectives' questioning but from her contact with, and loyalty to, Joyce. Cynthia realizes that she has projected her own anger at (and murder of) Jimmy onto Joyce, and she is persuaded to do right by Joyce. This plot is in keeping with the other films discussed so far in that it is a sense of sisterhood that propels the climax and the cure of the protagonist. The audience sees this realization and cure only when the protagonist does.

*Nobody's Fool* (1986) and *Sleeping with the Enemy* may appear more objectively rendered on film in that they follow more traditional observer camera shots and narrative formulas. Both films, however, involve flashbacks and voice-overs, and these are worth investigating for the possibilities they afford the protagonists' diegetic roles. *Nobody's Fool* centers on a small-town waitress (Rosanna Arquette) with a scandalous though comic past, and *Sleeping with the Enemy* shows battered wife Laura (Roberts) trying to start a new life. Both films ultimately shuffle the female protagonist from a "bad" man to a "good" man. *Nobody's Fool,* like *Heartburn,* offers a flashback in the form of a fantasy: a rewriting of the past from the perspective of present events. Cassie (Arquette), still living in her home town despite her notoriety, remembers the scene of aggression that ruined her reputation. As she passes the restaurant in which the scene occurred, she comments to the couple who accompany her that she "is not wanted in there." The ensuing flashback is an exaggerated and costumed version of what we are led to believe actually happened, now dressed up in Cassie's mind: Cassie told her high school sweetheart Billy (Jim Youngs) that she was pregnant. Although earlier he had promised to marry her, when faced with her pregnancy he declares that he wants no part of a family and suggests that he'll stay a bachelor. Cassie, screaming "I'll kill you," stabs Billy in the neck with a table fork. The film centers on Cassie's journey back to romantic health, undertaken with her own investigation of new flame Riley (Eric Roberts). She must decide whether Rilcy will be an appropriate replacement for Billy. Judith Williamson has dubbed this plot that of the *homme fatal* and notes that *Nobody's Fool* switches to a female subjective base in which men have become the unknown factor to be read (974). Although it is difficult to see the gender role reversal as complete in this film, Cassie's own reading powers are increasingly foregrounded.

In *Sleeping with the Enemy,* flashback and voice-over also play an important role. Laura stages her own death in a boating accident in order to escape her abusive husband, Martin. Martin believes that Laura is unable to swim, and a storm prevents him from serving as her rescuer. After the accident, there is a long sequence of water flashbacks, of drowning, and of learning to swim. Laura's voice-over explains that she died and that "someone else was saved" that night. What brought Laura to the point of escape were her secret swimming lessons at the YWCA with a group of caring women who helped her to overcome her fear of water. After eluding Martin (through the help of a conveniently hidden large stash of cash), Laura comes to terms with her past by describing her experiences as an abused wife to a female stranger. However, Laura tells the story in the form of a third-person narrative. She repeats the history of her "friend," the abused wife, to the old woman who is sitting next to her on a bus. Laura and the woman share an Edenic apple as Laura describes the "friend's" situation, saying that the friend thinks of herself as a coward. By the end of the conversation, the all-knowing older woman says, "A coward? Not a girl like that. . . . How long did you stay with him?" The women share an unspoken understanding of each other's lives, an understanding which, the film suggests, males cannot so easily grasp. *Fried Green Tomatoes* (1991) reverses and extends this narrative pattern, with the older woman (Mary Stuart Masterson) telling a fictional story of domestic abuse to a younger woman (Kathy Bates). The younger woman eventually discovers that the story is not fictional but autobiographical; both women are transformed by the telling of the story. Again, the protagonist (storyteller) effects a cure through her own volition, though always in the company of, and with the support of, other women.

In *The House of Games,* this "sisterhood" is again enacted to no small degree. An older woman psychiatrist, Dr. Littauer (Lilia Skala) plays a similar role in bringing about the confession and cure of her younger colleague, the protagonist Margaret. The older psychiatrist inadvertently gives advice that allows Margaret to forgive herself and to accept her perverse search for adventure. In addition, there is another female curative foil for Margaret. An institutionalized female patient (under the care of Margaret) shown early in the film also ends up serving as a mirror for Margaret herself. Margaret's adventure in a bar called the House of Games reduces her to an objectified position similar to her patient's: a victim of male psychological abuse. Margaret is used as a pawn in an elaborate scheme by con man Mike (Joe Mantegna), who also seduces her along the way as he carries out his manipulative plan to trick her out of thousands of dollars.

Margaret believes that she is studying Mike for professional reasons (as material for her next self-help book), while Mike is merely playing on her desire for adventure to further his own professional gain. In showing her his various small cons, Mike makes sure that the stakes (unknown to the viewer) get increasingly bigger, until Margaret finds herself in the middle of a staged police sting and murder, to which she believes she is an accessory. Of course, the entire arrangement—unbeknownst to Margaret (and, for some time, to the audience)—is an elaborate setup by Mike and his buddies to swindle the well-known and wealthy author and psychiatrist out of her savings. Though she is clearly attracted to the con artist's life and no longer just an academic observer, Margaret believes she buys her way out of the repercussions of her role in the "crime." Mike's error is in believing that Margaret will not want further contact with him. Margaret, however, returns to the House of Games, sees Mike with his buddies, and realizes the scam. Margaret, unlike her mentally ill patient, successfully takes the situation into her own hands and regains control over the course of the narrative. She ultimately becomes the prime mover of the film's climax, without the direct help of an outside curative reader.

When Margaret realizes that Mike has swindled her out of $80,000, she follows him to the airport, where he is about to make his escape. In this scene, Mike the con man and Margaret the psychiatrist engage in a battle of all-too-similar wills. The con and the psychiatric situation are shown to be analogous. Mike, in a sense, has been the "bad" psychiatrist of Margaret. He has manipulated her into a different (and criminal) worldview. When he realizes she's on to him, he says, "What do you want? You want your eighty grand back? I can't give it back; I split it up. What do you want, revenge?" Margaret says, "I gave you my trust." Mike's response is a completely professional one: "Of course you gave me your trust. That's what I do for a living. You asked me what I did for a living. This is it! Look, look. I'm sorry. I'm sorry I hurt you. Really. You're a good kid. Now, whatever it is you feel that you have to do . . ."

What Margaret feels she has to do is reduce Mike to a powerless position, one in which he is begging for his life. She says she may call the cops. Mike counters, "And tell them what? What are you going to tell them, stud? That the best-selling author of *Driven,* a guide to compulsive behavior, gave her fortune away to some con man? You see my point? But we've had fun; you must say that." When she accuses him of taking her money, he responds, "How naughty of me." When she accuses him of rape, of taking her under false pretenses, of using her, he says, "It wasn't personal . . . I used you. I did. I'm sorry. And you learned some things about yourself that you'd rather not know. And I'm sorry for that, too. You say I acted atrociously. Yes, I did. I do it for a living."

Margaret, momentarily switching roles to that of the criminal (just as Mike has momentarily switched roles to that of doctor), shoots him in a secluded section of the airport. In a controlled, deadpan voice that mocks the stereotypical female hysteric, Margaret says "I can't help it. I'm out of control." Mike, in a scene reminiscent of what Margaret has heard earlier from her female patient, says, "This is what you always wanted, you crooked bitch, you thief. You always need to get caught. 'Cause you know you're bad. . . . You're worthless, you know it. You're a whore. You came back like a dog to its own father. You sick bitch. I'm not going to give you shit." But unlike the female patient, who was abused, killed her abuser, and then was institutionalized, Margaret kills Mike without consequences and returns to her normal life. Margaret, with the help of friend Dr. Littauer and her experience with patients, "cures" herself, albeit criminally. The ending suggests that Margaret has sublimated her own compulsive behaviors only partially; however, she is seemingly successful and happy on her own terms.

The final authority of today's filmic narrative, these films would suggest, can only be the reader of *herself.* Therefore, an expert reader in the form of the doctor becomes superfluous; instead, reading is tied up in women experiencing different possibilities for themselves and in relating to their own past experiences in newer ways. These female protagonists become agents in their own right. Female subjects in these films must become highly self-literate. They must come to know themselves. This process and these conclusions can, then, be extended to those who view the film, *ad infinitum.* Women characters learn for themselves through the example, impetus, or direct help of other women characters. Women viewers of these films, in turn, may then take away the gendered, curative ideologies that these films espouse: and they tell two friends, and so on, and so on, and so on. These film women do not necessarily need men to effect their cures; they need only look inside themselves. A female subject becoming the object of her own knowledge is not the final word on her degree of agency or liberation, however, as Michel Foucault's work on the modern subject has suggested.

*Aggression*

The issue of aggression in these films sheds further light on the questions of agency and voice for the protagonists. If the talking cure film of the 1940s offered textual problems of medical reading and vision, elements of the gothic film of this period may be said to offer problems of violence, paranoia, and vision, with male violence as what is hidden from sight (Doane, *Desire* 134). These issues on the gothic romance of the 1940s are fruitfully discussed by Diane Waldman, who concludes that in this genre and during this period, female solidarity is transitory. In the more recent films discussed above, however, the female protagonist's aggression is surprisingly *not* encouraged through a (male) authority figure, nor is aggression exhibited in a stereotypical *femme fatale* manner. In each film, the woman takes up a weapon: a kitchen knife for Edna, a pie for Rachel, a fork for Cassie, a razor (from her hairdressing supplies) for Cynthia, and a gun for Laura and Margaret. Although these means of violence are largely domestic and often take place in a space of female authority (Edna's kitchen, Rachel's friends' dining room, Laura's foyer), the women carry out their intentional violence with no remorse.

The degree to which we are to identify with *Dancing in the Dark*'s Edna and her act of aggression against an unfaithful husband is, again, somewhat ambiguous. Instead of figuring solely as the victim or the *femme fatale,* Edna simultaneously fills the roles of victim and victimizer. The first sound after Edna stabs Harry is Edna's orgasmic reaction to the murder. When Edna's voice-over resumes, she explains her experience of the stabbing: "It was like I once thought making love would be . . . a soaring loss of consciousness and transcendence. . . . I'm free." Of course, Edna, unlike *Heartburn*'s Rachel, has legally as well as ideologically overstepped her traditional role here; she will be anything but "free" in a conventional sense. The final scene of *Dancing in the Dark* shows Edna in her institutional bedroom in a Zelda Fitzgerald–like moment of fumbling classical dance. Her aggression has "made her free," but she is "mad" and is as dependent in her role as a crazy, uncooperative patient as she was as Harry's pliable, obedient wife. Her increased narrative agency has had enormous ideological costs—costs that would seem to loom over the simple freedoms she claims she's reached.

In *Heartburn,* Rachel, too, takes her rage at her husband's infidelity into her own hands. At a dinner party, Rachel responds to her friends' unsuspecting and hypothetical queries about how it is possible for wives not to realize when their husbands are cheating. Rachel says that women who are being cheated on are living in a dream. Once they discover the illusion, one of their choices is to leave and to dream their own dreams, she claims. After this speech, Rachel serves one of her gourmet pies—right into Mark's face. This humiliation is what marks the end of their "dream" together. The film cuts to Rachel marching up to a plane, with their two children in tow. The last two shots are of Rachel singing "Itsy Bitsy Spider" with the youngest child and of the plane taking off. We are led to believe that she is "dreaming her own dream" at long last.

*House of Games'* Margaret signals her escape from the murder of Mike by abandoning her usually dour androgynous outfits for a brightly colored, floral print, feminine dress. Margaret sips a tropical drink in the restaurant and signs a copy of her book for an admirer. Dr. Littauer, who meets Margaret in the restaurant, is relieved to see her looking so well. Margaret tells Littauer, "You said when you've done something unforgivable, you must forgive yourself. And that's what I've done. And it's done." But Margaret has only partially taken Littauer's words to heart. Margaret—the happiest we've ever seen her—is not completely cured. The last scene shows her to be a kleptomaniac, stealing a lighter from a restaurant patron's purse, happily lighting her cigarette and blowing the smoke with a smile. Margaret's continuing crimes have moved to the realm of random and fairly insignificant. She can continue to live a normal life as well as an secret life of crime, preying on the easily duped, such as unsuspecting women in restaurants who are careless with their belongings. Margaret is transformed from a mannish workaholic who haunts dank offices and bars into a celebrity author who sports a new softer look and attitude. Her sordid experience with Mike, it seems, has made her a better con—in the form of a more properly feminine woman. We are, of course, supposed to see her as stronger, happier, sexier, and more "appropriately" compulsive as a result.

*Sleeping with the Enemy* and *Nobody's Fool* end by placing their female protagonists in the hands of new and improved male partners. First, Laura must endure the stereotypical slasher-genre hijinks in the form of a "he's-dead-no-he's-not-dead-he's-dead" scene. Laura's new love, Ben, gets knocked out by her abusive, estranged husband, Martin. Ben is lying stone cold on the floor. After Laura shoots Martin a good number of times—and after he reawakens to attempt to shoot her with a bulletless gun—Laura finishes off Martin. She immediately attempts to revive Ben. The last camera shot pans one end of the hallway to the other, starting with the embrace of Laura and Ben, tracing the outline of Martin's corpse, and stopping at his outstretched fingers. His fingers are reaching for Laura's (now superfluous) wedding ring. The promise here is certainly that she will need one again soon.

Domestic violence, then, is rendered an individual problem, not a social or institutional one, in *Sleeping with the Enemy.* Laura's problem is that she was inadvertently stuck with a (rich, handsome, controlling) madman. Ben, we are to believe, is an improvement. He's a small-town drama teacher who grows apples. He meets Laura after catching her stealing them from his lawn—another twist on the Edenic motif in the film. She bakes an apple pie for him, of course. Despite the seeming difference of Ben, however, he surprises her several times by showing up unexpectedly at her screen door, for example—leading the audience to believe that the "madman" Martin is again returning to the scene. Strangely, the film suggests that Ben's relation to Martin is not that of a polar opposite but perhaps the relation of a Dr. Jekyll to a Mr. Hyde. Laura's safety is not as clear-cut as the surface narrative of the film would have us believe. The promotional material for the film took this comparison between Martin and Ben a step further, posing the question, "Are *You* Sleeping with the Enemy?" to potential viewers. The idea of the enemy as a possible Everyman is thus reinforced; furthermore, the male figure in the ad is not Martin but Ben. The film's enemy, however, despite its attempt to play on women's fears, may not be a man at all. The enemy is primarily shown to be one's female self—one's own limitations and fears. These, the film suggests, may be overcome by squirreling away cash and taking swimming lessons. The best solution to domestic violence is self-empowerment—a partial solution at best and one that completely ignores economic imperatives, as does the film.

*Crimes of the Heart* concludes with all of the MaGrath sisters getting over old romantic wounds (and woundings) and entering into more promising relationships. Their "crazy" tendencies are transformed from criminal to benign with mere switches to "good" men. Again, the suggestion is that dysfunctional heterosexual relationships (which, apparently, are dysfunctional only for the angry women) are the fault of a few bad men, not of dominant ideologies that might call for revolution if not reform. The same is true of *Mortal Thought*'s Cynthia. Her murder of Jimmy, stabbing him as he rapes her, is also revealed at the end of the film. Jimmy, this film's "madman," is juxtaposed to Cynthia's husband, Arthur, the selfish entrepreneur who may not be perfect but who is offered as another potential Dr. Jekyll. We must assume that Cynthia's marriage to Arthur will also disintegrate. She is left almost as alone as *Dancing in the Dark*'s Edna, although Cynthia may perhaps be able to recover her friendship with Joyce. Cynthia is left knowing she did the right thing by confessing and clearing the name of her friend. The extent to which the murder was an act of sisterly loyalty—doing to Jimmy what his abused wife Joyce *should have wanted* to do all along—is left unexplored. The way these crimes (murder vs. rape) will be dealt with in the legal system is not followed through, either. Even with all of these unanswered questions, our sympathy is clearly with the film's women rather than the men. Similar interpretations and ambiguities have been explored in *Thelma and Louise* (1991), a more positive reading of which may be found in the insightful work of Patricia Mann.

Of course, many recent films in which the woman undertakes an aggressive act against a man do not show that aggression to be liberatory or curative. *Basic Instinct* (1991), *Fatal Attraction* (1987), *and Black Widow* (1987) all feature female "wackos" who need the law to step in to control them, thus allowing the reinscription of traditional and patriarchal values. In *Black Widow,* the "law" is a woman detective, Alexandra Barnes (Debra Winger), but even Alexandra must first be caught in a series of metonymic confusions with the criminal Catharine (Theresa Russell) before the law is able to set it all straight. *Fatal Attraction*'s reincarnations and plot changes made before its commercial release, and the ideologies that spurred on these changes, have been discussed at length by Susan Faludi and others. Such films deserve extended treatment in terms of the changes they offer in female narrative agency and voice, as they are dealing with somewhat different gender stereotypes. Clearly, not all recent women aggressors in popular film are heroines designed to be sympathized with or ultimately forgiven.

Increasingly, however, the *homme fatal* has emerged as integral to the woman's film genre. This theme has been explored outside of the talking cure genre to be sure, with *Thelma and Louise* and *Silence of the Lambs* (1991) as those films achieving the most notoriety. Both have been speculatively dubbed feminist and progressive for women. Critics who make these arguments often claim that these female protagonists are given much more narrative agency and control over their lives, control that was not often seen in earlier woman's films. Up to this point, I've offered a mixed reading of this narrative control as an emergent (and potentially positive) ideology of film women's subjectivity. I'd like to end with some tentative conclusions on the extent to which these changes might be viewed as the same old ideologies, albeit in new packaging.

### *Ideologies of Gender and Agency*

A shift can certainly be charted in recent woman's films in that the female subject has become an object of her own knowledge and not merely an object to an erotic or a medical gaze. The medium of the talking cure/woman's film in the last decade no longer requires that the protagonist be interpreted by an expert (usually male) reader or doctor. The knowledge these protagonists gain occurs either through confession or through metonymic experiences with other women and not, decidedly, through the technology of the psychiatric and/or medical profession. What ideological lessons are viewers to take away from this state of male/female affairs? We might wish to assume this as representational progress. The technology of gender in these films certainly seems to suggest historical changes in their representations of female characters. These films involve less mediated narrative agency for women. Such a conclusion only tells part of the story, though, because this historical shift unfortunately has not been accompanied by an equally radical shift in the conceivable roles women are shown to play.

The kinds of knowledge *Dancing in the Dark*'s Edna and *Heartburn*'s Rachel arrive at, for instance, are not finally that empowering or unifying. Both films' endings give a nod to the increased agency of the protagonist, as is evidenced by a climax that is both a show of strength and independence (aggression) and a "transcendent" moment of joy and song. These moments, however, must be seen as providing traditional reinings-in of the women's increased narrative agency. In other words, the knowledge these subjects gain is ideologically not far afield from what may have been given them by a traditional psychiatric reader. The familiar, traditional cures are offered not from the mouths of expert doctors but from the women's own mouths or the mouths of other women. This knowledge is no longer a medically disseminated, top-down version of "truth." Instead, it is a knowledge that springs up from within or that is passed on as oral narrative from woman to woman. We might say that it is an insertion of patriarchal knowledge into the minds and mouths of women—showing it to be (and to have been) "women's knowledge" rather than "men's" all along.

For all of their other differences, the recent films discussed here have outcomes that are in many ways similar to the classical Hollywood woman's films. Strong women are generally brought back into conservative social relations. Though some have argued about the extent to which these films' recuperative endings should be understood as providing the closure that audiences took away with them (see Basinger and Byars), downplaying the ideologies used to "resolve" filmic problems would seem to me to be wrongheaded in our attempt to gauge Hollywood's progress in its representations of film women. As I have argued, *Crimes of the Heart, Nobody's Fool* and *Sleeping with the Enemy* restore their female protagonists to stable heterosexual relationships with "more sensitive" men (who are sometimes themselves of questionable goodness). *Dancing in the Dark*'s Edna, like Irena in *Cat People,* is figured as a subject whose connections between sex and violence (in the guise of dangerous female sexuality) bring about the imposition of patriarchal norms. Edna is subdued from her foray into stereotypical male domains of agency (aggression) and language (narration or producing readings of herself). Both Edna's and Irena's "psychoses" lead to imprisonment with a small nod to freedom, in the form of an opened cage, a dance, etc. Similarly, in *House of Games,* although Margaret emerges triumphant, she is shown to be emerging as a stereotypical *femme fatale* in a newer, more feminine professional guise. In *Heartburn,* as in *Now, Voyager,* the protagonist ends up with no husband but with compensatory joy in a child. Rachel, then, is caught between discourses, in a sense. Is she a liberated career woman, "dreaming another dream," or is she locked into an older myth in which motherhood is the be-all-end-all of female existence? Clearly, the film shows her to be both. The notion that her primary identification could be outside that of wife or mother seems virtually unthinkable. These filmic ideologies serve to recommend the same outcomes for women that Haskell outlined for the woman's films of the 1940s: using self-pity and tears to reinforce the status quo for "good" women vs. "bad" women, wives and mothers vs. career women, feminine women vs. masculine women, cooperative women vs. competitive women.

The recent crop of commercial (still primarily "man-made") woman's films is undoubtedly authorized and made financially viable by the modest allotment of institutional legitimation for liberal feminism, as Teresa De Lauretis argues; she suggests that this so-called success has been bought at the price of oversimplifying the complexity and theoretical productivity of feminisms (138). Certainly De Lauretis has a point. Although we should be cheered by the move away from women's narrative passivity (and their more strictly objectified status), recent talking cure/woman's films further illustrate that many of the same ideological contradictions of decades past remain entrenched in our popular filmic conventions today. Film women are now more in control of refashioning their own subjectivities, but not accidentally, they arrive at precisely the same points that male psychiatrists and doctors traditionally might have taken them. As Elizabeth Traube has argued, "If Hollywood movies of the 1980s tend overall to reconstruct patriarchal symbols of men and women, the very fragmentation of images and the experimental aura of some of the new composites provides a potential resource, albeit a limited and highly compromised one, for reinventing gender identities" (25). To tie these brief readings into a larger critical project, then, we would have to continue to ferret out these contradictions and possibilities for female protagonists in contemporary popular films, both in their liberal concessions and perhaps in their more radical dislocations.

## Notes

1. For work that productively complicates subject-object/male-female investigations in current theoretical work, see Newman.

2. Ackerman's *Jeanne Dielman* was often cited as a similar film. I am especially indebted to Shelia Benson's review for making some of the connections that were an impetus to begin this essay (278).

3. Mimi White's work on women in recent adventure/romance films finds a shift in narrative function but no change in ending with a traditional romantic coupling. Not all of the films discussed in this essay follow this formula (see also Wexman). I suggest that generic expectations are crucial for these differences in endings. White suggests that the (quasi-) liberated female heroine is "afforded narrative agency" as well as being drawn back into postfeminist and neoconservative ideologies (41). Here our arguments overlap.

4. Gledhill briefly outlines the characteristics of voice-over conventions in film noir. See also Maureen Turim for a useful discussion of voice-over in film noir and melodrama.

## Works Cited

Ansen, David, and Karen Springen. "A Lot of Not So Happy Endings." *Newsweek* 13 Apr. 1992: 58.

Basinger, Jeanine. *A Woman's View: How Hollywood Spoke to Women, 1930-1960.* New York: Knopf, 1993.

Benson, Sheila. "*Dancing in the Dark.*" *Film Review Annual.* Ozer 277-81.

Byars, Jackie. *All That Hollywood Allows: Re-reading Gender in 1950s Melodrama.* Chapel Hill: U of North Carolina P, 1991.

Corliss, Richard. "*Heartburn.*" *Film Review Annual.* Ozer 575-76.

Cowie, Elizabeth. "The Popular Film as Progressive Text: A Discussion of Coma." *Feminism and Film Theory.* Ed. Constance Penley. New York: Routledge, 1988. 104-40.

De Lauretis, Teresa. *Technologies of Gender: Essays on Theory, Film and Fiction.* Bloomington: Indiana UP, 1987.

Doane, Mary Ann. *The Desire to Desire: The Woman's Film of the 1940s.* Bloomington: Indiana UP, 1987.

——. "The 'Woman's Film': Possession and Address." *Re-Vision: Essays in Feminist Film Criticism.* Ed. Mary Ann Doane, Patricia Mellencamp, and Linda Williams. Frederick, MD: University Publications of America, 1984.

Faludi, Susan. *Backlash: The Undeclared War Against American Women.* New York: Crown, 1991.

Foucault, Michel. *The Birth of the Clinic: An Archaeology of Medical Perception.* Trans. A.M. Sheridan-Smith. New York: Vintage, 1975.

Gledhill, Christine. "Klute 2: Feminism and Klute." *Women in Film Noir.* Ed. E. Ann Kaplan. Rev. ed. London: British Film Institute, 1980.

Haskell, Molly. *From Reverence to Rape.* 2nd ed. Chicago: U of Chicago P, 1987.

Mann, Patricia S. *Micro-Politics: Agency in a Postfeminist Era.* Minneapolis: U of Minnesota P, 1994.

Newman, Karen. "Directing Traffic: Subjects, Objects, and the Politics of Exchange." *differences* 2.2. (1990): 41-54.

Ozer, J.S., ed. *Film Review Annual.* Englewood Cliffs, NJ: Film Review Publications, 1987.

Sarris, Andrew. "*Heartburn.*" Ozer 572-73.

Silverman, Kaja. *The Acoustic Mirror: The Female Voice in Psychoanalysis and Cinema.* Bloomington: Indiana UP, 1988.

Traube, Elizabeth. *Dreaming Identities: Class, Gender, and Generation in 1980s Hollywood Movies.* Boulder, CO: Westview, 1992.

Turim, Maureen. *Flashbacks in Film: Memory and History.* New York: Routledge, 1989.

Waldman, Diane. "At Last I Can Tell It to Someone!: Feminine Point of View and Subjectivity in the Gothic Romance Film of the 1940s." *Cinema Journal* 23.2 (1983): 29-40.

Walker, Janet. "Couching Resistance: Women, Film, and Postwar Psychoanalytic Psychiatry." *Psychoanalysis and Cinema.* Ed. E. Ann Kaplan. New York: Routledge, 1990. 143-62.

——. *Couching Resistance: Women, Film, and Psychoanalytic Psychiatry.* Minneapolis: U of Minnesota P, 1993.

Wexman, Virginia White. *Creating the Couple: Love, Marriage, and Hollywood Performance.* Princeton: Princeton UP, 1993.

White, Mimi. "Representing Romance: Reading/Writing/Fantasy and the "Liberated" Heroine of Recent Hollywood Films." *Cinema Journal* 28.3 (1989): 41-56.

Williamson, Judith. "*Nobody's Fool.*" Ozer 973-75.

## Filmography

| Year | Film | Director |
|---|---|---|
| 1942 | *The Cat People* | Jacques Tourneur |
| 1942 | *Now, Voyager* | Irving Rapper |
| 1944 | *Lady in the Dark* | Mitchell Leisen |
| 1945 | *Spellbound* | Alfred Hitchcock |
| 1947 | *Possessed* | Curtis Bernhardt |
| 1948 | *The Guilt of Janet Ames* | Henry Levin |
| 1948 | *The Snake Pit* | Anatole Litvak |
| 1971 | *Klute* | Alan J. Pakula |
| 1975 | *Jeanne Dielman* | Chantal Ackerman |
| 1986 | *Crimes of the Heart* | Bruce Beresford |
| 1986 | *Dancing in the Dark* | Leon Marr |
| 1986 | *Heartburn* | Mike Nichols |
| 1986 | *Nobody's Fool* | Evelyn Purcell |
| 1987 | *Black Widow* | Bob Rafelson |
| 1987 | *Fatal Attraction* | Adrian Lyne |
| 1987 | *House of Games* | David Mamet |
| 1989 | *Steel Magnolias* | Herbert Ross |
| 1991 | *Basic Instinct* | Paul Verhoeven |
| 1991 | *Fried Green Tomatoes* | Jon Avnet |
| 1991 | *Mortal Thoughts* | Alan Rudolph |
| 1991 | *Prince of Tides* | Barbra Streisand |
| 1991 | *Silence of the Lambs* | Jonathan Demme |
| 1991 | *Sleeping with the Enemy* | Joseph Ruben |
| 1991 | *Thelma and Louise* | Ridley Scott |
| 1992 | *Final Analysis* | Philip Joanou |

# Surveying Popular Films of Oppression: The Ideological Construction of Women and Madness

**Jennifer A. Machiorlatti**

Images of madness and insanity have been popular for filmmakers ever since narrative storytelling began to develop and be portrayed on the screen. From D.W. Griffith's racist portrayals of "mad Negroes" in *Birth of a Nation* (1915) to the 1991 Oscar sweep of *Silence of the Lambs,* audiences have found continuing fascination with the dark recesses of the mind. Michael Fleming and Roger Manvell define madness in film to broadly include society and madness, institutionalization of the mad, possession as madness, eros and madness, murder and madness, war and madness, drugs and madness, paranoia and madness, madness as sanity, and madness and the psychiatrist. They find that "madness presented in film has a unique relationship to fluctuations in psychological and psychiatric theory and practice" (28), but they rarely look at larger social and ideological issues of race, class, and gender as roots of oppression in psychiatry and psychological diagnosis and treatment.

In *Couching Resistance: Women, Film and Psychoanalytic Psychiatry,* Janet Walker "describes how female deviance became an object of psychiatric expertise and how the interaction between psychiatry and female deviance became an object of fictional cinematic discourse" in films from World War II through the 1960s (*xv*). Walker examines how socially constructed gender stereotypes are reflected and perpetuated in mainstream film.

This chapter, operating much in the same sociohistorical framework as Walker's text, offers a survey of women's oppression through the portrayal of mental instability in American feature films. Because film can serve as a societal barometer of sorts, it provides a powerful visual record of problematic relationships based on dominance and power. In addition to identifying films that feature women as main characters who are labeled or portrayed as mentally ill like *Now, Voyager* (1942), *Play Misty For Me* (1971), or *Final Analysis* (1992), there needs to be more discussion on how these women are treated within the patriarchal institution of psychiatry and what may be at the root of their madness.

Some women, in reality and in film, may not only be oppressed because of their diagnosed madness, but their madness may have been caused by oppressive and dominating societal institutions.

This chapter also examines how women's representations in mainstream Hollywood films promote an acceptance of patriarchal norms. Women learn that their life choices are limited—they are supposed to find love, marriage, have children, and provide service in the domestic sphere. When they do not fulfill these expectations, they often are portrayed as "mad." Traditional definitions of femininity and masculinity are often what cause mental instability, because these definitions are far too limiting.

As more women entered the field of psychology, women's mental health became a prominent area of inquiry. Feminist psychology rewrites the way we understand women and their relations. Walsh (1985) suggests that the psychology of women reveals deficiencies in psychological research and theories relevant to gender. Popular media images often reflect these deficiencies in social scientific theory, therefore feminist psychology lends a useful perspective from which to examine the portrayal of women.

Feminist psychiatric theory points out the inequality in treatment and diagnosis of women and can be applied to women's representations in films that portray insanity. There are two approaches that feminists have offered concerning the relation between sexism and psychiatry that are useful in this analysis. Phyllis Chesler's historically significant *Women and Madness* (1972) suggests that sexism pervades psychiatry, its diagnosis and constructs. Psychiatry is seen as a fundamentally patriarchal institution that has always been oppressive to women in its sexist definitions and diagnosis of mental illness. Christina Robb argues that "when men devised a psychology that treated men's needs and preferences as normative goals for all people, then women's needs and preferences looked abnormal" (22). Chesler and others have examined the problematic relationship between psychiatry and sexism (Brodsky & Hare-Mustin, 1980; Penford and Walker, 1984; Russell, 1985). Insanity has been defined, albeit arbitrarily, by a male-dominated culture. This sociologically constructed view of madness provides a method to understand films that show the institutional incarceration of women (or attempt at institutionalization) who, because they exhibit behavior outside of their gender-prescribed role, have been labeled troubled, insane, or mad. Joan Busfield argues that women's behavior is more apt to be labeled disturbed, specifically based on the patterns of sex role performance and that "psychiatry, which is supposedly a helping profession, is fact oppresses women" (344).[1] Gostin agrees that psychology is socially constructed, writing that "mental illness is itself such an ephemeral and variable subject that it is much more liable to be interpreted according to the prevailing ideology" (15). And Jordan et al. write that "psychological theory, like any other cultural institution, reflects the larger Western patriarchal culture in the unexamined assumption that the white, middle class, heterosexual 'paradigm man' defines not just his own reality but human reality" (7).

Hilary Allen (1986) and Busfield (1989) offer an alternative approach to the study of sexism and psychiatry by examining "women's structural oppression" (Busfield 346). This perspective holds that the "oppression women encounter in their daily lives and on the way drives them into mental sickness. The emphasis here is less on mental illness as a social construct than on metal illness as a social product" (Busfield 344).[2]

*The Cracker Factory* (1979), a short film version of Charlotte Perkins Gilman's 1899 story *The Yellow Wall Paper* (1977), and *A Woman under the Influence* (1974), typify this phenomenon of being driven to mental breakdown because of societal forces. This second approach, mental illness as a social product, has gained popularity in psychiatric and feminist circles, but Chesler's original concern—psychiatry as a sexist design—cannot be ignored, especially in films that portray women who were incarcerated for behavioral problems—behavior that did not fit into what was socially prescribed for them. Gostin concurs with Chelser's assertion that psychiatry is inherently problematic because "its task has been to justify and make 'scientific' systematic discrimination against people who think and behave differently to the majority" which is in this case the male majority (14).

By incorporating the broad definition of madness outlined by Fleming and Manvell, we can locate a number of examples of films with "mad" women in central roles in American film history beginning in the 1940s. Insane female characters did appear before this decade, but a predominance of roles start to crop up at this time. This is partially explained by the social movement in the field of psychiatry. By the late 1930s and into the 1940s, the theories of Sigmund Freud, Carl Jung, Alfred Adler, Clara Thompson, and Karen Horney became known to the interested public and they were often examined in popular media (Fleming and Manvell 34). Horney was one of the first psychotherapists to argue that social and cultural factors influenced human psychic development. And it was her reactions to Freud that would provide the foundations for a psychology of women. According to Denmark and Paludi, Horney "was able to apply strict scrutiny to psychoanalytic theory and to refute androcentrism and sexist bias" (13).

*Now, Voyager* (1942) was one of the first films to have a woman central character who suffers a mental breakdown, is institutionalized, and eventually accepts her place in an imperfect world. The film not only portrays insanity and psychological treatment as a new subject matter, but also features a strong women in the lead role. Although melodramatic and merely skimming the surface of realism in its portrayal of insanity, the roots of madness as socially oppressive are present. The Bette Davis character (Charlotte Vale) represents a case where societal forces have driven a woman mad. Women who do not conform to traditional role expectations, in this case determined by her family and at the will of a domineering mother, are deemed insane. Mothers have frequently represented the traditional role of the passive, domestic, feminine woman, and their daughters who step out of this role have been thought to be conflicted, disturbed, even mad. The role of the mother in diagnosis of madness arises frequently, suggesting the continuity of this depiction.

The most influential film to treat mental illness in the 1940s was the first to question the poor treatment that mentally ill patients were receiving in state psychiatric institutions that often dated back to the late 1800s. *The Snake Pit* (1948) featured Olivia de Havilland in the lead role (Virginia) of the Mary Jane Ward novel. A contemporary look at this film illustrates both the gender bias of psychiatry and a greater ideological message that domesticity was a women's proper role, lest she go mad in pursuit of another.

During World War II many women left their domestic roles to work for the war effort on the homefront and abroad. This 'patriotic duty' was the first time a large percentage of women were receiving regular wages outside of the home. Following the war, most women returned home to lives of less intellectual and work-related freedom, in the traditional domestic sphere. According to Leslie Fishbein, feminist writer Betty Friedan (1963) argued that "Freudianism served to buttress a mystique of feminine fulfillment that cajoled women into abandoning their jobs to returning veterans in order to find satisfaction as wives and mothers" (135). It is this emphasis on Freudianism that sets *The Snake Pit* within the ideological concern about what happens when women "fall" from their feminine role. They go mad. Virginia's failure to balance housework with her professional writing, while trying to accept a husband who has failed as the traditional breadwinner are secondary to the character's journey through Freudian therapy.

Although the film does present the larger societal question of the treatment of the mentally ill by showing audiences scenes of overcrowding, radical treatment, and villain therapists, doctors, and nurses, it dilutes social criticism by offering, what Fishbein calls "a solution which celebrates the efficacy of psychoanalysis in restoring its heroine to mental health" (136), a mental health defined by male-dominated psychiatry. Fishbein suggests that the "films espousal of the feminine mystique seems far more energetic than its commitment to social reform" (148).

*Spellbound* (1945) features Ingrid Bergman as the psychiatrist who cures Gregory Peck. But more importantly, his love for her "cures" her heart. Although couched in the psychothriller genre, the film is really a love story between patient and therapist. Bergman is not the only female therapist to be involved in relations with her patients. This trend continues in *Prince of Tides* (1991), *Mr. Jones* (1992), and *Whispers in the Dark* (1992).

Two films of the 1950s, *Sunset Boulevard* (1950) and *A Streetcar Named Desire* (1952) feature mentally disturbed women in lead roles. Both women are psychologically trapped in the past where they were more glamorous, fulfilled, and youthful. Adoration by fans or suitors replaced motherhood, which was the more acceptable expression of feminity. The characters eventually pay for not having the lives of traditional wives and mothers. As their youthful beauty fades, so does their acceptance in a male-dominated world. Treatment for their mental illness is only tenuously addressed at the end of each film: Norma Desmond is allowed her final showbiz exit amid rolling film cameras, flashbulbs, and gawking reporters, before she is taken away by authorities. Blanche DuBois remains deluded that she is going on a vacation, although the kindness of the stranger who leads her out of Stanley and Stella's house is actually a sympathetic doctor, not a suitor. Neither film shows the true nature of mental illness or the psychiatric profession, but both offer dramatic glimpses of women who are shattered by failing to come to terms with the loss of youth, beauty, and attention from admirers. The emphasis in these films is on acceptance of these women by other people, usually men, in order for them to retain their self-worth and sanity. Yet both films suggest that women's reliance on socially constructed definitions of attractiveness and desire results in these characters' madness.

*The Three Faces of Eve* (1957), based on the actual clinical study of Eve White, was one of the first biographical films to examine mental illness.[3] Eve's story is about her three-way split personality and the "curing" of that illness. One of the first cases of multiple personality disorder to be realistically portrayed on the screen, Eve's characters are separated by behavior, costume, sexual expression, language, and personal aspirations—all of which are variations on traditional feminine expectations and roles. Through hypnosis and psychoanalysis, the personalities reveal themselves and the audience learns the cause for Eve's mental illness: a childhood trauma when forced by her mother to kiss her dead grandmother, a common folk-tradition. There is again a link between the maternal lineage and women's madness. After a memory flashback, Eve experiences a cathartic release and two of her 'inappropriate' personalities fade. The one that remains as the functioning personality is ready to marry and care for her daughter from a previous marriage. Finally cured, the healthy woman resumes a domestic and traditionally feminine role. The ideological message in the film is that women suffer from confusion, even madness, when they step outside of their traditional roles. But they find security and wellness as wife and mother. Walker notes that "at a time when women's roles were being widely discussed and challenged, multiple personality may have been read as an unconscious and expansive rendition of career and behavioral choices open to women" (77).

Instead of exploring real issues, mainstream films with female lead characters in the 1960s primarily utilized madness as a narrative device incorporating melodrama, sentimentality, and terror. *David and Lisa* (1962), based on actual case histories, is the story of mentally disturbed adolescents. The ease in curing the patients and the role that a love affair plays in treatment appears simplistic and sentimental. The heterosexual relationship appears to be the cure to their illness, further supporting the normalcy of traditional roles for men and women. Love is also central in *Lilith* (1964), based on the controversial J.R. Salamanca novel. Lilith's attractiveness is illustrated when a therapist trainee becomes enamored of her. What results is the suicide of another patient who also adores Lilith. The trainee eventually admits himself as a patient. Although love and control are at issue, a major theme is the definition of madness itself. Can madness truly be defined by those who do not experience it directly? Does its definition depend on the prescribed norms of a society that suppresses individuality? The focus on heterosexual love suggests that a person goes mad when these relationships go unfulfilled. The heterosexual relationship is the norm for a sane life. This social norm, along with feminine sexuality, is also reinforced in John Huston's biographical *Freud* (1962).

The treatment of alcoholism as mental illness appears in *Days of Wine and Roses* (1962). Although there is a realistic attempt to address the seriousness of this addiction, even introducing Alcoholics Anonymous as a treatment program, the film does not spare audiences in its use of sentimentality and melodrama. Both men and women succumb to addictions in this film, but the male character is the one who finds treatment. His character appears socially privileged because he succeeds at treatment, whereas the female character does not. Kirsten (Lee Remick), unable to fulfill the needs of her husband and care for her daughter, does not achieve success within the rigors of a treatment program. The film suggests that even with treatment, women's addictions are incurable.

Consumption of alcohol is portrayed differently in the Hollywood mainstream film based on gender difference. Men's alcoholism appears to be based on outside forces like war or stress from work, while women's addictions are often internal and personal. Alcoholism, even untreated, has been historically more socially acceptable for men than for women.

Madness, illustrated in the form of terror, has been one of the most prevalent mainstream representations in film. From the early Universal horror films, to possession films like *Dr. Jekyll and Mr. Hyde (1931)* or *The Exorcist* (1973), to the present-day slasher genre, the insane possession of a character gives justification for their gruesome acts. In films of the 1960s, this theme of madness is exemplified in *Whatever Happened to Baby Jane* (1962), a film that exploitatively uses mental illness to elicit suspense through horror.

Madness has also been defined through sexuality. *Marnie* (1964) continues the cinematic legacy of Alfred Hitchcock, whose films can be thematically linked on some level by their examination of the range of human neuroses. The severely disturbed Marnie is sexually "frigid" and suffers from traumatic reactions to the color red. These neuroses are traced to her childhood when her mother was forced to prostitute herself to take care of her daughter and herself, and when Marnie kills a young man in their house. Repression, guilt, and anxiety about familial relationships surface in many Hitchcock films.

One film from the 1960s does make an effort to examine new techniques in therapy and uncover the injustices of outdated techniques, as *The Snake Pit* attempted to do in the 1940s. In *The Caretakers* (1963), group therapy is shown as a means of encouraging patients to become nurturing to one another in the healing process, but the film continues to perpetuate oppressive representations of women. Although the introduction of group therapy accurately follows developments in psychiatric history, the emphasis placed on women in the traditional role of nurturer and caretaker follows the ideological goals of keeping women in the domestic sphere to care solely for husbands and children. As producers of ideology which often represent "model" gender roles, popular films like this one communicated to women that they would be happy and healthy in nurturing, mothering roles.

As we have seen, mainstream films have asserted that madness can result if women misalign themselves with nontraditional societal roles. Popular cultural images have also suggested that successful career women are troubled in some way, a sexist perspective seen in *The Caretakers.* The nursing profession is depicted in a manner not unlike that of *The Snake Pit.* The head nurse discourages any kind of new therapy and regards the patients as dangerous people who must be kept locked up like animals. She also requires her nursing staff to line up for rigorous drills and learn self defense for protection. Women in professional positions in *The Caretakers* are made a mockery of, portrayed as brutal, uncaring and nearly as paranoid as their patients. Nurse Ratched (Louise Fletcher), in *One Flew Over the Cuckoo's Nest,* exemplifies this characterization. Thus, careers outside of the home are not encouraged. These portrayals are interesting considering that psychiatry has always been a male-dominated profession with women relegated to supporting roles as nurses, assistants, and secretaries. Women who choose to work outside of the home in what seem to be "acceptable" subordinate professions are still portrayed as cruel and ignorant.

As Americans moved through the 1960s, women's social roles began to change along with the entire attitude of the country. The women's movement and the sexual revolution promised freedom and equity despite gender differences. However, the overwhelming ideological changes that loomed on the horizon never came to fruition and Hollywood films represented this. In feature films, women remained relegated to inferior roles and received inferior treatment in the mental health system. New themes did emerge in the portrayals of madness in the films of the 1970s: family dysfunction and family therapy, biography pictures of troubled artists, treatment of the mentally ill by women psychiatrists and mental illness from the patient's point of view. Women's alienation was also a prevalent theme in the 1970s, socially mirroring the fading energy of the women's movement and eventual defeat of the Equal Rights Amendment. However, alienation, as a social phenomena, was described several decades earlier and resulted in psychiatric developments in family therapy.

Beginning as early as the 1950s with developments in technology, consumer goods, and popular, affordable communication channels, the family unit started a slow but steady disintegration. Women were often blamed for this disintegration as they moved out of the home into personal and political activism and into the work force. It was within this context, in the late 1960s and into the 1970s, that family therapy was developed and practiced where "events were viewed within the context of the social system, as opposed to a linear, unicausal interpretation" (Fleming and Manvell 38). Family therapy has continued to gain momentum in the 1980s and 1990s. The term "dysfunctional" within family relations and development is now commonplace if not faddish. Films of the 1970s that began to examine family relations and individuals as a part of their environment, rather than separate from it, include *Summer Wishes, Winter Dreams* (1973), *A Woman under the Influence* (1974), *Looking for Mr. Goodbar* (1977), *Interiors* (1978), and *The Cracker Factory* (1979), a television movie.

*Interiors* places women at the center of attention. It also places them at the center of the cause and perpetuation of insanity and neurosis within the family. Although not directly about acute madness, this film embodies the mental neuroses which have come to exemplify Woody Allen films. Various degrees of mental illness can be defined and one could argue that the director uses these characterizations as harmless comic devices. But this film is part of the misogynistic history of many Hollywood films. The central character, Eve (Geraldine Page), is portrayed as an emotionally demanding mother and wife who cannot let go of an estranged husband or her adult daughters. Consequently, Eve's daughters' relationships with men reflect their mother's own troubled behavior. Her character spares no effort in trying to dominate family and friends, using emotional blackmail and an attempted suicide. In this film, women are the cause of familial dysfunction because they are domineering and emotionally irrational. Common neuroses are linked to insanity. *Interiors* illustrates Allen's and Busfield's arguments that social forces can drive women to madness. Insecurity, the loss of family, and the alienation that results from socially prescribed, conflicting feminine roles are part of Eve's troubles. But director Woody Allen places women at the root of all neurotic problems and shows that there may be no hope in breaking this cycle of sickness.

*A Woman under the Influence* (1974) again presents the domineering mother who drives women into madness. Although the mother-child relationship had been explored significantly in fields of psychiatry and mental health, the entire family unit was now being examined as contributing to its dysfunction. But according to Fleming and Manvell, "there is still a tendency to come back to the mother as the major provocation, if not the single cause, in the family's problems" (40). This portrayal has become a common one in popular film, placing women not only in roles of madness but blaming them for each other's, and their own, ill mental health. The central female character, Mabel (Gena Rowlands) is driven to a psychotic break primarily by both her own mother and her mother-in-law, although other family members do contribute to her illness, especially her husband Nick (Peter Falk). The film is a modern glimpse at the unending and hopeless isolation that families can experience from within. Susan Faludi writes that "the women who go mad in the 1970s women's films are . . . suburban housewives driven batty by subordination, repression, drudgery, and neglect" (58). And in *A Woman under the Influence* and *Diary of a Mad Housewife* (1970), the "wives' pill-popping habits and nervous breakdowns are presented as not-so-unreasonable responses to their crippling domestic condition—madness as a sign of their underlying sanity. What the male characters label lunacy in these films usually turns out to be a form of feminist resistance" (58).[4]

*Summer Wishes, Winter Dreams* (1973) and *The Cracker Factory* (1979) continue to portray how interrelationships within the family contribute to mental illness and in *Looking for Mr. Goodbar* (1977), an incestuous relationship at a young age affects a woman for her entire lifetime. Overall there is the lack of fulfillment and eventual isolation for women who cannot fit into the traditional gender roles that their parents experienced a generation earlier. Whether they are ridiculed by a contemptuous mother figure or other people in their social circle, their malaise is defined as mental illness and inevitably punishable. Although these films do not portray cases of severe madness, they communicate alienation, mental disease and even resistance among women as part of the family unit and what transpires because of their labeled emotional instability.

Artistic madness is a theme that has permeated literature and film for many years, but only recently have women been the subject of biographical films that examine this phenomenon. *Lady Sings the Blues* (1972) and *The Rose* (1979) are two biopics that examine women artists and mental instability, albeit not diagnosed insanity. Madness is defined here as a loss of control of one's own life and subsequent self-destructive behavior.

*Lady Sings the Blues*, based on the story of Billie Holiday, is set primarily in New York City. Alcohol and drugs were the escape for this gifted artist who not only had to suffer from gender discrimination in the music world but also was subjected to racial persecution. Rising up from a life of prostitution in Harlem, this African-American blues artist fought many battles in her life as a singer, but eventually lost herself in the madness of drugs and alcohol.

The talents of gifted women are often associated with a certain amount of instability. This is also seen in foreign films like *Camille Claudel* (France 1988) and *An Angel at My Table* (New Zealand 1990). These women artists' behavior is different from socially prescribed definitions for femininity, so they are defined as mad. Eccentricity, creativity, and independence are communicated in these films as unacceptable feminine qualities. These women were forced into isolating and harmful institutionalization for their unconventional personalities. Women artists have been treated similarly across culture, race, nationality, and history. Although *Lady Sings the Blues* is one of the first films to explore emotional problems with a racially diverse cast and leading character, it exploits every opportunity to sensationalize Holiday's tumultuous life including rape, violent sexuality, murder, drugs, alcohol use, and female hysteria. Holiday would likely have been institutionalized, like Frances Farmer, Camille Claudel or Janet Frame, if she had not died at an early age.

The same sensationalism is seen in *The Rose,* the story of a rock 'n' roll singer drawn loosely upon the life of Janis Joplin. Joplin rose to fame a decade after Holiday, but plays out her life much in the same way. The 1960s and 1970s brought much more publically visible drug use, including alcohol, marijuana, cocaine, heroin, and assorted pills. Musicians also came to be associated with this drug use and Janis Joplin fell into the heroic position of representing a generation of lost, rebellious youth who expressed their power through freedom along with Jim Morrison and Jimi Hendrix among others. But behind the facade of "the Rose" was a young woman starving for attention, love and acceptance from her fans, men and especially her rejecting mother. The loss of love and feelings of abandonment leave the main character (Bette Midler) empty, fragile and self-destructive. Escape into drugs offered a diversion from reality and thus a place of peace. Her death eventually comes when she is rejected by a man who she has been in and out of love with throughout the film. She accepts heroin from a fan, rushes to a football field where she was once gang-raped and calls her mother. When her mother refuses to attend her upcoming concert, rejected, she takes the fix and dies alone. The mother-daughter relationship is again central to the descent into madness.

*I Never Promised You a Rose Garden* (1977) serves to "correct" some of the portrayals of women and madness in film. By having a woman psychiatrist successfully rescue a troubled, schizophrenic and suicidal teenager, the mother figure is spared some of the blame in diagnosed madness. The psychiatrist replaces the "sick" mother with a "healthy," caring maternal figure. The image of women as psychoanalyst has not always been this positive. In *Spellbound* (1945), *Prince of Tides* (1991), and *Mr. Jones* (1992), women "fall" from their esteemed professional positions by getting romantically involved with their patients.

Women's domesticity has been a reoccurring theme in Hollywood films. In films, success in the role of wife, mother, and nurturer is thought to produce healthy families. Thus, madness within families almost always is portrayed as the result of the mother who, because of societal pressure, is left responsible for the well-being of the entire household but fails to adapt to this role. *Sybil* (1976), a television movie about a young woman with seventeen personalities, epitomizes the role of the mother in development of a mentally healthy child. Audiences see that Sybil's mental illness was caused by abuse at the hands of the maternal figure. But it is a woman psychiatrist who helps the distraught woman work her way through the emotionally disturbing trauma. The mother figure is either destroyer or savior.

The novel version of *The Snake Pit* portrayed mental illness from the patient's point of view. However the film version changed the perspective of the novel, focusing more on treatment and an overall ideological concern of women's social status, rather than what it felt like to be insane. *Images* (1972) finally offered audiences the subjective viewpoint of madness. Through cinematic means such as point-of-view shots and voice-over, we come to see how Catheryn (Susannah York) sees her troubled world. The narrative devices explore madness through self-reflexive cinematic techniques that call attention to the artifice of the film. The audience ends up uncertain about what is fantasy and what is reality. This serves two purposes: fulfilling what we imagine the mind of a mentally ill person is like while sensationalizing insanity.

In the 1980s, the range of the portrayal of madness was vast, although the treatment of women remained static. As in *The Rose* and *Lady Sings the Blues,* real life characters made for interesting reel portrayals. The biopic genre continued with *Frances (1982)* and *Gorillas in the Mist* (1988), offering consciousness-raising stories about social problems through the stories of well-known persons.

Frances Farmer's life as portrayed in *Frances* allows the viewer to see the cruelty of the male-dominated psychiatric establishment. Frances is repeatedly institutionalized by her mother during the 1930s and 1940s when experimentalization on mental patients was prevalent. There was massive institutionalization; deaf people, physically handicapped, depressed, diseased, stressed, and even politically outspoken individuals were placed in institutions.[5] The back ward patients were victims of water, heat, electric, insulin shock and radiation therapies as well as the new lobotomy procedure, as portrayed in the documentary *Asylum* (1988). Quick cures to mental dysfunction were desperately being sought. Overcrowding was also problematic and the rituals of daily life were reduced to spectacle. We can think of Frederick Wiseman's portrayal of clothing changes, bathing, and feeding in the controversial documentary *Titticut Follies* (1967), in which emotionally disturbed and criminally institutionalized men became herded animals, reducing their human dignity to a disgusting level.

*Frances* serves political functions as well as providing commentary on the gross practices within the mental health profession. The anti-Communist witch hunts, House Un-American Activities Committee (HUAC) hearings, and blacklisting of the late 1940s and 1950s quietly surface in the film. It is implied that because of Frances Farmer's personal grit and flamboyancy that there might have been a political conspiracy against her.

Frances Farmer is portrayed as a social misfit of sorts; winning an essay contest at sixteen years old with a controversial anti-deity paper, studying theater in Communist Moscow, acting with socialist Group Theater members, including an affair with Communist sympathizing playwright Clifford Odets, and eventually through her noncompliance with mainstream Hollywood and its sense of Babylonian stardom. Unlike her male counterparts, Farmer is not ignored or glorified in her eccentricities, she is punished for her "crimes" of nonconformity. The oppressive world she lives in frustrates her because it cannot accept the passionate and often deviant activist that she really is. Allen's argument, that society drives women mad is apparent. Farmer conducts her life as she wishes, even though her mother, Hollywood bosses, friends, and lovers think it abnormal. Frances Farmer was an individual in a world that did not allow individuality. The pressures of nonacceptance lead to her self-destructive behavior and eventual institutionalization.

Once labeled sick or ill, Farmer's life gets worse. "If you're treated like a patient, you're apt to act like one," she says. This is a strong case, as Chesler points out, for the historical sickness of psychiatry itself. The film "hints at a more radical idea, that treatment by the mental health profession is what causes mental illness" (Raushenbush 44). After her forced treatments with drugs, electroshock therapy, straitjacketing, rape by local soldiers who are let into the asylum by an attendant, and lobotomy, the blatant oppressiveness of state-run psychiatry cannot be ignored. Although it is a contemporary film that can safely criticize outdated treatment methods, the oppression of the past carries symbolically into our popular cultural present, suggesting that although there have been reforms in psychiatric treatment and the overall portrayal of women in film, there has been little reform in acceptance of women who are gifted, unafraid to speak against what is socially prescribed for them, and lead eccentric lives outside of what is considered normal.

*Gorillas in the Mist* (1988) is based on the life of Dian Fossey, the woman who was reportedly responsible for preventing the extinction of the mountain gorilla in Africa. She lived a secluded life in Rwanda, one that provided a place for her scientific accomplishments and genius to flourish.

As Farmer is portrayed in *Frances,* Fossey is also passionately driven in her work. She is determined, stubborn, not afraid to speak her mind, and protective of her research. Fossey's determination to save the gorillas from extinction becomes an obsession, causing people to think of her as a lonely madwoman. She may not have been clinically diagnosed as insane, but a dominating obsessiveness for her work consumes most of her adult life. In her story, we see that she also drinks, smokes, and is prone to fits of anger and aggression. This was certainly not the prescribed role for femininity, but quite acceptable for a male scientist or artist. Men are allowed to drink alcohol, be aggressive, fight for their territories, yet women are not. In Fossey's uncharacteristic behavior, she builds a legend—not only as a great scientist, but as a witch—a madwoman who thinks she owns the mountains and gorillas that inhabit them.

The biopic was not the only genre to examine madness or non-conformity in the 1980s. Fictional films like *Nuts* (1987) questioned the legal definition of insanity and action-thrillers like *Black Widow* (1986) often featured unbalanced, dangerous women in central roles. This sweep of psycho-thriller films offered no critique of madness as a social construct or ideological issue, rather madness served as a narrative/character device or as Davis suggests "to exploit primal male fears of female power" by portraying the "sexual female as destroyer" (47).

Barbra Streisand plays Claudia in *Nuts,* which tells the story of a high-priced prostitute who kills one of her clients after he becomes violent. The courtroom drama, more than portraying personal madness as its central element, examines the role of sanity or mental illness as social competency. The film raises questions about civil liberties, the role of the state, and the nature of sanity itself. It asks who is to judge who is "nuts" or sane? Claudia is controlled by those around her—her family, expensive lawyers, and the system of justice, all which speak for her, negating her voice. The systems of control, both personal and institutional, oppress Claudia because they judge her as incompetent. She is the victim of a male-dominated household, where a drunk mother turned her eyes away from a stepfather's sexual abuse, and an all-male courtroom that will decide her fate. In this case, Chesler's argument that psychiatry is sexist extends into other established societal units—the system of justice, the family, and work. *Nuts* remains an important film document about women, madness, and the structures of a society that continually subjugates persons based on their differences from the white male norm. The film was also one of the final ones of the 1980s to criticize definitions of madness instead of using it to stereotypically define characters.

In the 1980s a series of psycho-thriller films were released that featured women as emotionally disturbed central characters. Many of the films focused around issues of love and obsession. The predominance of portrayals of extramarital affairs, sexual obsession, and subversive sensuality all suggest a growing fear of women. Their ability to accept patriarchically defined, heterosexual relationships are central themes. Whether this is a backlash to the sexual revolution and feminist movement where women took control of their sexuality, a reflection of the greed and selfishness that permeated the Reagan presidency years, or a reaction to the beginning of the AIDS epidemic, films with love, obsession and madness changed the way audiences thought about casual sex and women. The major film to reflect this trend was *Fatal Attraction* (1987), although audiences did get a glimpse of obsessive love in Nicholas Roeg's *Bad Timing: A Sensual Obsession* (Britain 1980).

*Fatal Attraction* consistently underscores the theme that has been running through many of the films discussed in this essay. Women who stray out of their traditional roles in a patriarchal society are misdiagnosed as insane or are punished for their feminist transgression by indeed going mad, in this case becoming the dangerous female predator. After Dan (Michael Douglas) has a brief affair with independent, career woman Alex (Glenn Close), she stalks him and his family to force him to accept responsibility for her supposed pregnancy. Davis suggests that Alex "threatens what many men most fear, that if a feminist program succeeds, men can be held accountable, to a punitive degree, for what in fact they have no control over" (54). The film suggests that men must accept more responsibility for reproduction, both economically and emotionally. But that responsibility has taken the form of "patriarchal control over women's sexual activities and reproductive rights" (Davis 55). If a woman strays from her domestic, monogamous role she becomes the destroyer of human life rather than its creator. *Fatal Attraction,* with its demonic portrayal of Alex, the single, child-less, career oriented women, shifts the story from "male wrongdoing to female predation; what begins as a tale of a man's violation of the trust of his loved ones turns into a misogynistic rant against the social posture and sexual autonomy of the independent woman" (Babener 26).[6] James Conlon suggests that *Fatal Attraction* is more a film "about passion itself, about its powers and possibilities in human life" (150). Alex represents the element of passion, whereas Dan's wife Beth (Ann Archer), represents the safety of domesticity. In this argument, the film suggests that both men and women must keep their passions in check or go mad, "because there can be no union of passion and domestic security" (Conlon 152). Beth ends up killing Alex, the (passionate) part of herself "that inherently undermines domestic tranquility" (Conlon 153).

The psychodrama genre, which features women as mentally disturbed stalkers, continues into the 1990s with *Final Analysis* (1992), *Basic Instinct* (1992), *Whispers in the Dark* (1992), *Single, White Female* (1992) and *Hand That Rocks the Cradle* (1992). *Final Analysis* and *Whispers in the Dark* are two films that involve psychiatric treatment and the tormented relationship of patient-therapist. In most of the above-mentioned films, women's madness is central to character development and contributes as a narrative story device but rarely offers critique of gender relations and emotional instability. Women get the power they've been insisting on, but the overriding ideological theme is that this power is dangerous.

Although this essay is structured from a historical perspective, it is also informed by continuing themes that appear about women and madness in popular Hollywood film: the importance of the mother-figure in women's madness, the normalcy of domesticity, and the centrality of love and heterosexuality, which appears in *Benny and Joon* (1993). The theme of alcoholism as illness surfaces again in the 1994 *When a Man Loves a Woman.* And women psychiatrists continue to have relations with patients, curing them, while at the same time curing their own longing for a romantic partner. The most disturbing trend, the female as destroyer, persists in mainstream films like *A Dangerous Woman* (1993).

What audiences learn from these images certainly varies, but overall women's choices are limited, according to their portrayals in mainstream film—they are supposed to find love, have children, and live out fulfilled domestic roles. This supposedly contributes to their sanity. But the conflicting social roles that women learn in a patriarchal society are often those that cause alienation, anxiety, and mental distress. And it is no doubt that men fall into many of the same traps of societal pressures. But, the continual representation of unstable women as those who make choices outside of traditional femininity ideologically establishes male as psychologically normative. And although feminist psychology and psychotherapy techniques have prompted changes in the field by recognizing differences in behavior based on gender socialization, Hollywood films continue to ignore social changes and place women and men into defined roles which they cannot possibly fulfill—sanely.

## Notes

1. See also Chesler, *Women and Madness,* chapters 1 and 2.

2. Joan Busfield notes that this socially constructed mental illness was discussed earlier by Betty Friedan (1963) and Jessie Bernard (1971), Florence Denmark and Michele Paludi (1993), and Judith Jorden et al. (1991) anthologize writings on this subject based on groundbreaking works such as Jean Baker Miller's *Toward a New Psychology of Women* (1976), which identified women's psychological patterns and strengths rather than attempting to understand women from the dominant deficiency model. This model defined women's development and mental health to a patriarchal model rather than a matriarchal one. Thus, women were continually defined as deficient to the norm. Other subsequent works that contribute to the development of a female psychology include Nancy Chodorow's *The Reproduction of Mothering,* Carol Gilligan's *In a Different Voice,* and *Women's Ways of Knowing,* by M.F. Belenky et al.

3. The patient retells her story in *I'm Eve,* by Elan Sain Pittaillo for her cousin Chris Costner Sizemore.

4. Although Faludi reports that films of the 1970s offered some representations of feminist resistance by portraying housewives who "leave home, temporarily or permanently, to find their own voice" (58), during the 1980s and into the 1990s women's images regressed. Women characters' voices were taken away or muted, domesticity was revered and women were punished for not living up to traditional motherhood and spousal roles.

5. See also Gostin (1984), Rovner (1987), Asylum (1988).

6. The *Journal of Popular Culture* 26.3 (1992) is devoted to essays on *Fatal Attraction,* including discussion on the conflict between career and family for women, female identity and children, feminist discourse and politics, morality, and the trend of predatory-female films to emerge in the late 1980s. This trend, understood in many ways to be a backlash to feminism, continues in the 1990s with films like *Basic Instinct.*

Susan Faludi also comments on women's roles in Hollywood films in A. Alexander and J. Hanson's *Taking Sides,* as well as in her own *Backlash.*

## Works Cited

Allen, Hilary. "Psychiatry and the Feminine." *The Power of Psychiatry*. Ed. P. Miller and N. Rose. Cambridge: Polity, 1986.

*Asylum*. Dir. Sarah Mondale. Stone Lantern Films, 1988.

Babener, Liahna. "Patriarchal Politics in Fatal Attraction." *Journal of Popular Culture* 26.3 (1992): 25-34.

Belenky, M.F., B.M. Clinchy, N.R. Goldberger, and J.M. Tarule. *Women's Ways of Knowing: The Development of Self, Voice, and Mind*. New York: Basic, 1986.

Bernard, Jessie. *The Future of Marriage*. New York: World, 1972.

—. "The Paradox of Happy Marriage." *Women in Sexist Society*. Ed. V. Gornick and B.K. Moran. New York: Basic, 1971.

Brodsky, A.M., and R.T. Hare-Mustin, eds. *Women and Psychotherapy*. New York: Guilford, 1980.

Busfield, Joan. "Sexism and Psychiatry." *Sociology* 23 (1989): 343-64.

Chesler, Phyllis. *Women & Madness*. New York: Doubleday, 1972.

Chodorow, Nancy. *The Reproduction of Mothering*. Berkeley: U of California P, 1978.

Conlon, James. "The Place of Passion: Reflections on Fatal Attraction." *Journal of Popular Film and Television* 16 (1989): 148-54.

Davis, Kathe. "The Allure of the Predatory Woman in Fatal Attraction and Other Current American Movies." *Journal of Popular Culture* 26.3 (1992): 47-58.

Denby, David. Frances Film Review *New York* 13 Dec. 1982. Rpt. in *Film Review Annual* 1982: 467.

Denmark, Florence, and Michele A. Paludi, eds. *Psychology of Women: A Handbook of Issues and Theories*. Westport CT: Greenwood, 1993.

Faludi, Susan. *Backlash: The Undeclared War Against Women*. New York: Crown, 1991.

—. "Fatal and Fetal Visions: The Backlash in the Movies." *Taking Sides: Controversial Issues in Mass Media and Society*. Ed. A. Alexander and J. Hanson. 2nd ed. Guilford CT: Duskin, 1993. 55-64.

Fishbein, Leslie. "The Snake Pit (1948): The Sexist Nature of Sanity." *Hollywood as Historian*. Ed. Peter Rollins. UP of Kentucky, 1983.

Fleming, Michael, and Roger Manvell. *Images of Madness: The Portrayal of Insanity in Feature Film*. Rutherford, NJ: Fairleigh Dickinson UP, 1985/London: Associated UP, 1985.

—. "Through the Lens Darkly." *Psychology Today* July 1987: 26-34.

Friedan, Betty. *The Feminine Mystique*. 1963. New York: Dell, 1974.

Gilligan, Carol. *In a Different Voice: Psychological Theory and Women's Development*. Cambridge: Harvard UP, 1982.

Gostin, Larry. "Taking Liberties." *The New Internationalist* (Feb. 1984). Rpt. in *Social Issues Resources Series* 3.2: 11-12.

Lerner, Harriet Goldhor. *Women in Therapy.* 1988. New York: Harper & Row, 1989.

Miller, Jean Baker. *Toward a New Psychology of Women.* 1976. Boston: Beacon, 1986.

Mitchell, Juliet. *Psychoanalysis and Feminism: Freud, Reich, Laing and Women.* New York: Pantheon, 1974.

Penfold, P. Susan, and Gillian A. Walker. *Women and the Psychiatric Paradox.* Montreal: Eden Press, 1983.

Raushenbush, Burns. *Cineaste* 12.4 (1983). Rpt. in *Film Review Annual* 1983, 462-64.

Robb, Christina. "A Theory of Empathy." *Boston Globe* 16 Oct. 1988: 19+.

Rouner, Sandy. "A New Manual for Mental Disorders." *Washington Post* 12 May 1987: 8-9.

Russell, Denise. "Psychiatric Diagnosis and the Oppression of Women." *International Journal of Social Psychology* 31 (1985): 298-305.

Sizemore, Chris Costner, and Elen Sain Pittillo. *I'm Eve.* Garden City: Doubleday, 1977.

Strouse, Jean, ed. *Women & Analysis.* New York: Grossman, 1974.

Taylon, Paul. *Monthly Film Bulletin* Mar. 1983. Rpt. in *Film Review Annual,* 465.

Taylor, Debbie. "Madness & Badness." *New Internationalist* Feb. 1984: 7-15. Rpt. in Social Issues Resources Series 3.2: 7-11.

Walker, Janet. *Couching Resistance: Women, Film and Psychoanalytic Theory.* Minneapolis: U of Minnesota P, 1993.

Walsh, M.R. "The Psychology of Women Course: A Continuing Catalyst for Change." *Teaching of Psychology* 12: 198-203.

## Filmography

| Year | Title | Director |
|---|---|---|
| Women as central characters | | |
| 1942 | *Now, Voyager* | Irving Rapper |
| 1945 | *Spellbound* | Alfred Hitchcock |
| 1948 | *The Snake Pit* | Anatole Litvak |
| 1950 | *Sunset Boulevard* | Billy Wilder |
| 1952 | *A Streetcar Named Desire* | Elia Kazan |
| 1957 | *Three Faces of Eve* | Nunnally Johnson |

| | | |
|---|---|---|
| 1962 | *David and Lisa* | Frank Perry |
| 1962 | *Whatever Happened to Baby Jane* | Robert Aldrich |
| 1963 | *The Caretakers* | Hal Bartlett |
| 1964 | *Marnie* | Alfred Hitchcock |
| 1964 | *Lilith* | Robert Rossen |
| 1970 | *Diary of a Mad Housewife* | Frank Perry |
| 1971 | *Play Misty for Me* | Clint Eastwood |
| 1972 | *Lady Sings the Blues* | Sidney J. Furie |
| 1972 | *Images* | Robert Altman |
| 1973 | *The Exorcist* | John Boorman |
| 1973 | *Summer Wishes, Winter Dreams* | Gilbert Cates |
| 1974 | *A Woman under the Influence* | John Cassavetes |
| 1976 | *Sybil* | Daniel Petrie |
| 1977 | *I Never Promised You a Rose Garden* | Anthony Page |
| 1977 | *Looking for Mr. Goodbar* | Richard Brooks |
| 1977 | *The Yellow Wallpaper* | Marie Ashton |
| 1978 | *Interiors* | Woody Allen |
| 1979 | *The Rose* | Mark Rydell |
| 1979 | *The Cracker Factory* | Burt Brinckeroff |
| 1980 | *Bad Timing: A Sensual Obsession* | Nicholas Roeg |
| 1982 | *Frances* | Graeme Clifford |
| 1984 | *Committed* | Sheila McLaughlin, Lynne Tillman |
| 1986 | *Black Widow* | Bob Rafelson |
| 1987 | *Fatal Attraction* | Adrian Lyne |
| 1987 | *Nuts* | Martin Ritt |
| 1987 | *House of Games* | David Mamet |
| 1988 | *Gorillas in the Mist* | Michael Apted |
| 1988 | *Camille Claudel* | Bruno Nuytten |
| 1991 | *Prince of Tides* | Barbra Streisand |
| 1992 | *Final Analysis* | Phil Joanou |
| 1992 | *Mr. Jones* | Mike Figgis |
| 1992 | *Whispers in the Dark* | Christopher Crowe |
| 1992 | *Basic Instinct* | Paul Verhoeven |
| 1992 | *Single, White Female* | Barbet Schroeder |
| 1992 | *Hand That Rocks the Cradle* | Curtis Hanson |
| 1993 | *Benny and Joon* | Jeremiah Chechik |
| 1993 | *A Dangerous Woman* | Stephen Gyllenhaal |
| 1994 | *When a Man Loves a Woman* | Luis Mandoki |

Other films cited as portraying madness

| | | |
|---|---|---|
| 1915 | *Birth of a Nation* | David W. Griffith |
| 1931 | *Dr. Jekyll and Mr. Hyde* | Reuben Mamoulian |
| 1967 | *Titticut Follies* | Frederick Wiseman |
| 1991 | *Silence of the Lambs* | Jonathan Demme |

# The Ugly American Syndrome in Films of the Vietnam War

**Ralph R. Donald**

In the years since the war's end, historians, journalists, politicians, and political scientists have laid the blame for America's political and military failures in Vietnam on many causes. These include the American public's unwillingness to support the conflict, restricting the military's options in fighting the war, broadcasting the horrors of Vietnam into our living rooms nightly (thus affecting the nation's commitment), and other negative influences.

The purpose of this chapter is to present another set of influences that has been either underplayed or ignored in most contemporary analyses of our defeat in Vietnam. Ironically, these same influences may also have prompted analysts to overlook or undervalue their effects. A study of Hollywood's narrative feature films dealing with the Vietnam War points to a persistent pattern of attitudes and behaviors best described by William Lederer and Eugene Burdick in their novel, *The Ugly American.* This syndrome is chiefly characterized by arrogant American ethnocentrism and a bloated sense of United States national wisdom and omnipotence. Additionally, through America's dogged support of a corrupt, right-wing South Vietnamese government, this syndrome has caused America to be portrayed as an unwanted barbarian invader—in contrast to President Johnson's characterization of the United States as the "rescuer of Vietnamese democracy." These films dramatize why much of America's military failure, and indeed America's inability to win the "hearts and minds" of the Vietnamese people, can be attributed to various symptoms of the Ugly American syndrome.

### *The Novel and the Movie*

The 1958 novel is based on the authors' experiences in Asia working in the U.S. foreign service. While the 1963 movie adaptation's use of the term Ugly American is limited to the film's title, American audiences assumed from the story that United States Ambassador MacWhite, played by Marlon Brando, was the Ugly American character. In the film, MacWhite becomes the embodiment of the Sarkhanese (read Vietnamese) perception of Yanks as military and cultural imperialists bent on turning their country into a United States colony, dependent on the "white man" for all technology and progress, and subservient to American economic interests in the region. But MacWhite is *not* the Ugly American in Lederer and Burdick's book. Homer Atkins, a sympathetic character truly dedicated to unselfishly helping Southeast Asians, is Lederer and Burdick's Ugly American. The authors use this term because Atkins is physically unattractive, not because of his politics or his worldview. But because this is not explained at all in the motion picture, the popular understanding of the "Ugly American" is that the phrase describes the negative persona of MacWhite and others like him. For this reason, I choose to characterize the counterproductive behaviors described in this paper as the "Ugly American syndrome."

Lederer and Burdick write that, regrettably, there were very few Homer Atkinses in Southeast Asia before and during American involvement in that region. Rather, too many men fitting the descriptions of the authors' negatively stereotyped characters Ambassador Sears, Joe Bing, and Major Cravath mis-served their country with racist, elitist, thoughtless attitudes and actions, leading America down the path to its worst embarrassment in this century.

The authors claim that while the Soviet Union's foreign service personnel are well-schooled in the languages, cultures, religions, and customs of the countries to which they are assigned, Americans were not. As a matter of fact, as recent popular press articles will attest, most Americans are still geographically and culturally illiterate, assiduously avoiding opening their minds to the wonders found in other countries and cultures. Often, United States ambassadors are appointed through political patronage rather than by personal merit and diplomatic experience. United States foreign service personnel associate only with Americans, or with white Europeans, and conduct themselves in ways offensive to the native population, viewing themselves and their own customs as superior. Writing in 1958, Lederer and Burdick clearly warn that continuing this kind of United States representation in Southeast Asia could only play into the hands of the Communists.

Some chapters in the book dramatize the fact that the Ugly American syndrome is not solely a Yankee affliction. Schooled in Clausevitz at St. Cyr, overconfident French army officers were convinced that a ragtag band of Vietnamese could not devise tactics and strategies capable of defeating a European force superior in men, weapons, and logistical support. However, the book describes how the Viet Minh drove the French out of their country. Apparently no influential French officer respected his enemy enough to study the writings of Mao Tse-tung, which prescribed guerrilla tactics not found in European military textbooks. But these techniques proved devastatingly effective in a land war in Asia.

The authors created a stereotypical American army advisor named Major Cravath, and made him a witness to the French debacle. But Cravath's ethnocentrism keeps him from learning anything of value. Instead of bringing back a warning against American involvement in the area, Cravath reports to the United States Senate the following: "The Vietnamese just don't make very good soldiers. Their way of life doesn't make them susceptible to discipline, and if you give them a burp gun or a carbine, they'll sell it or take off with it into the hills." When unbelieving senators ask him how this successful guerrilla campaign against the French is being accomplished, Major Cravath responds that he believes that the Viet Minh are really Chinese communists, whom he considers "better fighters" than the Vietnamese.

These statements are symptomatic of the attitudes these farsighted authors warned the nation against in 1958. Unfortunately, throughout the next decade and a half, as both the history of the war and Vietnam War films indicate, the Ugly American syndrome became a major liability, effectively and unconsciously sabotaging United States interests in the region. Using the films Americans have made about the war as text, what follows is an analysis of a number of instances in which Americans of all kinds, protagonists as well as antagonists, demonstrate the symptoms of this syndrome, and suffer its consequences.

### *Racism*

American films about the Vietnam War were not the first to portray an Asian enemy as a subhuman, inferior race. Many United States movies produced during World War II made use of blatantly racist and dehumanizing propaganda appeals designed to slander the Japanese. Not surprisingly for propaganda, but curiously in retrospect, most of these films differentiated between an "inferior" Japanese enemy and the intelligent, courageous Chinese, Filipinos, and Burmese, America's allies. In contrast, Vietnam War films rarely make distinctions between the enemy and the population we were there to assist, since they were the same. To Americans, both the VC and our South Vietnamese allies were "gooks," "dinks," "scroungy little jungle buggers," "needle-dicks," "slopes," and "zipperheads" ("zips" for short).

In the documentary *Hearts and Minds* (1974), American Vietnam commander Gen. William Westmoreland says, "The Oriental doesn't put the same high price on life as does the westerner. Life is plentiful, life is cheap in the Orient, and as the philosophy of the Orient expresses it, life is not important." This shameful disrespect for the Vietnamese as human beings is expressed by soldiers throughout the chain of command in Vietnam War films.

Most of the plot of *Casualties of War* (1989) deals with this lack of respect for Vietnamese as individuals. In the film, soldiers kidnap a native girl to use "for portable R and R." All but one American participate in her rape and murder. In *Platoon* (1986), United States soldiers not only attempt to rape two children but also murder three apparently innocent villagers in retaliation for the deaths of three of their comrades.

These My Lai–type events don't always occur, close-up, on the ground. Sometimes they are callously ordered up from a safe distance. In *Bat-21* (1988), Col. Walker, circling in a helicopter over a Vietnamese village, has just seen the VC kill five of his men. Although the enemy holds scores of villagers hostage, he vengefully orders an air strike. The planes convert the village, mostly full of innocent men, women and children, into a fiery inferno.

Even when the killing isn't premeditated, Americans refuse to take responsibility. In *Born on the Fourth of July* (1989), Kovic and his men riddle a village with automatic gunfire, accidentally killing or wounding a hut full of innocent Vietnamese women and children. Kovic and others begin helping with the wounded villagers and call in a Medivac helicopter, but they are ordered to withdraw. The lieutenant tells his men, "They just got in the way, that's all." Then an artillery strike is called in on the village, killing the remaining wounded people.

In *Apocalypse Now* (1979), Col. Kilgore seems to be interested in only one thing: finding good waves for surfing. When he learns that a VC village has excellent waves, he mounts a bloody assault, gunning down or incinerating most of the local men, women, and children—but getting in a few good surfboard rides. Vietnamese property means little to Kilgore as well: After an earlier assault on a village, his men steal a villager's cow, and remove it by helicopter to be the guest of honor at the Americans' post-holocaust barbecue.

The television miniseries *A Rumor of War* (1980) displayed the difficulty the American command had in rationalizing the needless killing of civilians. Eventually, someone in charge created a policy to assist marines in both identifying the enemy and increasing the body count: "No Vietnamese is to be shot unless he's running: But if he's Vietnamese and dead, battalion says he's a VC." Less concern for good form is found in *Full Metal Jacket* (1987): A sadistic helicopter machine-gunner simply mows down any Vietnamese he sees. He explains to protagonist Joker how he determines who is the enemy: "Anyone who runs is a VC; anyone who stands still is a well-disciplined VC." Later, Joker sarcastically tells a television news interviewer why he is in Vietnam: "I wanted to see South Vietnam, the jewel of Southeast

Asia. I wanted to meet interesting and stimulating people of an ancient culture—and kill them."

In *Good Morning, Vietnam* (1987), two United States soldiers in a Saigon bar don't mind consorting with Vietnamese prostitutes, but object when Cronauer brings a young Vietnamese man named Twan into the bar. They won't allow a "gook" to sit at a table with white people in his own country. Later, Cronauer is indignant when he learns that this same young friend turns out to be "the enemy." Twan retorts, "*You're* the enemy, killing our people thousands of miles from your home. . . . Why? Because we're not human to you. We're only your enemies."

Reinforcing the view of many United States soldiers that the Vietnamese are not humans, or at least not of the same order of humanity as Americans, is Sgt. Oleonowski in *Go Tell the Spartans* (1978). In one scene, he tries to explain to an inexperienced officer how VC sappers can so easily penetrate defenses crisscrossed with barbed wire: "Lieutenant, the dinks don't feel any pain: The barbed wire just makes 'em itch a little." Instead of complimenting the VC on their courage and willingness to endure the wire, Oleonowski dehumanizes them to the point that they are presumed incapable of feeling pain.

*Not Worth Defending*

In these films, the South Vietnamese are often characterized as a population not really worth American intervention. Either their culture and mores are not considered "American enough" to preserve, or the South Vietnamese are not viewed as eager enough to defend themselves to warrant sacrificing the lives of United States troops. In the first scene depicting a Vietnam location in *Full Metal Jacket,* Joker and his friend Rafterman are accosted by a sleazy prostitute, and young Vietnamese thieves steal Rafterman's camera. "Do you know what really pisses me off about these people," he complains. "We're supposed to be helping them, and they shit all over us every chance they get." Throughout the movie, Rafterman never comprehends that Americans are viewed by most Vietnamese as just the latest army of barbarians occupying their country, and as such, are fair game for any kind of exploitation. Later in the picture, the squad of marines haggles with a South Vietnamese Army (ARVN) soldier/pimp for the price of his whore. "We'll be glad to trade you some ARVN rifles," one marine jokes. "Never been fired, and only dropped once." Likewise, in *Hamburger Hill* (1987), two sergeants, bathing with a pair of Vietnamese prostitutes, make cowardice jokes about "Marvin the ARVN." One prostitute says, "ARVN are tired of fighting your fucking war."

Indignant, one of the sergeants yells, "Our fucking war? Our fucking war?" The other sergeant, more of a realist, calms him down and states, "It *is* our fucking war."

In *The Iron Triangle* (1989), the ARVN officer, the government propagandist, and her bodyguard are all portrayed as hypocritical, savage, and cowardly, while the VC, although communists, are portrayed as more committed to their cause, and willing to fight and die for it. In *Go Tell the Spartans,* American advisors never consider their ARVN allies as equals. Pinned down during a firefight, Sgt. Oleonowski tries to prevent Lt. Hamilton from risking his life to rescue a wounded ARVN soldier. "He's *their* buddy, not ours," Oleonowski argues. Later, after their occupation of the Muc Hoa firebase provokes an en masse response by the VC, the American commander decides to "exfiltrate" all United States personnel and to "disperse the garrison." In nonmilitary language, this means that the Americans send in a helicopter to rescue all the United States troops, and leave the ARVN soldiers "holding the bag."

In *Good Morning, Vietnam,* while Cronauer plays Louis Armstrong's *It's a Wonderful World* over the radio, we see a contrasting montage of war images that includes a United States soldier accosting an unwilling Vietnamese girl, Vietnamese teenagers assassinated by vengeful American MPs, and the South Vietnamese police repressing a peaceful protest march with clubs.

An entire village—men, women, and children—is massacred by the VC in *The Siege of Firebase Gloria* (1988). Sgt. Maj. Hafner knows that this means an enemy buildup, and reports his assessment of the situation to headquarters in Saigon. They disagree: "Just another bunch of dead gooks—what else is new?" Later, when Hafner asks 1st. Sgt. Jones if his men are ready to fight, Jones replies, "I don't have anyone willing to trip over his guts for the Vietnamese way of life."

In *Gardens of Stone* (1987), Clell explains the folly of trying to end war in Southeast Asia. He laughs at the term "Peace-loving people of Vietnam. . . . That is the most bellicose race of people I've ever seen. They've been fighting for something like a thousand years, and they like it!"

### *The Language*

Among the symptoms of the Ugly American syndrome most easy to identify is the unwillingness of Americans to learn the language of the country they are visiting. Lederer and Burdick dramatized how the typical American overseas simply expects natives to learn to speak English. In one embassy, no American speaks the native tongue, making Americans entirely dependent on local translators. The same is often true in films. *In Go Tell the Spartans,* through "Cowboy," his native interpreter, young Lt. Hamilton tells his platoon of Vietnamese that they are going to Muc Hoa "to establish a fortress for liberty and justice." When Cowboy interprets Hamilton's speech to the men, they laugh uproariously. The lieutenant doesn't know why they laugh, and asks if he's said something funny. Cowboy simply lies and says, "No, the men are pleased." Sgt. Oleonowski explains: "Lieutenant, the dinks laugh all the time. Don't let it bother you.

In *Platoon,* during the previously mentioned vengeance raid on the Vietnamese village, the Americans seem oblivious to the fact that no one speaks English or understands the commands the soldiers bellow at them. When their orders are not obeyed, the Americans simply shout louder *in English,* as if the increased volume would make a frightened Vietnamese understand. In one instance, the men shout in English for villagers hiding in homemade air-raid bunkers to come out. Some do, but others are too terrified to move from their hiding places. They are killed when the Americans throw grenades into the holes.

Likewise, in *Bat-21,* downed flyer Hamilton chances upon a hut in the jungle. Entering, he examines the owner's belongings, and eats some rice he finds there. The owner of the house returns and discovers Hamilton there, and shouts threateningly in Vietnamese. Hamilton, still holding one of the man's few meager possessions in his hand, shouts "friend" over and over, and expects the man to understand that he's not a burglar. When the outraged homeowner attacks him with a knife, the American kills him. Then the man's family (including a boy whose face is scarred by napalm) arrives. All Hamilton can do is say, "I'm sorry, I'm sorry," which they also do not understand. Thus, another generation of revengeful VC is created.

In these films, Americans often make fun of the Vietnamese language. In "The Pass," an episode of HBO's award-winning mini-series, *Vietnam War Story* (1988), one soldier jokes that the Vietnamese method for selecting names for their children is to go out to the garbage and kick a can. The sound it makes, such as "bing, bang, clang," would be the child's name. The same GI also decides to name the three Vietnamese prostitutes serving them. He calls them "the *Lee* sisters: Ugly, Homely, and Scraggly." In *Good Morning, Vietnam,* Cronauer uses the Vietnamese language for off-color humor, such as describing the mythical city of "Con-dum." And in *Apocalypse Now,* Col. Kilgore sums up the American ethnocentric attitude regarding Vietnamese names. Not able to pronounce the name of a village, he quips, "Damn gook names all sound the same."

*If It's Different, It's Wrong*

Lederer and Burdick write that Americans are often disdainful of the cultural norms, values, and customs of Southeast Asians. In the *Vietnam War Story* episode, "An Old Ghost Walks the Earth," Matthews doesn't understand the Oriental need to save face. He clumsily prevents ARVN Sgt. Vinh and his soldiers from torturing a suspected VC, ignoring Vinh's subsequent loss of face in the eyes of his men. At the last minute, as the confrontation is about to escalate into gunfire, Matthews's buddy Bookman intercedes, striking a compromise that prevents Vinh from being embarrassed.

In many films, Americans make snide remarks about Vietnamese food and claiming that the VC smell of fish sauce. But in *The Iron Triangle,* we witness a VC political/social meeting around a campfire, in which the Vietnamese make fun of the Chinese, and joke about how bad the Americans smell.

In *Good Morning, Vietnam,* Cronauer does his best to bring American culture to his class of Vietnamese students who wish to learn English. He can never understand why, although they seem to like him, the Vietnamese consider him just "a crazy American." Cronauer also cannot understand why the Vietnamese girl he admires cannot be his friend—that she would be branded as a whore by her people for associating with an American, and both she and her family might be assassinated by the Viet Cong for collaboration with the enemy.

*Why Wouldn't They Want to Be Americans?*

Yanks in Vietnam often assume that the Vietnamese envy Americans, that they admire the United States and its culture, and should be grateful that we have come to rid them of the VC. In *The Iron Triangle,* Lt. Keene has become a prisoner of Ho, a VC soldier. Keene's hands are tied and Ho is leading him along a road. As they pass refugees, one of them stops, presenting Ho with a flower, and pats him on the back. The American can't understand why the VC merits this respect, so he finds within himself a relationship to help him rationalize the situation: "Flower power," he mutters, and shakes his head. The protesters at home, Keene's domestic enemy, are now lumped together with these "ungrateful" Vietnamese.

In *The Hanoi Hilton* (1987), navy flyer Williamson is being interviewed by American journalists about why he is at war. "The South Vietnamese," Williamson says, "want to establish a country with values similar to our own"—and he believes it. Later, Williamson is shot down, and these same people gladly turn him over to the North Vietnamese Army. But the most ridiculous of reasons for United States intervention in Vietnam comes from a marine colonel in *Full Metal Jacket,* who declares, "We are here to help the Vietnamese, because inside every gook, there is an American trying to get out."

### *America* Uber Alles

According to these movies, and with the possible exception of Hollywood's portrayal of Nazis in World War II propaganda films, there is no more arrogant, cocksure soldier than the American in Vietnam. Perhaps because the average 19-year-old American infantryman was raised on a diet of John Wayne war films and American military might, he arrives in Vietnam certain of eventual United States victory.

In *Born on the Fourth of July,* just before Kovic goes to Vietnam, he has a conversation in his living room with his parents. On the television, an arrogant army commander is being interviewed. Practically swaggering, he brags that one American air cavalry division is worth two or three divisions of NVA or VC: "No one can defeat us," he says. Later, when asked if the Americans can defeat the elusive VC, the commander states, "Anybody who lives in caves can be beaten." Kovic and his parents totally believe this myth.

In *A Rumor of War,* Caputo arrives in Vietnam. He narrates: "We didn't know what to expect: Rumors of screaming yellow hordes—but we were *Americans,* the first major force to land in Vietnam, and we were ready for anything." Capt. Keene has the same attitude in *The Iron Triangle.* Discussing the war with a French mercenary, both agree that the war isn't going well. But when the Frenchman says, "All is lost but the horror," the American retorts, "Nothing's *lost*, pal. We're talkin' stars and stripes." And in *Gardens of Stone,* young Cpl. Willow disagrees with Clell about the probable outcome of the war: "We beat King George, and we beat Hitler, and we beat everybody in-between. And we're not gonna go out and lose the first one to a bunch of gutty little Asian farmers." Similarly, in *The Hanoi Hilton,* Col. Cathcart insists that the United States will prevail over the Vietnamese for no other reason than that "we are Americans."

Probably the ultimate in arrogance and ignorance of history is to suggest that although other modern, well-trained, well-equipped armies were defeated in Vietnam, the United States would not be. But in *Go Tell the Spartans,* both Gen. Harnitz and Lt. Hamilton are cocksure America can't lose. The general is so ethnocentric that when Maj. Barker explains that his men are allowed to wear irregular uniforms to encourage esprit, Harnitz objects. He explains that he discourages the use of French words because "The French were *losers* here. That's not gonna happen to the U.S. Army." Later, frustrated with ARVN unwillingness to help the besieged garrison at Muc Hoa, the general yells, "The only way we're gonna win this war is to get United States combat troops in here." Sadly for a generation of Americans, Lyndon Johnson held the same belief.

Cpl. Courcey tells Lt. Hamilton that 300 French graves nearby attest to the futility of beating the VC. Hamilton responds, "Brave men, corporal. They fought the battle and lost—but we won't lose, 'cause we're Americans."

*John Wayne-ism*

As mentioned previously, in Vietnam War films, many young Americans appear convinced of the inevitability of United States victory because they were influenced by World War II films they viewed on television. Others, more experienced in the futility of the Vietnam war, speak of such films with sarcasm, as if betrayed by them. In *Full Metal Jacket,* from Joker's John Wayne imitation to frequent sarcastic references, the Duke's right-wing philosophy and macho ethic take quite a beating. For example, when filmed by newsmen, soldiers do a mock swagger, and make John Wayne jokes, comparing themselves to cavalry, and the VC to the Indians. This perhaps is Kubrick's veiled criticism of Wayne's own film, *The Green Berets* (1968), which treats the VC as though they were the savage redskins in one of John Ford's cavalry pictures. And in both *The Siege of Firebase Gloria* and *Platoon,* the term "John Wayne" is used as an adjective to describe stupid heroics guaranteed to get either one's self or a buddy killed.

*Clausewitz vs. Ho Chi Minh*

Americans of all ranks were unprepared for the kind of war waged by the VC and NVA. In *Go Tell the Spartans,* neither Cpl. Courcey nor Lt. Hamilton understand guerrilla warfare. Despite the fact that ARVN Sgt. Nguyen (Cowboy) explains that a refugee family they encounter is "a Cong family," Courcey befriends them, and gives them chocolate. He, like Hamilton, expects that they will find the VC with rifles, all carrying Mao's writings in their hip pockets. When Courcey brings the family back with him to the firebase for medical attention, Lt. Hamilton goes a step further. Although Cowboy insists that they are Cong, the lieutenant declares, "They don't look like communists to me." He reminds a protesting Sgt. Oleonowski that the United States is in Vietnam to "win the hearts and minds of the people." Hamilton takes them into their encampment and allows them to stay. Later, most of this family is killed trying to steal weapons for the VC, and the surviving daughter of the family leads the final, bloody attack on the garrison.

In *A Rumor of War,* the marines attack a VC location using the "classic hammer and anvil maneuver." However, the VC network of informants knows every move the Americans make when they leave their firebases. Instead of two groups converging to smash Charlie, the Americans' split forces come under heavy attack from the moment they touch down at their landing zones. When the surviving forces finally link up, Charlie is nowhere to be found. While the overconfident general who planned the operation announces to the press, "We have the enemy exactly where we want him," we cut to Caputo and his men pinned down by murderous artillery and small arms fire. Nearly the same thing occurs in *Platoon Leader* (1988). After Lt. Knight and his men kill a squad of VC in a firefight, command in Saigon announces that "the area is firmly in American hands." A short time later, the VC thwart an American sortie, double back on the Yanks, and destroy the village the Americans were assigned to defend.

In *The Siege of Firebase Gloria,* Hafner is furious after his repeated warnings about the upcoming Tet offensive are ignored by both the drugged-out officer in charge of the base and by headquarters. The officer is not worried about an attack during Tet, because "Every gook'll be on his way to his father's house for fuckin' fish heads and rice." Hafner sarcastically says, "H.Q. still didn't buy my analysis of the situation. Hell, they had *experts* sitting in air conditioned offices in Saigon who understood the war a whole lot better than *anyone* on the front line."

Similarly, both the *Vietnam War Story* episode "Separated" and *Full Metal Jacket* feature people whose racism doesn't permit them to take a Tet offensive seriously. In the former, Malone thinks that because Americans take time off to celebrate their holidays, the enemy will act the same way. In the latter, the public relations lieutenant dismisses the idea of a Tet offensive, saying, "The Tet holiday's like the Fourth of July, Christmas, and New Year all rolled up into one. Every zipperhead in 'Nam, North and South, will be bangin' gongs, barkin' at the moon, and visitin' his dead relatives."

### *Deceiving Ourselves*

Having been an Air Force public information (read propaganda) officer during the Vietnam War, I can attest to the fact that in attempting to convince the American people the war was being won, American military authorities in Vietnam eventually began to believe their own publicity. In *Full Metal Jacket,* the *Stars and Stripes* editor, a lieutenant, presides over a story session with his troops. He reminds them that they only write two kinds of stories, those in which Americans are winning the hearts and minds of the Vietnamese and those in which Americans are successful militarily. If any story didn't have enough of one of these elements, it was "juiced up" with fiction.

In *Go Tell the Spartans,* Gen. Harnitz begins to believe his own bluster about American superiority. He wants Muc Hoa defended simply because the VC attacked the outpost. Harnitz reasons that it must have some strategic value to the VC, or they wouldn't have attacked. "They don't want us in Muc Hoa," the general announces. But Maj. Barker clarifies, "They don't want us *anywhere,* sir."

In *Apocalypse Now,* the crew of the river patrol boat has just accidentally slaughtered a sampan full of innocent people. Aware that these incidents happened nearly daily in Vietnam, Capt. Willard narrates: "It was the way we had over here of living with ourselves: We'd cut 'em in half with a machine-gun and give 'em a band-aid. It was a lie. And the more I saw of them, the more I hated lies."

Lederer and Burdick write about several efforts to help Southeast Asian people with practical ideas, but higher authorities ignore these suggestions. Practical proposals for irrigation projects, assistance with poultry problems, and so forth, are not approved. Instead, American authorities convince themselves that huge but impractical projects will be most appreciated. They reason that building a highway or providing weapons to fight communist insurgents look good to the American public. Thus, these were the best ways to spend our foreign aid money. In *Vietnam War Story* episode "An Old Ghost Walks the Earth," a pacification company occupies a village "to protect people from the VC." Of course, the people don't want protection, and they fear the United States' presence. They know that when the Americans leave, the VC will savagely retaliate against anyone who was friendly to the Yanks. But an inexperienced soldier tries to find a real, practical way to help the people. A farmer himself, he suggests to his captain that they help the villagers with an irrigation problem. Later he is told that such things are not part of their mission: They protect the village, "but if we can't make it friendly, we waste it. . . . If we get sniper fire, a few ambushes, we have to figure it's a VC village, and we burn it down." Likewise, in *Platoon Leader*, Sgt. MacNamara explains what pacification means to him: "My job is getting people to change their minds [from the VC point of view to ours]. We're in the idea business. We sell ideas, and if you can't get a sale, if you can't place the right idea in their head, [he holds up a bullet], you place one of these in their body."

In *A Rumor of War*, Lt. Murphy, who has gone to great lengths to learn the Vietnamese language and culture, provides us with the perspective that his superiors largely ignore in their efforts to subdue the enemy: "Jungle warfare: You gotta play by the rules." "What are the rules," Caputo asks. "To learn his—forget ours—that the night can hide—that the ground is home. This is his land: He's been fighting for a hundred years. Only a fool hates his enemy."

*Concluding Thoughts*

Many armies have temporarily occupied Vietnam in the last thousand years. Eventually, the Vietnamese people always seemed to prevail. Stubborn nationalists, they were convinced that sooner or later they could also defeat their most recent invader. But, as Lederer and Burdick insist, Americans were equally convinced in our invincibility—in some cases, practically up until the day we evacuated the American Embassy in Saigon. And we're not much wiser today. Impressed with the myth of racial superiority and military omnipotence, Americans never seriously considered the possibility of our defeat in Southeast Asia. And overmatched victories such as America's recent foray into the Middle East do little to dispel this myth, and go a long way toward erasing memories of Vietnam, especially among our youth.

Americans expected to find an enthusiastic population of "little Asian friends" in Vietnam, ready to rally behind the representatives of the "Great White Father" to gloriously defeat our enemy, whom we also perceived was theirs. As both history and the films that have attempted to mirror this history demonstrate, these attitudes were major contributors to our undoing.

Unfortunately, officials responsible for American adventurism in Central America, the Middle East and Africa in recent years maintain that Vietnam was a fluke of circumstances, a situation unlikely to occur in future campaigns of a similar nature. Tell this to the families of American soldiers and airmen who died trying to Americanize Somalia. It appears that unless our country awakens to the dangers of the Ugly American syndrome, the same or a similar scenario may soon be played out again on some other continent. At this writing, Bosnia awaits.

To the Ugly American mentality, there is no difference between the media stereotypes of the indolent South American taking a siesta under his sombrero, the ignorant Arab on his camel, the poor, underfed African squatting in the sun, and the smiling little Asian bent over his crop in a rice paddy: All purportedly dream of the day when Uncle Sam will come to rescue them from their plight, bringing along the benefits of democracy, the Big Mac, Levi's jeans and VCRs.

At the risk of once again repeating George Santayana's old truism, those who ignore history are destined to relive it.

## Bibliography


Adair, Gilbert. *Vietnam on Film.* New York: Scribner, 1981.

Basinger, Jeanine. *The World War II Combat Film: Anatomy of a Genre.* New York: Columbia UP, 1986.

Clausewitz, Carl. *On War.* Princeton, NJ: Princeton UP, 1976.

Dick, Bernard F. *The Star-Spangled Screen.* Lexington, KY: UP of Kentucky, 1985.

Donald, Ralph R. "Conversion As Persuasive Convention in American War Films." *Beyond The Stars 2: Plot Conventions in American Popular Film.* Ed. Paul Loukides and Linda K. Fuller. Bowling Green, OH: Bowling Green State University Popular Press, 1991.

Furhammar, Leif, and Folke Isaksson. *Politics and Film.* New York: Praeger, 1968.

Hellman, John. *American Myth and The Legacy of Vietnam.* New York: Columbia UP, 1986.

Jacobs, Lewis. "World War II and the American Film." *The Movies, an American Idiom.* Rutherford: Fairleigh Dickinson UP, 1971.

Koppes, Clayton R., and Gregory D. Black. *Hollywood Goes to War.* New York: Free Press, 1987.

Lederer, William J., and Eugene Burdick. *The Ugly American.* New York: Norton, 1958.

Maynard, Richard A. *Propaganda on Film: A Nation at War.* Rochelle Park, NJ: Hayden, 1975.

McClure, Arthur F., ed. *The Movies, an American Idiom.* Rutherford: Fairleigh Dickinson UP, 1971.

Wilson, James C. *Vietnam in Prose and Film.* Jefferson, NC, and London: McFarland, 1982.


## Filmography

| Film | Year | Director |
|---|---|---|
| *Apocalypse Now* | 1979 | Francis Coppola |
| *Bat-21* | 1988 | Peter Markle |
| *Born on the Fourth of July* | 1989 | Oliver Stone |
| *Casualties of War* | 1989 | Brian De Palma |
| *84 Charlie Mopic* | 1989 | Patrick Duncan |
| *Full Metal Jacket* | 1987 | Stanley Kubrick |
| *Gardens of Stone* | 1987 | Francis Coppola |
| *Good Morning, Vietnam* | 1987 | Barry Levinson |

| | | |
|---|---|---|
| *Go Tell the Spartans* | 1978 | Ted Post |
| *The Green Berets* | 1968 | John Wayne |
| *Hamburger Hill* | 1987 | John Irvin |
| *The Hanoi Hilton* | 1987 | Lione Chetwynd |
| *Hearts And Minds* | 1974 | Peter Davis |
| *The Iron Triangle* | 1989 | Eric Weston |
| *Platoon* | 1986 | Oliver Stone |
| *Platoon Leader* | 1988 | Aaron Norris |
| *A Rumor of War* (TV miniseries) | 1980 | Richard T. Heffron |
| *The Siege of Firebase Gloria* | 1988 | Brian Trenchard |
| *The Ugly American* | 1963 | George H.England |
| *Vietnam War Story Episodes* | 1988 | Patrick Duncan, supervising producer |
| | | directors: |
| "An Old Ghost Walks the Earth" | | Michael Toshiyuki Uno |
| "The Pass" | | Kevin Hooks |
| "Separated" | | Todd Holland |

# Pacifism in Film:
# Exclusion and Containment as Hegemonic Processes

**Rick Clifton Moore**

Todd Gitlin once began an essay on television by stating that "every society works to reproduce itself" ("Prime" 426). The simplicity of his statement he freely admitted, calling it a tautology. To move to deeper levels of understanding, we must determine *how* societies reproduce themselves, which was Gitlin's point. He and a large number of other mass communication scholars have in recent years attempted to demonstrate that it is largely through ideology that societal reproduction takes place.

In this chapter, I suggest that an area of investigation that would deepen our understanding of societal reproduction is the portrayal of pacifism in cinema. More specifically, studying Hollywood cinema (a powerful mass medium) and pacifism (a specific ideological orientation) can help us better understand the way ideas are expressed, maintained, or dismissed by a society. Pacifism, as I use term here, is a worldview that sees violence as unacceptable, even when such violence is a means of defense. A study of pacifism in cinema thus allows us to look at media coverage of an unpopular ideology.

I will first examine the broader context in which film portrayal of pacifism is found, including films that vary in popularity and critical acclaim. One goal in discussing these varied films is to make a distinction between films that deal specifically with pacifism and those that do not. This affords some sense of the scope of the presentation of pacifism as an ideological orientation. An understanding of the presence or absence of pacifism as a subject in American film will tell us much about the acceptability of this ideological orientation. More important, films that explicitly deal with the subject permit analysis of common plot structures in those motion pictures.

With an analysis of context and content I will suggest that the relationship between the dominant American ideology and pacifism seems to be played out in two ways—through exclusion, that is, the scarcity of presentation of pacifism as a film subject, and through containment, the presentation of predictable formulas that frame arguments and lead to acceptable conclusions. Even so, the analysis that follows might suggest that neither of these two ideological constraints is completely predictable and that images of pacifism, though neither widespread nor positively presented, are available to viewers. Occasionally, positive images of pacifism are presented in the American media, images that strongly conflict with the dominant ideology.

*Cinema Violence as Context*

Critics have often noted that Hollywood cinema tends to wallow in violence. A watchdog group that monitored over one thousand films in 1987 found the majority of films contained violent images; in their summary, they stated that fifty-two percent of the motion pictures were either "extremely violent" or "predominantly violent" ("Films" 51). Numerous explanations are offered for this phenomenon. Producers of motion pictures argue that violence is what audiences want to see. Critics suggest that violence is deeply rooted in American culture as it was a necessary component of colonization and westward expansion (Prince; Gitlin, "Social").

Regardless of the origins of this violence, one of the strongest arguments that critics offer against it is that it is all too often seen as a means of solving problems. Characters (good and bad) face difficult situations and find their way out of those situations with the aid of guns and other weapons. One alternative to such representations would be characters who are confirmed pacifists. Yet such characters are uncommon. The nature of characters who *are* common in Hollywood film is the subject of the next section. (Given the overrepresentation of men in certain genres of film, the following discussion will predominately deal with male characters. An area for future investigation would be a specific analysis of women in such motion pictures.)

*Peace without Pacifism*

The observation that violence is ubiquitous in American cinema does not suggest the medium is completely devoid of the concept of peace. Though visions of violence assault us nearly every time we go to the theater, visions of peace are not completely wanting. After all, many definitions of peace suggest it is the absence of (or freedom from) war or violence.

There is a degree of logic, then, to the fact that the protagonists in most American motion pictures present a certain level of pacifism. At least, they believe in the concept of peace and hold it in high regard. Such characters are not pacifists as the term has been used here. They do, however, offer variations of pacifism if one wishes to see pacifism as existing on a continuum with legitimated violence.

For example, most action movies provide protagonists who hold firmly to the hope of peace. One can look at some of the most violent films (or even groups of films in sequel form) to see that this is the case. Clint Eastwood's Harry Callahan character demonstrates this. If antagonists would only cease their criminal activities, we presume that Dirty Harry would be able to sit peacefully and enjoy his hot dogs (which in one film he quickly gulps just before he has to shoot a malefactor). His aversion to the violence perpetrated by the antagonists leads him to his own violent actions. Note that the violence of antagonists does not fundamentally change the nature of the hero. Such violence simply presents the protagonist with what social critic Jacques Ellul calls the "necessity" of violence (85).

More recent films demonstrate that this necessity is still recognized. The popular action picture *Passenger 57* is a good example. Though John Cutter is an expert in security, he is in the bathroom of an airliner when a terrorist decides to commandeer the plane. With the exception of his combat skills, Cutter appears no different from any other passenger on the flight. He would probably rather attend to other business if the terrorist would only let him. Like Callahan, Cutter represents a hero who is led to violence by the acts of others. The extremely violent *Patriot Games* is a box office hit that offers another glimpse at this phenomenon. The film starts with peaceful scenes of Jack Ryan and his family. Only when Ryan coincidentally ends up in the middle of an assassination plot by an Irish terrorist organization does he show his violent side. The same character (created in Tom Clancy's novels) shows up again in *Clear and Present Danger*. Though not as graphic as *Patriot Games, Clear and Present Danger* reveals a similar protagonist. In the earlier film, Ryan was thrust into the violent confrontation early in the plot. In the latter, Ryan is distanced from much of the violence and ignorant of its causes. As it turns out, a Latin American drug cartel and clandestine CIA operatives (taking orders from the White House) are having a vengeful dispute and engaging in retaliatory strikes. Once Ryan knows the whole story, he takes an active part in settling things. The most interesting element of this film is that the resolution in Latin America is violent yet the resolution in the United States is not. In the first instance, he requires a helicopter and the protection of automatic weapons to succeed, in the second, he takes his case to a Senate Committee. *Clear and Present Danger* seems to intimate that in some contexts violence is less a necessity than in others. Given a context that does not necessitate violence, Ryan will abstain.

From a structural functionalist perspective this makes perfect sense. After all, societies cannot afford to glorify violence for violence's sake.

Rather, violence needs to be presented within the context of societal stability. This necessarily entails a concept of peace. Cinema protagonists do not randomly attack innocent victims, and we suspect that average film viewers will not do so as they leave the theater. As one summary of research on mass media violence stated, the media tend to "cultivate lessons about domination and submission" (Signorielli and Gerbner *xx*) more than they immediately incite violence.

Hence, what we find is a collection of cultural products that promote a form of peace, even though they might teem with violence. Characters in such films are not portrayed as pacifists by the definition presented above. They do in some ways strive for peace, though. We find in Hollywood cinema a wide variety of characters who could be categorized in such a way to demonstrate what distinguishes them from pacifist characters. In the next section I present some of those characters and the films in which they are presented.

### *Degrees of "Peacefulness" in Cinema Protagonists*

Innumerable characters in Hollywood motion pictures fall into the category mentioned above. They are "peaceful" protagonists who are required to fight for a cause. Some are law officers (e.g., Dirty Harry, Popeye Doyle, or the cop partners in the *Lethal Weapon* series). Some are common citizens (e.g., Charles Bronson's Paul Kersey in the *Death Wish* films). Bruce Willis successfully bridged this gap with the hero he played in *Die Hard* and its sequels. Though a police officer by trade, he is off duty when he finds himself the only one who can put an end to a terrorist conspiracy in the first film of the series.

Note that there are no indications that these heroes are bloodthirsty or enjoy violence for its own sake. They are always motivated by the actions of others. Granted, Bronson's Kersey character pushes our credulity in that he repeatedly finds himself victimized by social deviants. Moreover, one might argue that his quest for peace tends toward vengefulness. Even so, we presume he has not killed anybody during the fictional period that passes between each of the *Death Wish* films. These films and the others listed give indications that the chief characters will use violence only when it is necessary to keep the peace.

Occasionally, there are images of such peacemakers who come much closer to being true pacifists. James Stewart's Destry in *Destry Rides Again* represents such a character, as does John Wayne's Marlowe in *The Horse Soldiers*. In these two films (the first comedic, the second dramatic), the protagonist refuses to wear a gun. However, both characters seem content with their occupation and we assume that in a real world they would eventually find themselves in tight spots. Destry is a deputy, Marlowe an infantryman, yet little soul-searching takes place.

Another group of protagonists commonly found in American film consists of people who have legitimated violence in their past, but hope to escape it in the present. For example, John Wayne's final film, *The Shootist*, is about an aging gunfighter who wants to die in peace. Glenn Ford personified similar characters in two films. In *Fastest Gun Alive*, he played a gunfighter who is tired of killing and tries to retire as a shopkeeper. In *Heaven with a Gun*, he played an ex-gunfighter who decides to settle down and pastor a church in a small western town. A similar plot is presented in *The Peacemaker*, in which James Mitchell tries to clean up a town as a clergyman, not as the gunfighter he was earlier in his life. Obviously this desire to be able to escape the gunfighter persona is a major point of tension in the George Stevens classic *Shane* also.

Yet not all gunslinger protagonists in American cinema are at this stage of their careers. Even working gunslingers can fit the respectable-but-violent category listed above. Such gunslingers are American icons. They rarely draw first and usually act as guardians of the common citizen. Gunslinger antagonists, on the other hand, operate as desperadoes and minions of cattle barons. The retired gunslingers listed earlier are of the iconic variety. They were "good gunslingers," but now want to relax and avoid the stress of their profession. While not necessarily portrayed as pacifists (they have not denied the need to defend themselves, they have only abandoned the role of "gunfighter"), neither do they fit the mold cut by the standard hero of American film. Much like Greta Garbo, they just want to be left alone.

It is not uncommon for such isolationism to make its way into American motion pictures. Rick, the enigmatic character from *Casablanca* epitomizes this role. Jaded toward life by the rejection of a lover, he sticks his neck out for nobody, even innocent victims of the execrable Nazis. Such sentiments are not rooted in pacifism. But in American cinema isolationism can be blended with, or confused with, pacifism. Raoul Walsh's *Gun Fury* seems to manifest such confusion. His protagonist (played by Rock Hudson) appears at one moment to be a pacifist who feels the Civil War (from which he has just come home) could have been prevented if only negotiation and compromise had been used. His judgment of that conflict has no impact on his own life, however. He wants no more than to take his new bride to a ranch he has just bought. He feels that once he owns property with clear boundaries what happens across the river is none of his business. Of course, this is shown to be unrealistic. His bride is abducted by villains and he sets out to save her. What little pacifism the character embodied quickly disappears; he tries (twice within one minute of film time) to grab a gun to save his wife, showing no hesitation in this action. Eventually he does confront his isolationism, though. When he encounters difficulty raising a posse to help him chase down the bad guys, he concludes that what happens across the river should be everyone's business.

There are other characters on the screen who demonstrate a less-selfish perspective. One group of film protagonists who offer an appearance of pacifism are those who see beyond themselves and develop empathy for traditional enemies. These characters are not usually found in police or gunslinger dramas, but are occasionally presented in westerns that deal with land disputes with American Indians. James Stewart exemplified this role as Tom Jeffers in the 1950 motion picture *Broken Arrow*. After rescuing a wounded Apache boy, Jeffers decides the Native Americans are much more human than he ever imagined them to be. He even mentions that it never struck him that "an Apache woman would cry over her son like any other woman." Jeffers empathy is strong and he spends much of the rest of the film trying to strike a treaty between the Apaches and the government. Such treaty-making is occasionally presented as an admirable quality in film. It shows up again, for example, in *Battle of Rogue River*.

To a degree, empathy is (if not for any of the characters, at least for the viewer) the dominant emotion in *All Quiet on the Western Front*. Visions of the humanity shared between the two opposing groups of soldiers lead us to believe that the ensuing battle is unbearable. Yet this powerful motion picture relies just as much on a sense of futility to get its message across as it does on empathy. Futility plays strongly in a number of other films, for example in Stanley Kubrick's *Paths of Glory*. *Catch 22* and *Dr. Strangelove* offer some similar themes but in more comic form. Other motion pictures show futility or folly in regard to the weapons needed to fight a war, especially a modern war. This is certainly a part of *Dr. Strangelove*. Futility and folly can also be found in less critically acclaimed films such as *Deal of the Century* (which takes a comic look at arms dealers) and *War Games* (a teenager's view of the folly of computer-assisted nuclear warfare) as well.

But we are no longer analyzing characters who represent pacifism. Instead, we have veered into a discussion of film themes that promote peace. These films suggest some of the ways in which the concept of peace is woven into character and story in Hollywood cinema. What we have seen is that a wide range of characters and plot structures in some way promote peace without necessarily portraying true pacifism in any explicit form. Having examined the broad context into which any film that does offer an explicit rendition of pacifism must fit, we can look at cinematic images that clearly portray that ideology.

*Explicit Pacifism in Film*

A survey of reference books on film suggests that true pacifism is not a popular subject in the motion picture industry in the United States. There are a few notable exceptions. These exceptions cover a wide subject matter and an equally wide chronology. Among the films that include pacifist characters are *Angel and the Badman, Friendly Persuasion, Sergeant York, High Noon, Thunder in the East, Gandhi*, and *Witness.*

Some of these films deal with the subject of pacifism very briefly. *Gandhi*, for example, is such an epic endeavor that the leader's pacifism must be a relatively small part of the film. *High Noon* is a much different motion picture and a much different situation. More traditional in its Hollywood formula, the film follows a very narrative plot line. Part of that plot line is Amy Kane's (played by Grace Kelly) pacifism. In many ways, however, this element serves as window dressing to the major conflict between Will Kane (Gary Cooper) and the villains. Amy is just one of the many characters who appear ready to desert Will (for diverse reasons) before the bullets fly. After her Quaker religious convictions are revealed, little attention is given to them until the end of the film when we see her deny them.

Two of the films listed above are similar to *High Noon* in their traditional narrative plot structure but are not as widely known. *Angel and the Badman* and *Thunder in the East* both have characters who make clear declaration of their pacifist values. The films' endings are very different, however. In *Thunder in the East*, Charles Boyer's character turns his back on his beliefs after seeing a child victimized. As in *High Noon*, pacifist views seem to be easily abandoned. *Angel and the Badman* also shares similarities with *High Noon.* In both motion pictures it is a female character who is the pacifist; the male protagonist (clearly not a declared pacifist in either film) must listen to the pleadings of the female. In *Angel and the Badman*, John Wayne plays Quirt Evans, a wounded outlaw who receives aid from a Quaker family. Enamored of the daughter in the family, Evans considers settling down. Yet there are few indications that the bad man is considering becoming a pacifist. The director avoids tough questions when at the end of the film he has the marshall shoot two men who draw on Evans (who has set down his gun). The fuzziness of the ending in the film makes the viewer wonder just what the director might be saying. Like many of the films described thus far, *Angel and the Badman* does not seem to want to deal too deeply with the difficult ethical questions raised by a pacifist worldview.

Three films, *Sergeant York, Friendly Persuasion*, and *Witness* seem less timid. Each uses pacifism as a major element of the story and carries it through to the end. Moreover, these three films have a unifying theme (in addition to their shared subject of pacifism) which binds them together. In each of these motion pictures, key characters must deal not only with the issue of pacifism, but also with spiritual conversion. The tension of this spiritual conversion is a key element that drives the plots of these films. In addition, it is spiritual conversion that often affords the motivations of chief protagonists and affects the results of their actions. At this level the dramatic containment mentioned earlier takes place. The preceding paragraphs suggest that pacifism does not often receive thorough treatment in Hollywood cinema. In the following pages I will examine the type of treatment pacifism appears to receive once it becomes legitimate subject matter.

### Sergeant York: *Local Boy Makes Good*

The earliest of the three films is a fine example of the conversion theme. In fact, the protagonist of the drama, Alvin York, must face several conversion decisions in his life. The story in the film, though based on an actual historical figure, has clearly been structured and presented in thematic form. In the opening scenes of the film, we see York as a rowdy Tennessee farmer, shooting up the community, getting in fights, and drinking (much to the chagrin of his mother and family). When the mother sends the local pastor to speak to her son, Alvin explains that he knows his life is on a wrong track, but he is not a religious man. In Alvin's view, if religion is right for him, it will come and get him. Sure enough, religion does come and get him. While riding home from a night of drinking and fighting, a bolt of lightning knocks him off his horse. Alvin gets up off the ground and wanders toward sounds emanating from the local chapel where a night service is being conducted. When he enters the door of the building, he notes the presence of his mother and the pastor. The latter motions for him to come forward. To a chorus of "Give me that old time religion," York cautiously approaches the altar and soon finds himself encircled by a welcoming throng of Christians.

As the story is presented, Alvin suddenly lives a changed life. No longer the town bad boy, he even rectifies past misdeeds by doing favors for members of his community. He becomes a model citizen. In fact, it is his model citizenship that leads to problems. The major conflict of the film soon arises when the United States gets involved in Word War I. York, having determined from Bible study that killing is sin, sees himself a conscientious objector (although he does not use the term).

The pastor recognizes that trouble lies ahead for Alvin if he does not register for the draft, and he tries to persuade Alvin to formally apply for conscientious-objector status.

*Pastor:* Ya gotta register, Alvin.

*York:* I ain't gonna. I ain't gonta war. War is killin'. And the Book's agin' killin'. So war is agin' the Book.

*Pastor:* You're plum right, Alvin. You got the using kind of religion, not the meetin' house kind.

*York:* I got the kind you teached me.

*Pastor:* I know that. I hate to be tellin' you, but I don't want to see you get in no trouble. Now you got to register and there ain't no way you can get out of it.

*York:* You mean, they can make you go to war even if you think it is agin' what you think is right.

*Pastor:* No, No, No. They won't make you do that. That's what I want to tell you. Come here. [The pastor points to the draft notice on the wall]. Members of well recognized religious sects whose existing creed forbids their members to participate in war are entitled to request exemption from military service. (Finkel, Chandlee, Koch, and Huston)

Following that advice, Alvin decides to appeal his draft. The appeal, however, is denied and he is shipped off to training. Ironically, through his excellent marksmanship he wins another opportunity to maintain his pacifist stance. After York is pulled from the ranks to be commended for his skills, he is allowed to make another appeal. Upon hearing York's story, the commanding officer claims to have struggled with the same issues York has, and asks the recruit to take a little time off and consider how important national defense really is. York accepts the offer and returns to the backwoods to think things through. While sitting alone on a mountain, he begins to work through the different views he has heard. Audio flashbacks reveal the echoing voices doing battle in his mind, especially the voice of his friend the pastor and the voice of the commanding officer who has given him a different point of view. As the battling voices clash, a wind blows up the mountain and flips through the pages in York's Bible. Alvin picks up the scriptures and reads, "Render unto Caesar those things that are Caesar's."

With this image, the primary conflict of the scene is released. The ensuing resolution on the battlefield is a logical (or perhaps ideological) sequitur of the earlier events and in some ways (being physical rather than spiritual) unnecessary to the story. York's exploits in war—though they lend support to the views of the film—are not crucial. The main battle has already been fought. It was a battle between religious conviction and civic duty.

Friendly Persuasion: *War on the Home Front*

In *Sergeant York*, Alvin York's religious affiliation is not disclosed; he simply attends a Christian church with the Bible as its only creed. In *Friendly Persuasion*, however, the family of characters to whom we are introduced is clearly Quaker. Jess Birdwell and his family live in rural Indiana in the 1860s. His wife, Eliza, and three children live a quiet life on a farm, unprepared for the ravages of warfare soon to disrupt their home.

This idea is reinforced in a scene at a peaceful Quaker worship service (the members sit quietly, waiting for revelation) where the war takes a visible step forward. A Union officer walks into the meeting house and addresses the congregation. Much like York's commanding officer in the earlier film, this man has the task of persuading spiritual people (and the viewing audience) to engage in carnal warfare.

*Officer:* I have had the duty placed upon me of speaking to you Quakers about the war.

*Eliza:* It is a matter much on our minds and in our prayers.

*Officer:* But your men don't fight in it.

*Eliza:* Some of them have.

*Officer:* But you don't encourage them.

*Eliza:* We do not encourage them.

*Officer:* Ma'am, the union has endured two years of bloody civil war. Thousands have given their lives in battle to free our country from slavery.

*Eliza:* We are opposed to slavery. But we do not believe it right to kill one man to free another.

*Officer:* Ma'am, its not going to be a question of fighting for freedom or principle, but of protecting our own towns, our own homes from attack. . . . Would you men stand by while others die to protect you? [looks at Caleb, a burly young man]. You look like a boy who could give account of himself.

*Caleb:* Oh, I've been tempted to fight. Guess the good Lord knows why. I mean, sometimes I get the sinful wish to get in a good scrap. So I got to watch myself closer than most people. So I'll just stay away from the war. Cause if I ever got in it, I'd be a goner.

*Officer:* [to Josh Birdwell, Eliza's son] And you, son, are you ready to put up with looting and killing without lifting a finger? Are you afraid to fight?

*Josh:* I don't know.

*Officer:* Now, here at last is an honest answer. . . . I don't wish to offend, but how many of you are hiding behind your church to save your skins? Do you think it's right to let the others do the fighting for you, to protect your lives and property? Well! Why don't you speak up? (Wilson)

One member of the congregation, Purdy, speaks up quite loudly, not only declaring his dedication to pacifism, but also questioning Josh Birdwell's spiritual fervor. Jess defends his son, explaining that he too sometimes wonders how well he would hold up to the tests of war, especially if the war threatened his family. Purdy then expresses doubts about Mr. Birdwell's convictions.

The officer leaves the congregation, taking no eager volunteers with him. He has, however, planted seeds in the minds of characters. We sense that all of the characters face an internal conflict when thinking of the possible need to defend their homes.

In typical Hollywood form, that internal conflict is exacerbated when the war finally reaches their community. When Confederate troops begin attacking local farms, the Birdwells have tough decisions to make. Josh, the oldest son, is especially burdened by the conflict in his heart, as is revealed in dialogue with his parents, Jess and Eliza.

*Jess:* If thee has a sword in thy heart, son, thee must pull it out and use it. But there's no sword in my heart. No man is my enemy.

*Josh:* Well, any man who kills innocent people is my enemy, my mortal enemy.

*Eliza:* Josh. Thee has seen bad things today. Thee is upset. We've got more than we need here. It's high time we shared it.

*Josh:* If thee gives all thee has to thy enemy, thy friends will go hungry. What's good about that?

*Jess:* Josh. If thee wants to go out and fight, give thy life for what thee believes. Any of us here, I'm sure, is ready to do that. But that is not what thee will be asked to do. No Josh. What thee will be asked to do now is to kill.

*Josh:* I know that. I'll kill if I have to.

*Eliza:* [sternly] Thou shalt not kill!

*Jess:* Mother, I hate fighting. I don't want to die. I don't know if I could kill anyone if I tried. But I have to try so long as other people have to. (Wilson)

The next morning, Josh wakes up assured that he wants to go help defend against the Confederates. Even at this point, we are not sure how strong Josh's convictions toward actual fighting are. When we see him crouched in the battlefield with his comrades, we wonder whether he will ever pull the trigger. Our questions are soon answered, however, when rebel forces attack, killing a neighboring soldier. After weeping for a moment, the young Quaker picks up a rifle and begins shooting in succession at his enemy. The resolution of the drama quickly unfolds from this point.

### Witness: *Peace as a Means of Justice*

The third film tells the story of John Book, a tough Philadelphia cop who is sent to cover a murder in a train station. The only witness to the murder is a young Amish boy, Samuel. With the help of Samuel, Book discovers that the murderer was a police officer. Unfortunately, Book reveals his knowledge to a superior who turns out to be part of a ring of corruption. A crooked cop then shoots Book, requiring him to flee with the boy and his mother to the Amish community where they live with the boy's grandfather.

Once in this bucolic setting, the conflict moves in two directions. The violence-prone police officer struggles to coexist with the pacifist Amish, and the Amish try to survive the influences of the Philadelphia cop. Rachel, Samuel's mother, makes several references to Book's propensity for "whacking people." And in a crucial scene the boy's grandfather, Eli, speaks to the youngster about the policeman's firearm.

*Eli:* This gun of the hand is for the taking of human life. We believe that it is wrong to take a life. That is only for God. Many times wars have come and people have said to us, you must fight, you must kill, it is the only way to preserve the good. But Samuel, there is never only one way. Remember that. (Wallace and Kelley)

Samuel is placed in a similar position to that of Josh Birdwell, who had heard much preaching on pacifism and is now presented with a radically different view. Although the young Amish boy is not the protagonist in the film, he is noticeably perplexed by his respect for his tradition and his admiration for John Book.

This complex scenario suggests that in this film there is the possibility of conversion in several directions. The boy is obviously questioning traditional Amish values in the face of the influence of John Book. His mother is falling in love with the visiting police officer. She is even warned by Eli that she will be shunned by the community if she is not careful in her relationship with the stranger. Yet, clearly, Book is the protagonist of the film, and in this film the most important question of conversion is whether he can stop "whacking people" and become like the Amish. Though this possibility seems doubtful, toward the end of the film his attraction toward Amish life (sentimental as the film's portrayal of it might be) is growing. Most notable is the scene where Book assists in a community barn raising. Dressed in Amish clothing, he seems to fit right in with the group and works well as a part of their team. Moreover, when the task is completed, Book watches in admiration as the traditionalists pack up their things and join in song, celebrating a day of working together. The look on the Philadelphian's face suggests that his growing appreciation for the benefits of Amish life and his growing love for Rachel might just make him give up his life of violence and go native.

At this point we should note that in the earlier two films, the peaceful protagonists were threatened with the possibility of war and needed to decide how they would react to it. In *Witness*, the protagonist is threatened with the possibility of peace. The question is, can he accept it?

Just as the two earlier films had their crucial turning points where the heroes faced difficult decisions, *Witness* does also. In a trip to town, Book makes a phone call and learns that the corrupt cops have killed his partner. To make matters worse, on his way home he and his friends are harassed by a gang of young town thugs. Book soon loses his patience and returns to his true character, beating up the young men and leaving them strewn on the street. This incident in itself brings about his demise. The rural authorities tell the Philadelphia police about the ruckus. The next morning, the corrupt police officers show up on the farm to kill Book, Samuel, and anyone else who may stand as a witness.

### *Resolution as Ideological Determinant*

Each of these three films involves a rather traditional Hollywood formula: once it is revealed that the protagonist has certain psychological or sociological characteristics, he/she is thrust into in an environment where those characteristics are tested. Eventually, the character must either change him/herself, change the environment, or face the consequences.

In *Sergeant York* resolution clearly comes about by a change in the protagonist. Following his experience on the mountain, Alvin is sent to the front. He is thoroughly convinced that he will give his life for his country, yet uncertain whether he can kill for it. Once in combat, he chooses to fight, captures 132 German soldiers, and becomes a national hero. He explains that the German guns were killing thousands. In the heat of the battle, all he could think of doing was stopping the German guns.

In *Friendly Persuasion*, three key characters are presented with the options of changing their Quaker nature or changing some element of their environment. Josh Birdwell (the son) could be said to experience the greatest change. He fights, and in doing so is wounded in battle. When the younger Birdwell's horse returns home without a rider, Jess picks up his own gun and goes to save his son. This is, of course, a great change for the Quaker patriarch. While on his mission, Jess is shot and wounded (but only slightly) by a lone rebel soldier. After a moment of physical struggle, Jess takes control of the soldier's firearm. The young assailant, thinking himself condemned, begins to shake, and Jess becomes aware of his actions. Never before could we (or Jess himself) have imagined the peaceful father holding another man at bay by the threat of death. Catching himself, Jess tells the young man to move on, and allows him to escape. Back home, even Eliza—probably the most vehement defender of pacifism in the family—is faced with the consequences of holding to the courage of her convictions. When the men are away, rebel soldiers come to the house. For the most part, she assuages the travelers with food (an obvious reference to her earlier advice to Josh that they have more than they need), but she is greatly angered when one of them attempts to grab her pet goose. Losing her temper, she takes a broom and beats the young man with it. Even if this scene is played in a humorous manner, it reveals a change on the part of the character. Like her husband and son, she is not able to hold to her convictions given the new environment.

Finally, in *Witness* we see a film where the protagonist is not able to change and is not able to change his environment (or, in this case, his environments). John Book is not able to convert to being Amish (much as we might want him to). When the corrupt officials from the Philadelphia Police Department finally learn of his hideout, they show up and try to kill him. Book fails in an attempt to deal with the three attackers through violence. Though he does kill two of his combatants, Schaeffer (his boss) is left holding Eli and Rachel as hostages. Only when the Amish neighbors show up as a group does the final antagonist give up the battle.

The point to be noted here is that each of these endings leads to a sense of "rightness" about the world. Each character's reaction to a filmic environment leads us to believe that this is how things operate in our own environment. Here is where dramatic structure leads to ideological containment. Resolution in cinema can give us a sense of security in the dominant ideology of the culture. *Sergeant York* and *Friendly Persuasion* thus fit cleanly into the holes cut by our own culture's dominant ideology. York realizes the need to fight and defend his country. When he does, he is successful. In the final scene he returns home to his sweetheart and receives a coveted piece of land with a brand new home on it. In *Friendly Persuasion*, the Birdwells' decisions to resist their enemy have brought success, even if the film dodges its key issues in many ways. The denouement of American cinema is more than a lessening of tensions, it is an affirmation of a *weltanschauung*. The world is once again in its proper order. We see in these first two films a dramatic structure that quickly contains any ideological dissent that might be allowed by the presence of pacifism as counterideology. Clearly pacifism is presented in such a way that it can be easily dismissed at the end of the motion picture. Most critical media theorists would expect just that.

Yet, if one sees *Sergeant York* and *Friendly Persuasion* as the norm, *Witness* must be seen as the most radical of the three films. It starkly suggests that pacifism is a viable option to violence for solving problems. Where Book's solution fails at the end of the film, the solution offered by the congregation of Amish people succeeds. After the Amish community gathers around Book and Schaeffer (the latter holding a gun to the back of the former), Schaeffer throws down his gun, recognizing the futility of trying to kill the whole congregation. Moreover, in the final shot of the film, Book—the man who could not be converted and become like the Amish—ends up riding off alone. The woman he loves finally realizes that he cannot change and that his violent nature will only lead to sorrow. Given this assessment, she shuns him, gently turning her back on him when he stands before her to say goodbye. She herself had been threatened with such a means of justice. Now she practices it.

Clearly this film's ending contradicts many films we have seen on the screen. These are characters who hold to a metaphysical orientation suggesting that violence is not a necessity. And the final scenes do nothing to discount such a worldview. The Philadelphia cop does not get the woman. He does not get the riches. He has lost his partner. He returns to the city (a place of violence and anomie) by himself. Had he been able to change and become a pacifist, he could have stayed in the Amish community, a place of natural beauty and community. Rather than standing as an example of how the world works, Book is set up as an example of how it does not work, that is, how it is (in the mind of the auteur) dysfunctional. In *Witness,* then, the resolution, is not a resolution at all. The viewer is left with a continuing sense of tension. While most films leave us with conflicts that are quickly packaged and dispensed with, this one leaves the conflictual elements scattered. Further, to the extent that resolution is given, the viewer "knows" that the world outside the theater does not work like this. This is not the way things happen in the world as we know it.

### *Ideology, Hegemony, and Contradiction*

Certainly *Sergeant York, Friendly Persuasion*, and *Witness* allow for some interesting conjecture about the relationship between cinema and ideology. If nothing else we should note that on some occasions the Hollywood film industry does allow for the introduction of ideas that conflict with the dominant ideology in American culture. All three films deal directly with the issue of pacifism. All three films struggle with the relationship between individual conscience and community standards of justice.

In their simple plot structure, *Sergeant York* and *Friendly Persuasion* deal with these two subjects in a rather predictable fashion and the films are thus easy to place in the context of American culture. As their narration begins, they both appear to oppose dominant ideology, but any opposition they can offer to common ways of thinking crumbles in the end. In the face of the overwhelming value our culture lends to patriotism and military service, these two films could not likely end in a way other than they do. Alvin York must recognize the importance of physically confronting evil. The Birdwells must recognize the importance of protecting family and property. For these films to end otherwise would run contrary to what our culture sees as common sense.

At the same time, *Witness* not only introduces the controversial subject of pacifism but deals with it in a way that seems to invite a radical reading. Though there are clearly structural and social factors that diminish the film's message (Moore 195), the motion picture does demonstrate the ability for nonmainstream ideologies to receive positive treatment. Its solemn ending makes us yearn for the hero to be more like the pacifist Amish and less like his colleagues in the Philadelphia Police Department.

Whether the film makes us yearn for such a lifestyle for ourselves is another question. Given the plethora of film characters who model for us a life where violence is a necessity, our admiration for the Amish might be fleeting. And fleeting admiration of anything will not likely lead to significant change. If this is the case, Hollywood is probably doing a good job (for better or for worse) of reproducing the society in which we live.

## Works Cited


Ellul, Jacques. *Violence: Reflections from a Christian Perspective*. New York: Eerdmans, 1969.

"Films Violent Worldwide." *Christianity Today* 2 Sept. 1988: 51.

Finkel, Harry, Harry Chandlee, Howard Koch, and John Huston, screenwriters. *Sergeant York*. Dir. Howard Hawks. Warner Brothers, 1941. Dialogue was transcribed from the film.

Gitlin, Todd. "Prime Time Ideology: The Hegemonic Process in Television Entertainment." *Television: The Critical View*. Ed. Horace Newcomb. 3rd ed. New York: Oxford UP, 1982. 426-54.

—. "Social Breakdown: On Thrills and Kills." *Dissent* 38.2 (1991): 245-48.

Moore, Rick Clifton. "Pacifism as Narrative in the Mass Mediated Community." *Journal for Peace and Justice Studies* 4.2 (1992): 179-97.

Prince, Stephen. "Tom Horn: Dialectics of Power and Violence in the Old West." *Journal of Popular Culture* 22.1 (1988): 119-29.

Signorielli, Nancy, and George Gerbner, comps. *Violence and Terror in the Mass Media: An Annotated Bibliography*. New York: Greenwood, 1988.

Wallace, Earl, and William Kelley, screenwriters. *Witness*. Dir. Peter Weir. Paramount Pictures, 1985. Dialogue was transcribed from the film.

Wilson, Michael, screenwriter. *Friendly Persuasion*. Dir. William Wyler. Allied Artists, 1956. Dialogue was transcribed from the film.


## Filmography

| Film | Year | Director |
|---|---|---|
| *All Quiet on the Western Front* | 1930 | Lewis Milestone |
| *Angel and the Badman* | 1947 | James Edward Grant |
| *Battle of Rogue River* | 1954 | William Castle |
| *Broken Arrow* | 1950 | Delmer Daves |
| *Casablanca* | 1942 | Michael Curtiz |
| *Catch 22* | 1970 | Mike Nichols |
| *Clear and Present Danger* | 1995 | Phillip Noyce |
| *Deal of the Century* | 1983 | William Friedkin |
| *Death Wish* | 1974 | Michael Winner |
| *Destry Rides Again* | 1939 | George Marshall |
| *Die Hard* | 1988 | John McTiernan |
| *Dr. Strangelove* | 1964 | Stanley Kubrick |
| *The Fastest Gun Alive* | 1956 | Russell Rouse |
| *Friendly Persuasion* | 1956 | William Wyler |

| | | |
|---|---|---|
| *Gandhi* | 1982 | Richard Attenborough |
| *Gun Fury* | 1953 | Raoul Walsh |
| *Heaven with a Gun* | 1969 | Lee Katzin |
| *High Noon* | 1952 | Fred Zinnemann |
| *The Horse Soldiers* | 1959 | John Ford |
| *Lethal Weapon* | 1987 | Richard Donner |
| *Passenger 57* | 1992 | Kevin Hooks |
| *Paths of Glory* | 1957 | Stanley Kubrick |
| *Patriot Games* | 1992 | Phillip Noyce |
| *The Peacemaker* | 1956 | Ted Post |
| *Sergeant York* | 1941 | Howard Hawks |
| *Shane* | 1953 | George Stevens |
| *The Shootist* | 1976 | Don Siegel |
| *Thunder in the East* | 1953 | Charles Vidor |
| *War Games* | 1983 | John Badham |
| *Witness* | 1985 | Peter Weir |

# Film's Satirical Rogues at War

**Richard L. Stromgren**

Satire has always shone among the rest, and is the boldest way, if not the best, to tell men freely of their foulest faults.

—John Dryden, "An Essay Upon Satire"

The several complexities and challenges inherent in satiric observation have not prevented some filmmakers from showing how effective the film medium can be as a means of making some sort of satiric or ironic mischief. The history of film includes innumerable works by a surprisingly large number of filmmakers who fall into the satiric mode and reveal the diverse styles that have been employed, and the wide variety of "causes" or aberrations being queried, challenged, debunked, or condemned through the use of humor.

Film provides an especially flexible, complex, and subtle means of marshaling ironic and satiric language and imagery, and has become adept at confronting issues, making judgments, and even championing causes. Through film we discover the opportunity to balance the aesthetic experience and the spirit of playfulness with the shaping of an attack according to the disciplines of the medium.

It is the screen satirist who frequently makes it possible for us to overcome our reticence in accepting the humor in topics for which we expect respectful treatment, profound treatment, or no treatment at all. Wylie Sypher alludes to James Feibleman's *In Praise of Comedy* when he says in "The Social Meanings of Comedy," "Whenever we become aware that this is not the best of possible worlds, we need the help of the comedian to meet the 'insuperable defects of actuality'" (246). Comedy, he suggests, "can be the means of mastering our disillusions when we are caught in a dishonest or stupid society" (245). The use of comedy in such instances frequently comes under the label of "black comedy," and our response to it is what William Pechter, in "Why We Laugh at Buñuel," calls "a strategy for preserving sanity while contemplating the intolerable" (276).

One social ill that has roused and sometimes inspired the ranks of historians, philosophers, social critics, and comic artists alike, at least as far back as the conflicts on the plains of Peloponnesus, is warfare. It didn't take the filmmaker long to join the ranks in using the battlefield as an accommodating setting for high drama and heroics in both fabled and authentic lands—from Edison's crude reconstructions of campaigns of the Spanish-American War, Griffith's monumental *Birth of a Nation* (1915), and Milestone's *All Quiet on the Western Front* (1930) to the World War II epics and, belatedly, those of Korea and Vietnam. Though few can be classified as true antiwar statements, even fewer have been the effort of screen satirists. Those works that aspire to articulating the evils of warfare inevitably end up romanticizing the good cause or at least accepting the necessity of honorable engagement.

Where filmmakers have met the challenge of employing irony, parody, farce, or some other satiric mode to establish critical perspective, their agenda has been varied and frequently multidirectional. The more popular targets have included the nature of the military organization and elitist warfare as an extension of the class system; the mindlessness of drill and the madness of battle; the obscure and senseless reasons for going to war; the irony of protocol and civil pleasantries on the "killing fields"; and the romantic idea of heroism.

### *Madcap Mayhem*

A comic treatment of warfare would seem to invite instant censure, and many films have in fact come under attack for making light of a subject that is considered both sacred and profane. But an absurdist or surreal approach has enabled the skillful satirist to serve as both humorist and critic, sidestepping direct confrontation through hyperbole, ellipsis, and other distortions and disguises. The distancing that such manipulation provides gives license to laugh at what might otherwise be sober and sacred ground.

The Marx Brothers' *Duck Soup* (1933) is a prime example of complete lunacy that is today ranked among the more notable satiric commentaries on warfare. An anarchic response to authority, power, and ceremony is a prime ingredient of all Marx Brothers films. In *Duck Soup* the anarchy is directed, for a substantial period of time to the business of going to war. Although the film is basically apolitical and makes no direct reference to events or personalities of the day, it was produced the same year that Hitler became Chancellor of Germany and Harpo recounts listening to the tirades of the Führer on the radio while the film was in production. The primary intent may well have been to entertain, but the film inevitably becomes satiric, developing as a parody of national fervor, pomp and ceremony, dictatorial rule, the absurd reasons for going to war, and the mindlessness of battle.

National hysteria in preparation for war is turned into an elaborate musical production number combining barn dance, opera, blues, and minstrel show. The climactic scene becomes a surreal vision of battle-field insanity: Harpo is sent for replacements and paces the battlefield wearing a sandwich board—"Join the Army and see the Navy"; Groucho is advised that he is shooting at his own men and gives one of his officers a payoff to keep it under his hat; and Chico, as Secretary of War, decides to join the other side but returns because "the food is better over here." There are, of course, memorable sight gag routines that have nothing to do with war and politics—a confrontation between Harpo, Chico, and the proprietor of a lemonade stand; a "mirror" sequence in which Harpo mimics Groucho's gestures in front of an open frame to impersonate his reflection. Nevertheless, it is clearly the events leading up to and including the war between Fredonia and Sylvania that have won the film special recognition and prompted François Truffaut (among others) to include it among his choices of key parodies that do not "glorify war and render it in some way attractive" (Hughes 189).

Hollywood entries using the military establishment and battlefield as personae and setting for comic invention have been in ample supply through successive periods of war and peace. Films as varied in style and vintage as *You're in the Army Now* (1941), *Mister Roberts* (1955), and *Private Benjamin* (1980), have been generally accepted and enjoyed for their benign entertainment but would hardly rank as memorable satirical statements on the subject. Mike Nichols's *Catch 22* and Robert Altman's *M*A*S*H*  both made in 1970 at the height of the Vietnam War, and Barry Levinson's vehicle for Robin Williams, *Good Morning, Vietnam* (1987), have made considerable progress in demystifying the idea of the so-called just war. Through surrealistic imagery and unorthodox and trend-setting narrative construction, they convey something of the oxymoronic placement of rationality and purposefulness into a world gone mad. But *Catch 22* is set comfortably in World War II, *M*A*S*H* transposed to Korea, and *Good Morning, Vietnam* produced at the safe fifteen-year distance from the explosive issues of Vietnam. Still, all three harbor some of the darker shadows and bite of true social satire.

Some bite on the subject of military heroism is folded into the farce of both *Hail the Conquering Hero* (1944), written and directed by Preston Sturges, and *The Americanization of Emily* (1964), directed by Arthur Hiller from a Paddy Chayefsky screenplay. In *Hail the Conquering Hero* Sturges turns to heroism and motherhood for his and the audience's amusement—two subjects generally considered sacrosanct in this wartime era. Woodrow Truesmith, a Marine recruit, is medically discharged because of chronic hay fever. As the son of a World War I hero, he is ashamed to return home but is persuaded by a group of Marines returning from the war to assume the role of war hero for his mother's sake. With the help of a military escort, the "hero's" homecoming is carried off with brass band, parade, and hometown hero worship. Woodrow's feeble protests fail to prevent the tide of idolatry that reaches a fever pitch, and leads to promoting him as a mayoral candidate.

Charlie Madson, the young naval officer of the Hiller/Chayefsky film is also a victim of circumstances by which he becomes hailed as a war hero. It is the result of a determined, eccentric admiral's obsession that the first man killed on Omaha Beach during the Normandy invasion be a sailor. Unlike Woodrow Truesmith, who shows some heroics in admitting to the mistaken identity, Charlie accepts the accolades rather than be disgraced for cowardice and be separated from the English girl he loves.

Although both films have satiric thrust, the amalgam of farce and preachment in *The Americanization of Emily* clearly sent a mixed message. Partly the acquiescence of the protagonist, partly the choice of the tragic Omaha Beach landing to propel the plot, but mainly the portrayal of Charlie as a true believer of cowardice left the film open to charges of mixed signals and questionable values. Stanley Kauffmann, writing for *The New Republic*, found the picture to be "uncertain" and "contorted" (22). Hollis Alpert, in *Time* magazine, called it a movie that "cast one in a despair of confusion" (29). "A movie that goes only half way in a number of directions," reported Judith Christ of the *New York Herald Tribune* (17). It is likely that here, as in the Sturges film and others that attempt blending of farce and social import, the farcical treatment may neutralize, mask, or confuse the social purpose, leaving viewers embracing the comedy and missing the lesson. With *Emily* the lesson, by some, was simply rejected.

Few films have treated warfare in quite such a darkly comic and grandly absurdist and surreal manner as two works by British filmmakers—Richard Lester's *How I Won the War* (1967) and Richard Attenborough's *Oh, What A Lovely War* (1969). Richard Lester created his parodic vision of the Second World War in the tradition of the "campaign film." Developed through a free interchange of past, present, and future action, the narrative centers on the exploits of a British platoon led by an enthusiastic, good-hearted but dimwitted boy soldier—Lieutenant Goodbody (Michael Crawford). The two missions undertaken by the platoon are to build a cricket pitch for British officers behind enemy lines in North Africa, and to secure a strategic bridge over the

Rhine. Both missions are accomplished, though the entire platoon has been annihilated save its fearless leader and the platoon coward. We find Goodbody at the film's conclusion attending an aged veteran's reunion, declaring in nostalgic reverie, "But I won the war!"

Lester's mission here is to counter nearly twenty-five years of film's romanticizing over this "just" and popular conflict by dramatizing, in surreal and often absurdist imagery, the absurdity of war itself. As the cheery, overzealous, and totally inept leader of men, Goodbody takes the brunt of satiric salvos. His naivete, coupled with patriotic fervor, makes him more of a menace to the cause than the enemy, and while his platoon members perish, one by one, he survives by sheer dumb luck. It is an echo of many of the exploits of Buster Keaton but in a more deadly climate.

Playing off the enthusiastic bungling of Goodbody are the actions of the members of his platoon, fashioned as caricatures of those immortalized in other campaign films—the battle-hardened sergeant who barks orders and is brought down in battle only after being hit by repeated rounds of machine-gun fire; the prankster (John Lennon) who empties the precious water from a lawnroller to make it lighter; the overweight and out-of-shape grunt whose wife is cheating on him back home; the coward of the unit who survives only to be court martialed for capitulation to the enemy.

Though less broadly caricatured than the members of the British force, Colonel Odlebog, the Nazi officer who strikes a deal with Goodbody in the sale of the Ramagen Bridge, provides a more arresting image and statement of the surreal nature of war. Odlebog's tender care of greenhouse plants and his love of classical music provide an ironic contradiction to his offhanded admission to having killed "lots" of Jews. It is a reminder of both Renoir's characterization of von Rauffenstein in *Grand Illusion* (1937) and Resnais's documentation of Nazi cultivation and culture within the concentration camp community in *Night and Fog* (1955). The solicitous conversation between Odlebog and Goodbody reveals the two officers more as compatriots than enemies in their attitudes and values, a reminder once again of von Rauffenstein and his fraternal exchanges with de Boeldieu in the Renoir film. In their surreal exchange over the progress of the war, Lester's characters, like Renoir's, show a rapport with one another that belies their adversarial roles, at least for the moment. Lester's dedication to surprise and confusion is carried out in constant shifts from surrealism to naturalism to farce. The technique keeps viewers continually on edge while it reflects the very illogical and frequently absurdist and contradictory relationships of war's drama.

In *Oh! What a Lovely War* (1969), Richard Attenborough pushes the satire of war even further toward the surreal. The film is based on a stage play produced at London's Royal Court Theatre in 1963, one of a number of antiestablishment plays of the period using the British music hall as an inspiration for its style. The film adaptation, Attenborough's first directorial credit, suffers by comparison with the stage original. Several critics found it to be overproduced, with slick and elaborate production numbers that some believed distracted from the intent of the original. But putting comparisons aside, and allowing for something of a preoccupation with war as class struggle, the film provides some intriguing samplings of satirical invention. Its satirical bite comes largely through the contrapuntal linking of the horrors and sorrows of war with the stiff upper lip and cheery determination of both fighting forces and supporters on the home front. The stylized series of satirical vignettes alternates between the gaiety of seaside amusements and the bleak frozen trenches of British recruits fighting in France.

Dramatic personae are comprised of senior officers, "doughboys," heads-of-state, nurses, wives, and lovers. Aristocrats reveal their boredom over the war and a pretense of self-sacrifice: at an elegant dinner dance an upper-class wartime profiteer announces to his female companion, "I'm not using my German wine, not while the war is on." In one of the most chilling scenes of the film, a music hall routine featuring Maggie Smith becomes a recruiting session with men, young and old, lured to the stage by a chorus of beauties who sing of country and duty and a promise to wait for their return—"Oh we don't want to lose you but we think you ought to go." The men leave anxious mothers, wives, and lovers, smiling in anticipation of a kiss or hug from the seductresses and the promise of instant heroism. The smiles fade as they are herded into ranks by the blustering commands of a recruiting sergeant—"From now on your bloody life won't be worth living and you won't bloody die laughing either."

Throughout the film, the carefree carnival atmosphere of seaside amusements and the elegant formal dances give way to the horrors of war punctuated by the confusion and fatalism of the troops, the pomposity and indifference of commanding officers, and the sweet, caring encouragement of Red Cross nurses to men on stretchers—"Don't worry, we'll soon have you back at the front." Christmas in the frozen trenches brings a good-natured exchange of banter and carols between British and German troops. The two forces come out of their trenches to exchange smokes, drinks and news until artillery fire sends them scurrying back to their respective battle lines. The sequence is based on an actual event of the war, which came to be known as the Christmas

Day Truce. Such fraternization between members of opposing forces also has its antecedence in a number of films, ranging from Renoir's *Grand Illusion* to the Denis and Terry Sanders short dramatization of a lull in Civil War combat, *A Time Out of War* (1954). It still works as an arresting ironic commentary on warfare at its most personal level.

And there is more than a little irony in the exchange among heads of state concerning impending war that opens the film. The wife of the British Secretary of State for Foreign Affairs dismisses concern with, "Oh well, I mean, you know, who cares. Serbia is such a little country anyway, you know, and I mean, they're always up to something, aren't they." The French President answers, "Serbia is little, madame, but it will not be a little war."

These two British offerings are expansive "black comedies" on a particularly volatile subject and have been targeted by some critics for their broad parody, over-orchestration, and plain bad taste. But British film satirists, it seems, have always had a special talent for taking on the most sacred cows and, their detractors notwithstanding, are able to reflect, however obtusely, some profound human experiences in film that are more than innocent entertainment.

In both its lighter, fanciful and darker, more cynical forms, film is allowed to break with traditional perspectives on the social order, including the breaking of taboos. As members of the film audience, we view the unconventional critical perspective under the guise of artistic license while gaining reinforcement through the satisfaction of shared experience. Comedy, and satire in particular, puts the viewer into a conspiratorial relationship not only with the filmmaker but with other viewers as well, and the spirit of playfulness, even the darker variety, masks the threat of serious confrontation. The deflection or distraction from direct confrontation enables the comic artist to coax our indulgence. Though the aim of the satire may be the indictment of some aberration, or at times of some cherished belief, the route is by way of distraction or escape. It is this combination of putting the viewer on the offensive (challenging social ills) and also on the defensive (escape through humor) that allows the satirist to, in Sypher's words, "adjust incompatible standards without resolving the clash between them" (244).

### *Sterner Stuff: The Nazi Spectre*

Two war-related subjects that seem the least likely to lend themselves to comic treatment are the rise of Nazism—the social aberration considered the most horrific of the century—and the Armageddon via nuclear war. Our vision of the Nazi era comes largely through film: *Sophie's Choice* (1982), *The Pawnbroker* (1965), *The Damned* (1969),

*The Garden of the Finzi Continis* (1971), *Cabaret* (1972), and the television accounts such as *Holocaust* (1991). Though comedic treatment of the subject is understandably scant, there are the odd escapist fictions ranging from *Stalag 17* (1953), the prototype for the prison camp film, to the farcical offering by the Three Stooges, *You Nazty Spy* (1940) and *I'll Never Heil Again* (1940). The Billie Wilder film (*Stalag 17*), like most of his works, does generate a sense of cynicism through the character of the sergeant, played by William Holden, who is suspected of spying for the German command.

Documentaries like Capra's *Why We Fight* series (1942-45), produced before full realization of Hitler's "final solution," and Alain Resnais's 1955 commemorative short, *Night and Fog*, use documentary footage to provide a record of events leading up to genocide and frequently dwell on the ironies of the war. The Resnais work provides reflections on the fuller meaning of the Holocaust, including a frequently ironic vision of the events of the mid-1940s juxtaposed with the seemingly benign setting of the concentration camps ten years later.

In his article "Art and the Holocaust: Trivializing Memory," Elie Wiesel deplores the insensitive, superficial, and reductionist way in which the Holocaust has been "exploited" by film, theatre, and television. The examples he cites range from television docudramas like *Holocaust* to such darkly satiric fictions as Lina Wertmuller's *Seven Beauties* (1976), which I will deal with a bit later. These "cheap and simplistic melodramas," he charges, fail to meet the requirement that "this particular subject demands a special sensibility, a different approach, a rigor strengthened by respect and reverence and, above all, faithfulness to memory" (38).

Wiesel is certainly not alone in his sensitivity to the need for great care in approaching the subject of Nazism and the Holocaust. Where a comic treatment of Nazism is problematic at best, the Holocaust would seem strictly off limits. Yet, Rene Clair has observed, "The gloomier an era is, the more we find that humor, satire and laughter are the best witness we can bear to our liberty" (226). Works by two master screen satirists attempted to meet this challenge, though they were produced in ignorance of the horrors of genocide that were soon to be revealed. Chaplin's *The Great Dictator* (1940) and Lubitsch's *To Be or Not To Be* (1942) use satire as a weapon to attack the obscenities of the Nazi era and the more grotesque detail in word and action by which it was represented. The fact that both directors were using comedy to illustrate the aberration raised questions of propriety at the time of release and have continued to raise even more profound moral questions with the fuller realization of the Holocaust. It is doubtful that Chaplin would have made *The Great Dictator* had he known what was to occur at Auschwitz, Treblinka, and Buchenwald. But at the time *The Great Dictator* was released, Hitler and Chaplin were the two most famous men in the world and the parody of the one by the other is almost inevitable. In the dual roles of the Nazi dictator (Adenoid Hynkel) and the Jewish barber, Chaplin is able to represent the evils of Nazism and its victims but also provides a direct parody of Adolf Hitler. Particularly memorable—and evidence of Chaplin's satiric genius—are the speech to assembled masses and the globe sequence in which Hynkel dreams of world domination. In the course of the speech, the histrionics of the mad dictator are revealed in expression and gesture and particularly in the broken German/English that pays tribute to German youth and maidenhood and ends in a tirade against Jews. The globe sequence provides a marked contrast with the Hynkel speech. Here a silent and reflective dictator contemplates becoming ruler of the world while he both kicks and caresses an inflated globe to the strains of Lohengrin. It is arguably Chaplin's most accomplished ballet work in film.

There had been great anticipation of the film's release, and critical reaction was inevitably high profile and varied. Bosley Crowther, writing for the *New York Times*, is most laudatory, saying that Chaplin had "presented himself in triumphal splendor as The Great Dictator—or you know who," and speaking of "the superlative talent for ridicule . . . against the most dangerously evil man alive." He even suggests it was "perhaps the most significant film ever produced" (29).

While other critics were complimentary or at least respectful of Chaplin's comic genius, there is a general uneasiness about its dedication to such a somber subject and the blending of the "innocent," fun-loving comedy for which Chaplin was so much beloved and the ignominious social and moral specter raised. Writing for *The Commonweal*, Philip Hartung charges, "The grimness of the tragic situation does not mix well with the much-loved humorous Charlie Chaplin" (80-81). Otis Ferguson, writing in the *New Republic* identifies with those viewers "who will find the symbiosis of comedy and earnestness an unhappy state of union, detrimental to both; and I think these people will be right." Ferguson tempers his criticism with recognition of laughter as "one of the great and joyous healers of the spirit," but concludes that "the gulf between a kick in the pants and a pogrom is something even [Chaplin's] talent for the humorous-pathetic will not cross" (629-30).

Although the charges were mainly tied to the uncomfortable and awkward thematic mix and the minimizing of the Nazi threat, Chaplin's worst enemy here was his own reputation and legacy of films past—he had betrayed the expectations of his fans by taking on serious social purpose. In the final six minutes of the film, he steps completely out of *both* characters he plays and delivers an impassioned plea for world peace and human dignity. While defending the comic treatment of Nazism, both Crowther and John O'Hara gave up on the film's conclusion. "Chaplin's final appeal for reason," Crowther says, "is completely out of joint with that which has gone before." In his *Newsweek* review, O'Hara chastises critics who said this was no time for comedy: "No time for comedy? Yes, I say, time for comedy. Time for Chaplin comedy. No time even for Chaplin to preach as he does in those last six minutes" (60). Although nominated for top Academy Awards—best picture, best actor, best supporting actor, best original screenplay, and best original score—it won none and was withdrawn from circulation by Chaplin a short time after its opening until the war ended.

There is some irony in the fact that Chaplin had first ignored then mocked the "talking picture"—*City Lights* (1930), *Modern Times* (1936)—a decade after its arrival. And when he finally embraces it in *The Great Dictator,* he takes on the voice of two characters and then concludes in his own voice and an impassioned plea. Whether he would have fared any better with his critics had he stuck with his original conclusion is open to debate. The provisional script, copyrighted in November 1938, was subtitled "a story of a little fish in a shark infested ocean." In an epilogue following the concluding six-minute speech, the little barber wakes up back in the concentration camp to the menacing visage of a stormtrooper hovering over him and barking the tag line of the film, "Get up Jew! Where the hell do you think you are?" Chaplin disclaimed any role as social critic. Theodore Huff quotes Chaplin as saying, "There are those who always attach social significance to my work. It has none. I leave such subjects to the lecture platform" (208).

The criticism of *The Great Dictator* pales next to that launched against Ernst Lubitsch's *To Be or Not To Be*, released two years after the Chaplin film. Here, Lubitsch uses the invasion of Poland and a Warsaw theatre troupe's underground activities to provide the satiric sting. The reaction to this second classic satire of Nazism reveals the complex way conditioning and timing can affect how darker forms of satiric wit are perceived. Lubitsch had won a reputation in his earlier works for a certain spirit and visual style in dealing with manners and morals. The so-called Lubitsch touch was the filmmaker's approach to social conventions, particularly among the leisure class, and set within the drawing room and boudoir. His focus gradually began to center on the realities of personal and social conflict and finally on the political realities of the time. With *To Be or Not To Be*, the playful, sophisticated wit of earlier works gave way to a darker, more ironic blend of humor, anchored in allusions to actual events unfolding in Europe. In assessing the film for the *National Board of Review,* James Hamilton notes that the film "is mostly melodrama and farce of the recently popular kind that makes laughing matters of corpses and killings." He concludes by saying, "Chaplin's theory that the most serious matters are the best material for comedy gets a pretty tough test here. Sensitive people won't like it" (5-6).

Among the responses of such "sensitive" people were Bosley Crowther, writing for the *New York Times*, who found *To Be or Not to Be* guilty of three sins: mixing melodrama with comedy, treating Nazis too lightly, and using the occupation of Warsaw as a setting for comedy. Crowther speaks of "jangled moods and baffling humors . . . a subject which is far from the realm of fun . . . a spirit of levity, confused by frequent doses of shock . . ." Crowther goes on to accuse Lubitsch of reckless confusion between "comedy and grim excitement," and suggested the film lacked both taste and unity of mood (Crowther, *To Be* 13).

On the question of unity of mood it's interesting to note that Crowther's review referred to the striking contrast between the Lubitsch film and the two-reel documentary, *Churchill's Island*, which preceded it in many showings. Produced by the National Film Board of Canada, the short, inspirational film pays tribute to the heroics of the British R.A.F. using newsreel footage of both Allied and Axis powers. Unity of mood might well be called into question with this as a prelude to the Lubitsch mischief.

Philip Hartung, in his review of the film, said it "asks us to laugh at some of the very broad anti-Nazi satire while we are weeping over the sad fate of stricken Poland." Having complimented the acting, cinematography, and suspenseful screenplay, "the comedy is hilarious—even when it is hysterically thrilling," Hartung was clearly uneasy about the use of satire to dramatize Nazi occupation. "We should be able to take this kind of kidding of the Fuehrer and his boys, but perhaps we are still too close to his butchery to have the perspective that satire such as this and *The Great Dictator* demands" (Hartung, *To Be* 531).

Not all the critics were as caustic or cautious. *Newsweek* spoke of Lubitsch's "mastery of sly humor and innuendo" ("Farewell" 50). *Time* referred to the film as "a very funny comedy, salted to taste with melodrama and satire" (90). The change in perspective over time, alluded to by Hartung, is given a positive spin by *Life* magazine—"In years to come the fact that Hollywood could convert part of a world crisis into such a cops-and-robbers charade will surely be regarded as a remarkable phenomenon" (Mar. 9, 1942, 63). In his article "Comedy with a Bite," Andrew Sarris suggests that with this film, Lubitsch "succeeded in bridging the gap between humor and horror." In reflecting on the disparity of style, he says, "Nothing matches, but everything works" (62).

Whether or not one agrees with Sarris on the mismatches within the film, the timing of its release suggests at least a threefold mismatch and further explains some of the abuse Lubitsch received. First of all, the film had violated the unwritten rule resolutely defended by many critics. It is the rule reflected in all of the above-mentioned reviews of *To Be or Not To Be*—that comedy and horrific drama wear different masks and are generally considered incompatible. The commingling of the two, what was to be recognized and accepted as black comedy by the 1950s, was still an uncomfortable mix for critics and moviegoers generally in the early 1940s. In a 1942 review entitled "An Artistic Blunder by Lubitsch," *The Times* of London summed it up by proclaiming, "Lubitsch is determined on a disastrous attempt to reconcile two unreconcilable moods" (6). What seems to have made the film particularly problematic for some was that unlike Lubitsch's early works, known for their light, sophisticated wit, and elegant visual style—the celebrated "Lubitsch touch"—*To Be or Not To Be* coupled disturbingly realistic action with farcical incidents and wickedly ironic dialogue, much of it with a sexual connotation.

Aside from being ahead of its time in terms of aesthetic legitimacy of "dark humor," the film's release suggests a further mismatch in timing, coming, as it did, on the heels of two events that were inevitably to affect its reception. First, audiences viewing the film in the early months of 1942 had the image of conflagration at Pearl Harbor and the United States' direct involvement in the war foremost in their minds. Attitudes until December 7th had been strongly passive and even militantly isolationist. This change in perspective is a key factor in how differently Chaplin's *The Great Dictator* and the Lubitsch film were received. *We* were now at war with Germany and had detailed daily reminders of the gravity of our cause. By the time of the film's release, the German blitzkrieg had overrun the western front and Hitler had turned to the invasion of Poland. Although the full horror of Nazi atrocities was not yet known to most Americans, the realism of the scenes depicting the destruction of Warsaw coupled with the farcical encounters among theatre folk and the high command proved distasteful to many. In his review, Bosley Crowther charges that Lubitsch "has set his actors in performing a spy-thriller of fantastic design amid the ruins and frightful oppression of Nazi-invaded Warsaw. To say it is callous and macabre is understating the case" (*To Be* 13). Raymond Durgnat, in

*The Crazy Mirror*, calls it "the direct forerunner of bad taste comedy" (180).

It was the charges in the review for the *Philadelphia Inquirer*—"callous tasteless effort to find fun in the bombing of Warsaw"—that finally triggered a response by Lubitsch. In a letter to the critic he defends his treatment, suggesting that scenes depicting the destruction of Warsaw are treatments "in all seriousness," and that there can be no doubt concerning his attitude toward these horrors. "What I have satirized in this picture are the Nazis and their ridiculous ideology." In support of the bridge between laughter and horror, Lubitsch goes on to say, "The tragedy of Poland realistically portrayed as in *To Be or Not To Be* can be merged with satire" (*Philadelphia Inquirer*, Aug. 25, 1943). In a letter to the *New York Times* (Mar. 29, 1942) Lubitsch gives a generic label to reflect the bridge between comedy and horror—he calls the film " a tragical farce or a farcical tragedy."

The second untimely occurrence, coming between the film's completion and its release, was the death of one of its stars, Carole Lombard, in a plane crash during a war-bond-drive tour. There is an ethereal quality in Lombard's performance that must have been particularly unsettling for viewers who had read of her death only days and weeks earlier. It is clear that Lombard's spirit was haunting some of the critics. Still, the brief review in *Life* magazine ends with, "there is no chill when her blithe spirit animates the screen" (63). There is an irony and something of a chill in the way the *Life* review is tucked in among the benign and entertaining copy, ads, and photos that share space with the most gruesome accounts, including photographs, of Nazi horrors.

In something of an aside in his critique of the critics, Lubitsch mentions, "I have also satirized the attitudes of actors." Indeed, in a much more benign, even affectionate way, Lubitsch never misses an opportunity to satirize the egos and aspirations of the Polski Theatre entourage—Joseph Tura's anxiety over his image; the aspiration of Greenberg, a Jewish actor, to play Shylock; Bronski, the consummate ham, and others of the troupe engaged in an overzealous impersonation of Nazi officialdom. But it is the Nazi image that takes the stinging punishment. While making Nazis look both ridiculous and dangerous, Lubitsch makes their victims both heroic and very human with idiosyncrasies and foibles of their own. It is this unique blend of tragedy/farce, of the consortium of human and inhumane elements, that make the film such a durable property more than fifty years after its release.

The performance of the real Nazis, though less inspired, is no less interesting than that of the professional actors. The spy, Siletsky; the Nazi commandant, Colonel Ehrhardt; and his assistant, Schultz, all reflect the stultifying, humorless personae of the Gestapo. When humor is attempted, as in the case of the Napoleon brandy joke and the one that brought charges of tastelessness against Lubitsch—"What he (Tura) does to Shakespeare we are now doing to Poland," Colonel Ehrhardt observes—it is both sophomoric and in monumental bad taste. Siletsky's final performance, ironically, is played out on the stage of the Polski Theatre where he dies gasping a final "Heil!" It is finally stage illusion, which the Nazis cannot distinguish from reality, that defeats these ultimate ham actors—Colonel Ehrhardt, Siletsky, Shultz, and the Führer himself. The intrusion of reality on the illusory world is ironically illustrated, as already mentioned, by the death of Lombard and the United States entry into the war and unquestionably had an impact on how events of the film were perceived. The aging of a film, at least one with as strong a sociopolitical context as this, will inevitably modify a viewer's perception. Auschwitz, Bergen-Belsen, and the full realization of the Holocaust were to further complicate the way in which a viewer relates to the satire of the Lubitsch film. But it seems to me that in spite of the withering criticism at the time of the film's release and the changes in its reception over time, it is Lubitsch who has the last laugh. He saw, in the words of one critic, "the convoluted affinities between comic and Fascist rhetoric" (Tifft 1). The film is in a sense an answer to the Nazi commitment to the use of the medium as a most effective (albeit controversial) means of propaganda.

The charges of tastelessness leveled against Lubitsch may well have inspired Mel Brooks in his creation of *The Producers* (1968) and its "Springtime for Hitler" production number. Less successful in its invention and therefore more apt to raise questions of propriety is the 1983 scene-for-scene remake of the Lubitsch *To Be or Not To Be* in which Brooks and Anne Bancroft star.

### *The Bomb*

As sobering as "comedies" on conventional warfare and the Holocaust must finally be, those that anticipate the Armageddon through nuclear holocaust tend to be more complex in their appeal to viewers, simultaneously providing the ultimate in fright and amusement. While films like *On the Beach* (1959), *Fail-Safe* (1964), and *The War Game* (1967) were soberly analyzing the horror of nuclear annihilation, Stanley Kubrick's *Dr. Strangelove; or, How I Learned to Stop Worrying and Love the Bomb* (1963) addressed the subject with a relentlessly satiric perspective, and ranks as one of the darkest of black comedies. With the aid of scenarists Terry Southern and Peter George, Kubrick employs an arsenal of ironic devices. The basic irony evolves from the theme of man's subservience to the technology he has created and can no longer control, and which is about to destroy him. In narrative terms the conflict centers on the failure of the U.S. Strategic Air Command's fail-safe procedures to avert launching a nuclear strike and the resulting Soviet response with a "doomsday device." Within this narrative framework, the screenplay employs a dialectic approach that brings the representations of life, virility, sexual prowess in conflict with their opposites —death, sterility, impotence.

It is finally through characterization, dialogue and many touches in sight gags, setting, and sound that the satiric points are driven home. As an attack on the nuclear arms race and the U.S. military establishment, the film is without a protagonist but uses its eight principal characters to provide an ironic juxtaposition of rational judgment and lunatic leadership. But the rational judgment, in the face of nuclear holocaust, itself becomes ludicrous and we find the commander of the flight wing about to drop the hydrogen bomb, spurring his men on with the prospect of honors and citations; a Pentagon general worrying about the Soviet ambassador seeing and photographing "the big board"; and the base commander who ordered the attack worrying about the destruction of a Coca-Cola machine. The ironic pairing of virility and sterility is represented through many of the characters—most notably the virile Buck Turgidson, the impotent Jack D. Ripper, and even bronco-busting wing commander, Major Kong, who gives his crew an inspiring pep talk on duty and country and at the film's "climax," rides astride the hydrogen bomb to its target. The sexual imagery is used even in the opening scene of the coupling of bomber and refueling plane and the closing with its orgasm of a mushroom cloud. To the credit of the scenarists, much of the irony comes through dialogue, particularly in understatements and euphemisms. In an age in which garbage dumps have become "sanitary landfills" and the bombing of enemy cities is called "protective reaction strikes," the euphemism and understatement have become a means of protecting us from uncomfortable reality. Some of the lines given to Buck Turgidson, the commanding general, provide devilish examples. In reference to the penetration of U.S. air defense by a Russian nuclear strike he says to assembled brass in the war room, "I don't think it is quite fair to condemn a whole program for a single slip-up" and, in response to all-out nuclear war, "I'm not saying that we wouldn't get our hair mussed." Other characters also help to give the proceedings an ironic spin through understatement and gentle and evasive language. Peter Sellers as a British officer desperately seeking a rational solution to impending disaster attempts reason with the paranoid base commander who has just initiated the nuclear confrontation. His attempt to coolly defuse the situation without sending Jack D. Ripper further over the edge builds tension while serving as a gem of understatement. President Muffley as the rational, calm, but ultimately ineffectual commander in chief lends his own dimension to understatement, particularly in his conversations with the Soviet premier. The combined cool, rational and somewhat effete persona of Captain Mandrake and President Muffley stand in stark contrast to the blustering, knee-jerk, macho image of Buck Turgidson. But there is an even more ironic contrast between Buck and the cigar-chomping, sex-obsessed but ultimately impotent Ripper and the gung-ho Bat Guano who seems paranoid over what he suspects is Mandrake's sexual "preversion."

Dr. Strangelove, as the paraplegic, fascist scientist with an uncontrollable bionic arm, combines the ironic function of understatement with hyperbole. His histrionic performance combines with calm projection of survival through genetic engineering and winning of the "mine shaft gap." His twisted mind is revealed through the contortions of his body and the uncontrollable mechanical arm as he visualizes the amoral application of science run amuck.

The absurdity of character and situation threatens to send the work into an orbit of farce, but what finally keeps everything in check is the realistic, almost documentary style that the film adopts with voice-over opening narration, black and white cinematography, and the hand-held camera and general spontaneity of the attack on the air base. Jerry Palmer in *The Logic of the Absurd* suggests the film "illustrates the delicate balance between the plausible and implausible. This allows identification with the threat of nuclear annihilation by human error, while finding amusement in the idiosyncratic behavior of the several characters in responding to the frustrations confronting them" (192). Some would argue that humor in a film of such cataclysmic nature is in bad taste and therefore identification is impossible. To this, Andrew Sarris answers, "The great merit of *Dr. Strangelove* is its bad taste. . . . Responsible art is dead art, and a sane film on the bomb would have been a deadly bore" ("Dr. Strangelove" 181).

More recently, *The Atomic Cafe*, which is billed by its distributor, New Yorker Films, as "a film about the history and culture of the atomic age," was advertised in poster copy as a feature film "edited entirely from vintage propaganda to recreate the atmosphere of fear, conformity and official insanity which characterized the Cold War." It is another, perhaps the only other, film to deal in such broad satiric terms with the subject of nuclear attack. What is unique here is that the film is made up entirely of compilation footage taken from U.S. government educational shorts and indoctrination films of the 1940s and '50s (*How to Beat the*

*Bomb* and *Nuclearosis* are two samplings), which instruct Americans on how to adjust to the nuclear age. The film captures the innocence and gullibility of the American public for whom the original shorts were intended. The better informed audience of today will find the mission and perspective of the original footage particularly chilling while being amused by the arrogant, patronizing, and at times even romantic attitude it espouses. What makes the film of special interest is the fact that the satiric barbs are so often self-inflicted. With due respect to the production team that painstakingly assembled the footage over a five-year period, it is frequently the individual scenes from the original that provide the irony, not through their manipulation but in the light of current knowledge about nuclear testing and warfare. This is particularly true in scenes simulating the survivability of atomic warfare through the use of fallout shelters, tots in lead-lined snowsuits, soldiers charging onto ground zero seconds after an atomic test bombing, newsreel footage of Hiroshima survivors, U.S. Navy relocating the "friendly natives" in preparation for bomb testing, a cartoon turtle instructing school children in "duck and cover" drills that send them scurrying under desks for protection. A singularly morbid scene shows an Army chaplain describing an atom bomb detonation as "one of the most beautiful sights ever seen by man." If the film has a drawback, it is that its lunacy, while amusing, detracts from its timeless message: the power of official propaganda in a world of innocence. Still, it represents the quintessential example of taking years of official propaganda and turning the material on itself.

In his introduction to *The Comic Mind*, Gerald Mast observes that "the Twentieth Century is a comic century. Comic, ironic reaction is an understandably human, reasonable, and healthy response to the devastating chaos of Twentieth-Century life, politics, morality and science" (*ix*). Modern warfare surely represents a significant part of that chaos and has bedeviled and inspired some of our most illustrious screen satirists.

## Works Cited


Alpert, Hollis. Rev. of *The Americanization of Emily*. *Saturday Review* 24 Oct. 1964: 29.

"An Artistic Blunder by Lubitsch." *Times of London* 30 Apr. 1942: 6.

Byron, Stuart, and Elisabeth Weis, eds. *The National Society of Film Critics on Movie Comedy*. New York: Penguin, 1977.

"Carole Lombard's Last Movie." *Life* 9 Mar. 1942: 63.

Christ, Judith. Rev. of *The Americanization of Emily*. *Herald Tribune* 28 Oct. 1964: 17.

Clair, Rene. *Cinema Yesterday and Today*. New York: Dover, 1972.

Crowther, Bosley. "The Screen in Review: The Great Dictator." *New York Times* 16 Oct. 1940: 29.

—. "The Screen: To Be Or Not To Be." *New York Times* 7 Mar. 1942: 13.

Durgnat, Raymond. *The Crazy Mirror: Hollywood Comedy and the American Image*. London: Faber and Faber, 1969.

"Farewell with a Laugh." *Newsweek* 2 Mar. 1942: 50.

Ferguson, Otis. "Less Time For Comedy." *New Republic* 4 Nov. 1940: 629-30.

Hamilton, James. "To Be or Not To Be." *National Board of Review Magazine* Mar. 1942: 5-6.

Hartung, Philip. "That Funny Little Man Again." *Commonweal* 8 Nov. 1940: 80-81.

—. "To Be or Not To Be Laughed At." *Commonweal* 13 Mar. 1942: 531.

Huff, Theodore. *Charlie Chaplin*. New York: Pyramid Books, 1964.

Hughes, Robert, ed. *Film Book 2: Films of Peace and War*. New York: Grove, 1962.

Kauffmann, Stanley. "Spirits High and Low." *The New Republic* 5 Dec. 1964: 22.

Mast, Gerald. *The Comic Mind*. New York: Bobbs-Merrill, 1973.

The New Pictures. *Time* 16 Mar. 1942: 90.

O'Hara, John. "Charlie, Charley." *Newsweek* 28 Oct. 1940: 60.

Palmer, Jerry. *The Logic of the Absurd: On Film and Television Comedy*. London: British Film Institute, 1987.

Pechter, William S. "Why We Laugh at Buñuel." Byron and Weis 273-76.

Sarris, Andrew. "Comedy with a Bite." *American Film* Oct. 1986: 62.

—. "Doctor Strangelove." Byron and Weis 181-83.

Sypher, Wylie. "The Social Meanings of Comedy." *Comedy*. Garden City: Doubleday, 1956.

Tifft, Stephen. "Miming the Führer: 'To Be or Not To Be' and the Mechanism of Outrage." *Yale Journal of Criticism* Fall 1991: 1.

Wiesel, Elie. "Art and the Holocaust: Trivializing Memory." *New York Times* 11 June 1989: 1, 38.

## Selected Filmography

| Year | Film | Director |
|---|---|---|
| 1927 | *The Genereal* | Buster Keaton<br>Clyde Bruckman |
| 1933 | *Duck Soup* | Leo McCarey |
| 1937 | *Grand Illusion* | Jean Renoir |
| 1940 | *The Great Dictator* | Charles Chaplin |
| 1942 | *To Be or Not To Be* | Ernst Lubitsch |
| 1944 | *Hail the Conquering Hero* | Preston Sturges |
| 1953 | *Stalag 17* | Billy Wilder |
| 1958 | *Paths of Glory* | Stanley Kubrick |
| 1963 | *Dr. Strangelove* | Stanley Kubrick |
| 1964 | *The Americanization of Emily* | Arthur Hiller |
| 1967 | *How I Won the War* | Richard Lester |
| 1969 | *Oh, What a Lovely War* | Richard Attenborough |
| 1970 | *Catch 22* | Nike Nichols |
| 1970 | *M*A*S*H* | Robert Altman |
| 1976 | *Seven Beauties* | Lina Wertmuller |
| 1982 | *The Atomic Cafe* | Kevin Rafferty,<br>Jayne Loader,<br>Pierce Rafferty |
| 1987 | *Good Morning, Vietnam* | Barry Levinson |

# Diminishing Degrees of Separation: Class Mobility in Movies of the Reagan-Bush Era

**Carolyn Anderson**

In 1990, deep into the Reagan-Bush years, Benjamin DeMott published a persuasively argued and deeply troubling book entitled *The Imperial Middle: Why Americans Can't Think Straight About Class* in which DeMott maintains that a national inability to think straight and speak honestly about class has serious and destructive consequences for American society. DeMott reaches to several film examples to bolster his arguments, but his agenda is far broader than film criticism. This chapter inquires as to whether DeMott's claim of a disingenuous and even dishonest public discourse regarding class holds true in American films of the 1980s.

During a decade when affirmative action programs were dismantled because the time for their necessity had supposedly passed, when Americans were urged to "be all that you can be" despite the failed promise of a trickle-down prosperity, what sort of class discourse was enacted in popular movies? Does an ideology of an open class system, a system distinguished by great fluidity or even classlessness pervade the Hollywood narratives produced between 1980 and 1992? In this chapter I shall consider "the '80s" as a political and cultural unit of time, beginning in 1980 with the election of Ronald Reagan and extending through the administration of George Bush, when this nation was led by a man of great personal privilege who claimed that class is "for European democracies or something else—it isn't for the United States of America. We are not going to be divided by class" (qtd. in Will).

Is America divided by class? Although all social theorists agree that America is a stratified culture, the concept of social class means more than just social and economic differences; it implies cognitive categories or ways of thinking about class to which members subscribe. Some find that self-awareness lacking in the United States. More common is the attitude of sociologists Dennis Gilbert and Joseph Kahl, who assume an American class structure both material and perceptual. Their interpretation of 1990 United States census data places Americans, based on a combination of variables, including income, education and social status, in the following six classes: a capitalist class (1%), an upper-middle class (14%), a middle class (30%), a working class (30%), the working poor (13.5%) and an underclass (1.5%). They claim their scheme is congruent with empirical literature based on both demographic surveys and qualitative community studies and also "congruent with the way most Americans see the system and their place within it" (308-17; for other class permutations, see Ehrenreich, Eisler, Fussell, and Strauss).

Without necessarily knowing the term, most Americans recognize a concept that pioneer sociologist Max Weber called "life chances" to emphasize the extent to which chances for the good things—safety, education, good health, personal satisfaction—are shaped by social class. Most analysts describe the 1980s as a period in which life chances decreased for many Americans (Cassidy). Income, job opportunities, and political power shifted upward while the working class languished. The trend toward greater and growing social inequality was clear. According to the Census Bureau the income gap between the richest and the poorest American families was wider in the mid-'80s than at any time since the bureau began keeping statistics in 1946.

I do not suggest popular movies have an obligation to turn statistics into scenarios, but I am curious about what kinds of class discourse emerge in the Hollywood movies produced in the '80s by and for a highly stratified American population. If, as Graeme Turner does, we see film as "a social practice for its makers and its audience; [then] in its narratives and meanings we can locate evidence of ways in which our culture makes sense of itself" (*xiv-xv*). This chapter assumes that an important part of our subterranean national dialogue about class ironically takes place in the decidedly above-ground world of popular movies. What were movies of the '80s saying about class and "life chances" in contemporary America?

Class markers are ubiquitous in all films, from set design to costume selection to ways of speaking. Certain actors, especially supporting players, are so associated with class positions that the expression "casting against type" includes class expectations and thus the surprise of Meryl Streep (*Silkwood*) and James Spader (*The Music of Chance*) moving down and Robert DeNiro (*Guilty by Suspicion*) and Susan Sarandon (*Lorenzo's Oil*) moving up a class ladder. Still, the ideology of America-as-middle-class is so naturalized that movies are discussed as being "about class" mostly when central characters belong to the working class or the underclass or when class conflict becomes explicit. To give some shape to an unwieldy topic, I have narrowed my focus here to '80s films with contemporaneous United States settings that include explicit textual references to the notion of class *mobility*. Whether seen as dream or threat, reality or impossibility, upward (or downward) mobility seems an efficient and useful point of access into the complicated topic of class discourse in popular film.

According to Gilbert and Kahl, mobility mostly occurs between the upper-middle and the middle class and between the working poor and the underclass. They note that "the overall pattern of [inter-generational] mobility [of white men] has not changed dramatically over the last three decades. The most notable change seems to be between the 1970s and 1980s, when upward mobility dropped off, downward mobility correspondingly increased, and movement both ways across the blue-collar/white-collar line increased by a few percent" (153). The structural changes that fueled past upward mobility were waning in the 1980s and early '90s. What do popular movies made during this time of economic stagnation say about class mobility in America?

Several traditional Hollywood genres are wedded to mobility plots. *Dreams and Deadends* is a lucid analysis of the gangster genre and an apt description of the rise and fall structure that characterizes most gangster films, including such '80s examples as *Scarface* (1983), *Once Upon a Time in America* (1984) and *The Godfather Part III* (1990). The gangster film is far less trusting of the promises of the "American Dream" than other genres; here class resentments find expression in a criminality that is eventually punished and therefore contained.

Another genre committed to mobility is the biopic, which traces the trajectory of an individual life, usually a line of spectacular or admirable ascent and often an equally spectacular but less admirable descent. Both ascent and descent in the biopic are more often attributed to strengths and flaws of character, talent, or will than to something as structural as a class system or as amorphous as the fates. In contrast to the general optimism of '80s films, the biopics of the decade—*Raging Bull* (1980), *Coalminer's Daughter* (1980), *Frances* (1982), *Heart Like a Wheel* (1983), *Sweet Dreams* (1985), *Tucker: The Man and His Dream* (1988), *Walker* (1988), *Blaze* (1989), and *Bugsy* (1991)—often showed the dark side of achievement. More than any other genre, the life story is permeated with an ideology of self-creation and individual responsibility. Biopics are presented as evidence of mobility, their stories bolstered by historical authority and claimed authenticity.

At the other extreme of a reality continuum is the animated fantasy, which can give life to mobility myths with abandon. Two of the most popular films of the last decade were *Beauty and the Beast* (1991) and *Aladdin* (1992), slightly updated and imaginatively produced versions of two classic children's tales of virtue and intelligence rewarded. Both of these Disney films appealed to a surprisingly large adult audience; *Beauty and the Beast* became the first animated film nominated for a best picture Academy Award. But rather than consider genres predictable in their allegiance to mobility plots, I will concentrate on the more open forms of Hollywood comedy and drama as a way of tracking mobility in '80s movies.

According to DeMott, during the last decade in popular entertainment the

> idea of ascent has been modified and the three newish story patterns have emerged. The first pattern stresses discovery; characters who think firm class lines exist discover they're mistaken. A second pattern involves upendings; characters theoretically on the social bottom prove their superiority to characters theoretically on the social top. The third pattern dramatizes renunciations: characters belonging to the middle who are momentarily tempted by lofty visions of social-cultural ascent reject the temptation, realizing there are no higher satisfactions than those they already possess. (59-60)

In the following pages I will discuss a group of '80s films in which these "newish" patterns are expressed, joined, and complicated and then consider whether the three patterns outlined by DeMott sufficiently account for all the mobility stories I noticed in my review of '80s movies.

### *Discovery*

DeMott offers *Working Girl* (1988) as his primary example of the discovery motif (90-91). Bright, industrious, and dedicated to self-improvement as she may be, Tess McGill (Melanie Griffith) is discouraged by her friends from aspiring to rise from secretarial status in a Manhattan brokerage firm. They consider Tess's dream of moving from the word-processing pool to middle-management impossible. But Tess proves them wrong. Through a combination of luck, imagination, and guile, Tess takes both managerial position and corporate colleague-lover (Harrison Ford) from her patrician, dishonest boss Katharine Parker (Sigourney Weaver).

*Working Girl* was explicitly, and successfully, marketed to a largely adult female audience as a feel-good comedy about the upward mobility of a spunky heroine whose dreams all come true. In an adroit reading of the film, Elizabeth Traube finds a potent mix of class and gender politics masked as an unambiguous moral upending. While the manifest cause for Katharine's expulsion from the firm is her duplicitous professional conduct—claiming Tess's idea for her own—Traube argues that the film participates in the demonization of the independent woman, whereby the dutiful girl from the working class diffuses an imagined threat of female power (exerted by an upper-class woman). To Traube, Tess's success is compromised in a number of respects and is achieved only through the intervention of a paternal protector (Philip Bosco, as Oren Trask). The closing images of the film—revealing Tess's office window as one among many identical offices—have been much debated by audiences and critics. Traube sees these images as revealing Tess as more contained than liberated (112; also see Palmer 270-71).

*Down and Out in Beverly Hills* (1986) seems, at first glance, to take as its (satiric) subject the great class disparities in 1980s America. Wealthy businessman Dave Whiteman (Richard Dreyfuss) saves homeless and dissolute Jerry Baskin (Nick Nolte) from drowning himself in the swimming pool at Whiteman's Beverly Hills mansion. Against the protests of his wife, Barbara (Bette Midler), Dave invites Jerry to stay in their cabana and initiates him into his world of affluence. We expect a comedy of incompatibility; instead, we see the family and their maid discover that Jerry is the friend-father-brother-lover-comrade they have all needed. Soon after Jerry's disruptive arrival, Barbara voices the need to "overcome [her] middle-class prejudices" toward Jerry, but once he's cleaned up there's nothing to overcome. Left ambiguous is whether Jerry, whose beloved dog he had named Kerouac, had chosen a derelict life on the road. Jerry knows Balinese massage, practices Tai Chi, and plays Debussy (and may or may not be disingenuous when he offhandedly describes a past as a concert pianist). His abiding self-assurance also indicates he is a cultural superior to the anxious Dave and Barbara whose roots seem to be lower-middle-class Brooklyn. The insecurity surrounding their own past mobility and that of their neighbor (played at his usual high pitch by Little Richard) provides fodder for a constant stream of jokes based on the gullibility and vulgarity of the nouveau riche, but the fluidity and the luxury of the Whitemans' lives are ultimately embraced.

A consideration of the derivation of the story clarifies the choices Paul Mazursky made in his adaptation. *Down and Out* is based on the 1925 French play *Boudu Sauve des Eaux* by Rene Fauchois, in which bourgeois culture triumphs. In 1932 Michel Simon, who had played Boudu, hired Jean Renoir to direct a film version of the play. They kept the title and Simon again played Boudu, but Simon and Renoir made drastic changes. The film—a critique of bourgeois attitudes and a celebration of anarchy—so antagonized French audiences that it closed in three days. *Boudu Saved from Drowning* is now considered a classic, but its ability to antagonize continues. At the film's American release in 1967, Renoir identified its subject as "loitering," which he audaciously described as "the highest achievement of civilization" (qtd. in Sesonke, 113). In *Boudu* Renoir explored the loitering that society forbids, a loitering based not on activity, but status. Renoir's film ends with Boudu, on the way to his own wedding with his protector's maid, accidentally falling into the river. As others scrabble for the shore, Boudu gladly floats downstream, shedding the trappings of bourgeois culture. According to Simon, this Boudu "cannot integrate into society and so he has to leave it" (qtd. in Sesonke, 112).

Mazursky's film follows Fauchois, not Renoir. *Down and Out* is—to use Sidney Gottlieb's apt phrase—a "fable of integration." The harmony between Jerry and Dave temporarily breaks down when Dave learns that his daughter, wife, and lover (the maid) have all been bedded by the obliging houseguest. In a rage, Dave tries, unsuccessfully of course, to drown Jerry in the same pool that he had first pulled him from. Jerry disclaims any wrongdoing, saying he only "gave folks what they wanted," but he returns to his rags and leaves the house. After several steps and one garbage can, Jerry changes his mind. The cappuccino culture is ultimately irresistible. The family, smiling smugly, forms a reception line at the alley gate to welcome Jerry back into the luxurious bosom of Beverly Hills life.

*White Palace* also announces itself as a film in which class will matter in a passionate love affair between a middle-aged waitress, Nora Baker (Susan Sarandon), and a young advertising executive, Max Baron (James Spader). The lovers recognize the incompatibility of their class backgrounds as a serious hindrance to their relationship from the outset; it is brought to a moment of dramatic confrontation when Max takes Nora to dinner at a friend's home. When the topic of conversation turns to work, the hypocrisy of the guests—especially the host's affluent father who describes himself as working class—is more than Nora can tolerate. Before leaving in disgust, she bluntly asserts "*I'm* working class!" a condition that everyone at the table had immediately recognized, but evaded.

The lovers quarrel; Nora leaves St. Louis. When Max finds her, Nora is still waitressing, but now in New York at a tonier restaurant than the White Palace hamburger joint where they had first met. Nora is at first indignant at being tracked down and confronted publicly in a way that disregards how much such a display threatens her job, but her resistance is overcome by Max's declaration of love and his insistence that he loves her for who she is. He proudly announces that he has rented a cheap apartment nearby and plans to return to his former and more noble profession of teaching, where his true heart lies. It certainly pays less, which seems essential in the film's scheme of things. To further make his point, Max not only embraces Nora, but, in an extravagant gesture that demonstrates his new membership in the ranks of the passionate proletariat, Max pushes the dishes on the nearest table to the floor, dips Nora onto the table, climbs on top of her, and pulls his expensive topcoat over them to feign privacy for their lovemaking. Nora laughs in delight; the restaurant patrons clap. We in the audience are encouraged to clap, too, and with more reason than the gawking diners. We know this pair has been drawn together partly by loneliness and loss—Nora's son and Max's wife both died before they met—partly by shared sexual desire, but also by a growing mutual respect. Why not clap and wish them well?

Although not mentioned as one of Mark Crispin Miller's examples, the conclusion of *White Palace* fits his description of "Hollywood's new happy ending [once reserved for musicals, but in the '80s common across genres]: a moment of euphoric melding, as the audience within the frame looks on and cheers" (235). The plot resolution of *White Palace* also adds another instance to support Miller's contention of a more fundamental '80s trend: the melding of two "opposites" into a final unity, a trend Miller sees as partially resulting from the pernicious influence of advertising.

The discovery of *White Palace* is not that class lines are only imagined, but that they can be managed by a couple sufficiently resourceful and sufficiently in love. In Max Baron we see a character exercising the upper-middle-class option of downward mobility. This option, as we are reminded amusingly in *Lost in America* (1985), is not necessarily a permanent choice. Whether exercised or not, the option of descent is a form of personal renunciation and substantially different than the "doom" of downward mobility that Charlie (Taylor Nichols) direfully predicts for his UHB (Urban Haute Bourgeoisie) peers in *Metropolitan* (1990). Nevertheless, a common assumption runs through these films: characters who choose downward mobility do not exchange class; they become "declassed."[1]

*Upendings*

As Traube reminds us, "success ideology has never been static"; versions register and respond to historically engendered cultural tensions, but "[i]in all its versions success ideology has appealed primarily to the middle classes."[2] But various versions of success stories also have considerable appeal to the lower classes; one is the "upending" mobility pattern in which characters "upend" their social betters. I see "upendings" as less than the "newish" pattern DeMott describes and more a continuation of traditional American populist comedy, albeit modified to the hopes and anxieties of the '80s.

To illustrate the pattern of upending DeMott turns to *The Breakfast Club* (1985), *Pretty in Pink* (1986), and *Some Kind of Wonderful* (1987), all three produced and two directed by John Hughes. This popular trio joined literally hundreds of Hollywood teen movies produced in the '80s for the most devoted movie-going audiences of the era: 12-to-19-year-olds. Like many of the genre, these three were all set in public high schools, a perfect site for interrogating the American social ideal of a classless society. In films seen, often repeatedly, by huge numbers of American teenagers, Hughes presents class differences and hostilities as initial obstacles for the charming and talented working class protagonists, but these differences are finally exposed as superficial and easily overcome. DeMott summarizes: "The message is unvarying: the surface of things may look structured, and some members of the society may talk themselves into believing that escape from fixed levels is impossible, but actually where we place ourselves is up to us; whenever we wish to, we can upend the folks on the hill" (66).

*Mystic Pizza* (1988) continues the Hughes tradition, moving the setting slightly beyond high school to a pizza parlor in Mystic, Connecticut. Like many other New England towns, Mystic is a perfect locale for the display of class differences for it harbors both a traditional fishing industry and a vacation resort where the wealthy "summer." The film affectionately focuses on the lives and loves of three young women who work at Mystic Pizza: the Araujo sisters, Daisy (Julia Roberts) and Kat (Annabeth Gish), and their friend Jojo Barboza (Lili Taylor).

*Mystic Pizza* begins and ends with Jojo's weddings. There's no doubt she loves Bill (Vincent Phillip D'Onofrio), a Portuguese American fisherman. She's comfortable with her social class; Jojo's dilemma is whether she is ready to give up her "independence." The Araujo sisters, in contrast, have higher aspirations; both become involved with men outside their social class and ethnic background. By the film's conclusion the two privileged Anglo men are revealed as moral inferiors.

Daisy is determined not to be slinging pizza all her life. She frankly considers her looks as her way out. Presented initially as promiscuous, foul-mouthed, and jealous of her younger sister, Daisy turns out to be a person of integrity. She begins a romance with a rich WASP after meeting him at a local working-class bar (where Charlie claims the relaxed, downward access of the privileged that DeMott calls the "Omni Syndrome"). The moment of revelation or upending comes after a humiliating dinner at Charlie's family's home when Daisy voices her realization that Charlie (who was thrown out of law school for cheating on an exam and seems to be using her as a way to insult his parents) is "not good enough" for her.

Kat, who has been admitted to Yale with a (partial) scholarship, has already adopted upper-class mannerisms of dress, speech, and interest that separate her from her flamboyant sister and appeal to a married architect (and Yale grad) who hires her to baby-sit with his daughter while his wife is in England. Kat is bright, but sexually innocent. The warnings of her more experienced older sister fall on deaf ears; Kat is hurt, but—the film suggests—not permanently damaged by an involvement that ends abruptly when the wife returns home unexpectedly. It seems to go entirely unnoticed by a mother who sees Kat as incapable of doing wrong. In contrast, Mrs. Araujo warns Daisy that she is misleading herself with what is just a dalliance to a rich boyfriend; she "worries about" Daisy's future. Daisy admits she does, too. But, typically, these warnings are placed in the film only to be dismissed. And, after all, Daisy is played by Julia Roberts, soon to be America's sweetheart. By the end, Daisy has put Charlie in his place, sufficiently humbled into dishing ice cream in the kitchen at Jojo's wedding. But how long can we reasonably expect him to stay there?

The moral inferiority of the upper classes is presumed and enacted in *Scent of a Woman* (1992). The central story of the film is the relationship between an embittered blind retired army officer (Lt. Colonel Frank Slade/Al Pacino) and the boy (Charlie Simms/Chris O'Donnell) hired as a companion. An awkward, contracted relationship between the two grows into genuine affection. Charlie becomes the son Frank needs to make his life worth leading; Frank becomes the father Charlie has lacked. The old soldier teaches the boy many things—among them, how to dance the tango and drive a Ferrari, while enjoying a lavish trip to New York financed by Frank's disability checks—but mostly Frank teaches Charlie how to upend the uppers.

Charlie is a scholarship student at a prestigious prep school, distanced from the wealthy students not only by class but by character. Before he leaves for his Thanksgiving holiday job of assisting Frank, Charlie observes a prank set up to humiliate the headmaster. As a way of pressuring disclosure of the boys' identities, the headmaster offers Charlie the bribe of a scholarship slot to Harvard. Although Frank is contemptuous of the boarding school and its false values, he does not want Charlie dismissed. His surprise intervention in a highly improbable public hearing in the school auditorium serves as the climax of the film. When Charlie is threatened with dismissal for not revealing the pranksters' names, Frank takes the stage and delivers a rousing sermon on loyalty and courage as American virtues that must go rewarded. It's the kind of speech that, in the world of American movies, can make preppies cheer and school authorities change their mind. And win an Oscar for the actor who delivers it.

Few films of the '80s matched the aggressive upending of *Nine to Five* (1980), a revenge fantasy that takes as its premise class and gender inequities in the American workplace. The heroines are three pink-collar workers: an office supervisor, Violet Newstead (Lily Tomlin), an executive secretary, Dora Lee Rhodes (Dolly Parton), and the new gal in the secretarial pool, Judy Bernly (Jane Fonda). They unite in their hatred of an unfair and stupid boss, Franklin Hart, Jr. (Dabney Coleman). By film's end, the three women have managed to torture and humiliate him, introduce more efficient and humane work methods (for which Hart is "rewarded" and sent to Brazil), and earn themselves either deserved promotions (Violet) or a way out of the office (country singing for Dora Lee; marriage to a Xerox rep for Judy).

The casting is a marketing dream, for Tomlin, Parton, and Fonda are all popular performers with large, disparate constituencies. Although clearly a farce (and often a clumsy one), *Nine to Five* tapped a real rage in many women who crowded into mall theaters and responded to the upendings of *Nine to Five* with an uncommonly boisterous delight.

### *Renunciations*

DeMott provides no film examples of renunciations, using instead illustrations from other media to demonstrate the patterns he sees as occurring when characters belonging to the middle are momentarily tempted by visions of social-cultural ascent, but finally reject the temptations. It would seem that interclass love stories are potential sites of renunciation. We see such stories appearing in various '80s genres.

In the thriller *Someone to Watch Over Me* (1987) Tom Berenger plays Mike Keegan, a lower-middle-class policeman assigned to protect a wealthy murder witness (Mimi Rogers). (This clumsy plot device speaks to the difficulty for screenwriters of imagining situations in which people of different classes socialize.) Although Mike becomes involved in an affair with the socialite, he clearly belongs with his wife (Lorraine Bracco), a feisty, attractive ex-cop. Ultimately he realizes that fact.

In the romantic comedy *Crossing Delancey* (1988), Izzy Grossman (Amy Irving) is momentarily attracted to an urbane writer Anton Maes (Jeroen Krabbe) who frequents the Upper East Side bookshop where she works. Izzy eventually recognizes Anton's self-absorption and manipulation of her admiration and learns to appreciate the honest affection of Sam Posner (Peter Riegert), an unassuming "pickle salesman" from the Lower East Side. *Crossing Delancey* merges ethnic and class identities and then adds the twist that social status and income are not necessarily synonymous (for Sam runs a family business).

These renunciations do not leave the protagonist *alone*, but united or reunited with a partner who is a fitting class match. Whether such renunciations/happy endings support or challenge a notion of classlessness—as DeMott contends—is debatable, for such films confirm difference, while discrediting the educated and moneyed classes and rejecting the option of ascent. There is a substantial difference between implying there is no class system and not desiring to join a higher class. I offer two examples to demonstrate some of the contradictions that occur around the pattern of renunciation.

*Breaking Away* (1979), released at the cusp of the decade, offers a gentle contrast to many strident '80s films of social ascent. This low-key comedy presents the struggles of four young friends during the year after their high school graduation. They find themselves outsiders in their own hometown of Bloomington, Indiana. Dave (Dennis Christopher) and his three townie buddies are routinely insulted by the university students who run the town and have no use for "the cutters," a label that more accurately once described the boys' fathers and grandfathers who carved out the limestone in nearby quarries to erect the buildings of Indiana University.

Much of the delight of this comedy comes from watching Dave work out some sense of himself. His obsession with cycling turns into a devotion for all things Italian, to the bewilderment and irritation of his father (played with a deft comic touch by Paul Dooley). Presenting himself as an Italian exchange student, Dave courts an IU coed (who would never date a townie). His Italian connection is shattered when visiting Italian cyclists, heretofore his heroes, cheat him on the race track.

In their various ways, Dave and his friends seem to have come to a place of self-acceptance. Proudly labeling themselves "cutters," they become local heroes, however momentarily, when they defeat the Greeks in a climatic "Little 500" bicycle race in the university stadium. But the film does not end with this shared triumph. There is a short coda: Dave is now a student at the university. He meets a pretty exchange student from France. When Dave's father (now riding a bicycle) passes them, the greeting is "Bonjour, Papa!"

Does this coda make *Breaking Away* more or less honest in its treatment of class in America? (The film's director is British. Its writer, Steve Tesich, was born in Yugoslavia, came to the United States at 13, and later attended IU.) In a lighthearted film unusual in its unsentimental affection for working-class characters and in its sensitivity to their diminished life chances, would it have been more honest for Dave, clearly the brightest and most intellectually curious of the four boys, *not* to eventually take advantage of a great public university in his hometown? When I first saw *Breaking Away* in 1979 I thought the film had abandoned its class loyalties in that coda; in 1995 I have changed my mind and admire the earned optimism of a film that presents modest mobility without class renunciation. In a beautifully written and acted scene, Dave and his father walk on the IU campus. The father, now a used car salesman, recalls his experience as a "cutter" working on the university campus: "When I was finished, the damnedest thing happened. It was like the buildings were too good for us. Nobody told us that. We just felt uncomfortable, that's all." He tells his son "You are not a cutter" and urges him to go to college.

*Wall Street* (1987) would seem the most assertive example of mobility renunciation of the decade. Oliver Stone's moralistic version of the success myth teems with righteous indignation as it follows the rise and fall of Bud Fox (Charlie Sheen), an ambitious young stockbroker. Under the influence of a ruthless corporate raider, Gordon Gekko (Michael Douglas), Fox becomes a successful entrepreneur and, finally, through Gekko's betrayal, an indicted felon.

What seems at first a schematic class allegory between the good, honest (biological) father Carl Fox (Martin Sheen), an airplane mechanics union rep, and the scheming (symbolic) bad father Gekko turns out to be more complicated. Gekko is a self-made man, with a background much like Bud's; Lou Mannheim (Hal Holbrook) represents another kind of corporate father. Mannheim is a decent man of the old school whose sense of morality and class background separate him from Gekko. Michael Sprinker offers an interesting renunciation analysis of *Wall Street:* "At work here is Stone's conviction that the world of contemporary high finance and securities trading has been contaminated by the likes of Gekko, whose real sin is to have gotten beyond himself. One ought to stay in the class one is born to, the film asserts, and the world will be just fine" (366-67).

Sprinker argues that *Wall Street* is far from a radical critique. It renounces only a certain brand of corporate greed (and the aspirations to mobility that would lead one toward that greed) and presumes a greed-is-good mentality is atypical in the corporate world. *Wall Street* is dedicated to Lewis Stone, the director's deceased father, a stockbroker and economics writer. Through the character of Mannheim (and, less so, Sir Larry Wildman [Terence Stamp]), Stone implies that there are both destructive and productive styles of capitalism. The decent work to which Carl Fox refers in the last of many sermons in this film would seem to include work on the Street.

In the above examples I have explored how three story patterns of ascent—discovery, upendings, and renunciations—are displayed and complicated in some '80s films. I generally agree with DeMott that these patterns combine to dismiss the importance of class. Are there any '80s films of social ascent that don't fit these patterns? I offer the following examples as illustration of variance.

*Mobility and the Military*

No discussion of class would be complete without some attention to how '80s films presented the military, where class is rigidly codified. For my example, I offer an extremely popular, decidedly pro-military drama of ascent: *An Officer and a Gentleman* (1982). The film prologue introduces a drunken enlisted man who has presented his son with a prostitute as a college graduation present. When the son, Zach Mayo (Richard Gere) tells his father he's going to officer training school, the father laughs at his pretensions and tells him that "officers are not like you and me." The film then proceeds to prove the father wrong—in his doubt about his son's ability and determination to become an aviator—but also right: officers are different. They are better. What Zach needs more than instruction in aerodynamics or karate is a moral education. He needs to learn to be honest and to care for others. He does, becoming a new man: an officer and gentleman. A meritocracy operates here, but the upper class is not upended. The sufficiently worthy from the heretofore lower class are allowed to join. The film displays the same Calvinistic attitude, in a slightly different version, with the female characters.

Before their first leave, the trainees are warned by the all-knowing D.I. Foley (of course and ironically an enlisted man himself) about the young women who work in a nearby paper-mill and share a common desire to "marry an a-vi-a-tor." Predictably, Zach and his friend Sid meet two mill workers (at a dance hosted by the commanding officer and his wife, complete with a reception line for the women about whom they have just been warned). Quickly the film's moral compass begins pointing. One of these young women is morally superior to the other. The better one will deserve to become an officer's wife and share his status; the other one will not. Paula Pokrifki (Debra Winger) tells Zach she isn't looking for a husband, she just wants to "improve herself." In the moral universe of this film, that is not a joke. In an '80s version of a '50s attitude, the film offers sex on the first date, but expects true love. Paula's friend Lynnette accepts the film's dream of officer as object of desire but she is repudiated for wanting to be an officer's wife so badly that she would fake a pregnancy and then refuse to marry Sid when he dropped out of officers' training. Sid's suicide is presented as a consequence of her dishonesty. Paula's lie is a minor one that the film not only excuses but encourages: she had loved Zach "since she met him." Even though Paula is the illegitimate daughter of an officer candidate who abandoned her 17-year-old mother a generation before, she supposedly harbors no resentment toward or desire for officers in general, although she, like Lynnette, has been out with previous trainees.

The ending is old-fashioned Hollywood. When Zach strides into the paper-mill after his graduation, literally sweeps Paula off her feet, and carries her off, all the women on the factory floor, including her mother, cheer. Lynnette yells, "Way to go, Paula!" as the couple leave the factory, she wearing his officer's hat, to the strains of "Up Where We Belong." What are the women in the film (and, by implication, the film audience) applauding? True love? Or a reactionary female version of "be all you can be"?

*Mobility and Race*

Louis Malle, a French filmmaker who moved between United States- and European-based projects, made the serious and widespread tensions between working-class Americans and recent immigrants the subject of *Alamo Bay* (1985). Set in the fictitious town of Fort Alamo, the screenplay by Alice Arlen deals with the real problems of how Texas native shrimpers have reacted to the entrepreneurial zeal of Vietnamese immigrants. Arlen and Malle present three potential protagonists: Dinh (Ho Nguyen), an eager Vietnamese whose arrival in Fort Alamo begins the film; Shang (Ed Harris) a surly native shrimper and Vietnam vet, who lives in a trailer with his (usually crying) children and a wife "who got herself knocked up"; and Glory (played with great gusto by Amy Madigan), Shang's former (and for a short time current) lover. Glory has returned from the big city to help her ailing father (Donald Moffat) who runs a fish-processing factory that employs Vietnamese (possibly illegally).

As *Alamo Bay* progresses, the economic and moral complexities of the situation are flattened. Shang's legitimate economic terror of losing the boat ("American Dream Girl") necessary for his independence and livelihood is trivialized, with the film's attention riveted on his involvement with the Ku Klux Klan. By focusing on Shang's reprehensible racism and turning him and his buddies, also "Nam Vets of Texas," into yet another rabid band of hostile rednecks, the film squanders the opportunity to explore an important class issue. In contrast to the demonized native shrimpers, Dinh and the other Asians are treated with a respect that is distancing and ultimately patronizing. With one male too evil for our respect and the other too marginal, *Alamo Bay* becomes Glory's story. By the film's conclusion, she is forced to make a terrible and violent choice between Dinh and Shang. (This choice is not sexual, but moral; despite the fact that Dinh names his boat "Glory" and possesses the physical courage required of a traditional hero, Shang's jealousy is presented as paranoia.) When Glory, defending Dinh, shoots Shang, what might have been a tragic ending becomes merely melodramatic.

The conflation of race and class as historical reality and public perception is a complication that commercial filmmakers are more likely to exploit or ignore than explore. Even fringe films, such as *Mississippi Masala* (1991), often abandon the complications they introduce in a desire to please. *Mississippi Masala* presents rarely seen international political concerns—the expulsion of nonblack Africans from Uganda—along with an uncommon twist on a traditional love story, by featuring the romance between an Asian American woman (Sarita Choudhury) and an African American man (Denzel Washington). At a wedding reception early in the film, a wealthy Indian matron, in describing the chances of the dark-skinned Mina for a "good marriage," bluntly acknowledges race and class as obstacles: "one can be dark or one can be poor, but one can't be dark *and* poor." Although Mina's father was an attorney in Uganda, he seems unemployed in Mississippi, supported by his wife's store-clerking and Mina's cleaning and reception duties at a motel owned by another Indian family. The superficial alliance of people of color evaporates when men in the Indian community discover the affair between Mina and Demetrius. Their intervention results in the ruin of his carpet cleaning business. But rather than dwell on the depressing reality of how easily one can lose hard-earned entry into self-employment and self-reliance, the film ends with the two lovers striking out on their own, unencumbered by the race and class barriers the film has so well defined.

Since the mid-'80s Spike Lee has written, produced, and directed a series of films that have explored the intricacies of race and class with a bluntness and popularity unparalleled in American film.[3] His second feature, *School Daze*, confronts class divisions among African Americans. Lee presents economic, cultural, and political divisions among students at an all-black college as broadly comic and deeply serious. The "Wannabes" are light-skinned, politically conservative Greeks, all potential Buppies. Led by Dap Dunlap (Larry Fishburne) the "Jigaboos" are more concerned about pressuring the college administration to divest its stocks in South Africa than partying. By the film's (abrupt and largely unearned) resolution, Dap seems to have convinced everyone, including his nemesis, the Gamma pledge trainer (Giancarlo Esposito), to "Wake up." Filled with undergraduate humor and clearly aimed at a youth audience, *School Daze* also has moments of dramatic power. One such moment comes when Dap and his friends, while eating at a local Kentucky Fried Chicken restaurant, are taunted by a group of locals. A confrontation ensues in the parking lot: "You come to this town year after year and take over. We was born here, gonna be here, and die here and can't find jobs because of you." Dap replies, "Look, man, you've got a legitimate beef, but it ain't with us." Not mollified, the group's leader taunts, "College don't mean shit. You all are niggers and you're gonna be niggers forever, just like us." Dap responds, "You're NOT niggers."

Dap's heart-felt racial pride and his skill at street argument cool the situation and the Mission students leave without a fight. But the divisions of class are not so easily dispelled. Driving back to the campus, Dap's friends express opposing views of the young men they've just encountered: "You work or you starve; they've got to try" and (the line given the last word on the topic) "maybe they've tried [to better themselves] and have just given up."

*Boyz N the Hood* grows out of the parking lot scene from *School Daze*, in a number of senses, including the casting of Larry Fishburne, a commanding screen presence, to continue and deepen his position of "role model." In *Boyz N the Hood* Fishburne plays Furious Styles, the father of Tre (Cuba Gooding, Jr.), whose life is contrasted to those of his two friends, Doughboy (Ice Cube), and his half-brother Ricky (Morris Chestnut). *Boyz*, set in South Central Los Angeles, rejects two common ways out of the 'hood—the military and police work—but not a third: sports. Furious is a Vietnam vet who tells his son that "the black man's got no place in the army"; an African American policeman is presented as a race traitor. College is seen as a generalized good and a necessity for upward mobility. Ricky's football scholarship to USC is his way up, until a capricious shooting ends the life of the young athlete.

*Boyz N the Hood* embraces two quite different political attitudes and that duality may in part account for its great success. It is a politically conservative film in promoting the necessity of a stable home life, positive adult male guidance, education, and self-discipline for the upward class mobility that is clearly endorsed. That conservatism is joined by the angry recognition that many young African Americans live in neighborhoods where, no matter who much they work to gain some mythic American dream, they are in constant mortal danger.

Both of these attitudes—of the possibility of legitimate and respected mobility and the reality of its serious and unjust hindrances—are summarized in the brief epilogue with which John Singleton ends his film. Encouraging the heightened realism to which all such epilogues aspire, a printed text announces that Doughboy (whose loyalty to his brother resulted in deadly retaliation) was killed two weeks after his brother and that Tre went to Morehouse, his girlfriend to Spellman, in the fall.

*Impostors and Mobility*

As final examples of mobility, I offer a pair of comedies of deception: *Trading Places* (1983) and *Six Degrees of Separation* (1993). Eddie Murphy has built a successful movie career playing the clever trickster, a traditional figure in African American folklore and also a familiar figure in many comic traditions that recognize social inequities and feature various forms of upending. In *Trading Places* Murphy plays Billy Ray Valentine, an uneducated street hustler who "trades places" with Louis Winthrope III (Dan Aykroyd), a well-born presumably (but not demonstrably) well-educated executive in a commodities investment firm run by the Duke brothers (Ralph Bellamy and Don Ameche). The wealthy, miserly Dukes have set up this exchange of lives, unbeknownst to Valentine and Winthrope, to settle a dollar bet they've made on the relative importance of heredity and environment in determining life success.

The class (and race) politics of *Trading Places* are, like those of many popular films, convoluted. (That they often go undiscussed is perhaps due to that convolution but also to how overly earnest many feel in holding farce up to social scrutiny.) Although the centrality of environment wins the bet (when Winthrope, dressed as Santa Claus, is caught stealing food from a buffet table) and the "nature" brother (Ameche) seems one significant degree more evil than the "nurture" brother (Bellamy), the pleasures of capital are never questioned. When Valentine and Winthrope realize the mischief that has disrupted their lives, they plot revenge: "The best way to hurt rich people is to turn them into poor people." (The filmmakers must find some way to make Valentine discontent with the trade. He overhears Mortimer Duke [Ameche] saying to his brother, "Do you really believe I would have a nigger run our family business?") The unlikely pair, joined by mutual hatred of the Dukes, figure out a way to get justice by ruining the Dukes financially and making a nice profit for themselves. *Trading Places*, which plays "Get a Job" over its final credits, was a smash success.

Despite the casting of a popular young rapper and television star (Will Smith) in a leading role, *Six Degrees of Separation* does not have the mass appeal of *Trading Places*. Deftly directed by Australian Fred Schepisi, *Six Degrees* mainly attracts the sophisticated culture vultures it mocks. John Guare's screenplay of *Six Degrees* is based on his 1990 prize-winning play, which was inspired by an actual situation in which a young con man posed as Sidney Poitier's son and thus ingratiated himself into the lives of wealthy New Yorkers. Guare builds a witty and haunting drama out of that situation, as he explores the role of authenticity in contemporary life.

*Six Degrees*, as befits a drama of revelation, is intricately structured. It begins "mid-drama" and moves backwards and forwards in time to reveal various deceptions of Paul "Poitier-Kittredge" and the consequences of those deceptions on various lives, especially those of Flan and Ouisa Kittredge. The Kittredges (played with great subtlety by Donald Sutherland and Stockard Channing) make million-dollar art deals out of their luxurious Upper East Side apartment, but they actually live "hand to mouth on a much higher plateau" than the impostor who visits them. The young sage who recognizes the economic and social vulnerability of the parents of his prep school friends becomes Paul's coach and instructs him on how to enter the homes he plans to invade as a class equal.[4] Later in the film we see Paul repeating some of the same instructions of class ascent to a struggling young couple who befriend him and suffer tragic consequences.

Paul's real background is never revealed in the film. One assumes he is lower class because he is a street hustler, hanging out in a doorway when "introduced" (in a flashback); because he needs three months of instruction on upper middle-class manners and mores (as if that would be enough); and, probably, because he is black. A central joke and sorrow of the film is the fascination Paul's supposed relation to Sidney Poitier (a seminal figure of boundary crossing or race betrayal) holds for the self-styled liberals he cons. To all but Ouisa, Paul's scams become just a party anecdote. Ouisa's experience of genuine affection for Paul has made her realize the superficiality of her life. The film's conclusion suddenly drops its former cynicism and celebrates Ouisa's ability to feel authentically. Only she—to use the words of Paul's bogus thesis—has the imagination to make self-examination possible. She's not able to intercede successfully on Paul's behalf with the police, but the fact that she is concerned about him at all is presented as a moral breakthrough which is a sad reminder of the state of race and class relations in contemporary America.

### *Conclusion*

In the book that provoked this chapter, Benjamin DeMott describes a readiness throughout American society to at once embrace and reject class talk. I also found that dynamic operating in many popular films, with a misleading double talk the result. DeMott sees "the arts of exorcism and erasure practiced in the media [as shaping] four versions of class: as a fantasy from which the sensible and right-minded awake in good time; as a dress-up game enabling us to 'get out of ourselves'—turn omni, meet new people, have fun; as an unreliable, excessively subjective indicator, which, thanks to Science and Progress, need no longer be consulted; as a veil shrouding the real—i.e., moral/intellectual—differences in our midst" (124).

My examination of dozens of '80s films leads me to believe that the exorcism and erasures are powerful, but not complete. Characters in many Hollywood narratives seem to think of themselves and others as belonging to social classes. The prevailing ideology of '80s films is not so much an ideology of classlessness as an ideology of class fluidity, of class mobility, of meritocracy. But many popular films have complicated politics and project mixed messages regarding class.

During the Reagan-Bush years, at a time of growing social inequity, many Hollywood films dismissed the barriers of class and presented an America of diminishing degrees of class separation. Successful mobility was a recurrent theme. Why was this so? Some of the reasons are enduring. Hollywood narrative—with its emphasis on stars and individual action with its presumed dramatic necessity for conflict and change, with its obligation of a happy ending—deeply encourages a dominant ideology of mobility and meritocracy. Each of these abiding characteristics was intensified in the production and marketing of movies during the Reagan-Bush era, a period in which much American energy was committed to acquisition and personal material advancement. The public rhetoric produced during the Reagan-Bush administrations encouraged Americans to see success and failure in individual terms. Reagan was not only a president who argued from anecdote, but his own personal mobility story hovered over Hollywood dreams of the decade.

Many Hollywood films of the '80s acknowledged that social classes form the link between economic facts and social facts, but not surprisingly, these corporate entertainments rarely presented (let alone endorsed) class conflict. Conflict was instead routinely dramatized as the personal struggle of individuals; the message of most '80s movies, especially the comedies, was that class boundaries are hurdles that can be overcome by the best and brightest. The most common displays of class differences, tellingly, were in '80s comedies, which often featured outrageous upendings. Renunciations were far less common and appeared in less-popular films.

For a full understanding of how class mobility and immobility operate in film and beyond, one would need to recognize the nuances of these film texts and also go beyond the films to investigate the complexities of their construction and use. As Richard Johnson has forcefully argued, to understand popular culture one must move beyond text-bound analysis and study the circuit of production, circulation, and consumption of cultural forms.

What ideologies of class might shape the circuit of production, circulation, and consumption of popular movies? How committed to mobility myths is the producing community for these films? How much are class differences considered in developing marketing strategies for movies? What role do middle-class critics and academics play in perpetuating an ideology of meritocracy? And, most importantly, what do audiences of different social classes make of these mobility tales? Are readings class bound (as Andrea Press and Elizabeth Cole suggest)? Stuart Hall and other cultural theorists have given us a vocabulary with which to analyze differences in readings of cultural products, but what makes us initially and finally *care* about the class discourse in movies is a concern for the social world those movies reflect and enter.

## Notes

I thank Jeff Klenotic for sparking an interest that led to this essay, Lisa Henderson for her sympathetic reading of it, and scores of U-Mass students for reminding me that class matters.

1. See Stanley Aronowitz for a discussion of "declassed" status and working class portrayals in *Barfly*, *Someone to Watch Over Me*, *Dirty Dancing* and *Fame*. Aronowitz argues that the classes are "gendered" in cinematic representations and that successful "interclass sexual relations are possible only when the woman displays masculinity, which remains the privileged class position" (149).

2. Traube, 71. See Traube chapter 3, "Secrets of Success in Postmodern Society," 67-96, for broadly contextualized and deftly written analyses of four '80s mobility tales: *All the Right Moves*, *Ferris Bueller's Day Off*, *Nothing in Common* and *The Secret of My Success*. *Ferris Bueller* adopts a more cynical tone toward "upending" than the John Hughes films DeMott mentions. For further discussion of '80s mobility patterns, see Ward, and Palmer chapter 8, "The Yuppie Texts," 280-307.

3. The seminal book on the topic of race and class is *The Declining Significance of Race* in which William Julius Wilson argues that "[i]n the

modern industrial period fundamental economic and political changes have made economic class position more important than race in determining black chances for occupational mobility" (23). Based on focus group interviews with viewers of *The Cosby Show* Sut Jhally and Justin Lewis claim that "Americans are unable to think clearly about race because they cannot think clearly about class" (70). They found that focus group participants lacked a class discourse and, consequently, used racial descriptors to make class distinctions (i.e., the terms "white" and "middle-class" were used as synonyms).

4. The "instruction scene," often played broadly, is a convention in comedies of ascent, such as *Pretty Woman* and *Trading Places*. No instruction seems necessary for downward mobility, which makes sense if a person who chooses to descend (except as a disguise) is "declassed." *Street Smart* confirms this rule.

## Works Cited


Aronowitz, Stanley. "Working Class Culture in the Electronic Age." *Cultural Politics in Contemporary America*. Ed. Ian Angus and Sut Jhally. New York: Routledge, 1989. 135-50.

Cassidy, John. "Who Killed the Middle Class?" *New Yorker* 16 Oct. 1995: 113-24.

DeMott, Benjamin. *The Imperial Middle: Why Americans Can't Think Straight about Class*. New York: Morrow, 1990.

——. "In Hollywood, Class Doesn't Put Up Much of a Struggle." *New York Times* 20 Jan. 1991: H 1, 22.

Ehrenreich, Barbara. *Fear of Falling: The Inner Life of the Middle Class*. New York: Pantheon, 1989.

Eisler, Benita. *Class Act*. New York: Watts, 1983.

Fussell, Paul. *Class: A Guide Through the American Status System*. New York: Summit, 1983.

Gilbert, Dennis, and Joseph A. Kahl. *The American Class Structure: A New Synthesis*. 4th ed. Belmont, CA: Wadsworth, 1993.

Hall, Stuart. "Encoding/Decoding." *Culture, Media, Language*. Ed. Stuart Hall, et al. London: Hutchinson, 1974.

Jhally, Sut, and Justin Lewis. *Enlightened Racism:* The Cosby Show, *Audiences, and the Myth of the American Dream*. Boulder: Westview, 1992.

Johnson, Richard. "What Is Cultural Studies Anyway?" *Social Text* 16 (1986-87): 38-80.

Lapham, Lewis H. *Money and Class in America: Notes and Observations on Our Civil Religion*. New York: Weidenfeld & Nicolson, 1988.

Miller, Mark Crispin. "End of Story." *Seeing Through Movies*. Ed. Mark Crispin Miller. New York: Pantheon, 1990. 186-246.

Palmer, William J. *The Films of the Eighties: A Social History*. Carbondale: Southern Illinois UP, 1993.

Press, Andrea, and Elizabeth Cole. "Women Like Us; Working-Class Women Respond to Television Representations of Abortion." *Viewing, Reading, Listening: Audience and Cultural Reception*. Ed. Jon Cruz and Justin Lewis. Boulder: Westview, 1994. 55-80.

Sesonske, Alexander. *Jean Renoir: The French Films 1924-1939*. Cambridge: Harvard UP, 1980.

Shadoian, Jack. *Dreams and Deadends: The American Gangster/Crime Film*. Cambridge: MIT, 1977.

Sprinker, Michael. "Review of *Wall Street*." *Magill's Cinema Annual 1988*. 364-67.

Strauss, Anselm L. *The Contexts of Social Mobility: Ideology and Theory*. Chicago: Aldine, 1971.

Traube, Elizabeth G. *Dreaming Identities: Class, Gender, and Generation in 1980s Movies*. Boulder: Westview, 1992.

Turner, Graeme. *Film As a Social Practice*. London: Routledge, 1988.

Ward, Carol. "The Hollywood Yuppie: 1980-88." *Beyond the Stars, Volume 1*. Ed. Paul Loukides and Linda K. Fuller. Bowling Green: Bowling Green State University Popular Press, 1990. 97-109.

Will, George. "A Case for Dukakis." *Washington Post* 3 Nov. 1988: A 27.

Wilson, William Julius. *The Declining Significance of Race*. 2nd ed. Chicago: U of Chicago P, 1980.

## Filmography

| Year | Film | Director |
|---|---|---|
| 1979 | *Breaking Away* | Peter Yates |
| 1980 | *Atlantic City* | Louis Malle |
| 1980 | *9 to 5* | Collin Higgins |
| 1982 | *Fast Times at Ridgemont High* | Amy Heckerling |
| 1982 | *An Officer and a Gentleman* | Taylor Hackford |
| 1983 | *All the Right Moves* | Michael Chapman |
| 1983 | *Flashdance* | Adrian Lyne |
| 1983 | *Mr. Mom* | Stan Dragoti |
| 1983 | *Risky Business* | Paul Brickman |
| 1983 | *Scarface* | Brian DePalma |
| 1983 | *Trading Places* | John Landis |
| 1984 | *Beverly Hills Cop* | Martin Brest |

| | | |
|---|---|---|
| 1984 | *The Last Starfighter* | Nick Castle |
| 1985 | *Alamo Bay* | Louis Malle |
| 1985 | *The Breakfast Club* | John Hughes |
| 1985 | *Brewster's Millions* | Peter Yates |
| 1986 | *The Color of Money* | Martin Scorcese |
| 1986 | *Down and Out in Beverly Hills* | Paul Mazursky |
| 1986 | *Lost in America* | Albert Brooks |
| 1986 | *Nothing in Common* | Garry Marshall |
| 1986 | *Pretty in Pink* | Howard Deutch |
| 1987 | *Barfly* | Barbet Schroeder |
| 1987 | *Maid to Order* | Amy Jones |
| 1987 | *No Man's Land* | Peter Werner |
| 1987 | *Outrageous Fortune* | Arthur Hiller |
| 1987 | *The Secret of My Success* | Herbert Ross |
| 1987 | *Some Kind of Wonderful* | John Hughes |
| 1987 | *Someone to Watch Over Me* | Ridley Scott |
| 1987 | *Street Smart* | Jerry Schatzberg |
| 1987 | *Wall Street* | Oliver Stone |
| 1988 | *Big Business* | Jim Abrahams |
| 1988 | *Crossing Delancey* | Joan Micklin Silver |
| 1988 | *Cocktail* | John Sayles |
| 1988 | *Mystic Pizza* | Donald Petrie |
| 1988 | *School Daze* | Spike Lee |
| 1988 | *Stand and Deliver* | Ramon Menendez |
| 1988 | *Working Girl* | Mike Nichols |
| 1989 | *Pretty Woman* | Gary Marshall |
| 1989 | *Scenes of the Class Struggle in Beverly Hills* | Paul Bartel |
| 1989 | *Slaves of New York* | James Ivory |
| 1990 | *Bonfire of the Vanities* | Brian DePalma |
| 1990 | *Metropolitan* | Whit Stillman |
| 1990 | *Stanley and Iris* | Martin Ritt |
| 1990 | *Stella* | John Erman |
| 1990 | *White Palace* | Luis Mandoki |
| 1991 | *Boyz N the Hood* | John Singleton |
| 1991 | *City of Hope* | John Sayles |
| 1991 | *Dying Young* | Joel Schumacher |
| 1991 | *Gas Food Lodging* | Allison Anders |
| 1991 | *Mississippi Masala* | Mira Nair |
| 1992 | *Scent of a Woman* | Martin Brest |
| 1993 | *Six Degrees of Separation* | Fred Schepisi |

# Down and Out in Tinseltown: Hollywood Presents the Dispossessed

**William Brigham**

I have headaches almost everyday. I feel like I was born with them.
—10-year-old homeless girl (Stanford Center 19)

Let's go get a cup of cappuccino.
—No-longer-homeless protagonist
in *Down and Out in Beverly Hills*

In Gregory LaCava's *My Man Godfrey* (1936), a disillusioned millionaire eschews his life of luxury and joins the "real people" living in plywood and aluminum shanties along New York's East River. Two generations later, in *Life Stinks* (1991), Mel Brooks's millionaire protagonist wagers that he can survive on guts and instinct among a similar population on Los Angeles's skid row—the stakes being possession of a large chunk of prime Los Angeles real estate. In 55 years, the story line changed enough to reflect the shift in financial nexus from one coast to another, but remained constant enough to illustrate the seemingly unending plight of what Henry Miller called "the dispossessed in America." Even considering the differences in the solvency of the American economy during the Great Depression and what now precipitates the dilemma faced by millions of homeless people, and millions of housed but poor families, it is still clear that Hollywood is only superficially addressing (or not addressing at all) the elemental yet important causes of homelessness in America today: poverty, unemployment, and lack of adequate and affordable housing.

A content analysis of over three dozen films produced between 1934 and 1994 provides adequate illustration of the ideological distortions and simplifications employed by American filmmakers in their depictions of social class and social opportunity. Specifically, a review of the most recent films (1984-94) affords a set of images of homeless persons which, in most cases, is widely out of synch with just who "those people" actually are today. There is, however, a growing number of independent or limited release films that provide a more realistic and gritty picture of homelessness. First, a brief discussion of the early history of social problem films, and the sociocultural forces that virtually eliminated them, will serve as background to contemporary depictions of poverty and homelessness.

*The Loud Voice of the Silent Era*

Motion pictures dealt with matters of social reform almost from their inception, due primarily to the sociocultural climate of that day: "The movies were born into the era of reform which (roughly) opened with the inauguration of President Theodore Roosevelt in 1901 and closed with the entry of the United States into the First World War in 1917" (Brownlow *xvi*). Between 1911 and 1915, most "social" films (Brownlow) were made, coinciding with the advent of the feature film and the demise of the one-minute nickelodeon shows. Early directors were able to effectively portray the subjects of their reformist films through a new and ultimately very important element of filmmaking: "In the earliest days of projection . . . showmen stumbled upon the art of editing for social comment. Following a film of the fashionable Easter Parade on Fifth Avenue with one on the squalid streets of the Lower East Side, they made, without realizing it, the most powerful impact on their audience" (Brownlow 276). These films, made with considerable reformist zeal,[1] were produced—to a great extent—by recent émigrés to America, and for a similar audience. By 1910, each week 26 million people—primarily working class—were viewing films in nickelodeons, a practice considered by some as destructive to the moral fabric of society. And just as with temperance crusades (Gusfield), efforts to eliminate nickelodeons and their reformist films, were middle-class campaigns aimed at the working class and their newest addiction, "nickel-madness" (Brownlow *xviii*).

But social reform plots survived the nickelodeons, and feature films dealt with topics such as child labor (*The Blood of the Children)*, tuberculosis (*The Awakening of John Bond*), inequality in the administration of justice (*The Kleptomaniac*), child abuse/deprivation (*Kindling*), food speculation (*The Public Be Damned*), capital vs. labor (*The Struggle*), and loan sharking (*The Usurer's Grip*). Films with explicit Socialist agendas (*Why?*), although very limited in number, were also produced.[2] So many social films were made during this era "that a reviewer talked of a plot being 'typically sociological'"(Brownlow *xix*). But as movie theaters became larger and more hospitable venues, movie audiences broadened and a more middle-class audience began to predominate. This change in the consumers of film, as well as a much different social climate after World War I, led to considerable diminution in the social content of films: "As the poor became less important as the mainstay of the movie . . . the ideals and tribulations of the masses lost some of their importance as subject matter for the motion picture. . . . Pictures began to be devoted almost exclusively to pleasing and mirroring the life of the more leisured and well-to-do citizenry" (Lewis Jacobs qtd. in Brownlow *xix*).

Hence, entering the 1930s, Hollywood (filmmakers had all but abandoned New York by this point) was depending on pure and simple entertainment as its means to the most profitable end. The social reformist zeal of the early 1900s had been virtually decimated by the much greater (perceived) need to help Americans overcome the collective malaise brought about first by the horrors of World War I and now by the Great Depression.

### *Mass Culture As Ideological Agency*

The vast popularity and effective socializing tendency of motion pictures was not lost on its principal financiers, the elite banking houses of the East. Rockefeller, Morgan, and others recognized a profitable enterprise which also served to reinforce the values and myths that would ensure maintenance of the status quo. These myths served as the basis for the paradigms within which filmmakers operated during the Classic Period of Hollywood (see below). As Schiller (1973), Lazere (1987), McQuail (1987), and Herman and Chomsky (1988) have illustrated, the content of information produced by the mass media is structured and determined by myths and filters, devices embedded with the dominant ideology. The myths of individualism and personal choice, institutional neutrality, absence of social conflict and class divisions, personal rather than institutional responsibility for social ills and immoral or unethical behavior all function to govern the production of popular culture products. The themes, characterizations, and plots of popular film adhere to these myths in the interest of ensuring continued obeisance to a social structure and process that benefits the elites. If there is opposition to this dominant ideology, it is co-opted: "Popular culture absorbs oppositional ideology, adapts it to the contours of the core hegemonic principles, and domesticates it" (Gitlin 242). Thus, the apparently irreconcilable narrative conflicts that are established at the outset of a film (novel, play, etc.) are easily resolved according to the dominant ideology. This pattern was established during the period when a limited number of studios (i.e., banks) controlled the production of films.

*Social and Narrative Rupture in Classic Hollywood*

Film historians and critics refer to the "Studio System" of the 1930s and 1940s (Schatz), the "Classic Hollywood" of 1930 to 1945 (Ray), and other such appellations. All of which is to say that certain paradigms were dominant during this era, determining both the form and the themes of virtually all American film. And notwithstanding what might be characterized as either independent, nontraditional, avant-garde or countercultural filmmaking today, most elements of those "classic" paradigms are extant, most notably what Ray refers to as "the resolution of incompatible values" (55). This "narrative rupture" (Schatz 159-62), this ease with which Classic Hollywood solved these problems and reconciled apparently oppositional values, can be traced to Hollywood's tendency to convert "all political, sociological, and economic dilemmas into personal melodramas" (Ray 57). Once social structural matters have been reduced to the (relatively insignificant) problems of an individual, couple, family, or even community, resolution is quickly at hand. Social problems are not blamed on dominant institutions and no help is sought from those institutions.

The severe social ruptures wrought by the Great Depression, as well as other sociocultural matters, such as the far-reaching focus on issues of "morality," caused Hollywood to deal carefully with its representations of American values in films of the 1930s. Myths, which serve to help us understand and make sense of our reality, had to be underscored and/or reconstituted by Hollywood. These were myths that "provide[d] good, 'workable,' ways by which the contradictions in a society, the contrasts and conflicts which normally arise among people, among ideals, among the confusing realities, are somehow reconciled, smoothed over, or at least made manageable and tolerable" (Robertson *xv*). The Depression undermined that complex cultural myth we call the American Dream, as honesty, hard work, and "equal opportunity" no longer served to assure the middle class of their secure station in American life.

In 1933, estimates of homeless and "wandering" people ranged as high as 2 million (Miller 168); in one year alone—1932—the Southern Pacific Railroad ejected almost 700,000 people from its trains and property (Miller 167). American filmmakers (most notably Frank Capra and, to a somewhat lesser extent, John Ford) saw in this great social tragedy both the opportunity and the necessity "to revitalize and refashion a cultural mythology" (Sklar 196). Many of those films characterized as screwball comedies (Capra; Sturges; Hawks), as well as films which were generally celebratory of the American way of life (again, principally, Capra; Ford), served indeed to "revitalize" the dominant myths of America. The treatment in these films of class conflict, social problems, and individual responsibility contributed to the strengthening of a thematic paradigm that is still preferred in Hollywood today. The explosive growth of the film medium (and its mass audience) during the Classic period continued the supplanting of the written word—which had almost guaranteed a diversity of views and opinions in the era of "Typographic America" (Postman 30-43)—and substituted a homogenized and affirming portrayal of the American social structure and class system.

### *Class Conflict—Hollywood Style*

Aside from the dispossessed person, the most common character in the films I review below is a millionaire who is either alienated from his (or, quite infrequently, her) family, friends, and corporate comrades, and is struggling with some sort of angst. Most often, the agenda of these films is to illustrate how much this millionaire can learn from decent working-class folks and vice versa. In other words, the classes can and must get along; peaceful coexistence is in the best interests of all concerned. There is, however, no question as to who will continue to control and dominate whom; there is, in short, no intent to alter the class structure or to remedy its consequences. Capitalism has created and perpetuated a class system, but it doesn't have to be a system wherein ill feelings are harbored by the poor against the rich.

Six films that can be analyzed as examples of Hollywood-style class conflict—that is, class harmony; where millionaire meets and likes the downtrodden—range in time from 1934 to 1991, from Depression to "Recession": *It Happened One Night* (Capra, 1934), *My Man Godfrey* (LaCava, 1936), *Fifth Avenue Girl* (LaCava, 1939), *Sullivan's Travels* (Sturges, 1941), *Down and Out in Beverly Hills* (Mazursky, 1986), and *Life Stinks* (Brooks, 1991). The thematic paradigm that prevails in all these films is evidenced by (1) the reasons given as to why the dispossessed are in the predicament they are, (2) what happens to them by film's end, (3) what the future holds for the film's protagonist(s), and (4) what class or social structural change has been suggested by the film's ideological agenda. While an analysis guided by these questions provides few surprises for those familiar with American film, continued examination of popular cultural forces such as film contributes to an understanding of the ways by which "cultural institutions and practices institutionalize (settle, fix, secure, stabilize) a particular pattern of relations between the cultures and the classes in society" (Stuart Hall qtd. in Real 74).

*Whence Come the Dispossessed?* The dispossessed in Hollywood films are more often than not presented either as the victims of nebulous and disembodied economic forces (even if specific, recurring mention is made of "the Depression"), or their plight is neither explicitly or implicitly explained. Because four of the films at hand were made between 1934 and 1941, it was obviously not necessary to provide movie audiences with elaborate explanations of the *immediate* precipitating causes for the plight of the dispossessed being portrayed. So, in *It Happened One Night* and *My Man Godfrey*, films made during some of the darker days of the Depression, the homeless and unemployed are central to the stories because moviegoers knew the dispossessed really were in the streets, and they were there because of the Depression. There is, in other words, no suggestion that the "invisible hand" of capitalism has dealt a deadly blow to some participants, but not to others. No critical examination of the social and economic forces that wrought the Depression muddies up these glossy depictions of the dispossessed.

Even in *Sullivan's Travels*, made on the eve of World War II when the American economy was much stronger and employment much higher, the film's protagonist proclaims that there is "War in Europe, strikes here. No work, no food." This principal character, a successful Hollywood director, acknowledges class conflict but—in the end—does not believe the answer is to alter the class system, but rather to find something which will make each of the classes happy. In the more recent releases, *Down and Out in Beverly Hills* and *Life Stinks*, there is no explanation of just how—in the former—the protagonist became a transient eating out of garbage cans, or how—in the latter—the dispossessed encountered by the millionaire found their way to L.A.'s skid row—with the exception of the millionaire's love interest (see below).

Only in *Fifth Avenue Girl* are several specific references made about the "haves" and the "have-nots," capital and labor. Yet even in this case, the pseudo-Marxist chauffeur is ultimately co-opted by marrying his millionaire boss's daughter. Even the title character finds upper-class happiness by marrying the millionaire's son.

*Whither Goest the Dispossessed?* In all these films, the future of the downtrodden is as uncertain as the sources of their economic and social dilemma. In two cases, the very similar stories of *My Man Godfrey* and *Life Stinks*, concrete assistance is provided to the fortunate ones upon whom the respective millionaires had stumbled: *My Man Godfrey*'s millionaire opens an elaborate and chic nightclub by the river's edge, and employs his former neighbors from the shantytown he has torn down to build this new enterprise; in *Life Stinks,* the wealthy developer builds housing and provides it to the homeless free of charge, along with a new park and lake. In the first case, the remedy is extremely limited in scope and, of course, returns the millionaire to his rightful position of owner of the means of production, while his former homeless buddies park cars and wait on tables. In the latter, the millionaire's actions actually exceed those of government, in that all housing and amenities are offered free of charge and the taxpayer carries none of the burden—at least not in a direct way. The protagonist's profits from buying, razing, and redeveloping a large chunk of downtown Los Angeles are, of course, so massive that his contribution to the dispossessed is dwarfed. More to the point, he has made no effort to identify and/or remedy the social structural conditions—except some housing—which contributed to the homelessness and poverty he encountered.

In the other four films under review, there is no indication whatsoever as to the plight of the workers or dispossessed. In *Fifth Avenue Girl*, the chauffeur and the homeless girl each marry an offspring of the millionaire; presumably, these *individual* lives will improve. *Sullivan's Travels* ends with the director realizing that poor people need something to laugh about and, therefore, he ought to continue making the inane films he railed against before this epiphany. As the protagonists in *It Happened One Night* finally tear down the walls of Jericho, there is no mention of the poor and unemployed; the millionaire's daughter—who had initially eschewed her father and his fortune, but eventually came to her senses—was now happy with her new husband, a newspaper reporter—or now, perhaps, former reporter. Lastly, in *Down and Out in Beverly Hills*, none of the protagonist's street buddies (whom he cared so much about earlier in the film) are on his mind when—in response to the pleas of the millionaire and his family that he continue to live with them—he turns to his dog and, resignedly, says "Let's go get a cup of cappuccino."[3]

The protagonists in these various films all enjoy that sweetest of outcomes: Hollywood-type resolution. The millionaire "bum" in *My Man Godfrey* marries an heiress; in *Fifth Avenue Girl*, the poor girl gets the millionaire's son and the Marxism-spouting chauffeur marries the rich sister; the broke and struggling, yet very beautiful, actress marries the wealthy film director in *Sullivan's Travels,* after he sheds himself of his money-grubbing wife; in *It Happened One Night*, the brash and obnoxious reporter who is prone to drinking bouts, ends up with the millionaire's daughter; the bum who scoffed at the millionaire's lifestyle and family dysfunction ultimately decides he would rather not be *Down and Out in Beverly Hills*, and moves in; and, lastly, the millionaire developer in *Life Stinks* marries and enriches the bag lady who befriended him.

In sum, Hollywood's depictions of the dispossessed do not identify structural causes of poverty and homelessness, nor do they offer solutions in that sphere. In a quite prescient way, the earlier films foreshadowed the ideological agenda of the Reagan era, wherein the *individual* is seen as both the cause of, and the agent responsible for solving, problems of hunger, poverty, drug abuse, and homelessness, as well as global issues such as nuclear war (Brigham). All one need do is work hard and avail him/herself of the boundless opportunities in America's cornucopia. It helps, of course, if you befriend a millionaire, try to drown yourself in his swimming pool, or have one fall in love with you.

*Hollywood's Mirror: Contemporary Images of the Homeless*

How authentic are the portrayals of the down-and-out in American films? Given the considerable data available about the dispossessed in America, is Hollywood only contributing to the stereotypes that underpin our myths? To compare the most recent cinematic images of the homeless and poor with the data now available, I analyzed eight films released between 1986 and 1992: *Down and Out in Beverly Hills, Scrooged* (1988), *Life Without Zoe* (Coppola, 1989), *Life Stinks, Soapdish* (Hoffman, 1991), *The Fisher King* (Gilliam, 1992), *Curly Sue* (Hughes, 1991) and *Grand Canyon* (Kasdan, 1992). These films—by and large—meet the following criteria: (1) narrative, characterizations and dialogue that are generally free of offensive or extreme material, therefore of broad appeal to audiences, (2) high-profile actors in leading roles, thereby attracting larger audiences, (3) directors of some renown, (4) marketing and distribution sufficient to expose the film to a large number of people and, most importantly, (5) by film's end, resolution of the narrative conflict in concert with dominant sociopolitical norms and cultural values.

The centrality of the homeless and dispossessed to the narrative in each of these films is varied. In some cases (*Life Without Zoe* and *Grand Canyon)* there is only a single homeless person depicted and in others (*Scrooged* and *Soapdish*) a group of homeless people is depicted infrequently or trivialized. Two of the three principal characters in *Curly Sue* are homeless, but are the only ones so featured. In *The Fisher King*, one of the two principal characters is homeless and we are introduced—in two sequences—to his homeless comrades. The remaining two—*Down and Out in Beverly Hills* and *Life Stinks*—are stories focusing on homelessness as contrasted with middle- and upper-class values. I draw these distinctions as a cautionary note regarding what follows. This diversity of attention to, and inclusion of, the homeless in these films' narratives may place some limitations on the conclusions that can be drawn about contemporary cinematic depictions of the dispossessed.

While there are, in these films, some significant differences in characterizations of the homeless, a discrete image does emerge: Contemporary American filmmakers routinely and most frequently portray the homeless as middle-aged or elderly, single (that is, not accompanied by significant others) white males, who are dirty and/or disheveled, who are—in most cases—suffering from alcoholism and/or mental illness—and only occasional physical health problems, and who are homeless either for unexplained or probably apocryphal (*Down and Out in Beverly Hills*) reasons or, in two cases (*The Fisher King* and *Life Stinks*), because of the acts of individuals close to them—not due to the shortcomings of social institutions or the policies and power of the dominant social class.

A review of the literature provides a much different and certainly a more comprehensive picture of the contemporary homeless; a portrayal that brings to the fore the complexity of homelessness, the diversity of those who suffer in this way, and—in most cases—the misrepresentations and oversimplifications of American films dealing with this social problem.

*Causes of Homelessness*

In the films under study, little or no attention is paid to the reasons why the homeless characters have found themselves in such dire straits, but considerable research has been conducted to document the causes of homelessness. A review of these studies (particularly Waxman), as well as research and census data focusing on the distribution of wealth in America (Piven and Cloward; Antonio and Knapp; Hubler; Risen), suggests the following causes of homelessness: exacerbated maldistribution of wealth, unemployment and underemployment, poverty, lack of affordable housing, decline in entitlement expenditures, complexity of the entitlement system, substance abuse and alcoholism, and—specifically in the case of the mentally ill—deinstitutionalization, lack of a thorough discharge plan, discharge without appropriate housing, and problems with medications. Several of these causes warrant further discussion.

The rich in America have continued to get richer, while more of the poor and "near-poor" become homeless. The share of wealth held by the super-rich (the top .05% of families) went up by nearly 40% between 1963 and 1983, as the share of the wealth held by almost everyone else (that is, the bottom 90%) dropped by 20% during the same period (Zeitlin 147). While the relationship between *unemployment* and homelessness is rather clear and direct, the *underemployment* of millions of workers is also a significant contributing factor. A dramatic shift from a goods-based economy (52% of jobs in 1940) to one rooted in the low-wage service industries (72% of jobs in 1990) has occurred in the last several decades (Coser et al. 388). Approximately 20% of the homeless work full- or part-time at below subsistence wages (U.S. Conference of Mayors 1993 29).

Due in part to these quite considerable changes in the American economy, poverty increased dramatically during the 1970s and 1980s: "Between 1973 and 1983, the number of poor Americans rose by 54%, as over 12 million additional people joined the ranks of those deprived of basic housing, nutrition, and health care" (Antonio and Knapp 100). By 1991, the number of Americans living in poverty (approximately $14,000 per year income for family of four) had increased to 35.7 million, 14.2% of the United States population (Risen A1). Black Americans were disproportionately represented in this group due to median household incomes 62% that of whites (Hubler A21). More specifically, child poverty grew in the 1980s, to the point that "more than one-fourth of children living in cities with populations of 100,000 or more were classified as poverty-stricken in 1989" (Leeds A4).

Obviously, a lack of affordable housing is a principal cause of homelessness: "There is abundant evidence that homelessness is related both directly and indirectly to the shortage of inexpensive housing for poor families and poor unattached persons that began in the 1970s and has accelerated in the 1980s" (Rossi, "Why We Have Homelessness" 141). The legacy of the Reagan Era included cutting housing assistance in Reagan's first year in office by $11.6 billion, a 41% reduction (Piven and Cloward 18). In 1993, there was a national shortage of 2 million low-cost public housing units (U.S. Conference of Mayors 1993 57). The gentrification of the downtown areas of major urban cities resulted in the loss of from 25% to 50% of America's single-room occupancy housing (Rossi, "Why We Have Homelessness" 141).

One outcome of the Reagan era's call for individual responsibility was severe reductions in public assistance with resultant inadequate entitlement programs. By the end of Ronald Reagan's first term in office, he had cut Aid to Families with Dependent Children (AFDC) by $4.8 billion, child nutrition programs by $5.2 billion, and food stamps by $6.8 billion (Kozol 163). These reductions negatively impacted the ability of poor families to find and keep "affordable housing," which the Department of Housing and Urban Development considered to be that which rents for 40% or less of poverty level income. Even where public assistance was still available, the complexity of entitlement programs often served as an impediment to timely support for the needy. Dealing with the Kafkaesque bureaucracies of local, state, and federal agencies is a daunting prospect for the most well-prepared person.

The diversity, complexity, and deep-seatedness of these various causes of homelessness are in no way reflected in the films under study here. There is no information provided at all regarding the background of the homeless characters in *Scrooged, Life Without Zoe, Soapdish, Curly Sue* or *Grand Canyon*. The homeless protagonist of *Down and Out in Beverly Hills* offers several versions of his personal history, all of which sound too grandiose and self-serving to warrant serious consideration. In short, we just don't know how he ended up on the streets. In *The Fisher King*, the homeless protagonist was widowed when a malcontent opened fire with an automatic weapon in a crowded restaurant; devastated and with no motivation to work or do anything else, our character took to the streets. Only in *Life Stinks* do we find a representation of a realistic and common cause for an individual's homeless existence. The principal homeless character, Molly, was abandoned by her husband and, saddled by debt, ultimately resorted to a life in the streets. But in all, it is clear that these films fail to address the myriad causes of homelessness or to offer a truthful and comprehensive depiction of this complex issue.

*Gender Bias*. Those who were to rely upon popular films for an understanding of the gender of homeless people in America, would most certainly come away thinking that nine out of ten—or all—of the homeless are men. There are no depictions of homeless women in *Down and Out in Beverly Hills, Life Without Zoe, The Fisher King, Curly Sue* or *Grand Canyon*. Even in the other three films, the proportion of homeless women depicted does not correspond with research that suggests one in four homeless people are women (Rossi, "The Old Homeless" 957). Even in the one film that offers several, albeit fleeting, images of homeless women (*Scrooged*), there is no sense that these characters reflect reality: Most homeless women are mothers, average age 35 years, minority group members, high school dropouts, and have been homeless more than once in their lives (Milburn and Booth in Milburn and D'Ercole 1161). Moreover, many of these women became homeless after experiencing physical and sexual abuse and consequent psychological trauma (Goodman, Saxe, and Harvey 1219). And once on the streets, "homeless women [are] 20 times as likely to be assaulted sexually as U.S. women in general" (Ritchey, LaGory, and Mullis 34). These facts can be compared to the female protagonist, Molly, in *Life Stinks* who, although abandoned by her husband, was a trained and experienced dancer, as well as—in keeping with Hollywood's age-old image-making routines—a quite attractive woman.[4]

*Young, Old and In-Between.* While detailed information about the ages of homeless people is not readily available, we do know that about one-fourth of the homeless are children (accompanied by a parent or other adult) (Jordan & Reyes and Waxman in Foscarinis 1233). Another 3% of the homeless are "unaccompanied youths" (Waxman and Reyes 56). But in the films under review here, there is only one depiction of a homeless child or adolescent (*Curly Sue*).

Even in those films depicting large groups of homeless (e.g., in shelters)—*Scrooged, Curly Sue*, and *Life Stinks*—all the characters are adults, the majority middle-aged and elderly. Given that the average life expectancy of a homeless person in America is 50 years (Kiesler 1245), and considering the quite significant number of young children and their parents (i.e., young adults) who are homeless, the most common cinematic representation of middle-aged and elderly men is stereotypical and easily derived from the image of the hobo, vagrant, or "bum" of films made during, or depicting, the 1930s. While the vast majority of the homeless are adults (65-75%), they are marked by a diversity in age and gender—a diversity noticeably lacking in these films. In *Down and Out in Beverly Hills, Scrooged, Life Stinks,* and *The Fisher King*, the homeless are either middle-aged or elderly, with very limited depictions of young adults in the latter two. In *Life Without Zoe*, since we never actually see anything more than the hand of the homeless male living in a cardboard box, his age and mental/physical health are indeterminable, and in *Grand Canyon*, the somewhat fleeting images of the homeless man suggest that he is in his early- to mid-30s, but might be much younger.

*Where Will the Children Play?* This depiction of the homeless as middle-aged and elderly (males) allows the viewer (and filmmaker) to both continue the stereotype of the tramp or derelict and lessen the emotional impact that would certainly result from a more accurate portrayal of malnourished, undereducated, and sickly children and their mothers. One study of homeless children concluded, "When children's nutritional needs are not met, growth is affected, physical health deteriorates, mental health is adversely affected, behavioral problems increase, the ability to concentrate is compromised, and academic performance suffers" (Rafferty and Shinn 1176). One 10-year-old homeless girl said, "I have headaches almost everyday. I feel like I was born with them" (Stanford Center 19). Too many policymakers—and, apparently, too many filmmakers and film producers—want to add to the neglect already suffered by these children, by failing to portray their plight in contemporary films.

Arguably, those most vulnerable to the physical and emotional consequences of homelessness are those children who are absolutely absent from contemporary films. From birth, the life of a homeless child is in peril due to poor or no prenatal care, low birth-weight, inadequate or no postnatal care, and greater likelihood of contracting childhood disorders (e.g., upper respiratory infections, gastrointestinal disorders, ear disorders, minor skin ailments, chronic physical disorders) (Rafferty and Shinn 1170-71). In one quite telling and disturbing assessment, it was determined that 31% of homeless children are clinically depressed. The failure of American filmmakers to include in their treatment of homelessness any references to children cannot easily be explained. It may be simply that generic conventions are being employed; that is, the homeless "genre" eschews children and families. One of many advantages of such generic conventions are the economy of story line and characterization. A more cynical and critical interpretation would suggest that film producers and financiers will not unnecessarily encumber their budgets with legally mandated tutors and guardians for child actors, or negatively impact their production schedules with the legal limitations on how much time a child actor may work. And no doubt most directors would like to avoid professional dealings with young children. In short, whether for these specific reasons or not, economic considerations are the most likely explanation for this serious shortcoming in the depiction of homelessness.

*Family Affair.* Another facet of the stereotype to which American films are contributing is that of the single or "solo" bum. In fact, over 40% of the homeless are families with children (U.S. Conference of Mayors 1993), although the range is from 6% to 81% in the 30 cities surveyed (Waxman and Reyes 55); in New York City, the typical homeless family is comprised of a 27-year-old mother and two to three children with an average age of 6 years (Kozol 4). Of all homeless women, only 12% are single or solo (Waxman and Reyes 56). In only one of the films at hand (*Curly Sue*) was there a depiction of either a couple or a family on the streets; every other representation was that of a single or solo person, almost always a male.[5] In *Life Stinks*, there is a romantic linking of the millionaire protagonist and a homeless woman, but—because of his only temporary and self-imposed status—they are not a "homeless couple" and, in any event, she is saved from her life of poverty and desperation and whisked away by film's end in a gleaming white limousine. The "family" in *Curly Sue*—an adult male and a young girl—are not related biologically, although the man has cared for the child since birth.

*Reverse Racial Bias.* Given the tendency of the film and television industries to portray racial and ethnic minorities in a pejorative way (i.e., criminals, prostitutes, drug users, etc.), it is significant to note that the homeless depicted in these seven films are, in three cases (*Soapdish, Curly Sue* and *Grand Canyon*) all white or, in the others, predominantly white (i.e., perhaps 5 to 10% of the homeless depicted are blacks or other racial/ethnic minorities). This flies in the face of the 1990 United States Conference of Mayors report, which stated that almost half (46%) of the homeless are black, about one-third (34%) are white, 15% Latino, and the remaining 5% are largely Asian American and American Indian (Waxman and Reyes 56). Another study of homeless families in the San Francisco Bay Area concluded that 36% were Hispanic, 29% white, and 25% black (Stanford Center 10). This rather curious misrepresentation by American filmmakers may be explained in several ways: (1) If racial and ethnic minority advocates are correct, racial prejudice continues to affect casting, writing, and directing agendas in Hollywood—even when the characterizations (in this case, the homeless) demand a diversity of representation; (2) some perverted sense of "political correctness" has overwhelmed the filmmakers, and in an attempt to be sensitive to the plight of people of color, the filmmakers fail to accurately portray that very plight; and/or (3) the stereotype of the typical homeless person being a solo, middle-aged white male is simultaneously believed and reinforced by Hollywood. In any event, as with representations of gender and age, contemporary films provide an inaccurate and misleading portrayal of the racial and ethnic characteristics of American homeless.

*Mental Illness and Substance Abuse.* In the realm of what I am calling the "behavior" of the homeless, Hollywood has, sadly enough, come closest to actually depicting the extent to which the homeless suffer from mental illness and alcoholism and other drug use. *Life Without Zoe*, where we never see or learn anything about the single homeless person portrayed, is the only film with *no* indication of mental illness or substance abuse among the homeless. The single homeless person in *Grand Canyon* may or may not be suffering from mental illness; his physical appearance and mannerisms are intentionally meant to be menacing and possibly dangerous, but the filmmaker also wants to suggest that these are behaviors that others "see" in *all* the homeless. In the other films, a significant number of characters are blatantly mentally unbalanced. One study determined that over one-fourth (28%) of the homeless are mentally ill, ranging from 3% to 57% in a 30-city survey (Waxman and Reyes 56); another reports that one-third of single adult homeless people have severe mental illness (Dennis et al. 1129); and yet another that one-third to one-half of the homeless have a diagnosable mental disorder (Kiesler 1249). More serious problems befall 10% to 15% of the homeless who are "chronically mentally ill" (Kiesler 1249).

As to drug use, it is curious—given Hollywood's penchant for films and television dealing with the more dramatic elements of the drug trade (e.g., upscale dealers in *Light Sleeper* [Schrader, 1992], drug rip-offs and murder in *One False Move* [Franklin, 1992], or the entire *Miami Vice*-like *oeuvre*)—that in none of these films is there any evidence of the use of any drugs other than alcohol. In *Life Stinks*, the two characters who are the only homeless criminal types (in all these films) are engaged in the sale of what they tell their customers is cocaine, but there are no depictions or indications of their using drugs themselves. In fact, several studies have indicated that "[f]rom 25 to 50% of homeless people use illicit drugs and that rates of use exceed those reported for the general population" (Fischer and Breakey 1120). A 30-city survey of the homeless reflects a range of from 10% to 75% of the homeless as substance abusers (Waxman and Reyes 55). In some cases, of course, drug use was a contributing factor to the individual's eventual homelessness; alcohol and drug use was cited as the single most important factor leading to homelessness for 32% of the homeless population (McCarty et al. 1140). Again, as with depictions of race, American films curiously change their routines regarding the inclusion of drug references and eschew an accurate and complete portrayal of drug use by a significant number of the homeless. It is important to add, lest a stereotype be reinforced here, that although many homeless may use illicit drugs, the majority apparently do not.

The rate of alcohol dependence among the homeless (estimated to be from 58% to 68% among men; 30% among single women [Fischer and Breakey 1119]) is higher than that of other drugs, and the impact of alcohol abuse on physical health is quite considerable, resulting in serious health problems (Fischer and Breakey 1119). Given the prevalence of alcohol abuse and its concomitant array of health problems among the homeless, the depictions in these films are certainly incomplete. Alcohol use/abuse is portrayed in *Down and Out in Beverly Hills, Life Stinks*, and *The Fisher King*, but there is no indication or representation of the many health problems that accompany alcoholism. Indeed, as in films for decades, the drunk is a happy, friendly, and benign sort who usually provides comic relief.

*A New Wave of Social Problem Films?*

There have been some recent exceptions to the type of films examined above, although virtually all fail to meet the criteria listed at the outset. Most especially, these films are quite frank in their depiction of drug use, male prostitution, homosexuality, crimes against property and person, and adolescent/young adult angst and disillusionment.

Additionally, they do not enjoy the same wide exposure as the big budget, big name films; therefore, even if their subject matter is deemed of interest, far fewer viewers have access to them until and unless they are released on videotape. Finally, Hollywood-type resolution is offered in only one case. Gus Van Sant has released two of these grittier films, *Drugstore Cowboy* (1989) and *My Own Private Idaho* (1991), the latter featuring drifting young male street hustlers. (Even this film falls prey to the tendency to mythologize life on the streets—as did *The Fisher King*—with a Falstaffian subplot.) Martin Bell, the director of *Streetwise*, the trenchant 1984 documentary of Seattle street kids, revisited the Northwest in *American Heart* (1993). While not specifically on the theme of homelessness, *American Heart* includes a hard-hitting sequence reminiscent of Bell's earlier work, although a hopeful ending is included. Two films that offer more complete, honest, and realistic illustrations of the life of the homeless are *Where the Day Takes You* (Rocco, 1992) and *The Saint of Fort Washington* (Hunter, 1994). Although families and children are not adequately represented in either of these films, the depictions of "families" of teens and young adults in the former, and of single males in the latter are forceful, uncompromising, and realistically uncertain in their conclusions. That an examination of almost forty films results in such a statement about only two films accentuates the overarching argument of this chapter.

### *Conclusion*

Among the various theoretical perspectives on the function and purpose of the mass media are those of dominant class, media owners, and media audience (McQuail 51-78). The first, the role of the dominant class, considers the ways by which power is manifested and exercised through control of the mass media. Secondly, the role of the media owners (themselves members of the dominant class) reflects the centrality of the profit motive in media decision-making. Lastly, the media audience is using mass media as a primary source of information, indeed of "knowledge," as the font of what it understands our culture to be—or ought to be. When examining the ways by which Hollywood depicts homelessness—or any other social problem—these three perspectives provide some insight into, on the one hand, the extent to which media owners and other members of the dominant class determine and control media content and, on the other, the importance of popular mass media as the "window to the world" for most Americans—a window so opaque as to grossly distort reality. Challenges to the dominance of these decision-makers are defused through what Bennett (qtd. in Real 126-27), drawing upon Gramsci, sees as a process of negotiation, wherein divergent views and values are incorporated into, but still subsumed by, those of the dominant class. Whether these divergent views come from religious institutions, citizens' "watchdog" groups, or members of the media (film critics, editorial staff, etc.), their impact is indirect at best and limited in its scope.

Homelessness, due to the complexity and deep-seatedness of its causes, will not soon abate. Those who have studied this social dilemma project a quite dismal future. One study concludes that the number of homeless is growing by 25% each year (Reyes and Waxman in Foscarinis 1233), and another that by 2003, 19 million Americans may be without shelter (Kozol 204). Whether Hollywood will begin to fully and accurately inform and educate Americans about this problem is questionable. If the films discussed above are any indication, then most people's window to the world will become no clearer. What we do not see in these films is the reality of the poorest families in America losing ground while the richest only increase their wealth. What we do see is oversimplification, obfuscation, romanticization, and a self-contradictory celebration of the very social structure that delivered the dispossessed to their lives of hunger, fear, and loneliness. By admiring the "generosity" of the spoiled rich girl who gives a bag of candy to a faceless person living in a cardboard box (*Life Without Zoe*) or "gee-whizzing" at Terry Gilliam's ridiculously mythical view of the homeless (cavorting like Arthur's honorable knights in *The Fisher King*), the uninformed, and therefore uncaring, populace has only the life-threatening fat content of theater popcorn to worry about.

Few of the films discussed above are free from the oversimplification allowed by blaming the victim—by virtue of his/her alcoholism, mental illness, physical disability, or "choice" (*Midnight Cowboy* [Schlesinger, 1969], *Ironweed, Life Stinks)*, celebration of the "good life" available for all in America (*My Man Godfrey*, *Meet John Doe* [Capra, 1941], *Down and Out in Beverly Hills*), romanticization of life on the road—and on the run (*It Happened One Night, You Only Live Once* [Lang, 1937], *Bonnie and Clyde* [Penn, 1967]), and other narrative devices. At best, some of these films provide a satirical perspective on the bourgeoisie or on the super-rich (*Sullivan's Travels*, *Down and Out in Beverly Hills*, *Life Stinks*, *Curly Sue*) or on the dangers of fascism (*Meet John Doe*), but in the end there is neither a call for social-structural change nor an explicit abandonment of the bankrupt values that promote poverty and inequality. Filmmakers like Rocco, Van Sant, Hunter, and others may continue to chip away at the monolith that is the dominant paradigm of American filmmaking and provide more realistic images of the dispossessed in America. But the dictates of capitalism are such that if the product—whether soap or art—is not likely to be consumed, then it won't be produced.

## Notes

1. Principal players in the writing, directing, promoting, and producing of such films were *female* reformers. Social workers, concerned volunteer workers, and writer/directors like Lois Weber were largely responsible for bringing light to the various problems of the poor and the working class.

2. Upton Sinclair, the muckraking Socialist writer, some of whose work was translated to the screen (*The Money Changers, The Jungle*), was not impressed by the overall success of motion pictures in portraying social conditions: "The moving pictures furnish the principal intellectual food of the workers at the present time, and the supplying of this food is entirely in the hands of the capitalist class, and the food supplied is poisoned. . . . [T]he whole industry is so completely controlled by big business that there is practically no chance of breaking in with a true idea" (Brownlow 435).

3. Note that in Jean Renoir's *Boudu Saved from Drowning* (1932), the source for *Down and Out in Beverly Hills*, the protagonist ultimately walks away from his newfound comforts, rejecting the bourgeois life into which he had been delivered—and the wife he had wed only minutes before. Director Paul Mazursky, however, turns Renoir on his head in *Down and Out in Beverly Hills* and suggests that a life of comfort amid avarice, mendacity, and neurosis is better than one "on the bum."

4. *Ironweed* (Babenco, 1987), set in the Depression era, provides a much different and more realistic characterization in Helen, a quite unglamorous tubercular alcoholic who dies before film's end. A second female character, who refuses to avail herself of a bed in a "rescue mission," freezes to death in an open lot and is set upon by rats.

5. *Ironweed* focuses on a homeless alcoholic and his sometime female-companion, and *Trouble in Mind* (Rudolph, 1985) includes a young couple—the husband a criminal on the run—and their baby, living in a camper truck in a parking lot.

## Works Cited

Antonio, Robert, and Tim Knapp. "Democracy and Abundance: the Declining Middle and Postliberal Politics." *Telos* 76 (1988): 93-114.

Brigham, William. "Noncontentious Social Movements: 'Just Say No to War.'" *Peace Action in the Eighties: Social Science Perspectives.* Ed. Sam Marullo and John Lofland. New Brunswick: Rutgers UP, 1990. 155-66.

Brownlow, Kevin. *Behind the Mask of Innocence: Films of Social Conscience in the Silent Era.* London: Jonathan Cape, 1990.

Coser, Lewis, et al. *Introduction to Sociology.* 2nd. ed. San Diego: Harcourt, 1987.

Dennis, Deborah L. et al. "A Decade of Research and Services for Homeless Mentally Ill Persons: Where Do We Stand?" *American Psychologist* 46 (1991): 1129-38.

Fischer, Pamela J., and William R. Breakey. "The Epidemiology of Alcohol, Drug, and Mental Disorders Among Homeless Persons." *American Psychologist* 46 (1991): 1115-28.

Foscarinis, Maria. "The Politics of Homelessness: A Call to Action." *American Psychologist* 46 (1991): 1232-38.

Gitlin, Todd. "Television's Screens: Hegemony in Transition." *American Media and Mass Culture: Left Perspectives.* Ed. Donald Lazere. Berkeley: U of California P, 1987. 240-65.

Goodman, Lisa, Leonard Saxe, and Mary Harvey. "Homelessness as Psychological Trauma: Broadening Perspectives." *American Psychologist* 46 (1991): 1219-25.

Gusfield, Joseph R. *Symbolic Crusade: Status Politics and the American Temperance Movement.* 2nd ed. Urbana: U of Illinois P, 1986.

Herman, Edward S., and Noam Chomsky. *Manufacturing Consent: The Political Economy of the Mass Media.* New York: Pantheon, 1988.

Hubler, Shawn. "'80s Failed to End Economic Disparity, Census Shows." *Los Angeles Times* 17 Aug. 1992: A1+.

Kiesler, Charles A. "Homelessness and Public Policy Priorities." *American Psychologist* 46 (1991): 1245-52.

Kozol, Jonathan. *Rachel and Her Children: Homeless Families in America.* New York: Fawcett-Columbine, 1988.

Lazere, Donald. "Introduction: Entertainment as Social Control." *American Media and Mass Culture: Left Perspectives.* Ed. Donald Lazere. Berkeley: U of California P, 1987. 1-26.

Leeds, Jeff. "Child Poverty Grew in '80s, Study Finds." *Los Angeles Times* 12 Aug. 1992: A4.

McCarty, Dennis, et al. "Alcoholism, Drug Abuse, and the Homeless." *American Psychologist* 46 (1991): 1139-48.

McQuail, Denis. *Mass Communication Theory: An Introduction.* 2nd ed. Newbury Park, CA: Sage, 1987.

Milburn, Norweeta, and Ann D'Ercole. "Homeless Women: Moving Toward a Comprehensive Model." *American Psychologist* 46 (1991): 1161-69.

Miller, Henry. *On The Fringe: The Dispossessed in America.* Lexington, MA: Lexington, 1991.

Piven, Frances Fox, and Richard A. Cloward. *The New Class War: Reagan's Attack on the Welfare State and Its Consequences.* New York: Pantheon, 1982. 15-19.

Postman, Neil. *Amusing Ourselves to Death: Public Discourse in the Age of Show Business.* New York: Penguin, 1985.

Rafferty, Yvonne, and Marybeth Shinn. "The Impact of Homelessness on Children." *American Psychologist* 46 (1991): 1170-79.

Ray, Robert B. *A Certain Tendency of the Hollywood Cinema, 1930-1980.* Princeton: Princeton UP, 1985.

Real, Michael R. *Super Media: A Cultural Studies Approach.* Newbury Park, CA: Sage, 1989.

Risen, James. "Number of Poor in America Hits a 27-Year High." *Los Angeles Times* 4 Sept. 1992: A1+.

Ritchey, Ferris J., Mark LaGory, Jeffrey Mullis. "Gender Differences in Health Risks and Physical Symptoms among the Homeless." *Journal of Health and Social Behavior* 32 (1991): 33-48.

Robertson, James. *American Myth, American Reality.* New York: Hill and Wang, 1980.

Rossi, Peter H. "The Old Homeless and the New Homelessness in Historical Perspective." *American Psychologist* 45 (1990): 954-59.

—. "Why We Have Homelessness." *Crisis in American Institutions.* 8th ed. Ed. Jerome H. Skolnick and Elliott Currie. New York: HarperCollins, 1991. 140-54.

Schatz, Thomas. *Hollywood Genres: Formulas, Filmmaking, and the Studio System.* New York: Random House, 1981.

Schiller, Herbert. *The Mind Managers.* Boston: Beacon, 1973.

Sklar, Robert. *Movie-Made America: A Cultural History of American Movies.* New York: Random House, 1975.

Stanford Center for the Study of Families, Children and Youth. *The Stanford Studies of Homeless Families, Children and Youth.* Stanford, CA: Stanford Center for the Study of Families, Children and Youth, 1991.

United States Conference of Mayors. *A Status Report on Hunger and Homelessness in American Cities: 1993.* Washington, DC: U.S. Conference of Mayors, 1994.

Waxman, Laura DeKoven. *Mentally Ill and Homeless: A 22-City Survey.* Washington, DC: United States Conference of Mayors, 1991.

—, and Lilia M. Reyes. *A Status Report on Hunger and Homelessness in America's Cities: 1990.* Washington, DC: United States Conference of Mayors, 1990.

Zeitlin, Maurice. *The Large Corporation and Contemporary Classes.* New Brunswick, NJ: Rutgers UP, 1989.

## Filmography

| Year | Film | Director |
|---|---|---|
| 1905 | *The Kleptomaniac* | Edwin S. Porter |
| 1911 | *The Awakening of John Bond* | Charles Brabin |
| 1912 | *The Usurer's Grip* | Bannister Merwin |
| 1913 | *The Struggle* | George Melford |
| 1914 | *The Jungle* | Augustus Thomas |
| 1915 | *Kindling* | Cecil B. DeMille |
| 1915 | *The Blood of the Children* | Henry MacRae |
| 1917 | *The Public Be Damned* | Stanner E.V. Taylor |
| 1932 | *Boudu Saved from Drowning* | Jean Renoir |
| 1933 | *Lady for a Day* | Frank Capra |
| 1934 | *It Happened One Night* | Frank Capra |
| 1934 | *Our Daily Bread* | King Vidor |
| 1936 | *My Man Godfrey* | Gregory LaCava |
| 1937 | *You Only Live Once* | Fritz Lang |
| 1939 | *Fifth Avenue Girl* | Gregory LaCava |
| 1940 | *The Grapes of Wrath* | John Ford |
| 1941 | *Sullivan's Travels* | Preston Sturges |
| 1941 | *Meet John Doe* | Frank Capra |
| 1961 | *Pocketful of Miracles* | Frank Capra |
| 1967 | *Bonnie and Clyde* | Arthur Penn |
| 1969 | *Midnight Cowboy* | John Schlesinger |
| 1973 | *Scarecrow* | Jerry Schatzberg |
| 1973 | *Badlands* | Terence Malick |
| 1976 | *Bound for Glory* | Hal Ashby |
| 1981 | *Pixote* | Hector Babenco |
| 1984 | *Streetwise* | Martin Bell |
| 1985 | *Trouble in Mind* | Alan Rudolph |
| 1986 | *Down and Out in Beverly Hills* | Paul Mazursky |
| 1987 | *Ironweed* | Hector Babenco |
| 1987 | *Barfly* | Barbet Schroeder |
| 1988 | *Scrooged* | Richard Donner |
| 1988 | *Life Without Zoe* | Francis Coppola |
| 1989 | *Drugstore Cowboy* | Gus Van Sant |
| 1991 | *My Own Private Idaho* | Gus Van Sant |
| 1991 | *Life Stinks* | Mel Brooks |
| 1991 | *Soapdish* | Michael Hoffman |
| 1991 | *Curly Sue* | John Hughes |
| 1992 | *The Fisher King* | Terry Gilliam |

| | | |
|---|---|---|
| 1992 | *Grand Canyon* | Lawrence Kasdan |
| 1992 | *Vagrant* | Chris Walas |
| 1992 | *Light Sleeper* | Paul Schrader |
| 1992 | *Where the Day Takes You* | Marc Rocco |
| 1993 | *American Heart* | Martin Bell |
| 1993 | *It Was a Wonderful Life* | Michele Ohayon |
| 1994 | *The Saint of Fort Washington* | Tim Hunter |
| 1994 | *Twenty Bucks* | Keva Rosenfeld |
| 1994 | *A Home of Our Own* | Tony Bill |

# The Heart of the Order: The Success Myth in Baseball Biopics

**Howard Good**

> So that's it. Story of my life. Think we could make a movie of that? Well, maybe not. Too many things happened on the sidelines we couldn't put in. Right?
>
> —Lefty O'Doul, two-time
> National League batting champion

The biographical picture, more familiarly known as the "biopic," has been a Hollywood staple for decades. There have been scientist biopics (*The Story of Louis Pasteur,* 1934), Western biopics (*Buffalo Bill,* 1944), gangster biopics (*Al Capone,* 1959), literary biopics (*Young Cassidy,* 1965), entertainment biopics (*Lady Sings the Blues,* 1972), political biopics (*Gandhi,* 1982). Although the subjects of biopics have varied widely, the biopic form itself has been quite consistent. It typically—"painstakingly," one impatient critic said (Paget 188)—takes a chronological approach to a life.

Pulitzer Prize–winning historian Barbara Tuchman once explained that she used biography in her work "less for the sake of the individual subject than as a vehicle for exhibiting an age . . . or a country and its state of mind . . . or an historic situation" (133). The biopic, by contrast, focuses on the fortunes of the individual and ignores or obscures history and social relationships. Portraying in tightly ordered sequence the individual's formative experiences, temporary adversities, and ultimate triumph, it creates the impression that character is destiny (Joannou and McIntyre 147).

From the early 1940s to the mid-1950s, there was a string of biopics about baseball players: *The Pride of the Yankees* (1942), *The Babe Ruth Story* (1948), *The Stratton Story* (1949), *The Jackie Robinson Story* (1950), *The Winning Team* (1952), *The Pride of St. Louis* (1952), and *Fear Strikes Out* (1956). At least part of the explanation for this was, not surprisingly, monetary. Despite a Hollywood adage that sports films don't sell tickets, *The Pride of the Yankees* became a commercial as well as critical success (Sayre 182). It was among the top ten money-making films of its year and nominated for several Academy Awards, including best picture and best actor (Robinson 277). The baseball biopics that eventually followed it were imitations—sort of *The Pride of the Yankees* II, III, IV, V, VI—calculated attempts to recapture that old box-office magic.

Another factor in Hollywood's bringing to the screen the lives of ballplayers was the close fit between the films and the ideological needs of the postwar era. Carolyn Anderson observed that it was no accident that the most active period for the biopic as a genre, 1946-55, coincided with a notably repressive period in American politics (334). The country was scared coming into the '50s—scared of communist infiltration at home; scared of communist takeovers abroad; scared of an arms race with the Soviet Union; scared of general annihilation under billowing mushroom clouds (Dowdy 24, 60). "Do you remember," a middle-aged man wistfully asked a friend in a James Thurber cartoon in 1948, "when the only thing to fear was fear itself?" (qtd. in Huber 309).

Biopics were able to flourish in the pathological atmosphere of McCarthyism and the Cold War because they are conservative. Their subjects tend to be drawn from the past—Lou Gehrig, Babe Ruth, and Grover Cleveland Alexander were already dead by the time Hollywood told their life stories—and treated in safe, dependable ways. No other film genre so celebrates the traditional American belief that any person can achieve success through dint of his own efforts. The belief seems especially pronounced in baseball biopics, whose heroes played what is, after all, "the national game."

Americans have always been the world's most enthusiastic proponents of the self-made man (Cawelti 1). The success message was powerful box office long before there was ever a Hollywood. In the latter half of the 19th century, lecture halls rang with it, ministers sanctified it, schoolbooks taught it, and biographers cashed in on it. "The 'real-life' story of a well-known man soaring from obscurity to fame or from humble beginnings to great wealth was dramatic," Richard M. Huber noted. "Ideas are fatiguing, but ideas expressed through and by real-life people in a setting of romance and action are alive with the warmth of human interest" (50-51).

The 19th-century biographer saw his task as inspirational, the narration of a heroic, exemplary life for the purpose of providing a lesson and spur to dreamers of the golden dream (Pachter 10). Baseball biopics show a similar emphasis. And yet the social and material circumstances that once gave a certain plausibility to the saga of rags to riches—plenty of land, a competitive economy, a fluid class system—had changed radically by the mid-20th century. Now the individual was suspended in a complicated web of contacts and more dependent on institutions and other people (Goldman 263-64). It might be that the biopics, still preaching the old-time gospel of self-help and individualism, soothed audiences anxious about the loss of personal control in modern mass society.

Or it might be that the biopics themselves were less confident than either their makers or viewers realized. "There is," as Richard Schickel wrote, "the conscious movie, the one the people who created it thought they were making and the one we thought we were paying to see. Then there is the unconscious movie, the one neither the makers nor the viewers are consciously aware of, a movie that exposes the attitudes, neuroses, desires shared by both parties" (*viii*). A strange morbid streak runs through movieland's baseball season: Lou Gehrig (Gary Cooper) dies prematurely in *The Pride of the Yankees;* Monty Stratton (James Stewart) has a leg amputated in *The Stratton Story;* Grover Cleveland Alexander (Ronald Reagan) suffers epileptic seizures in *The Winning Team;* Jimmy Piersall (Anthony Perkins) goes insane in *Fear Strikes Out.* The portrayal of so much sickness and horror suggests that the biopics, for all their glorification of the self-made man, were struggling with doubts that secretly seeped in from the surrounding culture.

*"This Is a True Story"*

Which raises the question of whether these films are fact or fiction or a blend of both. *The Stratton Story, The Winning Team,* and *The Pride of St. Louis* each begin with a flat statement that "This is a true story. . . ." *Fear Strikes Out* makes the same claim, though more elaborately: "This is a story of one of America's leading sports figures, Jimmy Piersall, as taken from his own account of his life." However phrased, the written introductions position viewers to receive and be shaken by the "truth" of what they are about to see.

Other devices enhance the aura of factuality. Many of the films have an invisible narrator, the rumbly, omniscient voice traditionally associated with newsreels and documentaries rather than with Hollywood make-believe. Some films also present real-life ballplayers in bit parts. Lou Gehrig's teammates Babe Ruth and Bill Dickey portray themselves in *The Pride of the Yankees,* while *The Winning Team* includes appearances by big leaguers Bob Lemon, Hank Sauer, Al Zarilla, and Gene Mauch.

The documentary touches disguise the degree to which biographical material has been fictionalized. On the simplest level, the fictionalization involves minor errors or distortions of fact, such as giving Gehrig the nickname "Tanglefoot" when his actual nickname was "Biscuit Pants" because he looked ludicrous in the baggy baseball uniform of his day (Robinson 11). On a more profound level, it involves imposing a particular order and meaning—not to mention background music—on the life being depicted.

Ironically, filmmakers used the very devices that seemed to guarantee factual accuracy to mythologize their subjects. Consider the introductory note to *The Pride of the Yankees,* signed by journalist Damon Runyon:

> This is the story of a hero of the peaceful paths of everyday. It is the story of a gentle young man who, in the full flower of his great fame, was a lesson in simplicity and modesty to the youth of America.
>
> He faced death with that same valor that has been displayed by thousands of young men on far-flung fields of battle. He left behind him a memory of courage and devotion that will forever be an inspiration to men.
>
> It is the story of Lou Gehrig.

Runyon's worshipful prose transformed Gehrig the man into Gehrig the cultural monument. The ballplayer shed any ambiguities or quirks he may have possessed while alive and became thoroughly and uncomplicatedly heroic. His story as described here was true only in the sense that it had an all-American moral—practically italicized, underlined, and asterisked by Runyon—that rang true for wartime audiences.

In several films the voice-over narration picks up the myth-making where an introductory note leaves off. The narrator of *The Babe Ruth Story* calls Babe "the superman of baseball, the most famous and colorful athlete in the game's history," and boomingly adds that he was "American as the hot dog, soda pop, and chewing gum." Not to be outdone in either volume or clichés, the narrator of *The Stratton Story* declares at the end of the film: "As [Monty] goes on pitching, winning, leading a rich full life, he stands"—on one leg, remember—"as an inspiration to all of us. He is living proof of what a man can do if he has the courage and determination to refuse to admit defeat." These and other narrators don't just inform, they indoctrinate. And the sound of their great, godlike voices commands audience agreement with their doctrines.

Actors and acting styles represent still another aspect of fictionalization. Ronald Bergan pointed out that the stars of biopics "have substituted their own personalities for those of the persons portrayed" (22). Thus Lou Gehrig now has the earnestness and whole-some good looks of Gary Cooper; Babe Ruth is indistinguishable from clownish William Bendix; and Monty Stratton stammers like James Stewart. But even when a real-life ballplayer portrays himself, as Jackie Robinson did in *The Jackie Robinson Story,* the result can be curiously unreal. Robinson's brittle, self-conscious performance clashes with the more confident performances of the professional actors around him and highlights the "artifice of the biographical enterprise" (Anderson 333).

It is easy enough today to detect the many ways in which baseball biopics distort reality. And yet 40 or 50 years ago the films weren't nearly so transparent. The original viewers of the films were plugged into the same ideological circuit as the makers of the films. Back then the claim that these were true stories seemed valid, for the stories met one's idea of how life was supposed to be.

### *The Self-Made Men of Summer*

Baseball biopics of the 1940s and 1950s contain, paradoxically, few baseball scenes, and the few they do contain tend to lack excitement. The reason is twofold: (1) the actors impersonating the ballplayers were a bunch of dubs on the diamond; and (2) the films are less about the rewards and disappointments of a baseball career than about the rewards and disappointments of the American Dream.

The first point is illustrated by the comic difficulties Gary Cooper encountered in portraying Lou Gehrig. Gehrig, as every baseball fan knew, was a southpaw, but even after coaching from major leaguers Babe Herman and Lefty O'Doul, Cooper could barely throw and bat right-handed. "He threw the ball like an old woman tossing a hot biscuit," O'Doul observed of the actor (qtd. in Robinson 277). So the makers of *The Pride of the Yankees* used stand-ins for Cooper where possible. Where not possible—for example, in some batting sequences—they reversed the letters on Cooper's uniform, had him run to third instead of first base, and then flopped the image (Booth 45).

Obviously, there was a lot to be said for keeping actors off the base paths. To do just that, filmmakers often resorted to rear-projection process: a projector was placed behind an eight-foot-high translucent screen, and stock footage of a professional ballgame was projected onto the screen while actors scampered around in front of it (Harmetz 249). Real baseball was further avoided by using newspaper headlines—flashed over a montage of stands and diamonds or glimpsed in the pages of a scrapbook—to summarize a player's accomplishments.

In general, baseball biopics suggest rather than show the playing careers of their subjects. The films primarily tell the personal story of a baseball great. Yet, except for surface details, this story varies little from one biopic to the next. It is always cast in terms of what Irvin G. Wyllie called "the myth of rags to riches."

When we first meet Jackie Robinson in Hollywood's version of his life, he is literally dressed in rags—a sweater out at the elbows and pants torn in the seat. The boy who would grow up to break the color barrier in organized baseball doesn't even have his own mitt until the coach of a sandlot team gives him an old, discarded one. Other protagonists come from similarly humble backgrounds. Babe Ruth spends his turn-of-the-century childhood shuttling between his father's tough waterfront saloon in Baltimore and St. Mary's Industrial School, a sort of reformatory run by priests. Lou Gehrig, the son of a cook and a janitor, inhabits a New York neighborhood of crowded tenements and motley immigrant accents. Dizzy Dean quits school in the third grade to work in the cotton fields to help support his family. Jimmy Piersall shares a hovel with a tyrannical father and a sickly mother.

For centuries the American way was to blame the poor for their plight, attributing it to flaws in their moral makeup. Meanwhile, wealth was viewed—and defended—as a reward for virtue. "God gave me my money," John D. Rockefeller declared flatly (qtd. in Lord 84). In this cosmology the poor boy who made good had a special status. "He was," Richard M. Huber wrote, "a symbol of America's contribution to the world: the free man improving himself and his position in a land of freedom and opportunity" (34). That land lives on in baseball biopics. As the narrator of *The Jackie Robinson Story* says to the swelling strains of "America the Beautiful," Robinson's triumph over poverty and racial prejudice could occur only in "a country where every child has the opportunity to become president—or play baseball for the Brooklyn Dodgers."

Naive? Of course. But what else can you expect from films ideologically rooted in the 19th-century gospel of success? According to the gospel, the greater a man's climb to the top of his profession—from a log cabin to the White House, from a sandlot to Yankee Stadium or Ebbetts Field—the greater his character. It was character, not circumstances, that ultimately determined success or failure in life. I add "ultimately" because character itself was molded by external forces. Success writers of the post-Civil War era praised, for example, the role of a rural childhood in developing the health and morals on which achievement was supposed to depend (Wyllie 27).

Traces of the rural myth can be found in *The Pride of St. Louis* and *The Winning Team,* whose subjects were both country boys. *The Pride of St. Louis* opens in 1928 with Jay Hanna Dean (Dan Dailey)—he gets the nickname "Dizzy" a couple of years later—pitching on an improvised diamond in an Ozark cow pasture. There is a rising sense as the scene unfolds that this is how the national game originally was played, or at least should have been. We watch Dean, big and barefoot and with the tails of his uniform shirt hanging out, blow his fastball by batters. He is clearly a hick—and a heck of a pitcher. The film evokes through him America's strenuous agrarian past, "the heritage of the pioneer who swung the axe and left the steel and brawn of his arms to the sons who followed" (Crepeau 55).

Grover Cleveland Alexander is repairing a telegraph line at the start of *The Winning Team.* A friend standing below pleads with him to pitch for the locals against a professional ball club barnstorming around the Midwest. After some hesitation "Alex" climbs down from the pole and from the urban-industrial clamor of the new century. Country baseball belongs to an earlier era, an earlier and simpler America. The diamond where the game will take place isn't fenced or in any way modern, but a seamless part of the heartland. While Alex throws warm-up tosses, two boys drag a cow off the field, and the umpire informs the visiting players, "We got a ground rule here: if a fielder loses a ball in the grass, you only get one extra base."

*The Pride of St. Louis* and *The Winning Team* quickly establish the rural credentials of their heroes. Yet almost as quickly, the films show their heroes leaving home for the city to play big-league ball. It is a historical fact that organized baseball had urban origins. The first professional teams sprang up in mid-19th-century cities with populations large enough to support an entertainment business based on gate receipts (Goldstein 111). Moreover, a disproportionate number of the early players were drawn from the ranks of Irish-American and German-American city dwellers (Guttman 100-01). This began to change in the 1870s, when baseball fever spread to rural areas. By the end of the century the players who cavorted for the raging, booming, cheering public at urban ballparks often came from farms or small towns.[1]

Whether an aspiring ballplayer, lawyer, businessman, or artist, the country boy who sought fame and wealth had no choice but to migrate to the city. Success literature of the 19th century offered the consolation that his chance of failure was slight so long as he "remained faithful to the virtues that formed his country character" (Wylie 208). *The Pride of St. Louis* takes an identical view. Far from home, Dean is forever recalling the struggles and lessons of his hardscrabble childhood. "When I was six . . . ," he tells his future wife (Joanne Dru) on their first date, "I was planting in the fields behind a team of mules. Well, when I was going on ten, I could do a man's work. It weren't nothing for me to pick 400 to 500 pounds of cotton a day." His endless reminiscing in fractured English represents more than an absurd garrulity. Because he uses colorful country language—or, put another way, because he remains true to his roots—Dean enjoys a celebrated career as a baseball announcer after he hangs up his spikes.

But not everyone has the good fortune to be born and raised in abject poverty on a dust-bowl farm. Babe Ruth, Lou Gehrig, Jackie Robinson, and Jimmy Piersall grow up in urban slums. The beginning of *The Pride of the Yankees* suggests that this brutish environment can lead even a "nice" boy into the byways of crime. Young Lou accidentally breaks the window of a grocery store with a baseball. A policeman collars him on the sandlot and hauls him home. "I can't do anything without my wife," Lou's little immigrant father (Ludwig Stossel) whines. Forced to wait for Ma Gehrig (Elsa Janssen), the policeman stands over Lou and grimly twirls his nightstick. It is an oppressive scene, intended to convey the imprisoning circumstances of Lou's early life and the overwhelming odds against his ever escaping them.

That he does escape them is largely the work of Ma Gehrig. Beneath a mild appearance—white hair, rimless glasses, pendulous, grandmotherly bosom—she is a tough old bird. She loves her son, but in return for her affection he must listen to her success lectures. "Look at your papa, look at me," she says. "We didn't go to school, and what are we? A janitor, a cook. I want you to be somebody."[2]

Of all the external influences prodding the slum kid or country boy onward and upward, none had greater honor in the 19th-century cult of success than that of mother (Wylie 29). Freud notwithstanding, she continued to be glorified into the twentieth century—so much so that Philip Wylie complained in 1942 that "momworship has gotten completely out of hand." "Our land, subjectively mapped," he wrote,

> would have more silver cords and apron strings crisscrossing it than railroad and telephone wires. Mom is everywhere and everything and damned near everybody, and from her depends all the rest of the U.S. Disguised as good old mom, dear old mom, sweet old mom, your loving mom, and so on, she is the bride at every funeral and the corpse at every wedding. Men live for her and die for her, dote upon her and whisper her name as they pass away, and I believe she has now achieved, in the hierarchy of miscellaneous articles, a spot next to the Bible and the Flag, being reckoned part of both in a way. (198)

Wylie published his diatribe the same year *The Pride of the Yankees* came out. This seems symbolically appropriate, since the film is steeped in the "momism" he was attacking. In one scene Lou has just been voted into a college fraternity. He tells his mother that he is supposed to give his pledge pin to his "best girl." A shadow of worry darkens her face, but vanishes when he adds, "You're still my best girl, Ma, aren't you?"

Watching *The Pride of the Yankees* today, one is struck by the perversity of mother love in action. Ma Gehrig is "a good mother whose very goodness is . . . a threat, a loving mother whose love serves only to unman her son" (Fiedler 320). She expects Lou to go to Columbia University and become an engineer like his late Uncle Otto, and though Lou wants to be a ballplayer, he tries to oblige her. Perhaps he concludes from the crushed condition of Pop Gehrig that she would make a merciless opponent; certainly a modern viewer of the film does. At any rate, Lou attends Columbia until his mother falls ill. He then signs with the New York Yankees to get money for her hospital care. When she finds out about it, she isn't exactly grateful. "That's what we came to America for," she says with bitter sarcasm, "that's why you studied, so you can play baseball. After all my plans to follow your Uncle Otto."

Baseball isn't Ma Gehrig's idea of a respectable occupation, and she is right—up to a point. Sam Crawford, a star with the Detroit Tigers in the early 1900s, once told an interviewer: "Baseball players weren't too much accepted in those days. . . . We were considered pretty crude. Couldn't get into the best hotels and all that. And when we did get into a good hotel, they wouldn't boast about having us" (qtd. in Ritter 51). *The Pride of the Yankees* itself portrays players as overgrown boys whose antics include goosing the porter on a train and eating the brim of a teammate's new straw hat.

Until the 1920s the most admired examples of the self-made man were statesmen and businessmen. The '20s, however, saw sports figures and Hollywood personalities reach heights of prestige that would have shocked earlier generations (Huber 186-87). With the growth of tabloid newspapers and radio, a man or woman could achieve fame and wealth by becoming "an entertainment product that the public voraciously consumes as a luxury of its leisure" (Huber 289). Many baseball biopics feature ritualistic shots of reporters tap-tapping at typewriters in the press box or of announcers hunched over microphones in the broadcast booth and providing a sort of Greek chorus to the drama on the field.

Although the films condone the 20th-century means of attaining success, they still reflect the 19th-century meaning of success. Throughout the last century being successful wasn't simply being rich or famous. Most success writers, in fact, denounced the worship of mammon. They espoused material success only to the extent that it contributed to ultimate or "true" success, which they defined as happiness, the joy of living, developing yourself by doing your best with the faculties God gave you, leading a self-respecting life, peace of mind, service to others (Huber 96-97). In *The Pride of the Yankees* there is an exchange between sportswriters Sam Blake (Walter Brennan) and Hank

Hannemann (Dan Duryea) that locates Lou Gehrig within this older, conservative tradition:

*Hank:* I'll tell you something. A guy like that is a detriment to any sport. He's a boob with a batting eye. He wakes up, brushes his teeth, hikes out to the ballpark, hits the ball, hikes back to the hotel room, reads the funny papers, gargles, and goes to bed. That's personality, huh?

*Sam:* The best.

*Hank:* A real hero.

*Sam:* Let me tell you about heroes, Hank. I've covered a lot of them, and I'm saying Gehrig is the best of them. No front-page scandals, no daffy excitements, no hornpiping in the spotlight.

*Hank:* No nothing.

*Sam:* But a guy who does his job and nothing else. He lives for his job, he gets a lot of fun out of it, and 50 million other people get a lot of fun out of him.

*Hank:* You'd be right, Sam, if all baseball fans were as big boobs as Gehrig.

*Sam:* They are—the same kind of boobs as Gehrig, only without a batting eye.

Lou is the idealized common man—an earnest, somewhat gawky, courageous guy who doesn't let fame and money turn his head. Other subjects of baseball biopics aren't quite so steady. They need instruction in the moral responsibilities of success, and they generally receive it from their wives or fiancées. When Babe Ruth visits a children's hospital on Christmas Eve dressed as Santa Claus and drunk as a skunk, his bride-to-be (Claire Trevor) pops up to tell him: "Whether you asked for it or not, you represent the dreams and ambitions of millions of American kids. How you act, they act. Never forget that." Similarly in *The Pride of St. Louis,* Dizzy Dean's wife is appalled that he would hurt his team's chances and disappoint his fans by holding out for a bigger salary. "You just can't always have things the way you want them," she scolds. "Things happen that you have to adjust yourself to and that you haven't the power to change, unless you insist on twisting and bending and forcing things out of their natural shape."

Baseball biopics foster social quiescence by stressing the nobility of sacrifice and the grace inherent in hard work without thought of reward. The virtues the films preach—conformity, sobriety, humility—belong more to the good employee than to the rugged individualist. If the films inspire viewers to do anything, it isn't to fantasize about having a major-league career, but to push on with their own mundane lives.

*The Failure of Success*

Historically, as Irvin G. Wyllie noted, "success has been for the few, not the many" (174). It is perhaps the central ideological project of baseball biopics to help reconcile the many to this fact. The films negotiate the tension between class and mass in a number of ways: (1) their protagonists rarely seek to rise above the ordinary, but usually have fame thrust upon them; (2) once a Lou Gehrig, a Babe Ruth, or a Jackie Robinson achieves success, he continues to act as a friend or representative of the people; and (3) success often carries so heavy a price—from marital discord to mutilation, insanity, and death—that mediocrity seems preferable.

No matter how obviously talented they are, most protagonists of baseball biopics refuse to believe at first that they have been chosen for a special destiny. When sportswriter Sam Blake informs Lou Gehrig that the New York Yankees are interested in signing him, Lou thinks it is a hoax and throws Sam out the door. When Jack Dunn (William Frawley), manager of the Baltimore Orioles, offers Babe Ruth a spot on the team, Babe responds with an incredulous "Me?" And when Barney Wile (Frank Morgan), an ex-catcher who scouts Monty Stratton in the bush leagues, tells the lanky young pitcher, "You're ready [for the majors]," Monty exclaims, "You're joking!" The protagonists mustn't appear too eager to separate themselves from the anonymous herd—that would be antidemocratic. Rather, fame must arrive unbidden.

The ballplayers retain a democratic aura even after they become successful. Lou Gehrig marries Eleanor Twitchell (Teresa Wright) not with a lot of celebrity fanfare, but in a small, informal ceremony witnessed by the carpenters, painters, and other workmen who are fixing up the couple's apartment. Babe Ruth buys all the unsold papers of a half-dozen or more newsboys and then invites the ragamuffins into a posh restaurant to "put on the feed bag." He is warm, innocent, generous. "Money leaves me," he wryly remarks at one point, "like it was shot out of a cannon."

Were the ballplayers to use their fame and wealth for selfish purposes, their success might provoke the anger or envy of audiences, and so it is important that they be shown doing good works. Both Lou Gehrig and Babe Ruth serve on the screen as inspirational examples to youngsters, especially ill youngsters. During a visit to a hospital, Lou autographs a ball for crippled little Billy and promises to hit two home runs for him in a game that afternoon. Lou hits the homers, but the episode doesn't end there. Some years later a teenaged Billy greets Lou outside Yankee Stadium. With tears in his adoring eyes, he explains that he did what Lou said he should—he tried—and now he can walk again.

*The Babe Ruth Story* is full of similar miracles. Babe has only to wave and say, "Hiya, kid," for a crippled boy to regain use of his legs. In Babe's case, and Lou's as well, success isn't founded on secular qualities like initiative and aggressiveness or given a squalid cash interpretation. It is something far more ethereal—the outward sign of an inward grace.

Such religious overtones are muted in *The Jackie Robinson Story,* which deals sensationally with the issue of race relations. Jackie is the target of intense hatred when he breaks baseball's color line. "Hey there, big boy," one Southern fan shouts, "what y'all doing on a white man's field? You better get your carcass outta there before you get rode out." The players on opposing teams are just as bigoted, calling him "Sambo," "Nigger Lips," and other ugly names.

But neither Jackie nor Dodger general manager Branch Rickey (Minor Watson) can be intimidated into abandoning the "great experiment." Behind the scenes Rickey soothes fellow baseball executives who fear violence between whites and blacks and the smash-up of the league, while on the diamond Jackie strives to be, in his own words, "the best ballplayer they've ever seen anywhere." In the film's climax he doubles with two out in the bottom of the ninth, then steals third and home to clinch the pennant for Brooklyn. White and black fans happily shake hands, and teammates who once signed a petition to keep Jackie off the Dodgers congratulate him. His success brings Americans of different colors and creeds together. Let Lou Gehrig and Babe Ruth heal the lame; he heals an entire nation.

Success has its price, though. Under orders from Rickey to control his hot temper, Jackie silently suffers ostracism, slurs, and intentional spikings on his way to the top. The protagonists of other baseball biopics suffer even worse things after reaching the top—die young, lose a leg, go insane, become alcoholics. Players are always making comebacks in the films from injury or illness. In fact, Grover Cleveland Alexander comes back twice in *The Winning Team,* first from a beaning that leaves him with blurred vision and later from the combined ravages of epilepsy and drink.

Why did filmmakers choose as subjects only players whose careers were somehow blighted? One possible answer is that there was built-in drama in the story of achievement against the odds. Another is that viewers could be expected to find attractive the notion that famous lives were the same mixture of sunshine and shadow as their own lives. But perhaps the most comprehensive answer is that the scramble for success no longer seemed synonymous with the pursuit of happiness.

Post-World War II America was the richest country in history. By 1953 the United States, which contained seven percent of the world's population, produced two-thirds of its manufactured goods and owned three-fourths of its cars and appliances (Shames 30). The economic boom inspired a national faith in the "chrome and urethane prospects of modern consumerism" (Shames 32). And there was the rub. As affluence increased, so did material longings. Desires were continually running ahead of satisfactions. Eric Fromm described the dilemma well when he wrote, "The world is one great object for our appetites, a big apple, a big bottle, a big breast; we are the sucklers, the eternally expectant ones, the hopeful ones—and the eternally disappointed ones" (qtd. in Huber 424).

Of the seven baseball biopics made from 1942 to 1956, the most skeptical about the value of success was *Fear Strikes Out,* the last film in the cycle. Its subject, Jimmy Piersall, comes unglued in his rookie year with the Boston Red Sox and has to be institutionalized. The root cause of his breakdown is his father (Karl Malden), a factory worker who stands behind him from boyhood and pushes him to succeed on the diamond. An early scene shows father and son having a catch, but there is no pleasure or diversion in it for either of them. The father viciously whips the ball to the son, whose face contorts in pain as he suffers the stings of the throws. If this is the road to success, the film seems to be saying, then success isn't worth achieving.

What is worth achieving is self-knowledge, peace of mind, psychological freedom. Before his breakdown Jimmy half-attempts to escape the pull of his father and establish his own separate identity and family. He marries a pretty young nurse (Norma Moore), and they soon have a baby daughter. The trouble is that he takes them to live with his parents in the ramshackle house where he grew up and where he remains a prisoner of his father's dreams of the big leagues and big money. The makers of the film stressed his imprisonment in a neurotic past by repeatedly photographing him through chain-link fences or covered with striped shadows.

*Fear Strikes Out* can be included among the so-called "teen pics" of the '50s—*Rebel without a Cause* (1955) is the best known—in which sensitive sons struggle against callous or incompetent fathers (Considine 78). Jimmy's father may set some sort of teen-pic record for callousness. About the middle of the film he travels to Louisville to see his son play in the minors. "Fifteen games to go, and I'm batting third in the league," Jimmy greets him. "Well, it isn't first," dad characteristically replies.

Later Jimmy acts out an eerie, unconscious parody of his father's success message. He abrasively challenges his Red Sox teammates to get hits and squabbles with them when they don't. "I'm the only player on the team who plays to win, plays to win games," he says, a haunted look in his eyes and a strange lilt in his voice. One night the pressure to win finally proves too much for him. After walloping a home run he climbs the foul screen and yells at the fans, his father, the universe: "How was that? Was it good enough for you?" It was good enough to land him in a mental institution.

There, encouraged by a quiet and understanding psychiatrist (Adam Williams)—plus a few thousand volts of electroshock—he comes to realize just what a monster his father is. "You don't care about me," he tells bad old dad in a pivotal scene. "You never gave a damn. 'Win, Jimmy, win,' that's all you cared about. And you're killing me, you've been killing me for years." His father crawls off, and by the next spring Jimmy is fully recovered and playing again with the Red Sox. But we shouldn't be deceived by this happy ending. On the way to reaching it, the film has turned the conventions of the baseball biopic upside down.

Instead of a hero whose mother objects to his playing ball, *Fear Strike Out* presents a hero whose father drives him to make the majors. Instead of a hero who illustrates the rewards of hard work, *Fear Strikes Out* presents a hero who works so hard he cracks. Instead of a hero who cures sick children, *Fear Strikes Out* presents a hero who is "a pretty sick boy" himself. Instead of a hero who faces adversity without flinching—"Look, doc, stop throwing curves. Give it to me straight," a dying William Bendix says in *The Babe Ruth Story*—*Fear Strikes Out* presents a hero who withdraws into a catatonic trance. Instead of a saga of rags to riches, that is, *Fear Strikes Out* presents a saga of rags to wretchedness.

The film brought an abrupt and rather dark end to the cycle of baseball biopics that had begun in the early 1940s. As Peter Biskind pointed out, the Protestant ethic may have been fine on the frontier and in the days of cutthroat, competitive capitalism, but no more (252). An affluent consumer culture had little use for frugality or sobriety or other self-disciplinary virtues. "Do it, now!" was the motto of the credit-card-carrying public. The generation that came of age in the 1960s, and which preferred feeding their heads to getting ahead, further undermined the gospel of strive and rise. Nonetheless, the baseball biopic wasn't finished. It would return in the 1980s with a new kind of hero, one ideologically suited to a decade characterized by mega-wants, mega-deals, mega-bucks, and, beneath all the greed and glitz, an ineffable sense of loss.

### *The Yuppie Ghost of Shoeless Joe*

Is it just coincidence that three contemporary films—*The Natural* (1984), *Eight Men Out* (1988), and *Field of Dreams* (1989)—offer pseudo-biographies of Shoeless Joe Jackson? If it isn't, why has a player who was tarnished by scandal and banned from baseball become such a popular film hero? Where indeed have you gone, Joe DiMaggio?

Joltin' Joe has left and gone away to make television commercials. You might have seen him performing as a celebrity huckster for Mr. Coffee and the Bowery Savings Bank—a long step down from his glory days with the New York Yankees, but presumably a lucrative one.

Television is also where the old-fashioned inspirational biopic has gone. Since the late 1960s there have been made-for-TV movies about ballplayers Satchel Paige, Ron LeFlore, Jackie Robinson, and Babe Ruth. The traditional biopic is particularly well suited to the small screen. Its linear plot can be interrupted every 10 or 12 minutes for commercials without too much loss of coherence, and even more important to advertisers, its happy ending leaves viewers undisturbed by thought and in a buying mood.

Perhaps because of this special affinity to the wishful world of television, baseball biopics remained absent from the big screen for almost 30 years. And when they finally did return in the mid-1980s, no one seemed to notice, for they took a strange new form. The fictionalization that went on unannounced in the biopics of the 1940s and 1950s—Ronald Bergan wryly referred to these films as "fiction that dare not speak its name" (22)—now went on quite openly. It was part of the postmodern breakdown and blending of once-distinct categories, subjects, and styles in many areas of cultural production.

Novelist E.L. Doctorow, for example, has treated historical figures in his best-selling books *Ragtime* and *Billy Bathgate* as if they sprang entirely from his own imagination. Music videos have appropriated grisly news footage of the Vietnam War to decorate pop songs. News shows have re-created events with actors standing in for real people. Meanwhile, filmmakers have conjured up Shoeless Joe Jackson, surrounded him with fictional characters, placed him in fictional situations, and given him fictional dialogue—in sum, have imposed whatever fantasies they wanted on his unresisting ghost.

But before we get over our heads in ectoplasm, it might be a good idea to list a few biographical facts about the flesh-and-blood Joseph Jefferson Jackson:

- He was called "Shoeless" because that is the way he was playing when a major-league scout discovered him on a semipro team in Greenville, South Carolina. The nickname stuck because it fit the uncomplicated country boy who couldn't read or write (Gropman *xiv*, 35).
- Ty Cobb said Joe was the "greatest natural hitter" who ever lived, and Babe Ruth copied his swing. His career batting average of .356 is still the third highest of all time (Gropman 145).

- Joe was one of the Chicago White Sox—or, as they came to be known, "Black Sox"—who confessed to throwing the 1919 World Series to the Cincinnati Reds. Although acquitted in court, he and seven of his teammates were banned from organized baseball for life by the sport's first commissioner, Judge Kenesaw Mountain Landis (Coffin 95-99).

For many Americans the Black Sox scandal marked the end of innocence. Ring Lardner, then a sports columnist for the *Chicago Herald & Examiner,* was bitterly disillusioned by the fix. "My interest in the national pastime died a sudden death in the fall of 1919," he would recall, "when [manager] Kid Gleason saw his power-house White Sox lose a world series to a club that was surprised to even win one game" (68). Before the series, baseball had a bright, noble, superpatriotic image. It was the "Great American Game"; its stars were the idols of millions. After the series that image was shattered (Asinof 197-98). The now-famous words, "Say it ain't so, Joe," supposedly the cry of a little boy to Joe Jackson as he left the grand jury hearings, convey something of the shock and dismay that baseball fans of all ages felt (Smith 141).

Shoeless Joe's walk down the courthouse steps carried him out of history and into popular mythology. What he specifically symbolized there would undergo a remarkable change over the years. His role would evolve from that of a man who misunderstood the American Dream and betrayed the public trust to that of a victim of betrayal himself.

As far back as 1927, a Paramount comedy, *Casey at the Bat,* began the long, slow process of revision. In the film two gamblers (Ford Sterling and Sterling Holloway) offer "Home Run" Casey (Wallace Beery) a bribe to throw the game for the National League pennant. Casey turns them down cold. "If I strike out today," he declares via a title, "every kid in America would know I done it a-purpose." Yet strike out he does—after the gamblers slip a trick ball onto the field. His manager immediately accuses him of being crooked and adds, "You're out of baseball for life." That night Casey is recognized on the street by a newsboy with a stack of extras. "Please, Casey," the kid begs, "say it ain't true." It ain't, of course, and ultimately the gamblers are exposed, Casey is cleared, and the championship game is replayed.

*Casey at the Bat* combines Ernest L. Thayer's poem about the Mudville nine with the Black Sox scandal. The musical *Damn Yankees* (1958) combines indistinct memories of the scandal with the Faust legend. Here the hero is a middle-aged baseball fan (Robert Shafer) who sells his soul to the devil for a chance to be young again and play for his beloved Washington Senators. Shortly after he appears at the ballpark as 22-year-old slugger Joe Hardy (Tab Hunter), a reporter dubs him

"Shoeless Joe from Hannibal, Mo."—which, despite his secret bargain with the devil, is pretty much a misnomer. Unlike the original Shoeless Joe, this one has sold his soul to win. His teammates even sing about it: "He'll fight for us/He'll do right for us/He'll be a beacon light for us/Shoeless Joe from Hannibal, Mo."

More than a quarter century later, Joe was still hitting away. From 1984 to 1989 he or a fictional counterpart were featured in *The Natural, Eight Men Out,* and *Field of Dreams.* The films portrayed Joe rather curiously. One might have expected him to serve in the 1980s—"a time when 'success' was virtually synonymous with, and limited to, making money" (Shames 7)—as a cautionary figure, a symbol of the destructiveness of greed. But just the opposite was true. The player who sacrificed the game he loved for a "sleazy promise of dirty money" was called forth to receive absolution (Asinof 10).

*The Natural* takes its title, and little else, from a novel by Bernard Malamud. While the book ends with Roy Hobbs, a character modeled on Shoeless Joe, broken and disgraced, the film ends with Roy (Robert Redford) being conventionally heroic. He belts a prodigious home run with two outs in the bottom of the ninth and wins the big game for his team. Viewers never doubt Roy's will to resist the corruptions of commercial civilization, only whether his health—he has this old gunshot wound—can hold up through the pennant chase. At one point gambler Gus Sands (Darren McGavin), who is trying to bribe him, says, "You can't hang onto the game forever, kid." To which Roy sensibly replies, "You can't get back into it from jail either."

*Eight Men Out* is a fact-based account of the Black Sox scandal, and so closer in style than *The Natural* to the baseball biopics of the 1940s and 1950s—though still not too close. *The Pride of the Yankees, The Babe Ruth Story,* etc., were inspirational tales of players who struggled up from poverty and obscurity to fame and wealth. This is a sorry tale of players who risk everything—their reputations, their pride, their livelihoods—to make a dishonest buck. But the film doesn't necessarily blame them. There is the feeling that, whatever they did, they were treated unfairly both before and after the scandal.

The real culprits in the film are Sox owner Charles Comiskey (Clifton James), commissioner Landis (John Anderson), and professional gamblers "Sport" Sullivan (Kevin Tighe), Abe Attell (Michael Mantell), and Arnold Rothstein (Michael Lerner): Comiskey, because he is a cheap, double-crossing tyrant; Landis, because he exploits the scandal to establish the powers of his new office; and the gamblers, because, well, they are gamblers. With these sharks and snakes running baseball, the players are doomed. Black Sox pitcher Eddie Ciccote (David Strathairn) delivers what amounts to their eulogy: "I always figured it was talent that made a man big . . . if you were the best at somethin'. We're the guys they come to see. . . . Yeah, but look who's holding the money and look who's facing the jail cell? Talent don't mean nothin'. And where's Comiskey and Sullivan, Attell, Rothstein? Out in the back room, cutting up the profits, that's where."

Shoeless Joe (D.B. Sweeney) in particular emerges as a hapless victim. When the scandal breaks in the newspapers and he is called before the grand jury, he doesn't even know enough to get a lawyer. All he knows is how to play baseball. According to the film, Joe's greatest crime was his innocence.

*Field of Dreams* forgoes the historical approach of *Eight Men Out* to dabble in the supernatural. At the urging of a mysterious voice, Iowa farmer Ray Kinsella (Kevin Costner) plows under his corn and builds a ballfield, complete with arc lights and bleachers. Shoeless Joe (Ray Liotta) then returns from the grave, or from wherever he has been hanging out since he died in 1951, to play on it. Once more he is portrayed as having been railroaded by the lords of baseball. "He did take [the gamblers'] money," Ray notes, "but no one could ever prove he did a single thing to lose those games." Joe himself speaks poignantly of his banishment from the big leagues. "Getting thrown out of baseball was like having part of me amputated," he says. "I've heard that old men wake up and scratch itchy legs that have been dust for over 50 years. That was me. I'd wake up in the night with the smell of the ballpark in my nose, the cool of the grass on my feet, the thrill of the grass." His dialogue throughout the film is of this vivid, poetic sort, and quite anomalous for an illiterate. On the other hand, if he could vindicate his honesty in the afterworld, he could probably learn grammar there, too.

The pardon of Shoeless Joe by recent films seems connected in a roundabout way to the getting-and-spending frenzy that was the 1980s. "Success lost its reference to accomplishment, to high intent," Laurence Shames wrote of the decade, "and was recognized only in terms of its reward" (13-14). He added that "praising people for having money became almost a national reflex. . . . the real fan magazine was no longer *Rolling Stone* but *Fortune*" (105). Success literature of the 19th century had drawn a moral distinction between the investor who supplied capital for enterprises that fulfilled some human need and the speculator who bought stocks to make a quick killing (Wylie 77-78). The updated gospel wasn't so finicky. It "mattered less and less," Shames said, "how . . . money had been gotten, partly because, in an age of eroding values, every dollar was taken to be the same as every other, whether earned, embezzled, or inherited" (108).

If there was one figure that especially symbolized the 1980s, it was the "yuppie." The term originated as a political buzzword to describe the followers of Democratic presidential candidate Gary Hart and ended up as a derisive label for the most affluent faction of the nation's 75 million baby boomers (Shapiro 65). Yuppies were young, urban, greedy, affected —and always someone else. Still, when a certain lifestyle becomes the emblem of an era, that style insinuates itself (Shames 13). Yuppiedom didn't include just the nouveau riches who cruised around in BMWs, or drank Perrier with a twist of lime, or wore ventless Italian suits, but took in the many for whom ambition meant getting on a career track and success meant owning and consuming.

"Affluence causes difficulties," William L. O'Neill once observed, "even if they are more agreeable than those arising from poverty" (38). It is an observation that sums up the 1980s pretty well. In 1985, for example, the American Psychological Association held a symposium on a new syndrome, "the impostor phenomenon." Impostors were "men and women, generally in their twenties and thirties, who were successful in their careers, and yet felt like bluffers, vulnerable at any moment to exposure or disgrace" (Shames 126). The phenomenon indicated that people had adopted a version of success that turned out not to satisfy; that job promotions and a big paycheck didn't necessarily guarantee confidence and contentment; that the meaning of life in a mass society remained as perplexing as ever.

We now can let Shoeless Joe back into our discussion. Whether or not we want to believe it, the fact is that he accepted $5,000 from gamblers to throw the World Series. His greed and corruption resemble our own, which is why *The Natural, Eight Men Out,* and *Field of Dreams* whitewash his role in the Black Sox scandal. By exonerating Joe, the films exonerate us, we who grew up and sold out and called it being "realistic."

Nostalgia for lost illusions pervades these films. Both *The Natural* and *Eight Men Out* re-create the innocent America that existed just before the '20s started to roar. *Field of Dreams* identifies the good old days as rather more recent—the 1960s, to be exact. Ray, its baby-boomer hero, clings anachronistically to the vestiges of faded "flower power." He wears a Berkeley T-shirt, listens to the music of the Lovin' Spoonful, and drives a Volkswagen van with a peace-sign sticker on the windshield. On first meeting him, ex-radical author Terence Mann (James Earl Jones) cries in mock alarm: "Oh my god, you're from the sixties. Get back, get back, there's no place for you here in the future."

The problem for Ray is how to reconcile the hippie past with the yuppie present, idealism with materialism. He uses up all his savings to build the supernatural ballfield, and soon finds himself being hounded by creditors and in danger of losing his farm. But then his young daughter has a premonition. "We don't have to sell the land," she announces. "People will come." And, indeed, the last shot of the film shows a long line of cars approaching from out of the night. Hundreds who seek renewal are about to arrive, and thousands more will follow, and every one of them will pay to watch the ghostly ball game on Ray's field. The lesson seems to be that you can be a hippie and still be a yuppie, or be a yuppie and still be a hippie, or be dead and still be a ballplayer.

### *The End of Something*

With the American economy in turmoil and some of the most celebrated financial wizards of the 1980s in jail, the era of wanton consumption symbolized by the yuppie is now over. A "new frugality" may well define the closing years of the century (Marino 1D). As though to compensate or console us, Hollywood has rescued the traditional baseball biopic from limbo.

*The Babe,* released in 1992 and starring John Goodman, troops out all the old myths about Babe Ruth. Richard Schickel of *Time* magazine was just plain wrong in describing the film as "both antiheroic and antiepic, and thus a departure from the generally undistinguished tradition of the sports biopic" (66). Goodman's Ruth may punctuate his dialogue with belches and farts, but he is still a hero to small boys and an inspiration to grown men. "He ain't human, he's an animal," a Yankee teammate marvels after Ruth calls his shot on a home run in the 1932 World Series. "No," another replies, "he's a god."

Far from overturning the conventions of earlier baseball biopics, *The Babe* recycles them. There is the same introductory note that this is a true story; the same narrative pattern of rise, fall, and comeback; the same equation of success with inner strength. Why, Goodman even wears the same sort of Halloween makeup, including a grotesque putty nose, that William Bendix wore.

The baseball biopic persists while other film forms fade because it smooths out our crumpled dreams. When we are behind in the score, it encourages us to keep trying. When we are ahead, it assures us that we morally deserve to win. It suggests that in life, as in baseball, there are clear, recognized rules, and that the competition is fair and open and bathed in sunshine.

None of which is so, of course. In the real world hard work often comes to nothing, morals are an impediment, games get rained out. But we are taught, and perhaps need to believe, otherwise. If films portrayed the struggle for success as it really is—the desperation, the madness, the greed—who could bear to watch them?

## Notes

1. Hall-of-Fame outfielder Sam Crawford, who grew up in Wahoo, Nebraska, in the 1890s, recalled: "In those days baseball was a big thing in those little towns. The kids would be playing all the time. . . . I guess, when you come to think of it, we spent most of our childhood playing ball" (qtd. in Ritter 66).

2. Just how important a figure baseball biopics consider mother is perhaps best indicated by what happens to the city boy when she isn't around to protect or correct him. *The Babe Ruth Story* contains an opening scene—Babe swats a ball through the window of a Chinese laundry—very similar to the one in *The Pride of the Yankees.* But Babe, unlike Lou, has been in trouble before. The film explains his wildness by mentioning that his mother is dead and by showing that his saloon-keeper father hasn't the time or the interest to properly raise him. Instead of success lectures, Babe is treated to the drunken babble of his father's customers. He ends up in a reform school, there to be "mothered," so to speak, by the priests in charge.

## Works Cited

Anderson, Carolyn. "Biographical Film." *Handbook of American Film Genres.* Ed. Wes D. Gehring. Westport, CT: Greenwood, 1988. 331-51.

Asinof, Eliot. *Eight Men Out.* New York: Holt, 1963.

Bergan, Ronald. "Whatever Happened to the Biopic?" *Films and Filming* 7 (July 1983): 21-22.

Biskind, Peter. *Seeing Is Believing: How Hollywood Taught Us to Stop Worrying and Love the Fifties.* New York: Pantheon, 1984.

Booth, Stephen. "Hollywood Goes to Bat." *Video Review* Sept. 1989: 44-47.

Cawelti, John G. *Apostles of the Self-Made Man.* Chicago: U of Chicago P, 1965.

Coffin, Tristram Potter. *The Old Ball Game: Baseball in Folklore and Fiction.* New York: Herder, 1971.

Considine, David M. *The Cinema of Adolescence.* Jefferson, NC: McFarland, 1985.

Crepeau, Richard C. *Baseball: America's Diamond Mind, 1919-1941.* Orlando: U of Florida P, 1980.

Dowdy, Andrew. *The Films of the Fifties: The American State of Mind.* New York: Morrow, 1973.

Fiedler, Leslie. *Love and Death in the American Novel.* New York: Criterion, 1960.

Goldman, Eric F. *The Crucial Decade: America, 1944-55.* New York: Knopf, 1956.

Goldstein, Warren. *Playing for Keeps: A History of Early Baseball.* Ithaca, NY: Cornell UP, 1989.

Gropman, Donald. *Say It Ain't So, Joe!: The Story of Shoeless Joe Jackson.* Boston: Little, Brown, 1979.

Guttman, Allen. *From Ritual to Record: The Nature of Modern Sports.* New York: Columbia UP, 1978.

Harmetz, Aljean. *The Making of the Wizard of Oz.* New York: Limelight, 1977.

Huber, Richard M. *The American Idea of Success.* New York: McGraw, 1971.

Joannou, Mary, and Steve McIntyre. "Lust for Lives." *Screen* Apr.-May 1983: 145-49.

Lardner, Ring. "Some Champions." *Some Champions.* Ed. Matthew J. Bruccoli and Richard Layman. New York: Scribner, 1976. 67-71.

Lord, Walter. *The Good Years.* New York: Harper, 1960.

Marion, Vivian. "New Frugality: Is This the Future?" *Poughkeepsie* (NY) *Journal* 28 Nov. 1991: 1D+.

O'Neill, William. *American High: The Years of Confidence, 1945-1960.* New York: Free Press, 1986.

Pachter, Marc. "The Biographer Himself: An Introduction." *Telling Lives: The Biographer's Art.* Ed. Marc Pachter. Washington: New Republic, 1979. 2-14.

Paget, Derek. *True Stories?: Documentary Drama on Radio, Screen and Stage.* Manchester, England: Manchester UP, 1990.

Ritter, Lawrence S. *The Glory of Their Times.* New York: Macmillan, 1966.

Robinson, Ray. *Iron Horse: Lou Gehrig in His Time.* New York: Norton, 1990.

Sayre, Nora. "Winning the Weepstakes: The Problems of American Sporting Films." *Film Genre: Theory and Criticism.* Ed. Barry K. Grant. Metuchen, NJ: Scarecrow, 1977. 182-94.

Schickel, Richard. "All Appetite." *Time* 27 Apr. 1992: 66.

—. Introduction. *The Hollywood Hallucination.* By Parker Tyler. New York: Simon and Schuster, 1970. *v-x.*

Shames, Laurence. *The Hunger for More: Searching for Values in an Age of Greed.* New York: Times, 1989.

Shapiro, Walter. "The Birth and—Maybe—Death of Yuppiedom." *Time* 18 Apr. 1991: 65.

Smith, Leverett T., Jr. *The American Dream and the National Game.* Bowling Green, OH: Bowling Green State University Popular Press, 1975.

Tuchman, Barbara. "Biography as a Prism of History." Pachter, *Telling Lives* 132-47.

Wylie, Philip. *Generation of Vipers.* New York: Holt, 1942.

Wyllie, Irvin G. *The Self-Made Man in America: The Myth of Rags to Riches.* New York: Free Press, 1954.

## Filmography

| Year | Film | Director |
|---|---|---|
| 1927 | *Casey at the Bat* | Monte Brice |
| 1942 | *The Pride of the Yankees* | Sam Wood |
| 1948 | *The Babe Ruth Story* | Roy Del Ruth |
| 1949 | *The Stratton Story* | Sam Wood |
| 1950 | *The Jackie Robinson Story* | Alfred Green |
| 1952 | *The Pride of St. Louis* | Harmon Jones |
| 1952 | *The Winning Team* | Lewis Seller |
| 1956 | *Fear Strikes Out* | Robert Mulligan |
| 1958 | *Damn Yankees* | George Abbott, Stanley Donen |
| 1984 | *The Natural* | Barry Levinson |
| 1988 | *Eight Men Out* | John Sayles |
| 1989 | *Field of Dreams* | Phil Alden Robinson |
| 1992 | *The Babe* | Arthur Hiller |

# Hollywood's Ableist Agenda

**Martin F. Norden**

Anyone remotely aware of the mainstream movie industry's penchant for constructing warped social imagery should not be surprised to learn that this divisive behavior has extended as much to the depiction of people with physical disabilities as it has to other repressed social subgroups. As film historians Leonard Quart and Albert Auster have argued, "Hollywood, hardly noted for its realistic screen treatment of racial and ethnic minorities and women, has not been any more sensitive or illuminating in its portrayal of the disabled" (25). As powerful cultural tools, the movies have played a major role in perpetuating mainstream society's regard for people with disabilities, and more often than not the images borne in those movies have differed sharply from the realities of the disabled experience. This essay, a companion piece for several earlier *Beyond the Stars* entries (Vol. 1's "Victims, Villains, Saints, and Heroes: Movie Portrayals of People with Physical Disabilities" and Vol. 3's "Reel Wheels: The Role of Wheelchairs in American Movies"), explores the philosophical and historical beliefs that have informed the dominant society's strategies for dealing with its physically disabled minority in life and in the movies.[1]

The tendency of Hollywood moviemakers to isolate disabled characters from those representing mainstream society as well as from each other is the foundation for these cinematic constructions, and it generally coincides with the way mainstream society has treated its disabled population for centuries. "Prior to [the late 1960s and early 1970s]," wrote Andrew Grant and Frank Bowe, "being disabled almost assured social, educational and occupational isolation" (6). The process of mainstreaming—bringing disabled people out of institutions and into the mainstream of society, allowing them and able-bodied people to learn from each other—has by its very nature weakened the trend toward isolation, but unfortunately it has done little to vitiate the long-standing moviemaker tendency to characterize disabled people as isolated individuals. Paul Longmore's 1985 article on disability and film did not directly address the ways mainstreaming has affected moviemaker attitudes, but it is clear from its general tone that little has changed: "The disabled person is excluded because of the fear and contempt of the nondisabled majority. Still, even when the handicapped character is presented sympathetically as a victim of bigotry, it remains clear that severe disability makes social integration impossible. While viewers are urged to pity [such a character], we are let off the hook by being shown that disability or bias or both must forever ostracize severely disabled persons from society" (33).

The phenomenon of isolation is reflected not only in the typical story lines of the films but also to a large extent in the ways the filmmakers have visualized the characters interacting in their environments; they have often used the basic tools of their trade—framing, editing, sound, lighting, set-design elements (e.g., fences, windows, staircase bannisters)—to suggest a physical or symbolic separation of disabled characters from the rest of society. Audience positioning within the films becomes a critical issue, for more often than not moviemakers have photographed and edited their works to reflect an able-bodied point of view. By encouraging audience members to perceive the world depicted in the movies from this perspective and thus associate themselves with able-bodied characters, this strategy has the effect of further isolating disabled characters by reducing them to objects of spectacle for the able-bodied majority.[2]

This latter point deserves further examination, as it is the key to understanding why moviemakers create physically disabled characters at all. Joseph Stubbins once bluntly declared that "the toughest item on the agenda of disability is that modern America has no need for most disabled persons" (22), yet mainstream filmmakers, far from turning their backs on this minority, have constructed hundreds upon hundreds of cinematic portraits of disabled characters that reach back to the earliest years of the medium, and it's worth asking why. George Henderson and Willie V. Bryan suggested that "throughout history, people without disabilities have had a paradoxical repulsion-attraction for those with disabilities" (3), an observation that echoes the work of philosopher and sociocultural critic Leslie Fiedler. In his *Freaks: Myths and Images of the Secret Self,* Fiedler argued that people with genetic disorders (e.g., dwarfs, giants, hermaphrodites, Siamese twins) fascinate members of mainstream society because the former, simultaneously "others" and mirrors of the self, are akin to mythic icons that reflect the latter's dreams and fears. Though he distinguished people with genetic disorders from those with other disabilities (23-24), a number of his generalizations have particular relevance here.

Chief among them is Fiedler's observation that "human Freaks have, in fact, been manufactured for ritual aesthetic and commercial purposes ever since history began" (251). The majority society has always had a strong desire to see human anomalies, not always with the purest of motives, and entrepreneurial sorts within that society have all too willingly serviced that desire by creating "freaks," sometimes through mutilation, always through packaging and promotion. Though Fiedler was referring in the above quote to people who have been intentionally deformed ("the binding of feet by the Chinese, the stretching of the lower lip among the Ubangis"), it's an idea that easily transfers to the world of movies; filmmakers have quite literally manufactured disabled characters in the name of commercial gain. The people responsible for *The Hunchback of Notre Dame,* a 1939 film notable for its freakshow qualities, were so aware of mainstream society's fascination with deformity and ugliness that even as they went about constructing one of moviedom's most famous disabled characters they had no less a personage than King Louis XI acknowledge the topic. "The ugly is very appealing to man," said the monarch during the film's infamous fools' day festival sequence. "One shrinks from the ugly and wants to look at it. There's a devilish fascination in it. We extract pleasure from horror." Fiedler rightly asserted that movies have usurped the inglorious function of carnival sideshows, which despite occasional revivals have been in decline since the advent of movies: "Human curiosities [have], for most Americans, passed inevitably from the platform and the pit to the screen, flesh becoming shadow" (16). The moviemaker assault on people with physical disabilities is thus two-tiered: it tries to keep the minority isolated and at the same time frequently panders to the pathological needs of its able-bodied audience.

Since the practice of isolating disabled people in society as well as in the movies reflects a not-so-hidden political agenda—what better way to keep a minority under control than to divide and quarantine it?—it might be helpful to examine the general topic of political issues and their linkage with movies at this juncture. Briefly put, a mainstream society will do whatever it can to maintain itself in power, and its strategy of keeping minorities such as physically disabled people "in their place" and dependent by defining the issues represents a significant part of its self-continuance. Specialists in the rehabilitation field, an area dominated by able-bodied people, have certainly exhibited this perspective, as Joseph Stubbins has argued: "[Rehabilitation] professionals define the problems, the agenda, and the social reality of disabled persons in ways that serve their own interests more closely than those of their clients" (23). The movie industry, so intertwined with other institutions of the dominant culture, has likewise demonstrated this point of view. Its products constitute an important mode of discourse by which the culture perpetuates itself and its perspectives, and they operate on several levels in service to it. Not only do they frequently deal explicitly, if often misguidedly, with contemporaneous social concerns (the films of the 1940s and 1950s that examined the lives of disabled World War II veterans are obvious examples), but, more significantly, they also contain submerged ideological perspectives, or what Gerald Mast and Bruce Kawin have called "the unspoken, assumed cultural values of films—values that seem so obviously true for that culture that they are accepted as inevitable, normal, and natural rather than as constructs of the culture itself" (5). These values, which typically go undetected and unquestioned by mainstream audiences, often assume the form of stereotyped images that, though sheer repetition, eventually take on a ring of truth in that society.

In the case of people with physical disabilities, the movie industry has perpetuated or initiated a number of exceedingly durable stereotypes over the years as a part of the general strategy of isolation. Typically designed to inspire humor, pity, revulsion, awe, or some combination thereof, the following images are its more common representations:

- *The Civilian Superstar,* a world-class performer in such fields as sports, the arts, politics, and medicine who seldom allows his/her disability to interfere with career goals. E.g., *Dr. Kildare's Crisis, Edison, the Man, The Other Side of the Mountain, The Stratton Story, Sunrise at Campobello, With a Song in My Heart.*
- *The Comic Misadventurer,* whose disability causes self-directed problems, other-directed problems, or both. E.g., *Dr. Strangelove, Fire Sale, It's a Gift, See No Evil, Hear No Evil, Young Frankenstein.*
- *The Elderly Dupe,* an aged character, mostly limited to silent-era films, who because of a disability (usually blindness) is easily fooled by younger able-bodied types. E.g., *The Four Horsemen of the Apocalypse, The Jury of Fate, The Man and the Woman, The Miracle Man, The Show.*
- *The High-Tech Guru,* a wheelchair-using male who proves unusually adept at manipulating computers, communication consoles, and related paraphernalia. E.g., *The Anderson Tapes, No Way Out, Power, Starman, Three Days of the Condor.*
- *The Noble Warrior,* a disabled war veteran who made numerous appearances in movies immediately after WWI, WWII, and Vietnam. E.g., *The Best Years of Our Lives, The Big Parade, Born on the Fourth of July, Coming Home, Pride of the Marines, Till the End of Time.*

- *The Obsessive Avenger,* an Ahab-like character (most often, a doomed male) who does not rest until he has had his revenge on the person(s) responsible for disabling him and/or violating his moral code in some other way. E.g., *Freaks, The Hunchback of Notre Dame, The Penalty, Peter Pan, The Sea Beast, West of Zanzibar.*
- *The Saintly Sage,* another elderly character, especially prevalent in movies of the 1930s and '40s, who despite blindness can "see" things sighted people cannot and who dispenses much wisdom to his/her younger colleagues who ignore it at their peril. E.g., *Bride of Frankenstein, The Devil-Doll, The Enchanted Cottage, Heidi, Saboteur.*
- *The Sweet Innocent,* a child or young woman typically pure, godly, humble, asexual, and exceptionally pitiable, and who often receives a "miracle cure." E.g., *A Christmas Carol, City Lights, The Miracle Man, Orphans of the Storm, Pollyanna, Stella Maris.*
- *The Techno Marvel,* a person whose prosthesis (often a high-tech affair) frequently performs better than the limb, vision, or hearing it replaced. E.g., *Blind Date, The Empire Strikes Back, Innerspace, Star Wars, Stephen King's Silver Bullet.*
- *The Tragic Victim,* frequently a poverty-stricken social outcast, who expires by film's end, if not earlier. E.g., *The Blind Musician, The Faithful Dog, The Hidden, His Daughter's Voice, Kiss of Death.*

Such images typically bear little resemblance to the actual experiences and lifestyles of people with physical disabilities. After examining hundreds of disability-related film and television dramas, Lauri Klobas concluded that "an immense chasm exists between disabled people and their screen counterparts" (*xi*). It is a view shared by John Schuchman, a Gallaudet College professor immersed in deaf-related issues all his life: "The deaf characters I have seen on movie screens and on television bear little resemblance to the deaf people or community that I knew as a boy or that I know today as a professional in daily contact with deaf people" (*ix*). According to Klobas, the discrepancies between real-life disabled people and their movie portrayals are traceable to mainstream society's reluctance to recognize disabled people as a minority group suffering from discrimination:

> The "cultural" chasm between real-life and screen disability can be graphically defined by looking at disability not as a physical/personal problem, but as one of human rights. A simplistic parallel argument would be to state that the reason black Americans did not vote in previous decades, could not use all public bathrooms, and had to sit at the back of the bus was because they had not "accepted" the reality they were black. Their anger resulted from not "over-

> coming" their race. Obviously, this was never the case and it sounds ludicrous to state the same. However, it is happening to the nation's disabled citizens. Their social problems and individual idiosyncrasies are ignored, while easy emotional stories of "bitterness," "overcoming," and "courage" abound. (*xii*)

Appraising the situation in similar terms, Paul Longmore noted that the able-bodied majority views disability as

> primarily a problem of emotional coping, of personal acceptance. It is not a problem of social stigma and discrimination. It is a matter of individuals overcoming not only the physical impairments of their own bodies but, more importantly, the emotional consequences of such impairments. [The films] convey the message that success or failure in living with a disability results almost solely from the emotional choices, courage, and character of the individual. (34)

The people immediately responsible for this and other messages are, of course, the able-bodied folk who dominate the movie industry. Their attitudes toward disabled people as expressed in their films range from mildly insulting to overwhelmingly hostile and are often informed by an esoteric logic. For example, the silent-film director Rex Ingram recruited hunchbacked and short-stature performers to play minor characters in many films including *The Prisoner of Zenda, Trifling Women, Where the Pavement Ends, Scaramouche, Mare Nostrum,* and *The Magician* in part because, according to his biographer, he believed they would bring him luck (O'Leary 51, 73). A handful of Hollywood directors have had visual or auditory impairments, most notably, John Ford, Raoul Walsh, André de Toth, Tay Garnett, Nicholas Ray, and William Wyler, but little of their work—Wyler's *The Best Years of Our Lives,* Ray's *On Dangerous Ground,* Ford's *The Wings of Eagles,* maybe a few others—suggests any sensitivity to disability issues. People with disabilities occasionally act as advisors on a film, but ultimately the authorship of the movie rests with one or more able-bodied people. This is not to say the able-bodied can't have insights into the physically disabled experience, but far more often than not they warp the images to fit preconceived notions. The resulting films often have only the most tenuous connection to the world of people with physical disabilities.

Though members of the movie industry are obviously the front-line cultivators of these images, it would hardly be appropriate to suggest they have been operating independently of long-standing mainstream values. Though movies are intimately tied to the 20th century, they are informed to a large extent by negative attitudes toward disabled people that predate the cinema by centuries and have found their way into a variety of cultural expressions. They are certainly present in our language ("She's blind to that situation," "Their proposal fell on deaf ears," "That's a lame excuse," "He doesn't have a leg to stand on," etc.), for instance, as well as in the rules and regulations that have helped shape our society. In her analysis of pre-20th-century laws and public policy statements, Claire Liachowitz concluded that "the cultural practice of translating physical abnormality into social inferiority is so deeply rooted as to have had an almost certain impact on both the formulation and implementation of later public policy" (1). These same deeply ingrained attitudes toward people with physical disabilities have also served as the movie industry's basis for the disabled characters that populate its films.

Consider, for example, a typical moviemaker use of disability: to suggest some element of a person's character, a tradition that carries back to the earliest days of the medium. "A screenplay, remember, is a story told with pictures," wrote Syd Field, the dean of screenwriting teachers.

> Pictures, or images, reveal aspects of character. In Robert Rossen's classic film *The Hustler,* a physical defect symbolizes an aspect of character. The girl played by Piper Laurie is a cripple; she walks with a limp. She is also an emotional cripple; she drinks too much, has no sense of aim or purpose in life. The physical limp underscores her emotional qualities—*visually*" [emphasis in original text].

Field's prime justification for admonishing screenwriters to continue this contemptible tendency is its sheer longevity: "Physical handicap—as an aspect of characterization—is a theatrical convention that extends far back into the past. One thinks of *Richard III*" (27).

In a similar vein, screenwriting teachers Ben Brady and Lance Lee offered the hypothetical tale of a young Olympic skier who's hit by a car and left paralyzed from the waist down as a "good" example of a dramatic story. The woman's doctors and parents are skeptical that she will ever walk again, let alone ski, but through basic will-power abetted with physical therapy she eventually regains some feeling in her limbs. The story ends with the implication that this is only the first step toward a complete recovery. Embedded in this narrative is the unstated view that the stigma of a disability is something to be avoided at all costs, and that sheer determination will enable a person to return to the ranks of the able-bodied. They view disability not as a normal part of many people's day-to-day lives but something to struggle with and be cured of, as their comments make clear: "[Conflict] can come from within the protagonist, it can come from others outside, or it can come from some sort of physical or natural obstacle. . . . Sally is hurt: her obstacle is a physical one. She wants to ski again, but has to overcome paralysis" (11-12). If the beliefs of Brady, Lee, and Field are anywhere near the industrial norm, there is little mystery as to why such images continue to find their way into the movies.

The following sketch of mainstream society's attitudes toward disabled people prior to the 20th century should provide a basis of understanding for the disability-related movies that have followed.

In their book *Psychosocial Aspects of Disability,* George Henderson and Willie Bryan noted that people with disabilities were considered expendable in ancient societies for several reasons: they failed to contribute to the needs of the community, and they harbored evil *mana* or spirits who caused the disabling condition as a result of the individual's failure to appease the spirits:

> Mana encapsulates the primitive belief in a powerful, invisible, all-pervading force at work in the universe, which could cripple and kill at will. Thus, mental illnesses and physical afflictions were generally viewed as the work of evil mana, or spirits. If, after considerable coaxing, the spirits did not leave a possessed body, this was believed to be indisputable evidence that the individual was being punished. In order to prevent contamination, people possessed with evil spirits were to be either avoided or killed. (4-5)

People who experienced war-related disabilities were usually exempt from such despicable treatment. In ancient Athens, disabled soldiers received pensions while their Roman counterparts shared in the distribution of such items as food, money, and land grants. By the time of the Middle Ages, however, most disabled war veterans were reduced to roadside begging. If governments were no longer supporting them, they at least experienced a general exemption from mendicancy laws (Devine 19-49, Liachowitz 19-44).

Such profoundly ambivalent attitudes toward people with physical disabilities found expression in other forms. Leslie Fiedler noted that disabled people have been exhibited for the edification and amusement of audiences ranging from royalty to peasantry since antiquity and in latter years often enjoyed church sponsorship (279-80), presumably to show agog spectators the results of God's displeasure. In addition, many ancient works of literature contain sections that equate physical perfection with spiritual goodness and disability and illness with evil or punishment for evil. The Bible, a major defining text for Western civilization, includes numerous passages that suggest a linkage of disease and disability with punishment from God, as Nancy Weinberg and Carol Sebian have observed:

> In the Old Testament, God admonished people to obey all his commandments or he would inflict them with blindness (Deut. 27:27). The New Testament restates this same sentiment—that physical illness and disability are punishments for some religious transgression. Jesus, upon healing a man said, "See, you are well! sin no more, that nothing worse befall you'' (John 5:14). In another instance of healing he said to a man with palsy, "My son; your sins are forgiven" (Matt. 9:2). These teachings imply that the sick and disabled deserve to suffer as a punishment for having sinned. (273)

Weinberg and Sebian also underscored "the biblical tradition of giving alms to the disabled but not accepting disabled persons as equals"—a view that has changed little over the centuries (281).

Such perspectives on disability are deep-seated and continue to exert a powerful influence. As Henderson and Bryan further noted:

> Many of the ancient myths and stereotypes of people with disabilities still exist. Although few persons currently subscribe to abandoning or killing people with disabilities, many do associate disabilities with sin and the Devil. They either consciously or subconsciously think that *disability* is a synonym of *bad.* More often than not, *able-bodied* is associated with *good,* i.e., Christ and the angels, cleanliness, and virtue. None of the great artists ever created images of angels with disabilities. Conversely, persons with disabilities have been associated through the ages with all that is bad. (8)

Nowhere in literature are evil and disability so inextricably fused as in Shakespeare's infamous Richard Crookback, a character whose disability-informed identity is superseded only by his unremitting evil. Scholars have long been aware of the discrepancy between Richard's historical personage and Shakespeare's treatment of him. Marchette Chute's assessment is typical:

> Shakespeare's portrait of Richard does not have much resemblance to the real King Richard of history, any more than his portrait of a peasant witch has much to do with the real Joan of Arc. But it was the portrait he found in the only history books that were available to him, and he had no reason to question it. Moreover, it gave him the opportunity to show a complete villain in action and he made the most of it. (285)

The Bard introduced the treacherous character in *Henry VI, Part Two* and cranked up his wickedness in *Henry VI, Part Three* by having him slay King Henry to end the play. The words he utters over the dead monarch—"Then, since the heavens have shaped my body so, let hell make crook'd my mind to answer it"—not only set the stage for his consummate villainy in *Richard III* but have also served as a long-standing reminder of the disability-evil linkage.

Even as Shakespeare's villainous hunchback initially trod the boards, however, members of the able-bodied majority had begun moving away from the strategy of routinely disposing of its disabled minority and toward a more paternalistic perspective. Legal decrees such as the Elizabethan English Poor Laws of the late 16th and early 17th centuries helped protect disabled people, even to the point of offering financial assistance, while a number of Western societies began acting on the newfound view that people with disabilities, particularly deafness, were educable and could actually become contributing members of society. Education for people with physical disabilities had progressed to the institutional stage by the 1700s; facilities such as the Paris-based Institution Nationale, the place where Louis Braille developed the tactile form of printing that bears his name, were established during this time (Scotch 15).

These positive efforts were greatly hampered by the woeful levels of medical expertise, however, which remained inadequate until well into the 19th century. As Jeffrey Klenotic has pointed out,

> Any advances in the treatment of disabled persons brought on by the humanist and empiricist turns taken during the Renaissance were restricted by a lack of extant medical knowledge and facilities—a fact that severely limited the reach and quality of the era's goals for rehabilitation of the handicapped. (5)

By the nineteenth century, as medical knowledge and procedures were undergoing strong reforms (including the establishment of special hospitals for people with disabilities), various governmental and non-governmental entities explored other means of improving the lot of disabled people, particularly those injured in war. By the 1800s, Western societies such as Great Britain, France, and the United States had developed disability pension plans well beyond their primitive beginnings in the 16th and 17th centuries and had also begun establishing homes and other services for disabled veterans. In addition, the early decades witnessed the founding of private educational facilities dedicated to the needs of Americans with disabilities, including a Baltimore-based school for visually impaired people in 1812, Thomas Hopkins Gallaudet's school for deaf people in Hartford in 1817, and the Perkins Institute/ Massachusetts School for the Blind in 1823. By the latter part of the century, charitable organizations such as the Salvation Army, which commenced its work in Great Britain in 1878 and shortly thereafter formed a branch in the United States, and the American Red Cross, appearing in 1881, began making their important contributions as well (Devine 19-49, Scotch 15-16).

Significant as these advances were, mainstream society continued to perceive people with physical disabilities as freakish and socially peripheral. Leslie Fiedler suggested its interest in human "curiosities" such as those exhibited in the Barnum and Bailey circus peaked during the Victorian era (15), and its perception of their marginality found ample expression in the literary works of the day. In his study of 19th-century literature, Leonard Kriegel concluded that "the disabled, at best, served merely an ornamental function in the literature of early America." In support of this contention, Kriegel noted that the image that dominated American narrative writing during the 19th century and the first half of the 20th was the individual male, healthy in mind and body, who carves a sense of self out of a chaotic environment. A pure spirit and a strong body were such requisite traits that they became inseparable. As Kriegel put it, "Physical health and moral virtue were virtually synonymous during the nineteenth century in America writing." Such a literary preoccupation left little room in which physically disabled people could participate. "If the wilderness allowed ordinary men the opportunity to be heroic, to confront their inner selves and the external wilderness at one and the same time, what did it offer the crippled and the disabled?" queried Kriegel. "What the wilderness demanded as it offered itself for conquest, the cripple lacked" (16-17).

The few fictional characters with disabilities of the time, represented in the literary output of several Western societies, could be placed in two broad categories: what Kriegel has identified as the "demonic cripple" and the "charity cripple." Captain Ahab of Melville's *Moby-Dick* is a particularly vivid example of the former type—an obsessed male who will not rest until he has had revenge on the entity he holds responsible for his disability—while the latter is strongly represented in Victorian-era literary works such as Dickens' *A Christmas Carol* (that crutch-bearing cherub, Tiny Tim) and the stage hit penned by Adolphe Philippe d'Ennery and Eugéne Cormon, *Les Deux orphelines* (the blind ingénue Louise). These images did little to alleviate the sense of social marginality that has historically clung to people with physical disabilities; if anything, they encouraged audiences to continue regarding disabled people mainly in terms of fear or pity and served for better or worse (usually the latter) as the foundation for many a disability-related film.

The historical tendencies outlined above have led to numerous sociocultural influences still very much at work in our society. Hanoch Livneh has provided an excellent overview of these influences, such as the mainstream emphasis on "the body beautiful" and athletic prowess, which "are often institutionalized into cultural customs . . . to be conformed to by members of society" as well as the premium placed on personal productivity and achievement, and the general devalued status of a person bearing a disability (167-84). In addition, Livneh and a number of other social scientists have underscored mainstream society's need to symbolize what Kaoru Yamamoto has termed "evil, intangible dangers" to maintain its integrity and its strong tendency to bestow a sense of deviance on certain groups such as disabled people in pursuit of that desire. As Yamamoto further observed,

> Deviance is not inherent in any particular pattern of behavior or physical attribute. Society determines whether some individuals should be regarded as different by selecting certain facets of their being and then attaching to these facets degrading labels and interpretations. . . . The singled-out individuals personify the kinds of experience that fall beyond the boundary of the accepted group norm. In this sense, they preserve stability in society by embodying otherwise formless dangers. (186, 182)

Such time-worn constructs remain a conspicuous part of majority consciousness.

Even today, most members of mainstream society seldom perceive people with disabilities as minority-group members subject to alternating rounds of bigotry, paternalism, and indifference, in part because the latter lack a heritage and identity common to other oppressed groups. "While most minority groups grow up in some special subculture and, thus, form a series of norms and expectations, the physically handicapped are not similarly prepared," noted Irving Kenneth Zola. "Born for the most part into normal families, we are socialized into that world. The world of sickness is one we enter only later—poorly prepared, and with all the prejudices of the normal" (144). Majority members are more inclined to regard people with physical disabilities simply as hard-luck individuals who accept their "fate" only after a long personal struggle. Nancy Weinberg has observed that "the general public tends to believe that people with disabilities have suffered a terrible tragedy and are forever bitter about their misfortune" ("Another Perspective" 141), a view often at odds with the way disabled people themselves feel about their disabilities and adapt to them.

Such narrow perspectives are born from ignorance and misunderstanding—social scientists have long known that most able-bodied people tend to avoid interactions with disabled people because they are uncertain how to behave in their presence (Thompson 108, Yamamoto 180-89)—and nourished by the fear that a disabling circumstance may occur to anyone at any time. The movie representations of people with physical disabilities often reflect these concerns, as Paul Longmore has suggested:

> Disability happens around us more often than we generally recognize or care to notice, and we harbor unspoken anxieties about the possibility of disablement, to us or to someone close to us. What we fear, we often stigmatize and shun and sometimes seek to destroy. Popular entertainments depicting disabled characters allude to these fears and prejudices, or address them obliquely or fragmentarily, seeking to reassure us about ourselves. (32)

Such limited perspectives are not as immutable as they might appear. In another article, Weinberg suggested that continued intermingling of disabled and able-bodied people has the general effect of minimizing differences as perceived by the latter group. "As contact between able bodied and disabled is intensified, the stereotype of the disabled as different diminishes," Weinberg wrote. "There is a positive relationship between contact and perceived similarity: as contact increases, perceived similarity increases" ("Modifying Social Stereotypes" 123). Though Weinberg was writing about members of society in general, her observations suggest what undoubtedly will be the key to improved movie depictions of people with physical disabilities: disabled people working with able-bodied peers within and outside the movie industry.

Indeed, such collaborations are already underway. "I'm extremely proud" of *Born on the Fourth of July,* noted Ron Kovic, a disabled Vietnam veteran who co-wrote the movie's script from his like-titled autobiography. "I was able to see my story come out the way I wanted to see it and the way I felt it should come out," he said, adding that the able-bodied people with whom he worked "treated me with a great deal of respect" (Seidenberg 56). Another disabled person who has met with success in Hollywood is Neal Jimenez, a wheelchair-using screenwriter who penned the scripts for such movies as *River's Edge* and *For the Boys* and who wrote and co-directed a film based partially on his own experiences called *The Waterdance* in 1992. An unflinching look at the wide range of issues facing newly disabled males, *The Waterdance* won critical praise (Vincent Canby of the *New York Times* gave it a very favorable review, noting that "though small in scale, it is big in feelings expressed with genuine passion and a lot of gutsy humor") as well as several awards at the Sundance Film Festival that year (13).

Through the combined efforts of activists outside Hollywood (such as the deaf groups who lobbied hard for a deaf actor to play the role of a deaf character in 1993's *Calendar Girl*) and people within the industry like Kovic and Jimenez working with able-bodied counterparts, the movie image of people with physical disabilities will undoubtedly reflect refinements. It's an uphill struggle to be sure, but as their influence over the construction of Hollywood's social imagery continues to grow and as the Americans with Disabilities Act concomitantly brings people closer together, the sense of isolation that has haunted people with physical disabilities in life and in the movies may well become a thing of the past.

## Notes

1. This essay was adapted from sections of the author's *The Cinema of Isolation: A History of Physical Disability in the Movies* (New Brunswick, NJ: Rutgers UP, 1994).

2. Moviemakers are hardly different from their literary predecessors on this score. As Leslie Fiedler has observed, only a handful of pre-1900 writers—principally Victor Hugo and Mark Twain—ever wrote fiction that incorporated a disabled person's perspective (270-71).

## Works Cited

Brady, Ben, and Lance Lee. *The Understructure of Writing for Film and Television.* Austin: U of Texas P, 1988.

Canby, Vincent. "Heroism and Humor as Paraplegics Learn." *New York Times* 13 May 1992, sect. 3: 13.

Chute, Marchette. *Stories from Shakespeare.* New York: New American Library, 1956.

Devine, Edward T. *Disabled Soldiers and Sailors: Pensions and Training.* Carnegie Endowment for International Peace, Preliminary Economic Studies of the War, no. 12. New York: Oxford UP, 1919.

Fiedler, Leslie A. *Freaks: Myths and Images of the Secret Self.* New York: Simon and Schuster, 1978.

Field, Syd. *Screenplay: The Foundations of Screenwriting.* New York: Dell, 1982.

Grant, Andrew J., and Frank G. Bowe. "Watch Your Language!" *Handicapped Funding Directory.* 7th ed. Ed. Richard M. Eckstein. Margate, FL: Research Grant Guides, 1990.

Henderson, George, and Willie V. Bryan. *Psychosocial Aspects of Disability.* Springfield, IL: Charles C. Thomas, 1984.

Klenotic, Jeffrey. "Public Perception and Federal Policy: A Report on America's Response to Physical Disability." Unpublished paper, U of Massachusetts/Amherst, 1990.

Klobas, Lauri E. *Disability Drama in Television and Film.* Jefferson, NC: McFarland, 1988.

Kriegel, Leonard. "The Wolf in the Pit in the Zoo." *Social Policy* 13 (Fall 1982): 16-23.

Liachowitz, Claire H. *Disability as a Social Construct: Legislative Roots.* Philadelphia: U of Pennsylvania P, 1988.

Livneh, Hanoch. "On the Origins of Negative Attitudes Toward People with Disabilities." *The Psychological and Social Impact of Physical Disability.* 2nd ed. Ed. Robert P. Marinelli and Arthur E. Dell Orto. New York: Springer, 1984.

Longmore, Paul K. "Screening Stereotypes: Images of Disabled People." *Social Policy* 16 (Summer 1985): 31-37.

Mast, Gerald, and Bruce F. Kawin. *A Short History of the Movies.* 5th ed. New York: Macmillan, 1992.

Norden, Martin F. "Reel Wheels: The Role of Wheelchairs in American Movies." *Beyond the Stars 3: The Material World in American Popular Film.* Ed. Paul Loukides and Linda K. Fuller. Bowling Green, OH: Bowling Green State University Popular Press, 1993.

—. "Victims, Villains, Saints, and Heroes: Movie Portrayals of People with Physical Disabilities." *Beyond the Stars 1: Stock Characters in American Popular Film.* Ed. Paul Loukides and Linda K. Fuller. Bowling Green, OH: Bowling Green State University Popular Press, 1990.

O'Leary, Liam. *Rex Ingram: Master of the Silent Cinema.* New York: Harper, 1980.

Quart, Leonard, and Albert Auster. "The Wounded Vet in Post-War Film." *Social Policy* 13 (Fall 1982): 24-31.

Schuchman, John S. *Hollywood Speaks: Deafness and the Film Entertainment Industry.* Urbana: U of Illinois P, 1988.

Scotch, Richard K. *From Good Will to Civil Rights: Transforming Federal Disability Policy.* Philadelphia: Temple UP, 1984.

Seidenberg, Robert. "To Hell and Back." *American Film* Jan. 1990: 28+.

Stubbins, Joseph. "The Politics of Disability." *Attitudes Toward Persons with Disabilities.* Ed. Harold E. Yuker. New York: Springer, 1988.

Thompson, Teresa L. "'You Can't Play Marbles—You Have a Wooden Hand': Communication With the Handicapped." *Communication Quarterly* 30 (Spring 1982): 108-15.

Weinberg, Nancy. "Another Perspective: Attitudes of People with Disabilities." *Attitudes Toward Persons with Disabilities.* Ed. Harold E. Yuker. New York: Springer, 1988.

—. "Modifying Social Stereotypes of the Physically Disabled." *Rehabilitation Counseling Bulletin* 22 (Dec. 1978): 114-23.

—, and Carol Sebian. "The Bible and Disability." *Rehabilitation Counseling Bulletin* 23 (June 1980): 273-81.

Yamamoto, Kaoru. "To Be Different." *Rehabilitation Counseling Bulletin* 14 (Mar. 1971): 180-89.

Zola, Irving Kenneth. "Communication Barriers Between 'the Able-Bodied' and 'the Handicapped.'" *The Psychological and Social Impact of Physical Disability.* 2nd ed. Ed. Robert P. Marinelli and Arthur E. Dell Orto. New York: Springer, 1984.

## Filmography

| Year | Film | Director |
|---|---|---|
| 1907 | *The Faithful Dog* | unknown |
| 1907 | *His Daughter's Voice* | unknown |
| 1908 | *The Man and the Woman* | D.W. Griffith |
| 1909 | *The Blind Musician* | unknown |
| 1917 | *The Jury of Fate* | Tod Browning |
| 1918 | *Stella Maris* | Marshall Neilan |
| 1919 | *The Miracle Man* | George Loane Tucker |
| 1920 | *The Penalty* | Wallace Worsley |
| 1920 | *Pollyanna* | Paul Powell |
| 1921 | *The Four Horsemen of the Apocalypse* | Rex Ingram |
| 1921 | *Orphans of the Storm* | D.W. Griffith |
| 1922 | *The Prisoner of Zenda* | Rex Ingram |
| 1922 | *Trifling Women* | Rex Ingram |
| 1923 | *The Hunchback of Notre Dame* | Wallace Worsley |
| 1923 | *Scaramouche* | Rex Ingram |
| 1923 | *Where the Pavement Ends* | Rex Ingram |
| 1924 | *Peter Pan* | Herbert Brenon |

| | | |
|---|---|---|
| 1925 | *The Big Parade* | King Vidor |
| 1925 | *Mare Nostrum* | Rex Ingram |
| 1926 | *The Magician* | Rex Ingram |
| 1926 | *The Sea Beast* | Millard Webb |
| 1927 | *The Show* | Tod Browning |
| 1928 | *West of Zanzibar* | Tod Browning |
| 1930 | *Moby Dick* | Lloyd Bacon |
| 1931 | *City Lights* | Charles Chaplin |
| 1932 | *Freaks* | Tod Browning |
| 1934 | *It's a Gift* | Norman Z. McLeod |
| 1935 | *Bride of Frankenstein* | James Whale |
| 1935 | *A Christmas Carol* | Edwin L. Marin |
| 1936 | *The Devil-Doll* | Tod Browning |
| 1937 | *Heidi* | Allan Dwan |
| 1938 | *A Christmas Carol* | Edwin L. Marin |
| 1939 | *The Hunchback of Notre Dame* | William Dieterle |
| 1940 | *Dr. Kildare's Crisis* | Harold S. Bucquet |
| 1940 | *Edison, the Man* | Clarence Brown |
| 1942 | *Saboteur* | Alfred Hitchcock |
| 1943 | *The Enchanted Cottage* | John Cromwell |
| 1945 | *Pride of the Marines* | Delmer Daves |
| 1946 | *The Best Years of Our Lives* | William Wyler |
| 1946 | *Till the End of Time* | Edward Dmytryk |
| 1947 | *Kiss of Death* | Henry Hathaway |
| 1949 | *The Stratton Story* | Sam Wood |
| 1951 | *On Dangerous Ground* | Nicholas Ray |
| 1952 | *Peter Pan* | Hamilton Luske, Clyde Geronimi, Wilfred Jackson |
| 1952 | *With a Song in My Heart* | Walter Lang |
| 1956 | *Moby Dick* | John Huston |
| 1957 | *The Wings of Eagles* | John Ford |
| 1960 | *Pollyanna* | David Swift |
| 1960 | *Sunrise at Campobello* | Vincent Donehue |
| 1961 | *The Hustler* | Robert Rossen |
| 1964 | *Dr. Strangelove* | Stanley Kubrick |
| 1972 | *The Anderson Tapes* | Sidney Lumet |
| 1974 | *Young Frankenstein* | Mel Brooks |
| 1975 | *The Other Side of the Mountain* | Larry Peerce |
| 1975 | *Three Days of the Condor* | Sydney Pollack |
| 1977 | *Fire Sale* | Alan Arkin |
| 1977 | *Star Wars* | George Lucas |

| | | |
|---|---|---|
| 1978 | *Coming Home* | Hal Ashby |
| 1980 | *The Empire Strikes Back* | Irvin Kershner |
| 1984 | *Blind Date* | Nico Mastorakis |
| 1984 | *Starman* | John Carpenter |
| 1985 | *Stephen King's Silver Bullet* | Dan Attias |
| 1986 | *Power* | Sidney Lumet |
| 1987 | *The Hidden* | Jack Sholden |
| 1987 | *Innerspace* | Joe Dante |
| 1987 | *No Way Out* | Roger Donaldson |
| 1989 | *Born on the Fourth of July* | Oliver Stone |
| 1989 | *See No Evil, Hear No Evil* | Arthur Hiller |
| 1992 | *Jennifer 8* | Bruce Robinson |
| 1992 | *Passion Fish* | John Sayles |
| 1992 | *Scent of a Woman* | Martin Brest |
| 1992 | *The Waterdance* | Neal Jimenez, Michael Steinberg |
| 1993 | *Calendar Girl* | John Whitesell |
| 1994 | *Forrest Gump* | Robert Zemeckis |

# The Ideology of the "Red Scare" Movement: McCarthyism in the Movies

**Linda K. Fuller**

> McCarthy invented the Multiple Lie—the lie with so many tiny gears and fragile connecting rods that reason exhausted itself in the effort to combat it.
>
> —Richard H. Rovere

All too glibly, the current popular dialogue about "political correctness" is considered synonymous with the concept of "McCarthyism"—a term referring to the ideology of Senator Joseph R. McCarthy of Wisconsin, the demagogue who worked with the House Un-American Activities Committee (HUAC) during the 1950s, carrying out a witch hunt against suspected Communists.

This chapter aims to trace the phenomenon of "Red Scare" McCarthyism cinematically. First, some background on McCarthyism will be provided, particularly its symbiotic relationship to Hollywood. Although anti-Communism sentiments had long been engrained in the American value system, and it was estimated that at least 33 such motion pictures were made between 1947 and 1954 (Jones 300-01), filmic momentum related to the Red Scare movement actually began earlier with a number of pro-Russian films like *Mission to Moscow* (1943), *North Star* (1943), *Tender Comrade* (1943), and *Song of Russia* (1944).

A number of biopics, patriotic films, metaphorical movies, anti-HUAC and defensive-HUAC films, thrillers, comedies, documentaries, romances, and dramas relative to McCarthyism will also be discussed.

The context is the Cold War. The place: Hollywood, whose equanimity neither before nor since has ever been so threatened. The approach is a social scientific one, seeing film as a social artifact reflecting both fear and a concomitant defensive stance on the part of the motion picture industry; as such, quantitative data will be cited—chronologically tracing McCarthyism through three distinct phases: 1943-46 pro-Russian films; 1947-54 anti-Communist films; 1955-present anti-McCarthy/McCarthyism films.

*HUAC and Hollywood*

Hearings Regarding the Communist Infiltration of the Motion-Picture-Industry Activities in the United States, which began in October of 1947, included testimony by witnesses "friendly" to the work of HUAC: producers (Jack Warner, Louis B. Mayer), writers (Ayn Rand, Morrie Ryskind), actors (Adolph Menjou, Robert Taylor, Robert Montgomery, George Murphy, Ronald Reagan, Gary Cooper), directors (Sam Wood, Leo McCarey), critics (John Moffitt, Howard Rushmore), one mother (Mrs. Lela Rogers, mother of Ginger), one political science instructor (Oliver Carlson), and one animator-producer-director (Walt Disney), according to Gerald Mast (496).

Anti-Communism mania swept the country in the 1950s, particularly in the persona of Joe McCarthy, who produced names, "documents," innuendo, and outright fabrications to fuel the fire. Sensationalism spread throughout the media. Diana Trilling points out: "It was Joseph McCarthy who took anti-communism out of the realm of respectable discourse and created for people of liberal impulse an automatic association between any voiced opposition to communism and reaction" (32). While Edwin R. Bayley has questioned whether the press "created" McCarthy, Terry Christensen considers that the paranoia was a result of our trying to adjust to becoming a world power. The then-emerging technology of television was another factor: "As movies became less popular and influential, television attracted most of the moral surveillance once reserved for them . . . the ('Red Scare'/anti-Communist hysteria) witch hunt actually began in Hollywood before it did anywhere else" (Curran 95-96). Of that milieu, A. Scott Berg has yet another interpretation: "Anti-Communism may have been on their tongues, but anti-Semitism was on many of their minds" (433).

The second HUAC investigation, lasting some 15 months, took place beginning in March of 1951. Generating about 4,500 pages of testimony, it reviewed testimony from a number of Hollywood organizations, such as the Actors' Laboratory, Actors' Laboratory Theater, Associated Film Audiences-Hollywood branch, Citizens' Committee for Motion-Picture Strikers, Film Audiences for Democracy or Associated Film Audiences, Hollywood Anti-Nazi League or Hollywood League Against Nazism, Hollywood Independent Citizens' Committee of the Arts, Sciences, and Professions, Hollywood League for Democratic Action, Hollywood Motion-Picture Democratic Committee, Hollywood Peace Forum, Hollywood Theater-Alliance, Hollywood Writers' Mobilization, Motion Picture Artists' Committee, People's Educational Center/Los Angeles, Mooney Defense Committee-Hollywood Unit, Progressive Citizens of America, Hollywood Committee of the Arts,

Sciences, and Professions, Council of the PCA, Southern California Chapter of the PCA, and the Workers School of Los Angeles (Mast 552).

"We call it the Cold War but it was really three simultaneous conflicts," according to Victor Navasky, "a global confrontation between rival imperialisms and ideologies, between capitalism and Communism, between the United States of America and the Union of Soviet Socialist Republics" (3). HUAC's assault on Hollywood in a wider perspective has been alternately interpreted as a war on leftist liberals, the arts, intellectuals, and not merely on "communist subversives," as advertised.

### *Review of the Literature*

As Richard M. Fried reminds us, "The literature of 'McCarthyism'—that is, mid-century varieties of extreme anti-communism, generally attended by forms of political repression—is vast" (223). Many of those books are autobiographies and biographies of persons implicated in the Red Scare inquisition (Chambers, 1952; Faulk, 1964; Bessie, 1965; Hellman, 1976; Zheutlin and Talbot, 1978; Schary, 1979; Cole, 1981; Fast, 1990; Goodson, 1991). Others dealt with the HUAC hearings (Kahn, 1948; *Red Channels,* 1950; Carr, 1952; Goodman, 1968; Bentley, 1971; Trumbo, 1972; Navasky, 1980; Maltby, 1981). Still other publications dealt with the McCarthy era itself as a slice in time (Donner, 1961; Vaughn, 1972; Caute, 1978; Ceplair and Englund, 1980; Trilling, 1993). The references cited here represent only a small number of books about McCarthyism.

Of particular relevance to this media study is *Report on Blacklisting* (1956), published by John Cogley under the auspices of the Fund for the Republic while blacklisting was still in effect. Consisting of two distinct parts, the first on movies and the second on radio, television, and other entertainment fields, it generated such a controversy that HUAC began yet another investigation of blacklisting, this time focusing on how and why Cogley did the study rather than considering implications of his findings. Also, most critics would agree that Ceplair and Englund's *The Inquisition in Hollywood Politics in the Film Community, 1930-1960* (1980) is the definitive history of the blacklist era.

In general, this discussion of McCarthyism in the movies can be considered in three distinct time frames: the pro-Russian films of 1943-46, anti-Communist films of 1947-54, and the anti-McCarthy and anti-McCarthyism films from 1955 to the present.

### *1943-46 Pro-Russian Films*

Conceptions of Communism and Communists first began to emerge in Hollywood in the late 1930s, mainly taking the form of caricatures of

Soviet agents or plain peasant women, who were depicted as rather simple, unsophisticated, even silly types who might nevertheless be lured by our capitalistic treasures. The ideology itself was hardly threatening. A classic example would be 1935's romantic comedy *Red Salute*, where Barbara Stanwyck as a cute little coed with Communist sympathies travels cross country with an American soldier (Robert Young); it was dismissed by critics as a comment on campus agitators opposed to militarism.

Momentum for what became the Red Scare movement began with several films produced in the early 1940s that were considered, in retrospect, as pro-Russian. *Mission to Moscow* (1943) told of the Soviet career of United States Ambassador Joseph E. Davis, portraying the Russkies as our warmhearted allies. James Agee reviewed it as "A mishmash of Stalinism with New Dealism with Hollywoodism with opportunism with shaky experimentalism with mesmerism with onanism, all mosaicked into a remarkable portrait of what the makers of the film think the Soviet Union is like—a great glad two-million-dollar bowl of canned borscht, eminently approvable by the Institute of Good Housekeeping" (qtd. in *Halliwell's Film Guide* 682).

*North Star* (1943), based on a screenplay by Lillian Hellman, tells of a Russian village defending itself against a Nazi onslaught. Women welders bravely carrying on while their husbands are off at war is the subject of *Tender Comrade* (1943); written by Dalton Trumbo, one of the Hollywood Ten, the film was thick on sentiment. In *Song of Russia* (1944), Robert Taylor stars as a symphony conductor touring the USSR who is impressed by the citizens' war efforts and falls for a Russian girl. Initiated by the United States government as a propaganda tool for its allies, the film backfired against many of its participants, who were subsequently blacklisted. Two other Hollywood productions that were considered pro-Russian were *Objective Burma* (1945), a war film about an American platoon in the Burma campaign, and *Cloak and Dagger* (1946), which had Gary Cooper and Lilli Palmer involved in a mission of espionage.

### *1947-54 Anti-Communist Films*

During these years, "The movie industry in Hollywood engaged in its own miniature cold war. In general, the patterns of anti-Communist activity in the movie capital paralleled those developing throughout American society," according to Les K. Adler. "Yet because it existed on a highly visible pedestal, with the potential for a powerful impact on the public mind, Hollywood was in a unique position of both vulnerability and power" (242).

Sometimes the film industry's anti-Communism was expressed in films by means of portraying what happens with too much power. *Body and Soul* (1947), for example, used the power metaphor to show John Garfield as a boxer learning what can happen to racketeers—a lesson repeated two years later in *Force of Evil* (1949). Reds blatantly plot to produce biological weapons and take over the United States in Howard Hughes's anti-Communist melodrama *The Whip Hand* (1951). Marlon Brando in *On the Waterfront* (1954) represents what happens when one goes up against the powerful gang boss, with a twist; according to Terry Christensen, this was "not so much an anti-communist movie as a vindication of informers. Making an informer into a hero, however, was no mean feat. Stool pigeons had always been disdained in American folklore and movies" (93). The exploited working class, a staple of Marxist ideology emphasizing the oppressive power of the ruling bourgeoisie, this time in the personae of striking New Mexico mineworkers, forms the theme of 1954's *Salt of the Earth*.

Victims typically abounded in anti-Communist movies. *Crossfire* (1947) tells about innocent three soldiers suspected of an anti-Semitic murder by the police, while in *The Naked City* (1948), as the television series it later inspired warned, "There are eight million stories"—the idea being to watch out. *Gun Crazy* (1950) serves as a metaphor for what happens to victims, depicting a "lovers-on-the-run" duo who commit a series of robberies and eventually become wanted criminals. *In a Lonely Place* (1950) features Humphrey Bogart as a Hollywood writer wrongly suspected of murder—another classic symbol of its day. The 1955 Mickey Spillane saga *Kiss Me Deadly,* directed by Robert Aldrich, has the sleazy gumshoe Mike Hammer helping a girl who eventually ends up murdered; something of a cult classic, it is valuable as a mirror on the nuclear paranoia of 1950s America, a warning of what blind allegiance could lead to. In *My Son John* (1952), Helen Hayes as the mother in a devout Catholic family is devastated to learn that her son is a Communist; Bosley Crowther, writing in the *New York Times* of April 9, 1952, labeled the Leo McCarey film "cultural vigilantism." Les K. Adler calls Paramount's *My Son John* the best example of films dealing with domestic Communism:

> Unusually well produced and acted, *My Son John* contains the most complete presentation of Hollywood's perception of the nature of Communism, as well as one of its narrowest perceptions and presentations of Americanism. The studio went to great pains on the film, luring Helen Hayes out of retirement to star as the mother, Mrs. Jefferson, and putting together a case of Dean Jagger, Robert Walker, and Van Heflin as the father, son, and friendly FBI agent, respec-

tively. . . . This film, perhaps more than any other, expresses the spirit of McCarthyism and juxtaposes the frozen American perception of both Communism and Americanism while dramatizing in the most explicit manner the conflicts felt by a nation fearful not merely of the future but of itself. (255)

If characters were Communists in films during the 1947-54 period, by default they were bad guys, and they got their due. Witness, for example, Elizabeth Taylor's revulsion on finding out that her husband (Robert Taylor) was working with them in *Conspirator* (1949). Or how the evil, murderous Communists blackmail shipping executive Robert Ryan into helping them, threatening to reveal a crime from his past in *I Married a Communist* (1949, later retitled *The Woman on Pier 13*). *Time* magazine's film review of Oct. 17, 1949, referred to the film as "a celluloid bullet aimed at the USSR." The movie also attacked the West Coast dockworkers union, which at that time had Communist leaders, and "it was allegedly used to test the politics of various directors, 13 of whom refused to work on it" (Schindler 131).

The bad guys were easy to identify in the western *High Noon* (1952), produced by Stanley Kramer, a leading Hollywood liberal, and written by Carl Foreman, who was soon to be blacklisted. The anti-Red Scare collaborators "were commenting on the filmmakers' abandonment of their colleagues who were under attack by HUAC" (Biskind 49). In Elia Kazan's *Viva Zapata* (1952), when a Mexican revolutionary is betrayed by a friend, the bad guy is still understood as the "commie." *Man on a Tightrope* (1953) also is a Cold War story of betrayal, with a Czech circus owner trying to escape Communist authorities. In *Johnny Guitar* (1954) the "bad guys" are bad girls—Joan Crawford as proprietor of a gambling saloon versus Mercedes McCambridge as a banker, with a piece of land as the object to show how power can corrupt.

During this period in film history it was easy to identify the good guys. John Wayne as *Big Jim McLain* (1952), for example, is a special agent for HUAC routing out terrorists (i.e., Communists). About the film's spurious "110 percent Americanism," Joseph M. Curran wrote:

[*Big Jim McLain*] is a piece of crude, flag-waving propaganda sugared with romance and religion. The movie announced that it was based on HUAC files and made with HUAC cooperation. John Wayne is the Irish-American hero, a HUAC investigator who breaks up a Communist sabotage ring in Hawaii. Instead of handing over the culprits to the courts for trial, however, McLain brings them before HUAC, where they escape punishment by taking the Fifth Amendment against self-incrimination. This is a travesty of fact, not of our system of justice. But such misrepresentation enables McLain to assert that a constitution meant to protect "honest, decent citizens" should not serve to shield those who seek to destroy it. Denying to others the rights we claim for ourselves, betraying liberty while posing as its guardians—these things are the essence of McCarthyism. (100)

Leonard Quart adds that *Big Jim McLain* condemned Communists "more for their character traits [they were criminals, idealistic dupes, nymphomaniacs, or disturbed fanatics] than for their ideology. In fact, the ideology was never defined or explored. Communists were reduced to caricatures who saw human life as dispensable, had no room for private feelings, and were even in oppostion to God and motherhood" (46).

There were even a few anti-Communist biopics. *The Iron Curtain* (1949) told the story of Igor Gouzenko, a Russian official who helped corner a Canadian spy ring; it has sometimes been considered the first major anti-Communist film. Winner of an Academy Award for best picture of 1949, *All the King's Men* was based on the life of Louisiana Senator Huey Long (Broderick Crawford), who becomes absolutely corrupt with power. Director Robert Rossen "was himself a target of the McCarthyite hysteria that had gripped Hollywood in the form of HUAC hearings and studio blacklisting" (Lenihan 82). The underlying meaning from Robert Penn Warren's novel was clear: how an innocent victim can fall under the notion of absolute power, absolutely corrupting both him and the system.

*Guilty of Treason* (1950) is an account of the trial by the Russians of Hungarian primate Cardinal Mindszenty. *I Was a Communist for the FBI* (1951) stars Frank Lovejoy as the real-life undercover agent Matt Cvetic, who posed as a Communist to inform on Red activities in the United States.

While *The Iron Curtain* (1949) displayed the evils of Communism in a semidocumentary mold, *Walk a Crooked Mile* (1948) was a semidocumentary spy thriller showing British agents from Scotland Yard working with the FBI to investigate leakage of atomic secrets. *Walk East on Beacon* (1952), written by Leo Rosten, used a semidocumentary style to show the FBI exposing a Red spy ring.

Arch-conservative Ayn Rand's *Fountainhead* (1949) extols the many virtues of anti-Communism: an idealistic architect (Gary Cooper), modeled after Frank Lloyd Wright, stands by his American virtues, spewing lines written by the leader of the conservative Motion Picture Alliance for the Preservation of American Ideals. With the novel published to coincide with the 1947 HUAC hearings as a supplement to the MPAA's production code, its guide advised filmmakers not to "smear the free-enterprise system . . . success" or "industrialists," not to "deify the 'common man,'" and not to "glorify the collective" (qtd. in Cogley 11). Screaming the anticollective theme of man's personal integrity standing above the law, both the book and the movie caused quite a stir in their day.

*The Red Danube* and *The Red Menace,* 1949 examples of the continuing red-baiting Cold War charade, depicted, respectively, a political intrigue romance tempered by exile to Russia as a punishment and a discontented war veteran preyed upon by Communists. Samuel Fuller's *The Steel Helmet* (1951) is an action-adventure with the Reds in the early days of Korea, desperately trying to make a case for fighting Communism.

There are also some anti-Communist films from the 1947-54 era that defy categorization. *Red Planet Mars* (1952), for example, could be called the first "born-again" sci-fi movie, pitting Americans with the Russkies as they all respond to God's Voice of Radio Free Mars. Also, *It Came from Outer Space* (1953) and *Invasion of the Body Snatchers* (1956) are just two of many invasion films of the period that many scholars have claimed were representative of fears of Communism and the atomic bomb.[1]

### *1955-present: Anti-McCarthy/McCarthyism Films*

McCarthyism was in full bloom. Beginning around the mid-1950s, a rash of films appeared that moved from simple anti-Communism to vilifying both its emblematic personage and his message, warning the public so that such a phenomenon could never occur again. Anti-HUAC sentiments also lingered during this time. In *Storm Center* (1956), for example, Bette Davis plays a small-town librarian who is fired when she refuses to remove a Communist book from the shelves. While Andrew Dowdy dismissed it as "a sure loser as the only attack on HUAC ever made in a Hollywood studio" (184) Christensen points out: "*Storm Center* attacked the inquisitorial, guilt-by-association techniques of HUAC, but the message of free speech was so oversimplified that even the Daughters of the American Revolution endorsed it, and the movie was an unqualified flop" (95).

A *King in New York* (1957), Charlie Chaplin's last film, has the comic genius playing a deposed monarch who visits America during the McCarthy hysteria. Having survived a revolution, he seeks sanctuary in the United States, where he befriends a 10-year-old whose parents are under suspicion by HUAC because they refuse to squeal on their colleagues; as a tangential friend of the family, he too becomes a suspect.

Also in 1957 was Elia Kazan's *A Face in the Crowd*, about an Arkansas hick (Andy Griffith) whom television turns into a celebrity homespun philosopher—repeating again the power/corruption theme inherent in anti-McCarthyism. Based on a Graham Greene novel, *The Quiet American* (1957) tells of a hero duped into betraying his country for the Communists; throughout, ideological comments about the slimy villains, McCarthy-like symbols, are interspersed. Director Joseph L. Mankiewicz ensures that the Audie Murphy character's pro-American stance is underscored.

A documentary-style biopic about double agent Boris Morros (author of *My Ten Years As a Counterspy*), 1960's *Man on a String* is an anti-Communist exposé on the evils of Communist espionage; yet it underscores the more frightening fears of what an ideology like McCarthyism might bring. Stanley Kubrick's *Spartacus* of the same year uses the plot convention of the slave (Kirk Douglas) leading other oppressed persons out of bondage, a metaphor for anyone who had felt the same way about McCarthyism.

While brainwashing by the Reds is the overt theme in John Frankenheimer's brilliant spy thriller *The Manchurian Candidate* (1962), starring Frank Sinatra, Laurence Harvey, Janet Leigh, James Gregory (the perfect McCarthy demon), and Angela Lansbury, it is obvious who the evil Joe McCarthy character is. In film critic Pauline Kael's assessment, "Although it's a thriller, it may be the most sophisticated political satire ever to come out of Hollywood" (qtd. in Halliwell 652).

*Red Nightmare*, also of 1962, was a half-hour propaganda film produced for the Department of Defense by Warner Brothers that was both anti-Communist and anti-McCarthyism. Featuring the cast of television's *Dragnet* (starring Jack Webb), the story dramatized the Red Menace, as Communists conspired to take over a small town in America.

In 1964, Emile de Antonio directed *Point of Order*, a 97-minute documentary compressed from 188 hours of television coverage of the Army-McCarthy hearings some ten years earlier. Mitch Tuchman comments:

> To eyes schooled on content, *Point of Order* appears to be an elemental battle of Good and Evil, an archetypal confrontation between the ruthless, reckless senator Joseph McCarthy and the compassionate but cunning counsel Joseph N. Welch. A conventional filmmaker might have called it *Two Guys Named Joe*, but de Antonio named his film for a handy parliamentary ploy, because this is film not about distinctions between ends, but about similarities among means. (66)

*Point of Order* is divided into seven sections, representing a wide range of parliamentarian tricks: "From each side come charges and countercharges, interruptions and ridicule, challenges of propriety, name-calling, and bathetic appeals to integrity. The greatest difference between McCarthy and Welch was not ideology but demeanor" (66).

After the thrillers and political films of the 1960s like *Man on a String* and *Manchurian Candidate* came an onslaught of movies representing the "revenge of the blacklist."[2] The first of these films, *The Way We Were* (1973), directed by Sydney Pollack, was decidedly romantic, showing the college romance then marriage of Robert Redford as a novelist and Barbra Streisand as a Jewish bluestocking through a Hollywood of the 1930s to 1950s, including a McCarthy witch-hunt sequence. Under the strains of blacklisting, the marriage inevitably breaks up. Redford stars again under Pollack's direction in 1975's political thriller *Three Days of the Condor*, this time as a CIA agent paid to work for a covert, anti-McCarthy-like operation while all his associates are massacred.

Martin Ritt's *The Front* (1976) stars Woody Allen as a bookmaker fronting for blacklisted writers.[3] In this satire blending comedy and pain, the closing credits note that Ritt himself had been blacklisted, as also had been actors Zero Mostel, Herschel Bernardi, and Joshua Shelley, plus writer Walter Bernstein. "In the end, *The Front* said blacklisting was wrong not for political reasons but because it hurt innocent people," writes Christensen. "It and *The Way We Were* illustrate how political messages can be subverted or obscured by Hollywood's imperative to find an audience and make money. Both films took on political subjects, then backed away, the former toward romance and the latter toward comedy" (141).

Not surprisingly, a few documentaries have also been made about McCarthyism. *Hollywood on Trial* (1976), directed by David Helpern, Jr., had input from contributors including Walt Disney, Gary Cooper, Jack Warner, Adolph Menjou, Robert Taylor, Dalton Trumbo, and Louis B. Mayer. Narrated by John Huston, the story of "Red Scares Ignite Tinsel Town!" is the result of culled rare footage and other archival material, including print and radio interviews with the "Unfriendly 19," who refused to be witnesses against others, with the likes of Ring Lardner, Jr., Dalton Trumbo, and Edward Dmytryk.

The theme "Hollywood on Trial: Films from the Blacklist Era" was featured toward the end of 1992 at the Brooklyn (N.Y.) Museum, concomitant with a comment on its appropriateness during the current period that was witnessing increased attacks on the arts and freedom of expression. Patricia Bosworth, a daughter of one of six lawyers for

Hollywood on Trial's subpoenaed witnesses, tells of how "more than 50 anti-Communist movies were made very quickly between 1949 and 1954 to appease the right wing" (H1). After recounting her family's own saga, ending with her father's suicide, she adds:

> His story was not unique. Before the blacklist ended, it had spilled out into television, the universities, unions and the Government. Hundreds of families were disrupted, careers were ruined, and many men and women took their lives. By the time the blacklist era was over, more than 15,000 people had been directly affected, according to Katrina vanden Heuvel's study 'American Victims: A Study of the Anti-Communist Crusade.'
>
> The Hollywood blacklist system didn't stop until 1960, when Otto Preminger announced that he was hiring Dalton Trumbo, a blacklist victim who had been writing screenplays under pseudonyms for more than 10 years, to write "Exodus." And it was not until 1975 that the House Un-American Affairs Committee was abolished. (H23)

*Tail Gunner Joe* (1977), a semidocumentary film directed by Jud Taylor, stars Peter Boyle in a devastating examination of the rise and fall of the demagogue—McCarthy of course—and Burgess Meredith won an Emmy for his performance. The same year saw *Julia*, based on Lillian Hellman's autobiographical *Pentimento*, with Jane Fonda concerned about her politically active friend Julia (Vanessa Redgrave), who eventually is killed by the Nazis. It is particularly poignant that, like Hellman, both Fonda and Redgrave have suffered career setbacks because of their politics. Christensen states: "By giving both women a firm basis for their actions and by letting us see Lillian's maturation, *Julia* provided a politically stronger condemnation of HUAC and the blacklist than either *The Way We Were* or *The Front*, even though those films were more politically explicit" (142).

Probably the most ambitious anti-McCarthyism film ever undertaken was *Reds* (1981), which was written, directed, co-authored, and starred in by Warren Beatty. A biography of John Reed (played by Beatty), an American radical journalist who went with his wife, Louise Bryant (Diane Keaton), to Russia to participate in the revolution, and who wrote *Ten Days That Shook the World* (about the 1917 Bolshevik uprising), *Reds* won an Academy Award for Beatty as director and as actor, Vittorio Storaro for photography, Maureen Stapleton as supporting actress, Diane Keaton as actress, Jack Nicholson as actor, and nominations for best picture, screenplay, and editing. An epic more romantic than political, *Reds* is particularly distinguished by Beatty's innovative use of real "witnesses" interspersed throughout the film, reminiscing about Reed and the hideousness of the McCarthy era. Beatty's acceptance speech for best director, thanking supporters, is worth repeating:

> Your decision, taken in the great capitalist tower of Gulf & Western, to finance a three-and-a-half hour romance which attempts to reveal for the first time just something of the beginnings of American socialism and American communism, reflects credit not only upon you; I think it reflects credit upon Hollywood and the movie business wherever that is, and I think it reflects more particular credit upon freedom of expression that we have in American society, and the lack of censorship we have from the government or the people who put up the money.

Continuing chronologically, *Concealed Enemies* of 1984 was a four-hour docudrama originally aired on PBS's *American Playhouse* about the famous Alger Hiss (Edward Herrmann)-Whittaker Chambers (John Harkins) spy case, with its concomitant red-baiting atmosphere—Hiss being one of Joseph McCarthy's prime targets. The same year also saw right-wing ideologue John Milius's *Red Dawn*, with the Russians leading a violent invasion into Colorado until they are wiped out by the locals; anti-Communism persists.

A suspense film about a young 1950s political activist (Kelly McGillis) accused of involvement in a Nazi smuggling ring and a victim of McCarthyism, *The House on Carroll Street* (1988) was directed and produced by Peter Yates. The theme focuses on what happens to an idealistic young woman who refuses to answer questions at a 1951 Senate hearing about her membership affiliations. *Red Scorpion* (1989) deals with a Russian agent assigned to assassinate an African rebel leader, who instead teams up with the natives and helps drive out the Communists.

A made-for-cable offering, *Fellow Traveller* (1990) follows a Hollywood writer (Ron Silver) and an actor (Hart Bochner) who have fallen victim to 1950s witch hunters during the McCarthy era. Aligning the audience with sympathies for blacklist victims, one of the classic lines in the film says, "If we don't have our enemy in the room we just keep practicing on one another."

"McCarthyism is Americanism with its sleeves rolled up," said Joseph McCarthy in 1952. Some of its victims are depicted in a 1991 documentary, *American Inquisition*, directed by Helen Whitney. This was a personal endeavor, as she had known friends at Sarah Lawrence whose parents had been blacklisted and faculty who found freedom there. Whitney discovered in her directorial process that "McCarthyism was more than a Hollywood or Washington story. It was the little people who were caught up. There were signs of omission and commission. I talked to so many informants who were harsh on themselves, and whose lives have been exemplary ever since" (qtd. in Taubin 50).

While ostensibly 1991's *For the Boys* is a star vehicle for Bette Midler and James Caan, reviewing the story of two USO performers who entertain the troops from World War II to Vietnam, it also contains its own poignant comment about McCarthyism. Following the entertainers from Europe to North Africa, then to Korea, and finally to Vietnam, it also includes references people and places in the industry directly affected by the bloodbath of blacklisting.

*Guilty by Suspicion* (1991) demonstrates continued interest in McCarthyism as a filmic staple. It concerns a gifted, successful Hollywood director (Robert DeNiro) who is called to testify before HUAC during their 1950s witch hunts. Branded a "pinko," he soon finds himself at odds with the same studios that had been fighting for his services. Everyone turns against him, and he eventually loses all his belongings—learning that he has valued his "things" too much, and has loved his work too much. Stephen Prince adds an insight about the writer and director William Winkler:

> Winkler originally commissioned [leftish screenwriter-director Abraham] Polonsky to write the script, and in Polonsky's version real political, as well as social, issues were at stake: The character really was a Communist. Winkler, however, decided it would be more interesting, and more profitable at the box office, if the character was a political innocent, a non-Communist falsely accused of being a Communist. The Polonsky script was abandoned because Winkler did not believe he could get a contemporary audience to care about a Communist—as if that, rather than freedom of expression, was what the film ought to be about. (193-94)

*Guilty by Suspicion* also stars Annette Bening, George Wendt, Patricia Wettig, Sam Wanamaker, and includes a brief cameo by Martin Scorcese. The publicity for the film enticed with "All It Took Was a Whisper." Critical response to it varied: Roger Ebert hailed it as a "powerful statement against the blacklist" in *The Daily News*; Janet Maslin of *The New York Times* called it "a tragic evocation of terrible times"; Peter Rainer wrote in *The Los Angeles Times* that it was deserving of points "for dealing with a subject that, even today, is highly volatile and controversial."[4] In an article titled "Down by Law," *Entertainment Weekly* gave the film a C minus: "[It] is astoundingly flat and banal. Winkler serves up this infamous slice of our history as though it were breaking news, and his re-creation of early-'50s Hollywood is a real Scotch-tape job. The scandal of McCarthyism is too daunting to shake off. But *Guilty by Suspicion* leaves you wishing that someone would finally make a decent movie about it" (40).

The most recent film dealing with the McCarthy era has been HBO's *Citizen Cohn* (1992), an adaptation of Nicholas von Hoffman's 1988 biography about lawyer Roy Cohn, the "wonder boy commie catcher" who worked hand-in-hand with the Senator in the 1950s. Directed by Frank Pierson, it stars James Woods in a riveting performance as the hateful homophobe who, in an ironic twist, died of AIDS in 1986, a self-hating, paranoid homosexual. Undoubtably, there will be more movies to add to this filmography.

*Conclusions/Concerns*

From the number of biopics, patriotic films, metaphorical ones, anti-HUAC and defensive-HUAC films, thrillers, comedies, romances, documentaries, docudramas, and sheer dramas relating to McCarthyism outlined here, it is obvious that the Red Scare phenomenon had an enormous effect both on and by the motion picture industry.

As an ideology, perhaps it is instructive to review some comments made by Garry Wills in his introduction to Lillian Hellman's book *Scoundrel Time*. Preeminently considering that the ideology of the McCarthy era was based on the concept of "giving the Red-baiters their due," he points out how differences between liberals, socialists, radicals, and Communists is "a matter of degree within a continuum," as opposed to radicals. He states:

> Ideology is, by contrast, an *escape* from personal responsibility. Someone like Whittaker Chambers wanted to be told what to do, wanted to be History's slave. Ideologues want to be certified by others as respectable—if not by the Committee or the Party, then by the ADA. They want their hates to be dictated by the national program. The radical thinks of virtuous people, while the ideologue thinks of orthodoxy. The radical hates vicious and harmful people, while the ideologue hates heretical ideas, no matter how "nice" the possessors of those ideas may be. The radical tries to uphold a private kind of honor in a rotten world. (32-23)

Current concern focuses on the issue of whether conformity with the wave of "political correctness" that is sweeping the scene is not reminiscent of McCarthyism in a new form. Particularly in higher education, the debate rages.[5]

As Merle Miller, author of *The Judges and the Judged*, says of the McCarthy era, "While there are those who would like to pretend it never happened, it did, and we must remember it lest we repeat it."

Yet, the anonymous *Entertainment Weekly* reviewer of *Guilty by Suspicion* has posited a compelling question: "Why is it that whenever somebody makes a movie about the Hollywood blacklist of the '50s, it turns out like some soggy melodrama about the '50s?"[6] Despite the 60+ films listed here—including the pro-Russian period of 1943-46, anti-Communist movies from 1947-54, and anti-McCarthy and anti-McCarthism films from 1955 to the present—we await that honest depiction of what was truly one of the darkest periods of our history, but one that might reappear in a new guise at any time.

## Notes

1. Garyn Roberts writes of the sci-fi invasion film: "This formula initially achieved definition and articulation in 1951 in *The Thing from Another World* and culminated in 1956's *Invasion of the Body Snatchers* (130). Emanuel Levy makes the case that the latter film "differs from many sci-fi films because there is no immediate confirmation of the hero's report of the 'strange' phenomena by other witnesses: the conflict is between *one* individual and the entire community. And unlike other films, *Invasion* shows that the authorities, scientific and political, are neither trustworthy nor competent" (137).

2. A term used by Christensen in chapter 11 of his book *Reel Politics,* entitled " 'It Don't Worry Me': The Revenge of the Blacklist and the Emergence of Disillusionment" (137).

3. For more information on *The Front,* see Carlton Jackson's biography of Martin Ritt, *Picking Up the Tab,* published by Bowling Green State University Popular Press, 1994.

4. See Christopher Phelps, "The Second Time as Farce: The Right's "New McCarthyism," *Monthly Review* 43.5 (1981): 39+. Also reports from a symposium, James W. Carey et al. on "Communication Scholarship and Political Correctness," *Journal of Communication* 42.2 (1992): 56-149.

5. Phelps "The second time" 39+. Carey et al. "Communication," 56-149.

## Works Cited

Adler, Les K. "The Politics of Culture: Hollywood and the Cold War." *The Specter: Original Essays on the Cold War and the Origins of McCarthyism.* Ed. Robert Griffith and Athan Theoharis. New York: New Viewpoints, 1974. 242-60.

Bayley, Edwin R. *Joe McCarthy and the Press.* Madison: U of Wisconsin P, 1981.

Bentley, Eric, ed. *Thirty Years of Treason: Excerpts from Hearings Before the House Committee on Un-American Activities.* New York: Viking, 1971.

Berg, A. Scott. *Goldwyn: A Biography.* New York: Knopf, 1989.

Bessie, Alvah. *Inquisition in Eden.* New York: Macmillan, 1965.

Biskind, Peter. *Seeing Is Believing.* London: Pluto, 1984.

Bosworth, Patricia, "Daughter of a Blacklist That Killed a Father." *New York Times* 27 Sept. 1992: H1+.

Carr, Robert K. *The House Committee on Un-American Activities, 1945-1950.* Ithaca, New York: Cornell UP, 1952.

Caute, David. *The Great Fear: The Anti-Communist Purge Under Truman and Eisenhower.* New York: Simon & Schuster, 1978.

Ceplair, Larry, and Stephen Englund. *The Inquisition in Hollywood: Politics in the Film Community, 1930-1960.* Garden City, NY: Doubleday, 1980.

Chambers, Whittaker. *Witness.* New York: Random House, 1952.

Christensen, Terry. *Reel Politics: American Political Movies from Birth of a Nation to Platoon.* New York: Blackwell, 1987.

Cogley, John, ed. *Report on Blacklisting.* 2 vols. New York: Fund for the Republic, 1956.

Cole, Lester. *Hollywood Red: The Autobiography of Lester Cole.* Palo Alto, CA: Ramparts, 1981.

Committee on Un-American Activities, House of Representatives. *Citations by Official Government Agencies of Organizations and Publications Found To Be Communist or Communist Fronts.* Washington, DC, 1948.

Curran, Joseph M. *Hibernian Green on the Silver Screen: The Irish and American Movies.* Westport, CT: Greenwood, 1989.

Donner, Frank. *The Un-Americans.* New York: Ballantine, 1961.

Dowdy, Thomas. *The Films of the Fifties.* New York: Morrow, 1973.

"Down by Law." *Entertainment Weekly* 3 Mar. 1991: 40.

Fast, Howard. *Being Red: A Memoir.* Boston: Houghton Mifflin, 1990.

Faulk, John H. *Fear on Trial.* New York: Simon & Schuster, 1964.

Fried, Richard M. *Nightmare in Red: The McCarthy Era in Perspective.* New York: Oxford UP, 1990.

Fuller, Linda K. "Hollywood and HUAC: A Review of Motion Pictures about McCarthyism." Paper presented to the New England Popular Culture Association, Bates College, Lewiston, ME, 1994.

—. "How Much Like "McCarthyism" *Is* "Political Correctness"? A Cinematic Review." Paper presented to the 44th Annual Conference of the International Communication Association, Sydney, Australia, 1994.

Glazer, Nathan. *The Social Basis of American Communism.* New York: Harcourt, 1961.

Goodman, Walter. *The Committee: The Extraordinary Career of the House Committee on Un-American Activities*. New York: Farrar, 1968.

Goodson, Mark. "If I'd Stood Up Earlier . . ." *New York Times Magazine* 13 Jan. 1991: 22+.

Halliwell, Leslie. *Halliwell's Film Guide*. 7th ed. New York: Harper, 1989.

Hellman, Lillian. *Scoundrel Time*. Boston, MA: Little, Brown, 1976.

Howe, Irving, and Lewis Coser. *The American Communist Party: A Critical History (1919-1957)*. Boston, MA: Beacon, 1957.

Jones, Dorothy. "Communism in the Movies." Cogley 1: 300-01.

Kahn, Gordon. *Hollywood on Trial: The Story of the Ten Who Were Indicted*. New York: Boni, 1948.

Lenihan, John H. "Movie Images of Electoral Politics." Ed. Paul Loukides and Linda K. Fuller. *Beyond the Stars 2: Plot Conventions in American Popular Film*. Bowling Green, OH: Bowling Green State University Popular Press, 1991: 77-90.

Levy, Emanuel. *Small-Town America in Film: The Decline and Fall of Community*. New York: Continuum, 1991.

Maltby, Richard. "Made for Each Other: The Melodrama of Hollywood and the House Committee on Un-American Activities, 1947." Ed. Philip Davies and Brian Neve. *Cinema, Politics, and Society*. New York: St. Martin's, 1981.

Mast, Gerald, ed. *The Movies in Our Midst: Documents in the Cultural History of Film in America*. Chicago: U of Chicago P, 1982.

Navasky, Victor. "Has 'Guilty by Suspicion' Missed the Point?' *New York Times* 3 Mar. 1991: H9.

—. *Naming Names*. New York: Viking, 1980.

Perlman, William J., ed. *The Movies on Trial*. New York: Macmillan, 1936.

Prince, Stephen. *Visions of Empire: Political Imagery in Contemporary American Film*. New York: Praeger, 1992.

Prindle, David F. *The Politics of Glamour: Ideology and Democracy in the Screen Actors Guild*. Madison: U of Wisconsin P, 1988.

Quart, Leonard. *American Film and Society Since 1945*. 2nd ed. New York: Praeger, 1991.

*Red Channels: The Report of the Communist Influence in Radio and Television*. New York: Counterattack, 1950.

Roberts, Garyn G. "Revelation, Humanity, and a Warning: Four Motifs of 1950s Science Fiction Invasion Films." *Beyond the Stars 2: Plot Conventions in American Popular Film*. Ed. Paul Loukides and Linda K. Fuller. Bowling Green, OH: Bowling Green State University Popular Press, 1991: 130-42.

Schary, Dore. *Heyday: An Autobiography*. Boston: Little, Brown, 1979.

Schwartz, Nancy Lynn. *The Hollywood Writers' War*. New York: Knopf, 1982.

Shindler, Colin. *Hollywood at War.* London: Routledge, 1979.

Taubin, Amy. "Helen Whitney: An Insider Makes Movies about Outsiders." *Mirabella* Nov. 1991: 50.

Trilling, Diana. "How McCarthy Gave Anti-Communism a Bad Name." *Newsweek* 11 Jan. 1993: 32-33.

Trumbo, Dalton. *The Time of the Toad: A Study of Inquisition in America.* New York: Harper, 1972.

Tuchman, Mitch. "Freedom of Information." *Film Comment* July-Aug. 1990: 66+.

Vaughn, Robert. *Only Victims: A Study of Show Business Black-Listing.* New York: Putnam, 1972.

Zheutlin, Barbara, and David Talbot. *Creative Differences: Profiles of Hollywood Dissidents.* Boston: South End, 1978.

## Filmography

| Year | Film | Director |
|---|---|---|
| 1935 | *Red Salute* | Sidney Lanfield |
| 1943 | *Mission to Moscow* | Michael Curtiz |
| 1943 | *North Star* | Lewis Milestone |
| 1943 | *Tender Comrade* | Edward Dmytryk |
| 1944 | *Song of Russia* | Gregory Ratoff |
| 1945 | *Objective Burma* | Raoul Walsh |
| 1946 | *Cloak and Daggar* | Director: Fritz Lang |
| 1947 | *Body and Soul* | Robert Rossen |
| 1947 | *Crossfire* | Edward Dmytryk |
| 1948 | *The Iron Curtain* | William Wellman |
| 1948 | *The Naked City* | Jules Dassin |
| 1948 | *Walk a Crooked Mile* | Gordon Douglas |
| 1949 | *All the King's Men* | Robert Rossen |
| 1949 | *Conspirator* | Victor Saville |
| 1949 | *Force of Evil* | Abraham Polonsky |
| 1949 | *The Fountainhead* | King Vidor |
| 1949 | *I Married a Communist* | Robert Stevenson |
| 1949 | *The Red Danube* | George Sidney |
| 1949 | *The Red Menace* | R.G. Springsteen |
| 1950 | *Guilty of Treason* | Felix Feist |
| 1950 | *Gun Crazy* | Joseph H. Lewis |
| 1950 | *In a Lonely Place* | Nicholas Ray |
| 1950 | *The Red Danube* | George Sidney |

| | | |
|---|---|---|
| 1951 | *I Was a Communist for the FBI* | Gordon Douglas |
| 1951 | *The Steel Helmet* | Samuel Fuller |
| 1951 | *The Thing from Another World* | Christian Nyby |
| 1951 | *The Whip Hand* | William Cameron Menzies |
| 1952 | *Big Jim McLain* | Edward Ludwig |
| 1952 | *My Son John* | Leo McCarey |
| 1952 | *High Noon* | Fred Zinnemann |
| 1952 | *Red Planet Mars* | Harry Horner |
| 1952 | *Viva Zapata* | Elia Kazan |
| 1952 | *Walk East on Beacon* | Alfred Werker |
| 1953 | *It Came from Outer Space* | Jack Arnold |
| 1953 | *Man on a Tightrope* | Elia Kazan |
| 1954 | *Johnny Guitar* | Nicholas Ray |
| 1954 | *On the Waterfront* | Elia Kazan |
| 1954 | *Salt of the Earth* | Herbert Biberman |
| 1955 | *Kiss Me Deadly* | Robert Aldrich |
| 1956 | *Storm Center* | Daniel Taradash |
| 1956 | *Invasion of the Body Snatchers* | Dan Siegel |
| 1957 | *A Face in the Crowd* | Elia Kazan |
| 1957 | *A King in New York* | Charlie Chaplin |
| 1957 | *The Quiet American* | Joseph L. Mankiewicz |
| 1960 | *Man on a String* | Andre de Toth |
| 1960 | *Spartacus* | Stanley Kubrick |
| 1962 | *The Manchurian Candidate* | John Frankenheimer |
| 1962 | *Red Nightmare* | Warner Brothers |
| 1964 | *Point of Order* | Emile de Antonio |
| 1973 | *The Way We Were* | Sydney Pollack |
| 1975 | *Three Days of the Condor* | Sydney Pollack |
| 1976 | *Hollywood on Trial* | David Halpern, Jr. |
| 1976 | *The Front* | Martin Ritt |
| 1977 | *Julia* | Fred Zinnemann |
| 1977 | *Tail Gunner Joe* | Jud Taylor |
| 1981 | *Reds* | Warren Beatty |
| 1984 | *Concealed Enemies* | Jeff Bleckner |
| 1984 | *Red Dawn* | John Milius |
| 1988 | *The House on Carroll Street* | Dir/prod: Peter Yates |
| 1989 | *Red Scorpion* | Joseph Zito |
| 1990 | *Fellow Traveller* | Philip Savile |
| 1991 | *American Inquisition* | Helen Whitney |
| 1991 | *For the Boys* | Mark Rydell |
| 1991 | *Guilty by Suspicion* | Writer/dir.: Irwin Winkler |
| 1992 | *Citizen Cohn* | Frank Pierson |

# The Pleasures of Evil: Hedonism and the Contemporary Horror Film

**Gary Hoppenstand**

Though horror films have been a popular Hollywood staple since the earliest decades of commercial movie making, lately a number of films in this cinematic genre have undergone some revealing narrative transformations. The conflict between good and evil has always served as a fundamental plot type in the horror film, yet in recent years the definitions of good and evil have significantly altered. This chapter examines how the moral foundation revealed by the conflict between good and evil in many contemporary horror films has been diminished, and even abolished. In place of this moral foundation frequently there is utilized a more secular (and hence, a postmodern) interpretation of the defined boundary between good and evil that, in the traditional horror film, is based upon a violation of religious taboos (as in Tod Browning's *Dracula*) or a violation of the ethical limitations of scientific investigation (as in James Whale's *Frankenstein*). Indeed, hedonism, or the individual's quest for pleasure and self-gratification, has become the most important defining motif in the contemporary horror film. In this chapter a definition of hedonism will be outlined, a definition that offers specific applications to a critical discussion of the popular horror motion picture. Employing this understanding of classic hedonistic philosophy, a number of important contemporary horror films will be analyzed—including Alfred Hitchcock's *Psycho* (1960), Tobe Hooper's *The Texas Chainsaw Massacre* (1974), and Clive Barker's *Hellraiser* (1987)—in order to identify more precisely the social relationship between the popular horror film and its audience's cognitive understanding of a postmodern definition of morality (or the lack of morality).

Critically speaking, the horror film has always been viewed as subversive. In fact, among the various popular motion picture genres, the horror film is perhaps the most suspect artistically. The reasons for this critical suspicion are diverse. Some attack the exploitation factor of the horror movie, its use of violence to elicit a "cheap thrill" in its audience. Some attack the subversive quality of horror, arguing that its motivation is essentially antisocial, deviant, or sadistic. Many attack the horror film on artistic grounds, stating that horror does not enhance or illuminate the human condition, that it does not solicit philosophical reflection or contemplation, and that it denies levels of sophistication in its use of characters and plots. In other words, the horror film is not "art" because it does not look like art. Art has a message. It communicates fundamental social concerns. Its value is universal and eternal. The genre's critics may typically ask: "Which horror movie achieves these essential qualities of art?"

Perhaps the best way to address what the contemporary popular horror film offers (both as art and as entertainment) is to examine its use of violence, its politically subversive quality, its utilization of philosophical content, its use of characters and plot, and most important (for the purposes of this chapter), its social message—which is the redefinition of evil as a force that distances itself from a religious or scientific explanation, while moving toward a newly evolving (and very contemporary) social context that perceives both good and evil in hedonistic terms.

In *Pleasures and Pains: A Theory of Qualitative Hedonism*, Rem B. Edwards provides a general definition of hedonism. Edwards suggests that the philosophy of normative hedonism (e.g., an ideal type of action) claims that people generally seek pleasure (or happiness) and avoid pain (or unhappiness). Edwards goes on to outline the three elements of hedonism by stating that (1) pleasure is "intrinsically good," while pain is "intrinsically evil"; (2) happiness is achieved when there is a "surplus" of pleasure over pain; and (3) people should attempt to "maximize" happiness while "minimizing" unhappiness (18-19). Hedonism has always been an element of the classic horror film. Traditional monster movies such as *Frankenstein* (1931) and *Dracula* (1931) provide a reliable model of Edwards's definition of hedonism. The typical monster movie protagonist (the Henry Frankenstein character), after violating some norm or social taboo (playing the role of God by artificially creating life or assisting the Devil by providing succor for the Devil's agents), then spends the balance of the narrative attempting to avoid the resulting unhappiness (death and/or dishonor) while trying to preserve happiness (the security of family and friends and self-preservation). Hedonism in the traditional monster movie may not have been the single identifying characteristic of evil, but it was indeed a thematic motif in the overall narrative confrontation between the forces of good and evil.

By the early 1960s the moral definition of the horror film began to change, to evolve. The traditional monster movie of the 1930s was transformed by the commercially astute British Hammer Studios. Films such as *Horror of Dracula* (1958) and *The Curse of Frankenstein* (1957) subtly (and not so subtly) reconfigured their casts of characters and their plots in order to inject more substantial doses of sex and violence. The vampire's kiss became an obvious sexual act in the Hammer film. Repressed and dark emotions only hinted at in earlier films became more explicit. The Hammer Studios' motive was simple, and commercially viable—reinvigorate the old, worn-out monster formulas with a type of "peek-a-boo" titillation. Make what was once an implied sexual menace an overt sexual menace. Replace prudishness with passion. When the necklines on the female victims' nightgowns began to drop, the pursuit of pleasure became a perversion. In the process, Hammer helped to begin the horror film's redefinition of itself that eventually culminated in the seemingly grotesque contemporary "splatter films" (e.g., the Friday the 13th Series), in which violence itself became a pornographic act.

Graphic violence combined with sexual overtones began to dominate the content of the evolving contemporary horror film as it developed through the 1970s. William Friedkin's *The Exorcist* (1973) shocked its audiences with its grotesque special effects, while two years later, Steven Spielberg's *Jaws* (1975) reinterpreted Herman Melville's *Moby-Dick* in graphically vivisectionist, cinematic terms. And as the contemporary horror film defined itself in visual excess, its central characters also defined themselves along philosophically Epicurean lines (albeit a perverted and grotesque Epicureanism). John Watson states in his book entitled *Hedonistic Theories: From Aristippus to Spencer* that the philosopher Epicurus argued that hedonistic pleasure could only be achieved through much scrupulous planning or anticipation (47-72). This notion that pleasure must be carefully planned for is the fundamental attribute of the contemporary horror film, because the Epicurean quest basically establishes the motives of the hedonistic antihero.

In Alfred Hitchcock's *Psycho,* for example, Norman Bates (while in the throes of a schizophrenic fugue state) craftily plots the murder of Marion Crane as a means to diffuse his latent, hedonistic, sexual impulses. The cannibalistic, patriarchal family in Tobe Hooper's *The Texas Chainsaw Massacre*, in their hedonistic desire for good "food," murder and eviscerate (as they would cattle in a slaughterhouse) a group of young travelers in rural Texas. The sexual hedonist named Frank Cotton in Clive Barker's *Hellraiser* successfully deciphers the "Lament Configuration" puzzle box in his search for ultimate pleasure, though once he opens the mystical box—thus inviting the sadomasochistic Cenobites into the mortal dimension—he experiences a type of "pleasure" that he did not anticipate. The monstrous Hannibal "the

Cannibal" Lecter in Jonathan Demme's *The Silence of the Lambs* (1991; based on Thomas Harris's 1988 best-selling novel) is a morally inverted Sherlock Holmes character, who wants to "possess" his victims to the extent that he cannibalizes them. Lecter's hedonistic senses are so heightened that he can identify the brand name of FBI trainee Clarice Starling's skin lotion by a mere whiff from within his stone-and-plexiglass prison, and he is so intelligent that he employs traditional Holmesian observation and intellect to commit his heinous and savage crimes.

During the 1980s, as some people in American society became more absorbed in the wanton pursuit of wealth and in a shameless moral narcissism, hedonism as a perceived evil condition became equated with social class and social status. J.C.B. Gosling suggests in *Pleasure and Desire: The Case for Hedonism Reviewed* that one of the reasons why hedonism, as a philosophical doctrine, declined in popularity during the early part of the 20th century was that the larger moral issue that called into question an individual's "selfish" quest for self-gratification prevailed (6). And this attitude—the belief that the single-minded search for hedonistic pleasure is evil—embodied the driving moral force in the contemporary horror film that reached its culmination during the Ronald Reagan years, when this ultimate American political symbol of unbridled hedonistic consumerism was elected president of the United States. The Robert Zemeckis film *Death Becomes Her* (1992), for example, is fundamentally a horror story (from the tradition of W.W. Jacobs's "The Monkey's Paw" or Christopher Marlowe's *Dr. Faustus*) that has been repackaged as a "black comedy" about the Hollywood elite. Zemeckis's tale of vanity-gone-wrong mocks the Reagan era of trickle-down economics, junk-bond exploitation, and shameless profiteering. The high-class Beverly Hills zombies that haunt *Death Becomes Her* are a reflection of an American middle class's growing dislike of the self-absorbed, decadently wanton celebrity figure who populates the world of popular music, television, and film. Hollywood became synonymous with hedonism in the contemporary horror film (in an ironic, self-critiquing fashion), and hedonism subsequently became the prominent definition of evil.

The contemporary origin of hedonism as the central, defining factor of evil in the horror film can be found in Alfred Hitchcock's *Psycho*. Indeed, *Psycho* is a landmark movie that divides the modern horror film from the traditional horror film. Prior to *Psycho* the horror motion picture generally presented evil as an external force, outside of individual control. This external evil tended to be religious in nature or was scientific. Horror films with religious themes include such masterpieces of the genre as Tod Browning's *Dracula* (and its several Universal Studios sequels). A decade or two later, following the Second World War, scientific evil replaced religious evil as the foundation for the fundamental moral conflict that framed the horror film narrative. The motif of science as forbidden knowledge that was anticipated in James Whale's cinematic adaptation of *Frankenstein* (and in the resulting sequels from Universal Studios) re-emerged in the low-budget, science fiction/horror films of the 1950s. Patrick Lucanio discusses the significant relationship between science and horror in his book entitled *Them or Us: Archetypal Interpretations of Fifties Alien Invasion Films*:

> The alien invasion genre [of the 1950s] clearly focuses on science, and hence it is "science fiction." But in one aspect it shows us hope and aspiration, in another death and destruction. We can interpret these opposing attitudes toward science not as signs of dissension or confusion but . . . as complementary opposites that make for a sturdy balance. (53)

With *Psycho*—and the "slasher" style horror films that *Psycho*'s commercial success at the box office would soon inspire, such as the Texas Chainsaw Massacre movies and the Wes Craven films, including *Last House on the Left* (1972) and *The Hills Have Eyes* (1977)—evil became psychological, and thus became internal. Religion or science played a less important role in the typical horror film as it left the 1950s and entered the 1960s and 1970s. In the new psychological variant of the horror film, the location of evil was masked by the commonplace. Run-down motels on little-used highways (e.g., in *Psycho*) replaced the conventional gothic castle or the scientific laboratory as the place where evil tested humanity's resolve to survive. The traditional gothic narrative still exerted its influence upon this new psychological variant (after all, Norman Bates's house was situated upon the hill above the motel), but the way evil functioned had changed radically. The monsters were no longer the vampire or the mad scientist—external manifestations of our collective nightmares. They were the shy, unobtrusive, seemingly vulnerable, and very human sociopaths—the "Normal" Bates, internal representations of our own dark psyches and darker passions. Cinematic evil could no longer be vanquished by the crucifix, or the strand of garlic, or the square-jawed hero who could thwart the wild ambitions of the mad scientist, because evil could no longer be identified easily. It could no longer be linked to an external source. Instead, cinematic evil became more problematic, and subsequently more realistic. Because our popular movies internalized evil, it was less easy to defeat, and became impossible to eliminate.

What became interesting as the genre underwent this transformation is how the motivation of evil as a narrative device came to be defined. Rather than locating its thematic roots in religion or science, evil (by discovering its source within the individual) soon became equated with moral excess, as first evidenced in Hitchcock's *Psycho*.

Hitchcock based his film on the novel *Psycho* (1959), written by Robert Bloch. Bloch (1917-94) was a prolific author who, in addition to *Psycho*, had written widely in a number of different media—including story radio, film, and television—and in a number of different literary genres. He published extensively after his first book was released in 1945, but his finest work includes *The Scarf* (1947), *The Dead Beat* (1960), and *American Gothic* (1974). Bloch began writing horror stories in imitation of H.P. Lovecraft, yet soon developed his own unique literary voice. The best of Bloch's efforts are distinguished by his macabre sense of twisted humor and by his examination of the dark inner workings of the pathologically disturbed human psyche.

Bloch claimed that the inspiration for *Psycho* was the Ed Gein serial murders in Plainfield, Wisconsin, during the 1950s. Bloch discusses how the Gein killings became the literary catalyst for his imagination:

> I wondered how this man, never suspected of any kind of wrongdoing, in a town where if someone sneezed on the north side of town, someone on the south said "Gesundheit," was only *suddenly* discovered to be a mass murderer. I was also puzzled by how unanxious his neighbors were to speak about these crimes. I said to myself: "There's a *story* here." (Rebello 8)

Thus, Bloch's intent in his novel *Psycho* is to contrast the commonplace with the shocking, in the process generating a sense of horror in his readers because of the frightening and unexpected intrusion of violent evil in people's otherwise mundane lives. Hitchcock certainly incorporated Robert Bloch's fascination with the banal appearance of horror in the cinematic adaptation of his novel. Hitchcock's *Psycho* fundamentally changed how the film audience perceived evil and the motivations to commit evil deeds. Basically, two types of hedonistic behavior appear in the film's narrative: controlled and uncontrolled impulses.

The character Marion Crane (played by Janet Leigh) demonstrates an obviously hedonistic desire for a better life for herself. She is locked into a mundane occupation, and even more frustrating, she is committed to a dead-end relationship with beau Sam Loomis (played by John Gavin). Sam is unable (or unwilling) to wed Marion because he feels that he is financially incapable of supporting a new family (his father's debts and ex-wife's alimony payments are a major part of the predicament). Marion attempts to solve her problem by stealing $40,000 from her employer, money she feels will allow her and Sam to marry. After she escapes Phoenix, Arizona, with the money in hand and travels to Fairvale, California, in order to meet Sam, guilt begins to erode her hedonistic impulse. Finally, stopping at the Bates Motel, she becomes a reformed thief, intending to return the stolen cash. Thus, her hedonistic behavior is controlled, even blunted. Marion is able to thwart her desire for an immediate solution to her problems, and she becomes that archetypal figure that Americans really love in their melodrama—the reformed sinner.

However, as previously mentioned, Hitchcock's *Psycho* is a truly contemporary, truly bleak film. It is profoundly nihilistic in its use of a postmodern noir vision of the individual's fatal relationship with an indifferent, yet omnipotent, Fate. Morality is a meaningless concept in *Psycho*'s dark milieu. Marion Crane is senselessly and brutally murdered at that moment when she reforms, at that instant when she seems to have gained control over her "evil" hedonistic tendencies. Redemption is not rewarded. It is not even recognized. There is no clear-cut dichotomy between good and evil, only subtle variations of each. Marion, as a lesser evil person, is ultimately destroyed by a villain who is fundamentally evil, an individual who embraces a hedonism that is as uncontrolled as it is deadly.

Indeed, Norman Bates (played by Anthony Perkins) is an example of that worst type of monster; he masks his evil impulses behind a banal façade of innocence and naiveté. What makes Norman Bates such a fiend in *Psycho* is his uncontrolled passion. His voyeuristic impulses, as he views through his spy hole in the wall the unsuspecting Marion undressing, trigger his sexual libido. Sexual desire is then transformed into an uncontrolled hedonistic desire that quickly and violently manifests itself in his gender-crossing psychopathic split-personality (i.e., his Mother Bates persona). As a thematic device, this uncontrolled hedonism, as evidenced in Norman's character, subsequently became an important defining factor in the contemporary horror film. Uncontrolled hedonism eventually came to embody a number of the genre's most memorable villains, from *The Texas Chainsaw Massacre*'s Leatherface to *Hellraiser*'s Cenobites.

The notorious Ed Gein serial killings that provided Robert Bloch with the inspiration for *Psycho* also provided Tobe Hooper with the inspiration for the 1974 motion picture that he directed, produced, and co-wrote, *The Texas Chainsaw Massacre*. Basically, Hooper's film remakes *Psycho* (minus Hitchcock's suspense) in its utilization of pathological psychology; but whereas *Psycho* merely teases its audience with highly stylized glimpses of violence and necrophilia, *The Texas Chainsaw Massacre* bludgeons its viewers with grotesque images of cannibalism. As in *Psycho,* much of the violence is off screen or masked by cinematic technique. This technique, however, is employed effectively by Hooper in order to heighten his audience's sense of unease. The documentary technique that opens the film (the voice-over radio news report and the photographic flashbulb glimpses of the desecrated corpses), for example, creates a realistic frame for the monstrous series of events that follows. Hooper wants reality to intrude upon his fiction. He wants his viewers to understand that his Texas cannibal serial killers are but one short step away from today's news headlines. He wants verisimilitude to be his ally in his desire to create a frightening movie.

The plot of *The Texas Chainsaw Massacre* is deliberately sparse. A great deal of the narrative in Hooper's film concerns itself with scenes of victimization and pursuit. Sally Hardesty (played by Marilyn Burns) and her brother Franklin (played by Paul A. Partain) are traveling by van in order to make sure their grandfather's grave in Texas is undisturbed. News reports have indicated that a number of grave sites in the area have recently been vandalized, their occupants gruesomely defiled. Accompanying Sally and Franklin are Jerry (played by Allen Danziger), Kirk (played by William Vail), and Pam (played by Teri McMinn). While journeying to the deceased grandfather's old house, the group picks up a "Hitchhiker" (played by Edwin Neal). This Hitchhiker acts and appears grotesque. He seems to enjoy self-inflicted pain. After he is denied payment for taking a photograph of the travelers, he burns the photo (almost as if it were a sacrificial offering), slashes Franklin's arm with his razor, and marks the van with his own blood when he is thrown from the vehicle.

Hooper employs these early scenes to establish the boundary between the normal and the psychopathic. He encourages his audience to identify with Sally, Franklin, and the remaining group of traveling young adults by defining these characters as being either commonplace or vulnerable. For example, Sally, Jerry, and Kirk appear to be wholesome, "all-American." Pam, as the innocuous "New Age" advocate, passes the time by making astrological readings. Pudgy Franklin is handicapped, a paraplegic traveling in his wheelchair. All in all, these young people are emblematic of their middle-class culture. Their ideology reflects that of the mid-1970s American youth. Once this naive group of travelers has been established, the Hitchhiker is introduced, and normality is violated by extreme insanity. Initially, the Hitchhiker appears to be merely eccentric (being unwashed and wild-eyed), but as he continues to interact with the others, he soon demonstrates the perverse depths of his hedonistic passions by cutting his hand with Franklin's pocket knife. Thus, when Hooper violates the normality of the group by placing in their midst the sadomasochistic psychopath, he defines the Hitchhiker as evil because of this unsavory character's love of (or indifference to) pain. The Hitchhiker is the first encountered member of a patriarchal, cannibalistic family, a family whose desire for "special" food defines hedonistic excess in the most grotesque fashion possible. Indeed, *The Texas Chainsaw Massacre* violates one of the most sacred of social taboos (i.e., cannibalism), and this violation is motivated by hedonistic desire.

Following the early harrowing encounter with the Hitchhiker, when the group stops at a local gas station, they are told by the "Old Man" (played by Jim Siedow) who operates the station that he is out of gas. The Old Man also warns them not to investigate the grandfather's empty house, a warning the group soon ignores. After arriving at the grandfather's house, Kirk and Pam decide to go swimming in a nearby pond but, discovering the pond to be dry, instead wander off to another nearby farmhouse looking for gas, there to die horrible deaths. They both are attacked and killed by a large man (played by Gunnar Hansen) wearing a leather-like face mask (that looks as if it is constructed from a human face). Later, Jerry searches for Kirk and Pam, only to be killed as well by "Leatherface" while investigating the farmhouse. As Sally and Franklin join in the search for their missing companions, Franklin is attacked and killed by the chainsaw-wielding Leatherface. When Sally is pursued by Leatherface, she finds her way back to the gas station looking for help. Instead of providing help, the Old Man captures Sally and returns to the grisly farmhouse, picking up the psychotic Hitchhiker along the way. The viewer thus learns that Leatherface, the Old Man, and the Hitchhiker are all members of the same family.

Basically, director Hooper masks evil in his film with the façade of the mundane. The Texas farmhouse that is home to the cannibals appears from the outside to be a typical rural dwelling. But once the house is entered by Kirk and Pam, the veneer of normality is abruptly stripped away. Beneath the veneer, inside the house, images of the grotesque dominate. Bones and feathers hang from the ceiling and litter the floor. Curious furniture constructed of bone and skin decorates the rooms. A butcher shop, replete with hanging meat hooks and meat freezer, is situated behind a steel door. Like the disguised farmhouse, the Old Man who tends the local gas station appears to be normal. Yet this appearance, as with most other surface appearances in the film, is deceptive. The Old Man is as much the sadomasochistic hedonist as are the

Hitchhiker and Leatherface; though it initially appears that he does not like killing, he does enjoy torturing his victims for pleasure alone. The Old Man is a bit more sophisticated in his love of evil. He is better able to disguise his perverse desires, and this ability to appear normal perhaps makes him the most villainous of his "family."

The cannibals place Sally at their dinner table (set with food processed from their slaughtered victims), and later attempt to have their "Grandfather" (played by John Dugan) kill Sally with a hammer blow to her head. She escapes her captors and is pursued by Leatherface and the Hitchhiker. Sally eventually flags down a tractor-trailer (which runs over and kills the Hitchhiker), but still being attacked by Leatherface, she finally escapes in a pickup truck that is passing by.

What saves *The Texas Chainsaw Massacre* from being a simple exploitation film is director Tobe Hooper's utilization of sophisticated metaphor. As in Hitchcock's *Psycho,* an insanity that assumes monstrous proportions is the focal point of Hooper's cinematic narrative. Hooper builds on this by tempering the monstrous with the perversely humorous. The reason why the Texas cannibals have gone on a murder rampage (and the reason why they are desecrating the local graves) is because they have been "laid off" from work in a slaughterhouse. Improved technology has made their jobs obsolete. In essence, the Texas cannibals express their rage in the only way they know how, and Hooper thus incorporates a grim jest in his film, a jest that highlights the blue-collar worker's anger against the indifferent "system."

But Hooper's message is more than economic allegory. Hooper's intent in *The Texas Chainsaw Massacre* seems to be philosophical. He wants to create a new definition of evil, one that makes it problematic and thus postmodern. Hooper portrays insanity in his film as being nurtured, to a lesser extent, by external forces of nature (as represented by his persistent inclusion of the sun as a visual cinematic motif). To a greater extent, Hooper depicts human evil as being emblematic of the extreme, even pathological, function of the human senses: in particular, sight and taste. Hooper's Texas cannibals are cannibals because they are hedonists who have defined their quest for "pleasure" in the most socially offensive manner possible. The scene in the film, for example, in which the lethargic Grandfather is offered Pam's cut finger for a "taste" is illustrative of the hedonist's extreme senses. Grandfather prefers the taste of human blood, just as his progeny prefer the taste of human flesh, and these forbidden appetites define for Hooper's audience the hedonistic standards of evil and those who practice evil.

As in Hooper's *The Texas Chainsaw Massacre,* grotesque vivisection as an important thematic element also plays a crucial role in

Clive Barker's film *Hellraiser*. Drawing upon both literary and cinematic sources of hedonism for his work in fiction and film, popular fantasy author and motion picture auteur Clive Barker (1952- ) creates in *Hellraiser* several villains, both mortal and immortal, who embrace an uncontrolled desire for the ultimate hedonistic experience.

Barker began his professional career as a writer scripting plays for the British theatre. He became known as a major writer of dark fantasy with the publication of his epic six-volume Books of Blood anthology (the first three volumes were published in 1984; the last three volumes were published in 1985). His novels—including *The Damnation Game* (1985), *Weaveworld* (1987), *The Hellbound Heart* (1987), *Cabal* (1988), *The Great and Secret Show* (1989), *Imajica* (1991), *The Thief of Always* (1992), and *Everville* (1994)—have solidified his reputation as one of the most popular contemporary authors (along with Stephen King, Dean Koontz, and Anne Rice) of the macabre tale of the *fantastique*. Barker's directing credits thus far include three films—*Hellraiser*, *Night Breed* (1990; based upon his short novel, *Cabal*), and *Lord of Illusions* (1995; based on his Books of Blood short story "The Last Illusion")—and as he has helped to shape the direction of the modern horror story in fiction, Barker has influenced profoundly the direction of the contemporary horror film.

Barker adapted the screenplay of his movie *Hellraiser* from his short novel, *The Hellbound Heart*. In both the novel and cinematic adaptation of the novel, Barker establishes as the center of his plot a love triangle. Larry Cotton (played by Andrew Robinson) is to be married to Julia (played by Clare Higgins); as the wedding approaches, Larry's brother Frank (played by Sean Chapman) pays a visit. The viewer learns early in *Hellraiser* that "evil" brother Frank is a dedicated sexual hedonist. Frank purchases a mysterious, intricately designed puzzle box with the hope of uncovering new and unique areas of forbidden arousal. His purchase reveals more than what he bargained for; his quest for pleasure only brings him eternal pain. When Frank solves the puzzle box, this act summons the supernatural sadomasochists known as the Cenobites, creatures who are supreme hedonists, believing that pain is pleasure. Frank is literally ripped apart by the Cenobites, but his tormented soul still exists, desiring an entrance back into the mortal world.

With Frank and the Cenobites, Barker establishes two fundamental types of hedonists, one mortal and the other immortal. Frank's quest for hedonistic self-gratification is solely motivated by his enormous, perverse libido. He is depicted as a manipulating sexual ogre who will use women (such as his lover Julia) to obtain what he wants without regard to moral consequences. His sexual lust is destructive because it is so narcissistic. Barker initially suggests in Frank's character a lurking, barely contained sadism, a willingness to torment others. This sadism assumes grotesque proportions later in the film's narrative when Frank attempts to seduce his young niece, Kirsty (played by Ashley Laurence). Barker, of course, intends a grim irony in his narrative when he has Frank solve the riddle of the Cenobites' puzzle box. Frank thinks he is accessing a new form of sexual transcendentalism, but in reality he summons sadomasochistic monsters who are even worse than he is himself. He initiates his own destruction because he misunderstands the promise of the puzzle box. He brings to himself a searing, eternal pain, when he intended to discover the exact opposite; and thus, as a type of divine retribution, Frank suffers many times over the agony he has inflicted upon others. The creatures that he summons—the Cenobites (the name being a deliberate play on the word's religious connotation)—are the ultimate hedonists, powerful supernatural creatures who blur the distinctions of pleasure and pain into one "spiritual" experience. Barker intends the Cenobites to be angels of pleasure, albeit a pleasure that is founded upon intense physical suffering. Like Frank, the Cenobites are seekers of the ultimate hedonistic experience. Their bodies are tattooed with the scars of terrible self-inflicted wounds, and when summoned, as they were by Frank, they grant their special "favors" to their supplicants. They represent hedonistic desire taken to its ultimate, destructive extreme.

Early in the film, Larry and Julia move into the family home (with Frank mysteriously absent), an act that causes Julia (in a cinematic flashback) to remember her first encounter (via an intimate photograph that Julia discovers in the house) with brother Frank at her wedding, an encounter that quickly leads to Frank's seduction of Julia. Julia subsequently pledges herself to Frank, and Larry knows nothing of this infidelity. When Larry cuts his hand during the move, the blood that drips on the floor in an upper bedroom helps to resurrect Frank's physical form. But Frank's body has only partially returned from the dark realm of the Cenobites. He needs more blood to complete his transformation and convinces Julia to lure men into the room, there to murder them for their blood. After several murders, Frank is almost whole again, but a new problem arises. Kirsty, Larry's daughter by his first marriage, has returned home to visit her father. Her love for her father and her innate distrust of her stepmother eventually lead her to become involved in Frank's and Julia's vile schemes. Kirsty not only fails to save her father's life (Frank and Julia kill Larry, and Frank uses his brother's skin to complete his physical metamorphosis), she has to confront an evil even greater than her vile uncle's or wicked stepmother's. By accidentally solving the same puzzle box that trapped Frank, Kirsty unwittingly summons the Cenobites. She can save herself only by promising the Cenobites to lure her uncle into admitting the fact of his escape. Frank is eventually recaptured, and Kirsty exorcises the Cenobites by working the puzzle box back into its original configuration.

With Julia, Barker parodies the wicked stepmother figure in the traditional fairy tale. Barker typically employs a parody of other narrative traditions in his fiction and motion pictures in order to establish a familiar frame of reference for his audience. Once this point of reference is created, Barker swiftly moves away from mere parody into startling new territory. Barker thus celebrates past traditional narrative formulas by employing them in his work, while also underscoring the conventional limitations of these stories by demonstrating how they can be used to create a new variant and a new perspective. Julia may start out as a wicked stepmother in *Hellraiser*, but she eventually becomes something much more evil and more frightening. From the start, Julia is deceptive, conniving, and extremely crafty. Her antagonistic relationship with her stepdaughter, Kirsty, is hinted at early in the film, but toward the end of the film, as Julia learns to murder (becoming a serial killer), she assists her lover Frank in attempting to seduce Kirsty, a seduction that viewers understand will eventually lead to Kirsty's own murder.

Like Frank, Julia is a sexual hedonist; but whereas Frank's nature is inherently evil, Julia has to learn how to become evil. Julia takes her first steps toward damnation when she succumbs to Frank's amorous advances. She completes her moral transformation (as Frank is completing his physical transformation) when she lures middle-aged men—who themselves are minor-league sexual hedonists—to their sacrificial death. Barker's message in *Hellraiser* is both moral and allegorical. His film is a contemporary morality play warning against the dangers of rampant hedonistic desires. There are many levels of hedonistic evil in the film's narrative, (no fundamental black-and-white moral frame, but one possessing many shades of gray), and Barker's implication is that there exists but a short step from the minor sexual perversion of Frank's and Julia's initial adulterous relationship to the type of diabolic aberration as represented by the Cenobites. Barker's dark message is that everyone has a Cenobite locked away in the shadowy corners of their psyches, and if passions are given their freedom, if the Cenobites are summoned, then literally all hell will break loose.

A number of today's film critics consider the contemporary popular horror film to be a grueling exercise in excess. Graphic violence, rather than suspense, has become the standard narrative offering, as each new motion picture attempts to outdo its predecessor by invading and pushing the extreme boundaries of social taboos. It may be conversely argued, however, that rather than pandering to the most visceral elements of an inane teenage film audience, motion pictures such as *Psycho, The Texas Chainsaw Massacre,* and *Hellraiser* attempt to critique the larger culture by attacking the perceived moral excesses of that culture. These movies, to a greater or lesser extent, portray evil in hedonistic terms. They criticize a society whose members have grown ever more self-serving through the recent decades, and more narcissistic. Alfred Hitchcock's *Psycho* revealed a pronounced break with previous horror films in its handling of evil. Instead of depicting evil in religious or scientific terms, *Psycho* suggested that moral aberration was internally motivated, driven by psychopathic, hedonistic actions. Tobe Hooper extended Hitchcock's depiction of hedonism as the central motivating force that explains the actions of the human monsters in *The Texas Chainsaw Massacre*. Social taboos were shockingly violated by characters who defined themselves in Hooper's film by their grotesque desires. Clive Barker has utilized perhaps the most sophisticated treatment of hedonism in *Hellraiser*. His "love triangle" gone wrong details the variety and depth of hedonistic passions that bind people to their desires. Barker's Cenobites are the perfect symbolic representation of a larger society that worships immediate gratification to the exclusion of other ennobling ambitions or motivations. Indeed, as illustrated in a large number of contemporary horror motion pictures, hedonism—as a thematic narrative motif—now functions as the predominant metaphor of the postmodern horror film.

## Works Cited

Edwards, Rem B. *Pleasures and Pains: A Theory of Qualitative Hedonism.* Ithaca: Cornell UP, 1979.

Gosling, J.C.B. *Pleasure and Desire: The Case for Hedonism Reviewed.* Oxford: Clarendon, 1969.

Lucanio, Patrick. *Them or Us: Archetypal Interpretations of Fifties Alien Invasion Films*. Bloomington: Indiana UP, 1987.

Rebello, Stephen. *Alfred Hitchcock and the Making of Psycho*. New York: Harper, 1991.

Watson, John. *Hedonistic Theories: From Aristippus to Spencer*. Glasgow: James MacLehose, 1895.

## Selected Filmography

| Year | Film | Director |
|---|---|---|
| 1960 | *Psycho* | Alfred Hitchcock |
| 1971 | *The Vampire Lovers* | Roy Ward Baker |
| 1972 | *Frenzy* | Alfred Hitchcock |
| 1972 | *Last House on the Left* | Wes Craven |
| 1974 | *The Texas Chainsaw Massacre* | Tobe Hooper |
| 1975 | *The Rocky Horror Picture Show* | Jim Sharman |
| 1977 | *The Hills Have Eyes* | Wes Craven |
| 1978 | *The Fury* | Brian De Palma |
| 1980 | *Dressed To Kill* | Brian De Palma |
| 1981 | *The Howling* | Joe Dante |
| 1981 | *Scanners* | David Cronenberg |
| 1983 | *The Hunger* | Tony Scott |
| 1983 | *Psycho II* | Richard Franklin |
| 1983 | *Videodrome* | David Cronenberg |
| 1985 | *The Hills Have Eyes, Part II* | Wes Craven |
| 1985 | *Silver Bullet* | Daniel Attias |
| 1986 | *Psycho III* | Anthony Perkins |
| 1986 | *The Texas Chainsaw Massacre 2* | Tobe Hooper |
| 1987 | *Hellraiser* | Clive Barker |
| 1987 | *The Lost Boys* | Joel Schumacher |
| 1987 | *Near Dark* | Kathryn Bigelow |
| 1988 | *Dead Ringers* | David Cronenberg |
| 1988 | *Hellbound: Hellraiser II* | Tony Randel |
| 1988 | *The Unholy* | Camilo Vila |
| 1990 | *Leatherface: Texas Chainsaw Massacre III* | Jeff Burr |
| 1990 | *Psycho IV: The Beginning* | Mick Garris |
| 1991 | *Scanners II: The New Order* | Christian Duguay |
| 1991 | *The Silence of the Lambs* | Jonathan Demme |
| 1992 | *Candyman* | Bernard Rose |
| 1992 | *Death Becomes Her* | Robert Zemeckis |
| 1992 | *Hellraiser III: Hell on Earth* | Anthony Hickox |
| 1992 | *Scanners III: The Takeover* | Christian Duguay |
| 1994 | *Interview with the Vampire: The Vampire Chronicles* | Neil Jordan |
| 1995 | *Candyman: Farewell to the Flesh* | Bill Condon |
| 1995 | *Lord of Illusions* | Clive Barker |
| 1995 | *Species* | Roger Donaldson |
| 1995 | *Vampire in Brooklyn* | Wes Craven |

# Discounting the ’60s: Hollywood Revisits the Counterculture

**Greg Metcalf**

> The ’60s hadn’t really hit yet in our little town in Maryland, even though they were almost over. I mean that in the sense that nothing much had changed.
>
> —Scott, *1969*

> Beulah: I experienced the ’60s.
> Annie: No, I think you had two ’50s and moved right on into the ’70s.
>
> —*Field of Dreams*

> I’ve never taken drugs because I missed the ’60s. I was an accountant.
>
> —Peter Banning, *Hook*

“The ’60s” of post-1960s Hollywood film is a romantic and marginalized period in American history. By focusing on individual relationships and family strife and settling on a checklist of conventional signifiers of the era, Hollywood films set in the ’60s translate the social and political events of the day into background details for more conventional stories of young people coming of age in a harsh world. In the process, the distinct ideals and politics of the ’60s are presented as secondary to the youthful self-indulgence of those who embraced those values. Similarly, films set in the post-1960s feature the image of “ ’60s leftovers” as the drugged-out, the dropped-out and the sold-out. Both approaches to the ’60s tend to characterize “ ’60s people” as naive, irrelevant, or ridiculous. While some films suggest that such naivete is superior to the cynical realism that followed, it is also shown to be impractical in the present.

This is not to say that filmmakers are intentionally trying to dismiss the ’60s. Rather, these films translate the complicated political and social events of the period into the form and conventions of the Hollywood film. In the absence of a vocabulary for directly addressing political issues, these films rely on a traditional Hollywood focus on individuals and on happy endings. These narrative choices shoehorn rebellion into a structure of family conflict and stress the forced resolution of interpersonal relationships, resulting in a sort of individualized nostalgia for the period, and a treatment of the period as a "coming of age" drama often exaggerated by directors who stress the roots of these films in their own lives. Such films take the experiences of the individual very seriously, but that emphasis on maturation—whether of the individuals or the society—recasts the social and political ideals of the era as youthful excesses whose time has passed.

The consequences of this focus on maturation in films set during the '60s are seen most clearly in the second body of films to be discussed here, Hollywood films about '60s leftovers. If the conventional assumption is that '60s rebellion was a youthful indiscretion that must end in mature reintegration into mainstream society, then the unreintegrated '60s character is a dysfunctional aging child, either naively immature or despondently self-obsessed. Regardless of which, these Hollywood films stress the same convention of the alienated individual's inevitable reintegration into the community. Only the magic realism of *Field of Dreams* (1991) can achieve the fantasy of living in the present without abandoning the idealism of the '60s by allowing its hero to mature while also returning to a child state.

While the ideals of the '60s are almost always presented as impractical to a contemporary audience, the marginalization of the '60s as generic youthful rebellion does allow one opening for advocating their validity. A few films turn the dismissal of inevitable youthful rebellion on its head and find a happy ending in conclusions suggesting that '60s people may have failed but a new generation of youth might (however temporarily) carry on the struggle.

A note on terminology: The working definition of the '60s within these films is the counterculture associated with young, mainly white, middle-class Americans from the mid-1960s to about 1972. It includes activism—from the Students for a Democratic Society (SDS) and its successors, the Weathermen and the yippies, drug use, the rock music scene, with civil rights activism, the women's rights movement, the free speech movement, the antiwar movement, the conscientious-objector movement, the sexual revolution—and in-activism, those who tuned in, turned on and/or dropped out. In a word, the '60s mean "rebellion," albeit with widely varying personal meanings.

*Hollywood's '60s: The Personal, Not the Political*

> People are gonna look back on 1969 and say that's the year that everything changed. That's the year they got rid of all that shit, prejudice, fighting, poverty, fighting, disease, they'll say it was a year of miracles. Scott Denny got laid. Maybe.
>
> —Scott, *1969*

Throughout films about the '60s made after the '60s, there is a focus on individuals rather than causes. While the personal may be political, in these films it tends to obscure the broader context. Whether Scott (Keifer Sutherland) in *1969* (1988) loses his virginity is exactly as important as any political issue. The Vietnam war is a cause for battle between Scott and his father (Bruce Dern), a threat to the friendship of Scott and Ralph (Robert Downey, Jr.) and a threat to Scott's parents' marriage because of the strains due to their other son, Alden's, being in Vietnam. While Alden's being in the war tears the family apart, his eventual death in Vietnam also acts as the catalyst for bringing the family back together.

Even Oliver Stone's declared attempts to counter the Hollywood presentation of the '60s in such films as *Born on the Fourth of July* (1989) and *The Doors* (1991) return to the convention of parent-child struggle. In *Born on the Fourth of July,* the crises of Ron Kovic (Tom Cruise) are attributed to his mother's domination and denial, his redemption is gained in revolting against her values. While the mother-son struggle is not resolved in the story, the film's final scene creates the appearance of resolution as Kovic's preparation to address the Democratic National Convention is juxtaposed with a voice-over that repeats his mother's early prediction of his greatness. While the parents are seen only in sepia-toned memories in *The Doors*, the denial of Jim Morrison (Val Kilmer) of the existence of his parents, especially his father, who is an admiral, is revealed as his great, defining, hidden secret.

Such a focus on the individual within the family universalizes '60s rebellion in a way that both increases the accessibility of the film to a non-1960s audience and minimizes the uniqueness of the events of that period into a, perhaps unintended, "kids will be kids" subtheme. The '60s are, simply, another generational conflict, an Oedipal struggle writ large. *1969, '68* (1988), *Four Friends* (1981), *Running on Empty* (1988), *The Big Fix* (1978), and *Field of Dreams* (1989) all focus on the family as the central struggle of the 1960s. This centrality of the family also allows the films to achieve cinematic closure in a parent-child reconciliation as the film fades out.

Minor variations occur in *More American Graffiti* (1979), where the conflict is between insurance salesman Steve Bolander (Ron Howard) and his radical student brother-in-law Andy Henderson, with Steve's wife, Laurie (Cindy Williams), playing the mediating maternal role. The film shows us the intolerance of the radicals (Laurie: "Don't you believe in democracy, Andy?" Andy: "With qualifications") but it also allows Andy and the parent-surrogates to reconcile over the issue of police overreaction, when they are all trapped in a police riot. As in the film *1969,* the unjust arrests are overturned by a good man, Steve, somewhat magically releasing all the prisoners. And Steve and Laurie achieve a renewed commitment to their marriage by having been touched by a broader social crisis. *The Big Fix* shows the price of a lack of reconciliation: a murder, several attempted murders, and a kidnapping result from a father's refusal to reconcile with his once-activist son. The film *'68* finds the father alone with an alienated wife at the end, having chased away his homosexual son, his antiwar son, his mistress, and his friends.

In *Daniel* (1983), the antiwar activism of Susan (Amanda Plummer) is seen as a failed attempt to resolve her conflicted feelings toward her pre-'60s radical parents (a fictionalized version of Ethel and Julius Rosenberg). Daniel (Timothy Hutton) finally realizes that he can't find answers about his parents for his sister or himself, and returns to New York to reconcile with his wife and their child in a joyous protest march as a Melanie folk song plays on the soundtrack. The message of this march is unclear, made more so by the use of aerial shots of Central Park filled with people, which now seem to refer less to protests than to the free concerts by Simon and Garfunkel, Paul Simon, and Diana Ross. Nonetheless there is the sense, as in *1969,* that the family that can protest together can stay together.

The film *1969* seems to distill most of the other '60s films. It focuses on two young men: Scott, a sincere, antiwar "bad son" and his neighbor Ralph, an acid-dropping, dark-side nutcase who flunks out of college. They get picked up by a homosexual man who propositions Ralph. The duo drive their hand-painted VW van to California, where they have "naked people giving us free food." The parents and children break into separate worlds. Scott becomes the lover of Ralph's sister (Winona Ryder), which adds to the strain. Scott smokes marijuana, loses his virginity, admires Eugene McCarthy, and reads Kurt Vonnegut. Scott's father loses his "good" son in Vietnam, has an affair with Ralph's mother, wants his antiwar son arrested and throws him out of his house. In the end, after Ralph is arrested for breaking into the draft board, Ralph and Scott fall out because Scott is sleeping with Ralph's sister,

Scott almost goes to Canada but returns to embrace his father at Alden's funeral and lead the entire community, including his father, in a march on the city jail. There the policeman releases Ralph, and Ralph and Scott make up. A soundtrack of '60s rock hits is used to verify the film's authenticity.

If the preceding paragraph appears list-like, it reflects a "rebellion-checklist" quality in many films dealing with films about the '60s. Certain symbols of rebellion become icons of the era. Marijuana and LSD usage, for example, have become prime signifiers of the era. Marijuana is present in almost every film that invokes the '60s. Those set in the 1960s tend to present marijuana smoking, like losing one's virginity, as connected to a growing political enlightenment or at least maturity. Typically, as Peter in *'68* becomes politically active and socially aware, he smokes marijuana. Non-drug-users are "Narcs," the epithet hurled at Steve Bolander in *More American Graffiti* when he goes looking for his radical brother-in-law. Films set in the post-1960s tend to stress the malaise and negative effects of drug use in the present while being nostalgic over drug use in the past.

Sexual liberation and sexual coming of age are similar key touchstones. *Four Friends, Willie and Phil* (1980), *The Return of the Secaucus Seven* (1980), *More American Graffiti, Class Action* (1991), *Far Out Man* (1990), *Rude Awakenings* (1989) and *The Doors* (1991) offer variations on a casualness in sexual relations, with increasing emphasis on the callousness of male partners of the '60s and the suggestion that sexual relationships can't be as casual as the ideology insisted they should be.

While these films tend to be extremely male-centered, women are presented, within limitations, asserting individual identity. In *More American Graffiti*, Laurie is a conservative housewife trying to break out without rebelling. Similarly trapped housewives are seen *'68, 1969,* and even in Oliver Stone's *The Doors*, and the convention of the woman bridling at being forced to stand by her man is used in almost all '60s survivor films from *Between the Lines* (1977) to *Class Action* (1991). *Graffiti*'s Debbie (Candy Clark) gains her sexual, romantic, and career fulfillment as she moves from having a sleazeball boyfriend while working as a stripper to gaining a studly and monogamous musician (Scott Glenn) who also gives her a job playing a tambourine with his rock band.

The issue of nascent women's liberation is often wrapped up with sexuality. *Coming Home* (1978) links Jane Fonda's ability to achieve orgasm (through "nontraditional" sex) with her growing self-awareness and antiwar sentiments as she shifts her romantic orientation from a husband who is an active duty officer in Vietnam to a lover who is an antiwar veteran. Alana (Mirlan Kwun) of *'68* is defined by her control of the sexual relationship with Peter (Eric Larson) as much as by her radical political sophistication. More often than not, a '60s blending of female sexuality and rebellion against traditional roles emerges in a caricatured form like that in *Bird on a Wire* (1990), where Rick (Mel Gibson) chances to look up her dress and asks his '60s girlfriend-turned-corporate-lawyer, Marianne (Goldie Hawn), "Since when did you start wearing underpants?"

Escalating *1969*'s father-son conflict over Vietnam, the father-son battle in *'68* is over both the war and the homosexuality of the son Sandy (Robert Locke). Like Scott, Peter is thrown out of the house by his father (Sandor Tecsi) for his politics, Sandy for his sexuality, while an understanding mother silently sympathizes, and dad has an affair. The implicit argument in these parental affairs is that the un-hip people in authority are hypocritical because they don't live up to the standards they demand of their children. While this can be read as a metaphor for the social and political situation of the day, the films do not develop these points. Instead, the focus remains on the personal. Peter's grief over the Robert Kennedy assassination is quickly superseded by his father's falling victim to a hospitalizing illness, turning him back to familial conflict and responsibility as he takes over the family business.

These films also approach protests in terms of individual relationships. In *More American Graffiti,* getting caught in a police riot saves the Bolanders' marriage. A police overreaction to a protest in 1969 defines Scott's role as protector to his mother and to his soon-to-be lover. As in *Daniel,* when *'68*'s Peter is thrown out of his father's house he joins his girlfriend in a protest march.

In fact, these films tend to suggest that political action has a lot to do with the pursuit of sex. In *'68* Peter becomes politically active in pursuit of a doctrinaire radical woman. As already noted, *Coming Home* draws a tight connection between sex and political activism, with the strong possibility that hormones guided ideology. Among the post-1960s crowd, *The Big Fix*'s Moses Wine (Richard Dreyfuss) gets involved in a political campaign in pursuit of an old girlfriend, Lila (Susan Anspach), propositioning her with the line, "Why don't we just pick up where we left off in the days of protest? We could pretend there's tear gas coming through the door . . . put on an old Buffalo Springfield album." In *Teachers* (1984), Alex Jurrel (Nick Nolte) returns to activism in response to equal parts of shaming and sexual invitation from his former student (Jo Beth Williams). Of course, in most of these cases, the rock music soundtrack is *de rigueur*. In *'68, 1969, Flashback* (1990), *The Big Chill*

(1983) (with a Motown-dominated playlist for a group of ex-Ann Arbor, Michigan, students), and *Rude Awakenings* feature soundtracks of '60s hits, some rerecorded for a modern audience. *Running on Empty* (named after a Jackson Browne song) and *Bird on a Wire* (named after a Leonard Cohen song) also draw on the classic rock playlists. While the music itself may be seen as establishing "authenticity" for the film, the compilation of a pervasive rock soundtrack itself refers back to a movie that many see as an archetypal 1960s film about the '60s *Easy Rider*, with its titles-to-credits collection of rock music.

The music, the drugs, the sexual freedom, protest scenes, even the Volkswagen—especially the "microbus"/van (as seen in *1969, Daniel, '68, Field of Dreams*, and *More American Graffiti*), preferably hand-painted—become distilled symbols of '60s rebellion. Such symbols carry a significant portion of the rebellious content in '60s films, especially as they are often used in conjunction with story lines that present mixed, if not nonrebellious, messages. Symbolic rebellion is paired with conservative narrative.

This approach to youth rebellion is not unique to post-1960s films about the '60s. In fact the two most famous youth rebellion films—*Rebel without a Cause* (1955) and *Easy Rider* (1969)—utilize the same mix of symbols of rebellion and a story line that arrives at a very mainstream conclusion. The transcendent image of James Dean, the rebel, has largely obscured *Rebel without a Cause*'s story, which shows the failure of young people rebelling against the hypocrisy of their elders. The teenagers, Jim Stark (Dean) and Judy (Natalie Wood), who think they could make a better family than their own parents end up abandoning their "child," the teenager Plato (Sal Mineo), and indirectly cause his death at the hands of the police. The alienation and rebellion of suburban youth—the signifying jackets and jeans, the boots, the switchblades, and chickee runs—were presented to its audience, but the film's story toed the line of safest resolution as Jim, returned to the bosom of his family, introduces his new girlfriend to his supportive parents, as his father finally stands up to his mother and takes the authoritative role toward wife and son that Jim had requested.

Similarly, the '60s film some see as embodying the era, *Easy Rider*, was intended by its makers as a critique of the failure of its central characters, although the cocaine-smuggling motorcyclists came to be embraced as counterculture heroes. Even if we read the closed-minded and paranoid Wyatt (Dennis Hopper) and the detached Billy (Peter Fonda) as heroic figures and ignore that Billy's final judgment on their experience is that "We blew it," we are still faced with their shotgun deaths at the film's end. Even if the duo are the heroes, their death at the film's end reiterates the danger of challenging the system and, at best, suggests a mixed message.

### *The '60s Leftover: Drugged-Out, Burned-Out, and Sold-Out*

> Oh my God! You're from the '60s! . . . Get back! . . . There's no place for you in the future!
>
> —Terence Mann, *Field of Dreams*

The second, larger pocket of films about the '60s are those dealing with '60s leftovers, survivors of the period who generally fall along a spectrum including the drugged-out, the burnt-out, and the sold-out. While Marilyn Quayle and Peter (Robin Williams) from *Hook* (1991) may not have dropped out or protested in the '60s, in Hollywood film they are in the extreme minority. It is the rare character identified with the '60s who does not fall into one of those categories.

### *The Drugged-Out*

> Back in the '60s he was part of the Free Speech Movement at Berkeley. Frankly, I think he did too much LDS . . .
>
> —James T. Kirk, *Star Trek IV: The Voyage Home*

If film is to be believed, the "stoned hippie" image of the '60s will have an incredible staying power. In *Star Trek IV: The Voyage Home* (1986), when Admiral Kirk (William Shatner), temporarily in the late 20th century, must account for Spock's strange behavior, the 23rd-century resident turns to '60s drug use. Kirk may have garbled the name of the drug but apparently the drugged-out stereotype and the linkage of drugs with the activism of the free speech movement will survive some three hundred years into the future.

The stereotype has been played out in the broad caricature of the stoned hippie, codified in many ways by the recordings, and later the movies, of Cheech and Chong. While most of their films contain few explicit ties to the 1960s as such, their entire personae are those of the "burned-out, leftover 1960s druggie" (to use Leonard Maltin's words from his movie and video guide. Along with George Carlin and his Hippie Dippie Weatherman, Cheech and Chong's '60s dopers became the successor of the Foster Brooks-style drunk, but they have become an embodiment of an era in a way that the drunk act never did.

In *Outrageous Fortune* (1987), George Carlin plays this character in his supporting role as Frank, an unkempt hippie gone "native," "a bloodbrother to the Chicatacawa since 1968" with a horse named Frodo. Carlin befriends two women Lauren (Shelley Long) and Sandy (Bette Midler) who are caught between a couple of intelligence agencies and a rogue agent who has stolen a tube of biological warfare material. Frank's response to Sandy's news of an unbelievable conspiracy, "Gee, the '60s were good to you," reveals his point of reference as that of a '60s drug-user experienced in paranoid flashbacks. Just such a character, named only Hippie, appears in *The Abyss* (1989), where he is dismissed by a fellow crew member for thinking everything is a conspiracy. *They All Laughed* (1981) and *Bad Influence* (1990) ring minor variations on the stoned-hippie character in the supporting characters of Arthur (Blaine Novak) and Pismo (Christian Clemenson). In *Rude Awakenings*, Cheech Marin plays Jesus Montaya, a hippie whose mind was rewired through the CIA's LSD experiments in the 1960s and who has spent the last twenty years in Central America smoking enormous joints and hallucinating that fish were talking to him.

Tommy Chong extended, if not expanded, the Cheech and Chong doper when he wrote, directed, and starred in the 1990 eponymous film about Far Out Man, a '60s roadie who, according to his daughter (Rae Dawn Chong), "got hit by a Rolls Royce. He was so stoned he didn't feel a thing, but he got tons of money 'cause they thought he suffered brain damage." The literally brain-dead Man has spent the last ten years smoking dope, living in squalor, listening to very loud rock music and pining after Tree (Shelley Chong), his ex-girlfriend and the mother of his second child. Man is unable to find her because he doesn't know her last name.

Like *The Big Chill*'s druggie Nick (William Hurt), these characters are drawn with an emphasis on their child-like qualities, their essential optimism and innocence. *Outrageous Fortune*'s Frank and *Rude Awakening*'s Jesus, Far Out Man, and *The Big Chill*'s Nick all see the simple truth that others miss. This insight, however, is purchased at the price of an inability to completely comprehend or function in the complexities of the post-1960s world.

> Why don't you grow up? There's nothing to win. It all ended when the War ended.
>
> —Annie to Gus the bomber, *Running on Empty*

The films about '60s leftovers also offer a sampling of radical activists who never gave up. Just as Susan in *Daniel* pursues radical causes until she ends up in a mental asylum and dies, Arthur (Judd Hirsch) and Gus (L.M. Kit Carson) continue the fight in *Running on Empty*. Gus, the violent radical, keeps on fighting the war after it's been lost and, in the process, threatens the marriage of Arthur and Annie (Christine Lahti) and the safety of their family. Fortunately, the film suggests, Gus is killed fleeing a failed bank robbery. Arthur is less violent but just as driven as Gus. Even on the run, Arthur organizes unions, fights toxic waste, and sets up a food co-op. But although he is a loving father, his obsession with "the cause" is destroying his family and has destroyed his marriage.

*The Big Chill* relates a gathering of '60s leftovers for the funeral of Alex (Kevin Costner), their group's activist. As the film comes to an end, Chloe (Meg Tilly), Alex's last girlfriend, reveals that his suicide may have been related to his recent reassessment of his activism. Alex had come to believe that he shouldn't have rejected a tainted academic fellowship, his exemplary act of protest, that his life of protest had meant nothing, and that he should have sold out.

While not consciously self-destructive, Fred Wook (Eric Roberts) in *Rude Awakenings* shows another danger of '60s activism. Wook went to Central America in the 1960s to keep the spirit of the counterculture alive in an expatriate commune. After twenty-five years of an idyllic hippie lifestyle, Wook discovers plans for a secret CIA war and returns to America to stop it, only to end up causing an even bigger war.

As Annie suggests to Gus in *Running on Empty*, these leftover '60s activists are more immature and childish than the child-like hippies. They are selfish, unrealistic, and in the end, self-destructive. As with the most positive reading of *Easy Rider*, the rebels end up dead or destroyed. Only Wook of *Rude Awakenings* is offered the possibility of a role as a mentor to a new generation of proto-radicals.

These two version of the '60s survivor—doper and activist—often end up paired in Hollywood film. *Rude Awakenings* offers Jesus and Wook as stoner and activist who return to America after twenty-five years in Central America to find their former comrades have sold out. *The Big Chill* makes this pairing implicit in Nick's close kinship with the unseen activist. At the film's end Nick ends up with Alex's coat, his papers, and his cabin, and his ex-girlfriend. In stepping into Alex's life, Nick is also seen as beginning to redeem his own. In *Flashback*, Huey Walker (Dennis Hopper) fits both descriptions; the escaped fugitive is an activist who turns out to have been just a doper who became a counterculture hero by mistake.

*The Burnt-Out and Sold-Out*

> I’m part of a lost and a restless generation. What do you want me to do? Run for the Senate?
>
> —John Winger, *Stripes*

The two other options for a ’60s leftover, the marginalized burnt-out cynic and the sold-out activist, can found in *The Big Fix*. Moses Wine (Richard Dreyfuss) is a private detective with a failed marriage and a total disinterest in who wins elections. Because of his erstwhile contacts with the Berkeley student underground, Moses is hired to find Howard Eppis (F. Murray Abraham), a hippie radical who has been underground for the last seven years. (Like Huey Walker [Dennis Hopper] in *Flashback*, Eppis is clearly based on yippie activist-jester Abbie Hoffman.) Moses discovers that the former agitator has taken a new name and become a tool of the capitalists, advertising the life he once condemned. Now Eppis has been made the scapegoat for a father (Fritz Weaver) attempting to destroy his son, Oscar, Jr. (John Lithgow), by smearing the gubernatorial candidate who is the focus of his son’s mainstream political activism. The father’s hostility was inspired by Junior’s own ’60s radicalism.

In the *Big Fix* we touch most of the major post-1960s themes: everyone has sold out—except perhaps Lila Shea (Susan Anspach) who ends up dead. Moses’s first moment alone on screen has him lighting a joint; other drug references follow, including a request for hash brownies and a question about whether Moses is “back on the pipe.” Moses also drives a convertible yellow VW and joins in with Eppis and their children as they dance around the swimming pool while chanting slogans from the ’60s.

As with the drugged-out hippies and the burnt-out activists, Moses is presented and treated as an overgrown child, even by his own children. Moses’s desire to be a detective rather than a lawyer is portrayed as part of his childishness, both through explicit comments from other characters and by his practice of “perfecting his craft” by playing the game Clue. His attempts to recapture the ’60s of his youth—through his old girlfriend Lila (who is murdered), through tracking Eppis (who has sold out), and through talking to a pair of radical bank bombers (who are imprisoned for life)—leads him back to the same point again and again: the ’60s are dead, and Moses needs to start acting his age.

Moses becomes an adult through avenging the death of Lila, the last pure example of his ’60s. Lila’s idealism helps Moses climb out of his isolated, cynical, and reactive childhood. The reinspired ’60s burn-out is also seen in *True Believer* as Ed Dodd (James Woods) is reinvigorated by a naive young lawyer (Robert Downey, Jr.) who appeals to Dodd's lost '60s idealism to take on a case on principle after years of cynically defending well-paying drug dealers. Similarly, Alex Jurrel is reinvigorated by his idealistic former student, Lisa, to lead a lost cause battle against a corrupt public school administration in *Teachers.* Lauren and Sandy eventually win Frank's assistance against international supertoxin thieves in *Outrageous Fortune*. Jesus and Wook convince the sold-out Sammy (Robert Carradine) and Petra (Julie Hagerty)—who have gone from food co-ops to co-op apartments—to climb out of their consumerist lethargy to fight a lost-cause battle against the CIA conspiracy. Just as, in *Bird on a Wire,* Rick, still committed to social equity, eventually convinces the sold-out Marianne, wife to "the Napalm King," to turn her back on her bourgeois yuppie values and help him fight against a corrupt Justice Department official.

It is worth noting that each of these revitalizations does not launch the character into a renewed life of '60s-style activism. Instead the characters are reintegrated into mainstream society in the service of mainstream values and definitions of justice. Otherwise, '60s-style activism is acceptable only at the distance of a conventionalized nostalgia. Moses gets teary-eyed watching television videos of Howard Eppis leading antiwar demonstrations. In a moment that viewers may recognize from traditional Hollywood portrayals of people looking at scrapbooks or home movies, *Flashback*'s home movie sequence shows John/Free (Keifer Sutherland) breaking down to images of his childhood days at the commune with his loving hippie parents. Ray Kinsella (Kevin Costner) demonstrates similar responses to the photocopies he compiles of the '60s career of Terence Mann (James Earl Jones) in *Field of Dreams*. In *The Return of the Secaucus Seven*, Jeff (Mark Arnott) gets teary-eyed listing his record of previous (protest) arrests for a police report when the gang is erroneously arrested for deer-jacking. Similarly, central scenes of reminiscence over '60s activism are featured in *The Big Chill, Between the Lines, Class Action, Rude Awakenings* and *Flashback.*

> Hell, if you can write "Rip It Off" you can write soap commercials. . . . You know why no one lasts as a revolutionary in this country? Because it's like being a spoilsport at an orgy. All those goodies spread out in front of you and you feel like a shit for saying no.
>
> —Howard Eppis, *The Big Fix*

Generally, the triumph moment of the '60s survivor films is found in the reinvigoration of the leftovers and a restatement of their connection to the community. While the films set during the '60s tend to focus on the disruption of the biological family, '60s survivor films tend to reconnect the leftover with a much more broadly defined extended family.

While "sold-out" characters populate many '60s survivors films—including Sammy, Petra, and Ronnie (Louise Lasser) of *Rude Awakenings*, Marianne of *Bird on a Wire*, Michael (Stephen Collins), Lynn (Jill Eikenberry), and the publisher of the once-underground "Back Bay Mainline" in *Between the Lines* and, by self-definition, most of the characters in *The Big Chill* and *The Return of the Secaucus Seven*—the film and its individuals decide that it's not so much selling out to the system as "maturing."

At the end of *The Big Chill*, with the value of the '60s protest rejected by its most ardent advocate, the film settles instead on the timeless quality of the generosity among friends, symbolized by both their Ann Arbor group house and the house in which they now reunite. The cause may not survive, but the friendships will.

### *Society's Children*

> Revolution is a young man's game.
> —Huey Walker, *Flashback*

The final twist on—or perhaps confirmation of—the idea of the '60s as a time of youthful indiscretion is seen in the reiteration of Huey Walker's claim in a wide range of films. *Field of Dreams, Running on Empty, Flashback, Lost in America, The Return of the Secaucus Seven, Between the Lines,* and *The Big Chill* all make the point that you can't help but outgrow rebellion.

Revolution is shown to be for the young and, implicitly, rebellion is of the young. The '60s was just a natural cycle of youth challenging authority. No longer youthful, the one-time rebel's enlistment in the system is seen as a proof of maturity—not necessarily a good thing, but a natural thing. Staying outside the system remains proof of childishness, not necessarily bad, but unnatural.

In *Lost in America*, Albert Brooks plays David, an upwardly mobile advertising man who loses a promotion to senior vice-president and responds by deciding, too late, to regain his lost youth by hitting the road in homage to the film *Easy Rider*, apparently his only graspable vision of the '60s. But David's version of reliving the '60s is to hit the road in a

Winnebago with his wife and a $125,000 nest egg, to "touch Indians" and "have sex right here, right now."

The paltriness of David's cinematic symbol of '60s rebellion is finally laid bare when the couple are pulled over for speeding. Linda (Julie Hagerty), David's wife, talks the highway patrolman out of giving them a ticket because it turns out that *Easy Rider* has also shaped his life, inspiring him to the very non-'60s goal of becoming a highway patrolman.

David and Linda in *Lost in America* are just too set in their "bourgeois" lifestyle to return to youthful rebellion. Even the activist Arthur in *Running on Empty* is too old, cracking from the strain of a lifetime on the run.

Once again, the '60s boils down to relations between fathers and sons, but now the fathers are children of the '60s. The idea that the '60s was just part of a normal cycle of generational rebellion is argued in films like *Far Out Man* and *Running on Empty*, where the child of stoned hippies and the child of radical activists both rebel against their parents' dominant values and turn from rock and roll to embrace classical music, study, and other trappings of "bourgeois white skinned" middle-class culture. In the end, *Far Out Man*'s rebellious son Kyle (Paris Chong)—his chosen name, although his given name is Jimmy Henry Clapton Chick Hooker Lee John Charles Berry Richard Fahey—joins the family rock band. *Running on Empty*'s radical father allows his son to go study classical piano at Julliard. The major plot twist of *Flashback* revolves around the fact that the rigidly conservative John Buckner is, in fact, Free Buckner, a child who rebelled against his hippie parents to become an FBI agent. That film ends with Buckner quitting the FBI, buying a motorcycle, and heading out to see his parents at their food co-op in Santa Monica. The vegetarian food co-op-owning doper parents of *Valley Girl* (1983) get the sort of daughter the title suggests, although there is no real strain between them. In *Class Action*, the daughter of a '60s radical lawyer (Gene Hackman) becomes a corporate lawyer for a major automaker, the antithesis of everything her father stands for, before seeing the corruption from within and returning to her father's values.

The rebellion of these "grandchildren of the '60s" comes to a less comforting resolution in *Repo Man*, where the stoned childishness of the '60s parents of Otto Madd (Emilio Estevez) has lead them to become mindless devotees of a television minister. Their anti-idealist son takes work as a car repossessor before climbing into a time machine to escape into the past. Otto's escape seems only a more pessimistic version of the more metaphorical escape into a past of '60s activism by the son of the sold-out Sammy at the end of *Rude Awakenings*.

### *The Successful '60s Leftover*

> He was in Civil Rights, reshaped a generation, hung out with the Beatles and it wasn't enough. He needed baseball.
>
> —Ray Kinsella, *Field of Dreams*

It may be that the only place where the idea of the '60s is allowed to continue untainted in Hollywood film is on the surreal plane. In *Field of Dreams*, Terence Mann is the radical writer who inspired Ray Kinsella in the '60s but then gave up on his dreams and learned to hate the '60s. Ray Kinsella, the vision-driven Iowa farmer helps Mann remember the optimism of the '60s in a cross-country trip in a VW microbus. The film distills much of the Hollywood version of the '60s into its plot and, in doing so, confirms the somewhat conflicted meaning that the '60s have in Hollywood film.

The '60s in *Field of Dreams* is wrapped up with the unattained personal dreams of unfulfilled Americans; for Mann that means baseball, for Kinsella that means that he and his father parted in anger during the '60s and he never got to tell his father that he loved him before he died. These are the dreams of young American males grown old(er).

The '60s ideals lead to the fulfillment of the two men's dreams as both men achieve a child's utopia out of touch with the realities of the present day. At the film's end Mann, the burnt-out activist, is rewarded for his activism in ascendance to heaven without death, as he goes off into the afterlife with the greatest (white) baseball players of all time. The dropped-out Kinsella family is reinvigorated as Ray's daughter explains how her father's '60s vision can support the family; his wife (Amy Madigan), who has kept the home fires burning, is now making dinner while Ray gets to make up with his dead father by sharing the childhood security of a father-son game of catch. Meanwhile, just over the hill are thousands of people who are coming to share Kinsella's nostalgic dream and make him rich.

Even as it presents the '60s ideals with sympathy, *Field of Dreams* confirms the Hollywood treatment of the '60s as a period whose causes were secondary to father-son conflicts, whose survivors ended up burnt-out, or dropped-out, hurting their families and incapable of functioning in the post-1960s world. It is only through divine intervention, or fantasy, that '60s idealism doesn't lead to economic and familial failure. Instead Ray Kinsella prospers, still confirming the cinematically conventional use of the '60s. Kinsella is allowed to have it both ways, but they are both Hollywood's ways; the '60s leftover reaps the benefits of selling out while remaining an innocent child.

## Filmography

| Film | Year | Director |
|---|---|---|
| *Rebel without a Cause* | 1955 | Nicholas Ray |
| *Easy Rider* | 1969 | Dennis Hopper |
| *Between the Lines* | 1977 | Joan Micklin Silver |
| *The Big Fix* | 1978 | Jeremy Paul Kagan |
| *Coming Home* | 1978 | Hal Ashby |
| *More American Graffiti* | 1979 | B.W.L. Norton |
| *The Return of the Secaucus Seven* | 1980 | John Sayles |
| *Willie and Phil* | 1980 | Paul Mazursky |
| *Four Friends* | 1981 | Arthur Penn |
| *The Big Chill* | 1983 | Lawrence Kasdan |
| *Daniel* | 1983 | Sidney Lumet |
| *Valley Girl* | 1983 | Martha Coolidge |
| *Teachers* | 1984 | Arthur Hiller |
| *Lost in America* | 1985 | Albert Brooks |
| *Star Trek IV: The Voyage Home* | 1986 | Leonard Nimoy |
| *Outrageous Fortune* | 1987 | Arthur Hiller |
| *1969* | 1988 | Ernest Thompson |
| *'68* | 1988 | Steven Kovacks |
| *Running on Empty* | 1988 | Sidney Lumet |
| *The Abyss* | 1989 | James Cameron |
| *Born on the Fourth of July* | 1989 | Oliver Stone |
| *Field of Dreams* | 1989 | Phil Alden Robinson |
| *Rude Awakenings* | 1989 | Aaron Russo |
| *Far Out Man* | 1990 | Tommy Chong |
| *Flashback* | 1990 | Franco Amurri |
| *Bird on a Wire* | 1990 | John Badham |
| *Class Action* | 1991 | Michael Apted |
| *The Doors* | 1991 | Oliver Stone |

# *Dances with Wolves* and *Unforgiven*: Apocalyptic, Postrevisionist Westerns

**Philip J. Skerry**

Several years ago, I wrote a paper on the western film entitled "The Western Film: A Sense of an Ending" (*New Orleans Review*), in which I argued that the western as a genre appeared moribund. Since I wrote that paper, however, a mini-renaissance of the western film has developed, heralded by two extraordinary films, *Dances with Wolves* and *Unforgiven,* both winners of Academy Awards for best picture. After viewing these two films—and other revisionist westerns featuring African Americans (*Posse*) and women (*Ballad of Little Jo*)—I believe I was premature in my pessimistic prognostication for the western film. Whether this resurgence signals a new "golden age" of the western, though, is not yet clear. What is clear, however, is that both *Dances with Wolves* and *Unforgiven* reflect a new state of consciousness about the western film genre: I call that consciousness apocalyptic postrevisionism.

### *Apocalyptic Postrevisionism*

What does the term "postrevisionist" mean? I again turn back to my earlier paper, in which I sketched the evolution of a genre: (1) establishment of conventions; (2) repetition of conventions and creation of icons; (3) full flowering of conventions and icons and development of formula; (4) theme and variations on formula; (5) critical questioning of conventions; (6) sense of ending of conventions; (7) ironic reversal of formula and icon; (8) satiric treatment of icon, formula and conventions (Skerry 14).

The final stages of evolution usually involve a revisionist interpretation in which the former conventions of the genre are turned upside down, and the icons are employed in unexpected ways. A vivid example of this revisionist reversal is Arthur Penn's *Little Big Man* (1970): Custer is the megalomaniac villain; the Indians are true "human beings"; Buffalo Bill is an environmental terrorist; Wild Bill Hickok is paranoid, and so on. This same revisionist trend can be seen in the final stage of the evolution, the satirical, in which formula, icon, and convention are presented in self-consciously humorous and burlesque ways, such as in *Blazing Saddles.*

Postrevisionism represents a further development on my evolutionary scale, for although postrevisionism involves a self-conscious view of the genre, this self-consciousness is not treated satirically but rather seriously, even profoundly. In addition, postrevisionism incorporates an awareness—perhaps meta-awareness would be a better term—that is contained in an apocalyptic moment—a genre-clarifying epiphany—in the film. I believe this apolcalyptic, postrevisionist moment grows out of two major visions inherent in western films.

The first vision is one that is traditional to the American western film and that develops out of the facts of American history: the depiction of the trek westward and the opening of the frontier as America's great national epic, similar to the defining national epics of Homer and Virgil. The category of western films presenting epic visions features heroes and villains who embody national mores, customs, and actions, and who define a national character. The heroes presented in films like *The Plainsman, They Died with Their Boots On, My Darling Clementine* are well known: Wyatt Earp, Wild Bill Hickok, George Armstrong Custer. The villains also take on epic dimensions—Jesse James, Billy the Kid, the Clantons. Within this epic category is also a third group—the indigenous people of the region—the Native Americans—Sitting Bull, Crazy Horse, Geronimo. Frequently the Native Americans are portrayed as savages, as extensions of the wildness of the frontier. At best, they are a natural force; at worst, they are embodiments of unbridled savagery. In any case, their depiction acts as a kind of social Darwinism: they are obviously not worthy of survival in the struggle for the control of the frontier and of the eventual "civilizing" of the West.

The second vision of the western film is just as important as the epic, and this is the morality play. In this vision, the western is depicted as a vehicle for the playing out of moral forces as starkly metaphorical and symbolic as those of *Everyman.* This thematic layer has been part of the western since its very beginning. *The Great Train Robbery* (1903), for example, uses the western (actually, New Jersey) as a setting for a story of crime, pursuit, and retribution, the basic trinity of the morality play western, during which the "bad" train robbers are tracked down and captured by the "good" posse. These allegories of good and evil account for many confrontations between the evil gunfighters and the good sheriff. The most allegorical of these morality play films is of course, *High Noon,* which uses the western setting ostensibly to tell a tale of personal courage and collective cowardice in the face of the pure evil of Frank Miller and his gang, but in reality to relate a political tale of heroism in the face of the McCarthy threat. If Native Americans are depicted in these morality-play westerns, the Indians are usually symbolic of the savagery of the wilderness. They are, in effect, extensions of a kind of Calvinistic view of fallen nature. The chief, Scar, along with his Commanche tribe, is portrayed in this way in John Ford's *The Searchers.* Scar's slaughter of the Edwards family and his abduction of Ethan Edwards's niece, Debbie, are indicative of the savage ruthlessness that threatens the thin veneer of civilization set up by the early settlers. Ethan's rescue of Debbie, then, is actually her salvation. In fact, Ethan would rather have her dead than become a "commanch."

What makes the western the quintessential American film genre is that these two visions—the epic and the morality play—are frequently embodied in the same film, providing the audience with a defining national epic, underscored, or underlain, by a moral allegory that informs and interpenetrates the epic. The classic period of the western genre, I believe, is one in which the two visions support and enrich one another when, in other words, the heroes of the national epic are identified with the forces of goodness in the morality play. In the revisionist stage of the genre, then, the two visions collide, as the characters of the national epic reflect a reversal of those in the morality play. In this case, the formerly heroic characters such as General Custer now become the villains of the morality play (in *Little Big Man,* again); or characters from the epic that were villains in the morality play—Billy the Kid or Jesse James—now become complex antiheroes (e.g., in *The Left-Handed Gun; The Great Northfield Minnesota Raid*) or non-heroes (e.g., *For a Few Dollars More*). In the revisionist western, the third group—the Indians—who played various roles in the classic western, sometimes representing extensions of the natural landscape and frequently playing the role of villains, now become associated with the forces of goodness in the morality play. Concomitantly, Indians are portrayed in the national epic as victims of white, Eurocentric imperialism, now clearly the evil force in the morality play.

## Dances with Wolves

*Dances with Wolves,* at first glance, seems to fit into the revisionist pattern described above. On the national epic level, the push westward is interpreted as an imperialistic expansion. In the book that accompanied the release of the film—*Dances with Wolves: The Illustrated Story of the Epic Film*—Kevin Costner states of the film, "It's a romantic look at a terrible time in our history, where expansion in the name of progress brought us very little and, in fact, cost us deeply" (*viii*). On the level of morality play, the Sioux Indians are portrayed as Rousseauian noble savages, and the white soldiers are embodiments of evil and exploitation. As the film develops, Lt. Dunbar begins to realize that white culture is predatory, destructive, and imperialistic. Inexorably, he is drawn to the life-enhancing and virtuous culture of the Sioux Indians. This metamorphosis is accompanied by a symbolic shedding of part of his cavalry uniform and his adopting of a Sioux warrior's clothing. He becomes a true Sioux warrior when he states after the battle with the Pawnees: "As I heard my Sioux name being called over and over, I knew for the first time who I really was."

*Turner and Postrevision*

As revisionist as *Dances with Wolves* seems to be, there is a crucial scene in the film that points it in the direction of postrevisionism and that draws on the moral implications of Frederick Jackson Turner's influential essay, "The Significance of the Frontier in American History," delivered to the American Historical Association in 1893. The thrust of Turner's thesis is well-known among western film scholars. As of 1890, the frontier was officially closed. Early in the film, after Lt. Dunbar's nearly suicidal act of courage in the skirmish against the Confederates, he is posted at his own request to the frontier and reports for his orders to the demented Major Fambrough:

*Fambrough:* It says here you've been decorated and they sent you out here to be posted?

*Dunbar:* Actually, sir, I'm here at my own request. . . . I want to see the frontier . . . before it's gone.

Those three words, "before it's gone," have significant implications for the thesis of this chapter, for those words pinpoint that apocalyptic moment—that genre clarifying epiphany—that makes *Dances with Wolves* a postrevisionist western.

The apocalyptic moment described above, in which Dunbar foresees the end of the frontier, is different from Dunbar's thoughts about the frontier in the novel *Dances with Wolves.* In Michael Blake's 1988 novel, Dunbar wishes to see the frontier because of its romantic symbolism of the eternal: Blake says of Dunbar's experience of the unspoiled land:

And he was there. It was beyond the reach of his imagination, and at the same time he knew that this was why he'd come, this was at the core of his urge to be posted on the frontier. This, without his knowing it before, was what he had yearned to see. For those fleeting moments he became part of something so large that he ceased to be a lieutenant or a man or even a body of working parts. For these moments he was a spirit hovering in the timeless, empty space of the universe. For these precious few seconds he knew the feeling of eternity. (99-100)

In Blake's screenplay, however, Dunbar's awareness of the end of the frontier adds a new dimension to the film version of the novel—a dimension that incorporates Turner's thesis into the film text. Dunbar's epiphanic realization of the frontier's end takes place in 1863; thirty years later (1893) Turner's thesis claims that the frontier had ended by 1890; one hundred years later Costner's film appears. This concatenation of dates is more than coincidental, I believe. Dunbar's consciousness of an inevitable apocalypse identifies him with the consciousness of 1990, not 1863, the time of the story; his awakening to the possibilities of the end of the frontier coincides perfectly with the knowledge that film viewers of 1990 had not only of the closing of the frontier, but also of the decline of the western film. In other words, Dunbar's narrative knowledge thrusts him outside the context of the story and consequently makes him a narrator with knowledge that he could not possibly have as a narrator within the story itself.

This knowledge provides credibility for Dunbar as the film's voice-over narrator. Dunbar's methodical and compulsive journal writing provides a means by which Dunbar's voice-over acts as a commentary on the actions we are seeing on the screen. Dunbar's apocalyptic vision is also shared and deepened by the Sioux Indians' realization of the ending of their way of life. Kicking Bird states: "But the whites are coming. Our friends the Shoshone and the Kiowa, even our enemies, agree on this—the whites are coming." Later in the film, Dances with Wolves says to Kicking Bird: "You have asked me many times about the white people. . . . You always ask how many more are coming. . . . There will be a lot of my friends . . . more than can be counted." Kicking Bird responds, "Help me to know how many," and Dances with Wolves replies, "Like the stars" (Costner, Blake, Wilson 34).

Dunbar's postrevisionist narrative stance is enhanced in the film by images of death, destruction, and abandonment. The film opens with Dunbar's death-wish ride in front of the Confederate lines; Major Fambrough commits suicide just after posting Dunbar to the deserted Fort Sedgewick; the Fort itself is abandoned, its deadness symbolized by the rotting carcasses Dunbar finds in the pond. The two most potent symbols of death, though, are the buffalo—Tatonka—the veritable life-blood of the Sioux, and Two Socks, the wolf totem of Dunbar. These animals become associated with the eventual disappearance of the Sioux culture in the film. It is significant that the death of the buffalo and the wolf comes at the hands of the white man, who plunders the land and wastes its natural resources. Dunbar writes in his journal after he has seen the rotting buffalo carcasses:

> Who would do such a thing? The field was proof enough that it was a people without value and without soul, with no regard for Sioux rights. The wagon tracks leading away left little doubt, and my heart sank as I knew it could only be white hunters. (Costner, Blake, Wilson 59)

The final scenes of the film also underscore this sense of loss. Dances with Wolves and Stands with a Fist have decided to leave the Sioux's winter camp because their presence endangers the Sioux and also because Dances with Wolves hopes to talk to whites who might listen to the Indian's plight. His words show just how far he has moved from his position at the beginning of the film, when his brave, but suicidal ride helped his fellow soldiers. Dances with Wolves says, "Killing the soldiers at the river was a good thing. It made me free, and my heart was big to see my friends coming to help me. I did not mind killing those men. I was glad to do it" (Costner, Blake, Wilson 129).

### *Subverting Turner's Thesis*

I have claimed above that *Dances with Wolves* incorporates Turner's thesis into its text; in reality, though, *Dances with Wolves* subverts Turner's thesis and becomes postrevisionist, not in the sense of revising the western epic and morality tale, but in revising Turner's interpretation of the significance of the frontier. Turner's thesis is evolutionary; the progress from savagery to civilization requires the conquering of successive frontiers as Americans push west in their quest for new land. Turner claims:

> The history of our political institutions, our democracy, is not a history of imitation, of simply borrowing; it is a history of the evolution and adaptation of organs in response to a changed environment, a history of the origin of new political species. . . . In this sense, therefore, the west has been a constructive force of the highest significance in our life. (Turner 64)

*Dances with Wolves*, however, subverts Turner's thesis even as it incorporates its theme of the sense of an ending of the frontier. For the trek west in *Dances with Wolves*, which represents our great national epic, is actually a move from one imperialist venue to another. There is no evolutionary advance. In fact, there is actually a decline. The Sioux culture, as presented in *Dances with Wolves,* is clearly superior to white culture in almost every way, but mainly in environmental consciousness. In destroying Sioux culture—and the culture of the Native Americans in general—white Europeans clearly were guilty of genocide and environmental terrorism.

Seen in this way, then, *Dances with Wolves*'s apocalyptic post-revisionism is actually a millennial ideology, one aspect of a general millennialism that has taken root in many aspects of popular culture, from the conspiracy theories of Oliver Stone's *JFK* to the boyhood experiences of Indiana Jones in George Lucas's television series, during which young Indiana encounters some of the cultural icons of the 20th century—Freud, Einstein, Teddy Roosevelt—before they have become cultural icons. This apocalyptic self-consciousness partly derives from what, for want of a better term, we call environmentalism, the belief that our destructive and wanton ways with the earth will surely lead to an environmental catastrophe that could wipe out human life, just as the inevitable trek west wiped out Sioux culture.

### Unforgiven: *A Dark Morality Play*

Clint Eastwood's *Unforgiven,* I believe, also contains an epiphanic moment, but this moment is a reflecton of the film as a starkly post-revisionist morality play. It is on this second vision—the western as morality play—that I take issue with Jane Tompkins's thesis in *West of Everything.* Tompkins initiates her analysis of the western with a discussion of the significance of death in the western. Her claim is that the omnipresence of death is evidence that the western is in essence an anti-Christian narrative, formulated in reponse to the post-Victorian narratives of Christian salvation written by female novelists of the late 19th and early 20th centuries. Tompkins claims that "Christianity had to be forcibly ejected," in part because of its "doctrines of a feminized Christianity" (32-33). As a result, Tompkins believes, male violence, symbolized by the ubiquitous gun in western culture, comes to replace "the church and the home, in two places women could call their own" (44).

I believe Tompkins's thesis is provocative, but I also hold that it is essentially mistaken in its interpretation of the role of death in the western. Tompkins's historicist orientation blinds her to the fact that death is a major (but not the major) theme in western film and fiction precisely because the threat of death clarifies and intensifies the struggle between good and evil and because at death the soul confronts its ultimate destiny.

Hence, rather than being a non-Christian narrative (and hence not a morality play), the western film is the morality play par excellence, for it situates the play of good and evil in a starkly metaphoric setting—the frontier, the desert, the plain—but a setting that is quintessentially and mythically an American one. Thus questions of good and evil, right and wrong, are inextricably connected to our historical development as a nation and to our cultural assumptions. The western is perhaps the only genre that has been able to reflect the moral dilemmas we have faced: the McCarthy threat in *High Noon*, imperialism in *Little Big Man,* genocide in *Dances with Wolves*. And now, even our romance with the gun and the gunfighter in *Unforgiven*.

Given Tompkins's assertion that the western is a non-Christian narrative, what would she make of this scene from *Unforgiven*, with its hero's ruminations about death? Will Munny has just been savagely beaten by Little Bill Daggett, sheriff of Big Whiskey. Will is taken by Ned and the Schofield Kid to a hideout in the mountains to recuperate.

*Will:* (moaning) Claudia, Oh!
*Ned:* Claudia's not here, Will.
*Will:*: Claudia, Claudia. I seen him, Ned. I seen the angel of death. It's got snake eyes.
*Ned:* Will, who's got snake eyes?
*Will:* Oh, Ned, I'm afraid of dying.
*Ned:* Easy partner, easy.
*Will:* I see Claudia, too.
*Ned:* Well, that's good, Will. It's good you saw Claudia.
*Will:* Her face was all covered with worms. Oh, Ned, I'm, scared. I'm dying. You won't . . . don't tell nobody. Don't tell my kids none of the things I done.
*Ned:* All right, Will.

Certainly, the "vicious, intemperate" William Munny is now facing death and thus the full force of his conscience, as represented by his physically absent but spiritually present wife Claudia. Munny's fear of death is not a fear of nothingness, but rather of the "angel of death." Tompkins holds that women are mainly absent from westerns because men banished them and their special places. Yet, although Claudia Munny is not physically present in *Unforgiven*, her spiritual presence is everywhere in the film, most importantly in her inculcation of Munny's conscience.

*The Apocalyptic Moment in* Unforgiven

One definition of the morality play is that it is the dramatic depiction of the struggle for an individual soul by the forces of good and evil. Given this definition, I assert that *Unforgiven* is indeed a morality play since the film dramatically depicts the struggle within William Munny between the demons of his former life as a bandit and gunfighter and the angels of his wife Claudia's Christian morality. The fact that Munny's demons win out over his angels in no way banishes Claudia or diminishes her importance. Rather, Munny's recidivism is in keeping with the pessimism of the revisionist and postrevisionist westerns in general.

It is at this point that the epiphanic moment in *Unforgiven* comes into play. This moment, I hold, functions in the same way as does the moment in *Dances with Wolves,* when Dunbar tells Major Fambrough that he wants to be posted to the frontier before it is gone. The complementary moment in *Unforgiven* takes place just after the Schofield Kid has killed the second cowboy in an outhouse. Munny and the Kid are on a rise just outside of Big Whiskey waiting for their reward for the revenge killing of the cowboys, one of whom had cut up the prostitute.

*Will:* It's a hell of a thing, killing a man. You take away all he's got and all he's ever gonna have.
*Kid:* Yeah, well, I guess they had it coming.
*Will:* We all have it coming, Kid.

At the end of the scene, the Schofield Kid decides to give up the gun at the same time that Will Munny decides to avenge Ned's death by killing Little Bill Daggett.

The implications of this scene are manifold. Eastwood has structured the film so that the killing of the two cowboys raises questions about the morality of killing for revenge—challenging the Old Testament injunction of an eye for an eye. During the killing of the first cowboy, Ned Logan, Will's partner, cannot pull the trigger. He has had his fill of killing, and therefore, no longer has the stomach for it. Will takes Logan's Spencer rifle and kills the cowboy, but it is clear from his actions that it is a distasteful task. The second killing, though, crystallizes the postrevisionism of the film. Not only is killing an ugly, distasteful, unheroic thing, but the mythical quality of killing—the gunfight—is also decidedly unheroic and unglamorous. This idea is forcefully brought home in many ways. W.W. Beachamp, the eastern writer of penny novels glamorizing the west for an eastern audience, is given the true story of the "Duke of Death's" (English Bob's) exploits by

Little Bill. The Duke is drunk during his famous confrontation with Two-gun Corky, just as Munny was drunk during his evil days. Munny's climactic gun fight with Little Bill and his deputies is not really a test of skill and courage but rather of coolness and calculation, both of which are heightened by Munny's return to the bottle. Munny's cold-blooded killing of the wounded, prostrate Little Bill reinforces the ugliness of the gunfight. Little Bill says, "I don't deserve this. I was building a house." Will responds, "'Deserve's' got nothing to do with it."

To reinforce the postrevisionism of his western, Eastwood draws upon other famous westerns. From *The Left-Handed Gun,* Eastwood borrows the character of the eastern writer who glorifies psychopathic killers and thus romaticizes the West; from *Shane,* Eastwood borrows the famous showdown between the herioc Shane and the Striker Brothers; from *Ride the High Country,* Eastwood draws upon the bonding of the older and younger gunfighter in the passing on of a heroic tradition. Yet Eastwood revises and subverts the classic westerns *Shane* and *Ride the High Country,* while at the same time he reinforces the revisionist view of *The Left-Handed Gun.* The conversation between Munny and Schofield quoted above reflects the same kind of self-conscousness as Dunbar's realization of the end of the frontier. The significance of the end of the frontier was brought home only after the frontier had ended; thus Dunbar's realization of the significance of that ending thrusts him outside the chronology of the narrative. Munny, too, in his statement, "We all have it coming, Kid," demonstrates an awareness of the de-romanticizing and the de-mythologizing of the West that would begin to occur in the western film in the late 1950s and reach its full flowering in the mid-'60s.

Eastwood's film, I conclude, is indeed a morality tale; its dark conclusions about the essentially fallen nature of humanity align it with works like Conrad's *Heart of Darkness.* To imply that the western is not a moral narrative but a vehicle for male fantasy and violence, as Tompkins does, is to reduce a genre that has spoken and continues *to speak to us as a people* to a genre that speaks to us only of our gender.

### *Conclusion*

In tracing the evolution of the western genre, one can say that the western actually initiated the narrative film with the release of *The Great Train Robbery* in 1903. It has been my contention in this paper that the western plays an equally important role in the defining of the American character and landscape through the ideology of the epic and morality play. In the 1990s this ideology has taken on a paradoxical quality. On the one hand, the postrevisionism of *Dances with Wolves* asserts a positive, optimistic *Zeitgeist* in the life-enhancing traditions of Native Americans.

In casting the imperialistic Anglos in the role of destroyers of truly American virtues embodied by the Sioux, Costner has reestablished the edenic qualities of the American continent. Eastwood's *Unforgiven,* however, presents its postrevisionism in much darker terms, for all humans are fallen in the bleak landscape of this American morality play.

## Works Cited

Blake, Michael. *Dances with Wolves.* New York: Ballantine, 1985.

Costner, Kevin, Michael Blake, and Jim Wilson. *Dances with Wolves: The Illustrated Story of the Epic Film.* New York: New Market Press, 1990.

Skerry, Philip. "The Western Film: A Sense of an Ending." *New Orleans Review* 17.3: 13-17.

Tompkins, Jane. *West of Everything.* New York: Oxford UP, 1992.

Turner, Frederick Jackson. "The Significance of the Frontier in American History." *Frontier and Section: Selected Essays of Frederick Jackson Turner.* Englewood Cliffs, NJ: Prentice Hall, 1961.

## Filmography

| Year | Film | Director |
|---|---|---|
| 1903 | *Great Train Robbery* | Edwin S. Porter |
| 1936 | *The Plainsman* | Cecil B. DeMille |
| 1941 | *They Died with Their Boots On* | Raoul Walsh |
| 1946 | *My Darling Clementine* | John Ford |
| 1952 | *High Noon* | Fred Zinneman |
| 1953 | *Shane* | George Stevens |
| 1956 | *The Searchers* | John Ford |
| 1958 | *The Left-Handed Gun* | Arthur Penn |
| 1962 | *Ride the High Country* | Sam Peckinpah |
| 1965 | *For a Few Dollars More* | Sergio Leone |
| 1970 | *Little Big Man* | Arthur Penn |
| 1972 | *The Great Northfield Minnesota Raid* | Philip Kaufman |
| 1974 | *Blazing Saddles* | Mel Brooks |
| 1990 | *Dances with Wolves* | Kevin Costner |
| 1992 | *J.F.K.* | Oliver Stone |
| 1992 | *Unforgiven* | Clint Eastwood |
| 1993 | *Ballad of Little Jo* | Maggie Greenwald |
| 1993 | *Posse* | Mario Van Peebles |

# Afterword
# Film Convention Studies: A Topographic Model for Film Study

It is the thesis of this series that a particularly useful approach to film studies can be developed through documenting and interpreting the conventional elements of film. Instead of taking traditional approaches such as looking at film genres, film directors and/or film auteurs, film history, film personalities, the language or semiotics of film, film audiences, film styles, or even the film industry itself, it is time to document and analyze the complex cultural assumptions that are embedded in film conventions themselves. Film convention studies, an evolving methodology, is a means of penetrating into largely unexamined layers of film that can lead to a better understanding of the interrelationship of popular film to American culture.

Film convention studies go beyond aesthetics and personal response to consider connections not only between many varieties of film but also the connections between film conventions, social phenomena, and social reality. The film convention textual model includes, but is not limited to, the close documentation of the following elements: filmic characters, themes, objects, places, plots, and narrative conventions.

*Character Conventions*

Both central and lesser movie characters form the focus of this area of study. Those characters can be professors or prostitutes, babies or broadcasters, athletes or army recruits, comedians or country folk, doctors or mechanics, computer nerds or hairdressers, or any of the scores of stock characters who play familiar roles in film. Conventional characters and stereotypes evolve in ways that reflect both enduring social values and changes in the social fabric.

While sensitivity to minority viewpoints has encouraged deeper dissection of various typical filmic character types, particularly of women and minorities, the exercise of exploring even minor and noncontroversial filmic character conventions has value in helping to explain and explore the cultural milieu from which particular conventions emerge. Conventional characters reflect our sense of social roles and appropriate behavior; on the most fundamental level, character conventions are a reflection of whom we choose to see.

*Plot Conventions*

Conventions of plot, which in themselves are key indices of cultural assumptions about our physical and social worlds, are further guideposts to revealing the symbiosis between film and the society it services. Whether the narrative attests to our fascination with the rise and fall of the sports hero, our faith in the last-minute rescue, or our belief in personal redemption, the box office brings us parables to please our sense of acceptable narratives.

We know, for example, that cinematic killers, with few exceptions, will nearly always get caught. We count on the underdogs in sport films to achieve either real or moral victory, despite the odds against them. We know that couples that are meant to be together will somehow find a way, just as we can count on the moral sheriff or cop to survive the final shootout. But we have also come to recognize that in contemporary films one or more innocent young people are likely to die in a movie about life in the urban ghettos of America; in today's films, cops in the war against drugs may become corrupt or addicted; corporate America may try to betray the public interest in the pursuit of profit. Film convention studies help to reveal and explore the changing and the fixed patterns of popular film narratives.

*Conventions of the Material World*

The material world of motion pictures, its "stuff"—both used and abused—is probably the most obvious and at the same time one of the least analyzed elements of film texts. How well is America's love affair with automobiles reflected in the movies where destroying autos is commonplace? Food, in film, as in life, has many functions. From pizza to escargot, food choices have meaning. Or consider how images of cigarettes have evolved, from the macho mannerisms of Humphrey Bogart to today's association with nervous losers. Clothing, computers, weapons, cocaine, chaise lounges, pianos, paintings, snapshots, and the myriad things of contemporary life—all provide invaluable clues to understanding our society and what it values at any given historical moment.

*Conventions of Place*

Locales—whether London, laundromats, or literary hideaways, provide much more than setting in the telling of a story. Conventional locations like prisons, residential suburbs, nightclubs, churches, the

West, Vietnam, bedrooms and kitchens, the Bronx, ballparks, race tracks, highways, and strip joints reflect the changing landscapes of America and the ways in which both real and imagined changes in those landscapes are reflected in American popular film.

The examination of how beaches and steelmills, churches and Watts, hair salons and fight arenas, borders and bookstores have been used in popular film both past and present helps us understand the intersection of social reality and filmic representation.

*Filmic Themes and Ideologies*

Thematic or ideological conventions—the "isms," doctrines, leitmotifs, and ways of thinking about the world—provide yet another way that the study of film conventions encourages looking at cultural assumptions. Popular films have dealt with antiestablishment themes, hedonism and horror, pacifism, anticommunism, American success mythology, spiritual regeneration, homelessness, consumerism, alienation, racism, Ugly Americanism, ageism, class conflict, and so on.

Even a cursory examination of the history of popular film suggests how certain themes and ideologies seem to persist and/or evolve, while others have only a relatively brief life in movie consciousness. What, if any, are the enduring themes of American film? What forces lead to changes in the ideological and thematic dimensions of film? These are questions yet to be answered.

*Film Topography and the Intersection of Conventions*

While the essays in this series have largely focused on documenting and analyzing single conventions (of plot, character, place, objects, or thematic motifs) the intersection or interrelationship of various conventions is also important to our understanding of cultural patterns.

No convention exists in isolation; rather, individual conventions intersect and interrelate to all of the other dimensions of film. Is it accidental that contemporary shootouts very frequently have an industrial rather than, say, a residential setting, or that the firepower conventions of urban showdowns have changed since the days of the 1930s gangster films? The plot (or box office) may call for a sex scene, but will sex take place in a bedroom, a stairwell, a sylvan glade, or an elevator? Will there be displays of sexy apparel or the use of ropes or handcuffs? Will condoms be mentioned or shown? Will premarital or extramarital sex be condoned or condemned? Will both parties be physically attractive? The conventions of film intersect and interact in complex ways.

We must, at some point, recognize that even a simple scene provides us with whole sets of questions and insights into the cosmology of American culture. Let us examine, as an example, a generic scene in which a detective hero, wearing a gun and a beeper, is having an alfresco lunch of hotdogs with his lover when his beeper signals. He apologizes to his love, kisses her, gets into his Jeep Cherokee, and drives away.

The scene, which serves some minimal dramatic function in the screenplay, also reveals an enormous range of cultural choices that are so deeply embedded in the matrix of ordinary life as to be nearly invisible without the conscious decision to see them as cultural elements. The ballpark frank is a quick, acceptable meal in our mainstream culture, but it is an act of very different meaning to a vegetarian. The public kiss does not offend our sensibilities as it might a film censor in India. Carrying a gun suggests that whole sets of religious, ethical, and cultural choices have already been made and the Jeep Cherokee, both in its name and in its actuality, tells us a great deal about the world and the culture in which our hero operates. The beeper, now appearing with some regularity in American popular films, is, in some ways, the pivot point of the scene; more importantly, it is, like the other elements in the scene, a complex and potent symbol whose cultural dimensions call for analysis. For example, should we not notice how the beeper signals the conflict between the obligations of job, career, or social responsibility and the demands and rewards of love, romance, and potential family values? Should we not at least speculate that our detective's willingness to even wear a beeper suggests a whole set of cultural assumptions about power (he is at the beck and call of whom or what?), individuality (he has chosen to abandon that degree of personal freedom offered by being unreachable), and time (the beeper insists that the urgent is, of itself, more important than what can wait). Does it seem misguided to see in the beeper a cultural sign of how even fairly modest technological changes can, and do, affect the very patterns and assumptions in which we live?

These are, perhaps, legitimate questions that can lead us further into an understanding of our culture. The problem, of course, is that until there are many more of us willing to look at beepers or purses or kisses or eating scenes or traffic or public spaces or ritual greetings or any of the thousands of unexamined conventional bits and pieces that are unemphatically embedded in popular films, we will continue to have only a very limited and narrow view of what popular film can tell us about the minds and lives of those who produce and consume American movies.

It is our hope that the essays in the five volumes of the Beyond the Stars Series will help to lead others to document and analyze still other elements of the complex matrix of American film conventions. If we are ever to truly understand the intricate relationship between film and social reality, we might do well to continue looking at the patterns of creation, alteration, and destruction of the most familiar elements of American popular film.

Paul Loukides
Linda K. Fuller

# Contributors

**Carolyn Anderson** is associate professor and Graduate Program director in the Department of Communication at the University of Massachusetts at Amherst, where she teaches film history and criticism. She is coauthor, with Thomas W. Benson, of *Reality Fictions: The Films of Frederick Wiseman* and *Documentary Dilemmas: Frederick Wiseman's* Titicut Follies.

**Parley Ann Boswell** teaches English at Eastern Illinois University in Charleston, Illinois. In addition to her work on mothers in the movies, she has contributed essays to *Beyond the Stars 1, 2,* and *3,* and is currently co-writing a book on rituals in Hollywood movies with Paul Loukides. She has an interesting mother of her own, and she became someone's mother in 1993.

**William Brigham** is currently a lecturer in the Sociology Program at California State University, San Marcos. His primary area of interest is mass media, with particular focus on news media and film. His essay "Whatup in the 'Hood? The Rage of African American Filmmakers" was published in the anthology *States of Rage* (NYU 1996), Renee Curry and Terry Allison, eds.

**Mark J. Charney** teaches film and literature at Clemson University, where he is working on a biography of D.W. Griffith for the University of Virginia's Minds of the New South Intellectual Biography Series. He is author of a critical study of southern author Barry Hannah, and has directed a professional video documentary, *Red to the Rind*, chronicling the formation of an "extended family" who meet each year in New Orleans for Jazz Festival. He is married to Sappho Charney, writer of adolescent novels, and has recently adopted twin daughters.

**Ralph R. Donald** is professor and chair of the Department of Communications at the University of Tennessee at Martin. He earned his B.A. and M.A. at California State University, Fullerton, and Ph.D. at the University of Massachusetts. Research interests include propaganda and gender-related issues in mass media, and film history. He is also editor of the *Mid-Atlantic Almanack*, the journal of the Mid-Atlantic Popular/American Culture Association.

**Linda K. Fuller,** coeditor of this series, is an associate professor in the Communications Department of Worcester (Massachusetts) State College. She is the author of *The Cosby Show: Audiences, Impact, Implications*; *Community Television: Your Guide to Public, Educational, and Government Access*; *Chocolate Fads, Folklore, & Fantasies*; and *Media-Mediated Relationships*; coauthor of *Communicating Comfortably: Overcoming Speaking and Writing Anxieties*; and *Communicating about Communicable Diseases*; and editor of *Media-Mediated Aids*. For 1996, Dr. Fuller has been awarded a Fulbright to teach and do research in Singapore.

**Howard Good** is a professor of journalism at the State University of New York at New Paltz—and a Mets fan. He is the author of *Acquainted with the Night: The Image of Journalists in American Fiction, 1890-1930* (1986); *Outcasts: The Image of Journalists in Contemporary Film* (1989); *The Journalist As Autobiographer* (1993); and *Diamonds in the Dark: America, Baseball, and the Movies* (forthcoming).

**Gary Hoppenstand** is an associate professor teaching in the Department of American Thought and Language at Michigan State University. He has written numerous books and articles on a variety of topics ranging from American literature to popular culture studies. His most recent book, *Clive Barker's Short Stories: Imagination As Metaphor in the "Books of Blood" and Other Works*, was published by McFarland in 1994. He is currently at work on two projects: an analysis of Sir Arthur Conan Doyle's "Professor Challenger" adventures for the Borgo Press and a textbook anthology for HarperCollins entitled *Popular Fiction*.

**Devoney Looser** is an assistant professor of English and Women's Studies at Indiana State University. Her essays have appeared in *Rhetoric Review, Style, European Romantic Review*, and *a/b: Auto/Biography Studies*. She is currently at work on a book-length project on postmodernism, feminism, and film.

**Paul Loukides** is a professor of English at Albion College, where he teaches courses in film, creative writing, and literature. He is particularly interested in the conventions of popular film and is currently at work on a book about rites of passage in American film.

**Jennifer A. Machiorlatti** teaches at the University of Michigan-Flint and Michigan State University and is a documentary and experimental filmmaker. Book reviews appear in *Journal of Film and Video* and *Journal of Popular Culture*, and the essay "Julie Dash as a Postmodern Afrocentric Griot: The Theory of an Interactive and Mobile Aesthetic" is part of the anthology *Afrocentric Notions: Studies in Culture and Communication.*

**Greg Metcalf** is a visiting professor of American Studies at the University of Maryland, Baltimore County, and a lecturer on cultural texts at Johns Hopkins University and the Smithsonian Institution. He also makes pop-up books.

**Rick Clifton Moore** lives in Boise, Idaho, with his wife, Kim, and children, Emily and David. He holds a Ph.D. from the University of Oregon and is currently an assistant professor in the Department of Communication at Boise State University. His research interests include pacifism, environmentalism, and the social theory of Jacques Ellul.

**Martin F. Norden** teaches film as a professor of Communication at the University of Massachusetts at Amherst. His articles on moving-image media have appeared in many journals and anthologies, including two prior volumes of *Beyond the Stars*. He is the author of *The Cinema of Isolation: A History of Physical Disability in the Movies* (Rutgers, 1994), and *John Barrymore: A Bio-Bibliography* (Greenwood, 1995).

**Philip Skerry** is a professor of English and Film at Lakeland Community College in Mentor, Ohio. He has published several articles on westerns in *The Journal of Popular Film and Television* and *The New Orleans Review*. He is also a contributing author to the book *Superman at Fifty*.

**Richard L. Stromgren** is an associate professor of Communication at the University of Massachusetts at Amherst, where he teaches courses in film history, genre studies, and film persuasion and propaganda. He has coauthored two books on film: *Light & Shadows: A History of Motion Pictures* and *Movies: A Language in Light*. His current research involves studies in social imagery and stereotyping and the evolution of screen satire. His essay on Chinese and Chinese American stereotypes—"The Chinese Syndrome"—appears in Volume 1 of *Beyond the Stars*. In Volume 3 he is represented by "Hitchcock's Gourmet and Gourmand Offerings."